P9-CAJ-356

# The Body Betrayed
## Women, Eating Disorders, and Treatment

# The Body Betrayed
## Women, Eating Disorders, and Treatment

Kathryn J. Zerbe, M.D.

Washington, DC
London, England

**Note:** The author has worked to ensure that all information in this book concerning drug dosages, schedules, and routes of administration is accurate at the time of publication and consistent with standards set by the U.S. Food and Drug Administration and the general medical community. As medical research and practice advance, however, therapeutic standards may change. For this reason, and because human and mechanical errors sometimes occur, we recommend that readers follow the advice of a physician directly involved in their care of the care of a member of their family.

Books published by the American Psychiatric Press, Inc., represent the views and opinions of the individual authors and do not necessarily reflect the policies and opinions of the Press or the American Psychiatric Association.

Copyright © 1993 American Psychiatric Press, Inc.
ALL RIGHTS RESERVED
Manufactured in the United States of America on acid-free paper
97 69 59 49 38    7 6 5 4 3 2 1
Published by American Psychiatric Press, Inc.
1400 K Street, N.W., Washington, DC 20005

**Library of Congress Cataloging-in-Publications Data**
Zerbe, Kathryn J., 1951–
    The body betrayed: women, eating disorders, and treatment /
Kathryn J. Zerbe.
        p.    cm.
    Includes bibliographical references and index.
    ISBN 0-88048-522-1
    1. Eating disorders.    I. Title.
RC552.E18Z47    1993
616.85′26′0082—dc20                                                                    93–5737
                                                                                                          CIP

**British Cataloging in Publication Data**
A CIP record is available from the British Library.

"I Dreamed a Dream"
(From *Les Misérables*)
Music by Claude-Michel Schönberg
Lyrics by Herbert Kretzmer
Original Text by Alain Boublil and Jean-Marc Natel
Music and Lyrics Copyright © 1980 by Editions Musicales
    Alain Boublil
English Lyrics Copyright © 1986 by Alain Boublil
    Music Ltd. (ASCAP)
Mechanical and Publication Rights for the USA Administered
    by Alain Boublil Music Ltd. (ASCAP) c/o Stephen
    Tenenbaum & Co., Inc., 605 Third Ave., New York, NY 10158
    Tel. (212) 922-0625, Fax (212) 922-0626
International Copyright Secured. All Rights Reserved. This
    music is copyright. Photocopying is illegal.
All Performance Rights Restricted.

"I Won't Last A Day Without You"
Lyrics by Paul Williams   Music by Roger Nichols
Copyright © 1972 Almo Music Corp. (ASCAP)
All Rights Reserved—International Copyright Secured

*For my mother*
*Ethel Schreckengaust Zerbe*
*and*
*for the memory of my father*
G. Frank Zerbe, M.D.

*The case histories in this book have been thoroughly disguised to preserve confidentiality.*

# Contents

# Acknowledgments

L ife can change in a moment's time. It's funny how sometimes seemingly trivial events can make us rethink issues or revise our goals. We are forced to look at life with a fresh eye, and although it is difficult, we adapt and grow. Life forces us to change.

In 1986, I was asked to lead a workshop on the psychology of women for the United States Rowing Association's annual convention in Topeka, Kansas. The audience was attentive to the general topics of that presentation, which dealt with the problems of combining a career and marriage, developmental impasses and sexual conflicts, and the nature of success and performance inhibitions. It seemed like standard and plausible fare to my listeners.

This particular group of health-minded and competitive men and women seemed particularly troubled, however, by the dearth of information about a behavioral problem they encountered almost daily in fellow athletes. With increasing alarm, they had noticed the pervasiveness of self-restrictive dieting, bingeing, and purging among rowers. Often after coaches and athletes confronted a rower with such a problem head-on in the locker room, they were alienated by the anger and surreptitiousness of the individuals they were trying to help. They wondered how people who were overtly developing and caring for their bodies could simultaneously betray them by repetitive self-abuse.

These rowers noted that they felt helpless whenever they tried to intervene with athletes who had eating disorders. They were quite aware that the behavior they witnessed in the locker room also occurred frequently in nonathletes. Observing a more generic, societal concern about disturbed eating and body image patterns, they questioned how the psychiatric profession understood and treated persons with these potentially life-threatening symptoms. They were anxious to know when to leave well enough alone and when to refer an athlete with an eating disorder to a mental health professional. Their perceptions about this important health problem were key in raising my own consciousness as I began to learn more about these pervasive and often secret disorders.

Gradually, I became aware of how many women patients seemed to be perplexed by disordered eating and body image problems. Even if they did not come for psychiatric treatment with an overt eating disorder, they worried about their attractiveness, size, and shape. I found myself asking patients more directly about problems with eating and dieting, only to find that they often kept their concerns and their symptoms to themselves for years. One college student in therapy confided how her dormitory had special bathrooms for the "binge-and-purgers," a fact she had shamefacedly withheld for 2 years despite her frequent use of that facility. Subsequently, many other women shared their stories and taught me much about the variety of self-esteem issues that culminate in the disordered eating and bodily betrayal that is rife in contemporary society. I am particularly grateful to all those individuals who courageously revealed their personal struggles in mastering their eating disorders and engaging more effectively in life.

I am also indebted to a number of colleagues and associates who encouraged me to study and refine concepts and therapeutic strategies throughout my career. Robert Conroy, M.D., saw the need to develop a specialized unit for eating disorders at The Menninger Clinic. He urged staff members to find new ways to creatively address these challenging problems while he fostered each individual's growth and particular contribution. After the unit had been in operation for 4 years, Stuart Averill, M.D., then Hospital Director, appointed me its Section Chief. His commitment to furthering psychological health and individual development in patients nurtured my desire to more fully understand and treat those whose very lives and autonomous strivings were imperiled by their eating disorders.

During my 5 years as Section Chief of the Eating Disorders Program, I worked with a most devoted and talented interdisciplinary staff. Although space does not permit me to acknowledge each individual by name, my gratitude for their caring, teaching, tenacity, and dedication to the treatment of patients is heartfelt. I am particularly appreciative of Gabriella Adorino, M.S., A.T.R.; Johanna Logan, A.S.C.S.W.; and Regina Sebree, R.N., M.S., A.R.N.P., for their solid leadership, clinical wisdom, and unwavering friendship. I have also benefited greatly from working on the unit with Shirley Allen, R.D.; Sarah Bremer Parks, M.A.; C. Alton Barnhill, M.D.; Elizabeth Hatcher, M.D., Ph.D.; Jennifer Kennedy, M.D.; Steven Kowalski, M.D.; and Susie Massoth, M.D. Each provided useful feedback at various phases of this project and fresh perspectives in the care of patients. At a time when regulatory agencies, legal issues, and reimbursement concerns greatly affect the practice of medicine, the contributions of Edward Zoble, Ph.D.; Glenn Leonardi, M.S.; and Marilyn Young, M.B.A., our hospital administrators, went largely unsung but are essential to our work.

Invaluable in the birth of any book is the total ambiance in which one lives and works. The Menninger Clinic is a unique setting that strives to offer its staff as many opportunities for growth as it does its patients. As a student and then faculty member in the Karl Menninger School of Psychiatry and Topeka Institute for Psychoanalysis, I have been exposed to educational and clinical opportunities that have been personally and professionally enriching. My personal analysis with Leonard Horwitz, Ph.D., provided particular understanding, insight, and momentum to pursue my own path. Although many gifted teachers have touched my life, I am especially grateful to John Cokeley, M.D.; Glen Gabbard, M.D.; W. Walter Menninger, M.D.; Irwin Rosen, Ph.D.; and the late Paul Pruyser, Ph.D.; and Donald B. Rinsley, M.D. Each gave thoughtful clinical guidance at crucial moments in my career. Their belief in their students' potential and encouragement to test one's wings by writing has been a vitalizing force for many, including myself.

A number of other colleagues have been kind enough to offer anecdotes, lend support and enthusiasm, and read drafts of chapters at various stages of the manuscript's development. Their thoughts and suggestions were indispensable in helping bring this work to fruition. I wish to thank Alice Brand Bartlett, M.L.S.; Marci Bauman-Bork, M.D.; Bonnie Buchele, Ph.D.; Mary Cerney, Ph.D.; Patricia Harper, M.D.; Phyllis Ragley, D.P.M., J.D.; and Meredith Titus, Ph.D., for all they have contributed to make this book more thorough, useful, and readable. An inestimable degree of appreciation is accorded Kelli Holloway, M.D., who generously read each chapter from the first draft to the final galleys, offering excellent advice and unflagging support. Harriet Lerner, Ph.D., has provided astute guidance about the world of publishing and the merit of writing for a general audience.

Special recognition is due to Mary Ann Clifft, Director of Scientific Publications at Menninger, whose talent for editing is only equaled by her ever-present encouragement. I also wish to thank Philip Beard and Eleanor Bell for their editorial contributions and the staff of the Professional Library at The Menninger Clinic for their tireless efforts in tracking down even the most obscure references. Finally, my Administrative Assistant, Janice Bays, typed and proofread every page from the first to final draft, all the while immersed in additional responsibilities. Her concern for our patients made itself known in a variety of ways—from the coordination of admissions to the Eating Disorders Unit over a period of 9 years, to her meticulous preparation of manuscripts.

My broader support system in the field of eating disorders has added leavening wisdom and unstinting commitment to patients and fellow colleagues. So many workshop participants and new friends sparked fresh ideas that found later expression in this book. I especially wish to thank Judi Goldstein, M.S.S., Renfrew Center; Laura Hill, M.D., National Anorexic Aid Society (NAAS); Craig Johnson, Ph.D., Laureate Psychiatric Center; Marcia Marcus, Ph.D., University of Pittsburgh; Patricia Santucci, M.D., Anorexia Nervosa and Associated Disorders (ANAD); and Rosalyn Weiner, Ph.D., Tufts University, for their encouragement of my writing and teaching over the years.

I owe a considerable debt to the staff of American Psychiatric Press, Inc. Carol Nadelson, M.D., Ron McMillen, Claire Reinburg, Pam Harley, Jon Jensen, Melissa DiGiacomo, Jane Davenport, Anne Friedman, Maria Lavorata, and Stephanie Selice shepherded the entire publication process, maintaining a firm commitment to widely dispersing what contemporary psychiatry offers patients and their loved ones.

It is perhaps more difficult to adequately acknowledge the life-giving force of one's early teachers and the role education plays in setting one's course. From secondary school at the Harrisburg Academy through

Duke University and Temple University School of Medicine, I have grown from the emphasis that was placed on the power of the pen in expressing one's own ideas and values. I am especially grateful for the inspiration of scholarship tempered with concern for other people provided by Fred Rogers, M.D., Temple University School of Medicine.

The completion of any project is made much richer by the love, interest, and generosity of family and friends. Their pivotal presence reaffirms the importance of how change and growth, although difficult, are made easier by relationships that unselfishly promote them. For all they have given to sustain, encourage, guide, and nourish my life over the years, I wish to acknowledge Lance Hamilton, Oscar Laskin, Phyllis Ragley, David Beale, Carlene Benson, John Dillingham, Kelli Holloway, and the late Thomas Dann. I have also been blessed by the irrepressible spirit and advocacy of my uncle, Frank "Skip" Schreckengaust, whose love of the arts guided my own early on. My mother's enthusiasm and feminist strivings convinced me that women can do much of what we want to do and need to do, given the right opportunities and willingness to make difficult choices. With so much to be thankful for, one regret is that my father did not live to see the book to completion. His generosity of spirit, broad intellectual interests, and unselfish devotion to others will always serve as my most abiding source of inspiration.

Kathryn J. Zerbe, M.D.

# About the Author

Kathryn J. Zerbe is the Director of the Adult Outpatient Department, Medical Director of the Women's Program, and a staff psychoanalyst at The Menninger Clinic. Dr. Zerbe completed her B.S. degree in zoology and history at Duke University and her M.D. degree at Temple University School of Medicine. She was the Section Chief of the Eating Disorders Unit at The Menninger Clinic for 5 years and continues to teach and consult on eating disorders. Dr. Zerbe is a faculty member of the Karl Menninger School of Psychiatry and has published numerous professional articles on eating disorders, women's issues, psychotherapy, and psychobiographies of artists. She is a Fellow of the American Psychiatric Association.

# 1

# The Spectrum of Eating Disorders

Diseases of the soul are more dangerous, and more numerous, than those of the body.

Cicero
*Tusculanarum Disputationum*

"I believe we're a little lost. Can you help?" asked Mr. Hamilton as he pulled over to the curb to seek directions to the clinic.

A bit startled by the temporary interruption of her own thoughts, the doctor looked up and tried to orient him. "It's right around the corner. If you park in that paved lot, you won't have any trouble finding your way."

How simple it is to ask for help or to give directions when the questions are clear and the path seems easy to follow! And how much more difficult to find your way when you or a loved one confronts a serious, potentially life-threatening problem. Immediately, you worry if you are doing all that should or can be done. You wonder if those who are trying to be helpful really understand the complexity of the situation that has bewildered you for so long. You naturally feel irritated and upset when you find no relief from your burden. And if your problem involves a serious medical illness, you struggle all the more with concerns about the ultimate physical outcome and psychological toll: "What can be done? Where do I turn for help? Am I responsible for what has happened? Will I survive?"

Your questions, which may not even be spoken to those you love the most, reflect how perils of the body always seem to make us search our souls. We are forced to ask ourselves over and over what is most meaningful in our lives. We wonder what we must change so that we can get well, and if we will have the strength to do it. Questions about how to take care of our bodies ultimately encompass how we care for all aspects of ourselves and those we love.

Such was the soul-wrenching situation for the Hamilton family. Like so many parents of patients with eating disorders, Mr. and Mrs. Hamilton had become quite confused and beleaguered in their attempts to help their daughter, who struggled with a severe eating disorder. The more they tried to help Greer, the more she felt they were trying to take over her life. The three of them avoided talking about conflict at all costs, but each silently worried about the eventual state of the other two. They had all read many books and pamphlets about eating disorders, had worked hard in individual and family therapy, and were willing to do just about anything to try to change the manifest problems. Nothing seemed to work. Their loss of physical direction to the clinic mirrored their inner loss of direction. Each member of the family silently and sadly wondered, "Can I do anything else to change this eating disorder and put life on a better track? Why is it that we always start out with such purpose to modify our behavior and end up with flat-footed failure?" Perhaps the greatest burden is the silent weight of guilt that all of them felt for not doing more—or not doing better.

From 21-year-old Greer's perspective, success seemed like a birthright. She was proud that she always seemed to accomplish exactly what she set out to do in school, but she always had two very big worries. One was her weight. She never seemed to be thin enough or attractive enough. The other worry was her family. She never was able to please them enough—not to her satisfaction at least. It seemed impossible to let them know how hurt she was that her achievements never garnered their approval.

Greer sensed that her mother turned to her for comfort and companionship while her father retreated to the den to place business calls. He attended to his work, not to his wife's emotional needs. Greer wished her parents could intimately share their troubles with each other, rather than with her. Greer had few friendships with people her own age because her mother seemed to demand so much of her daughter's attention.

Mrs. Hamilton was very concerned about Greer's restless pursuit of thinness to the neglect of other life accomplishments. Somehow, she seemed to sense that for years Greer had kept secret episodes of dieting and bingeing. All the while, Mrs. Hamilton had tried to be the "perfect mother," not only ministering to her immediate family but also taking care of her own mother, who lived just a few blocks away. She had her own secrets, too. Mrs. Hamilton felt bitter about how she had sacrificed her talents to care for her family. Still, she was perplexed because her devotion had given her much gratification throughout her life, yet now Greer was not doing well.

In contrast, Mr. Hamilton was more walled off from his feelings. He seemed to be totally devoted to his work and would often go for days (or so it seemed to his wife and daughter) without taking a break. Greer and her older sister Elyse experienced their father as devoted but distant, caring but too caught up in his own world for them to count much. Yet Mr. Hamilton perceived himself as being continually preoccupied with the plight of his family. Like most parents, he said his heart's desire was to be a better parent than his own parents had been to him. To provide what he believed were the financial and spiritual requirements for a successful family life, he sacrificed his own pleasures and even side-stepped several promotions.

Nonetheless, Mr. Hamilton's wife and daughters seemed chronically irritated with him; they believed that he did not regard any of them with the depth of respect they deserved. They felt unheard and unaccepted. Although Mrs. Hamilton still loved her husband, she longed for the tender passion of their courtship and the esteem with which he had held her when they first met. Greer and Elyse knew none of this; the glimmers of sexuality and courtship were suppressed in this proper, emotionally muted family.

By the time the four had found their way to the clinic's entrance, each shuddered about the evaluation they knew would soon occur. On the outside, they seemed composed and compliant; on the inside, they fretted about what they would be asked to reveal and admit to. Like other eating disorder patients and their families, they worried that they would be blamed for the "sin" of causing or having an eating disorder. They had come to expect that the treating clinicians might not be direct with them and would always assume the worst. Thus, when they were met at the door by a staff member who simply began to take their history nonjudgmentally, they were immediately relieved. Treatment had begun.

The plight of the Hamilton family is not unique. Patients with eating disorders and their mothers, fathers, and siblings all struggle with shame and guilt about having the illness in the first place. They blame themselves and—instead of believing that mental health professionals know that they have done their best—they nevertheless assume they will be found guilty of a series of crimes they unknowingly committed. Although the context for starting treatment appears to be changing for the better, professionals have contributed much to the fear and lack of confidence that families face when seeking help. Psychiatric care has not always been user friendly. In the past, psychiatrists, psychologists, and social workers sometimes seemed to have a haughty attitude toward their patients and the patients' families, and these therapists sometimes came across as distant, uncaring, hurtful, or even cruel.

This perception of mental health professionals and their judgments of patients has held true for those with a variety of emotional illnesses, but it is particularly common in those with eating disorders. These disorders, which occur 90%–95% of the time in women, have been understood as arising from faults within the family system. No doubt family therapy has been an important source of help for such families, but blaming them has not been so helpful. Little wonder that patients and their families have tried to avoid professional guidance until it is absolutely necessary.

To enter treatment, families like the Hamiltons must muster their courage. They must be willing to take a hard look at themselves as well as at each other. Admitting one has flaws and makes mistakes is never easy; forgiving errors of the past, which must occur for treatment to be successful, is even harder. Thus, treatment that emphasizes from the first the strengths and potential of each family member, while acknowledging the complexity and difficulty of the illness, is bound to start off on a much better footing.

The Hamiltons were encouraged by an approach that de-emphasized blaming and encouraged a thorough understanding of the problems at hand. They were aware that their family, like all families, had problems and conflicts. Although they wanted to become less rigid and more able to deal openly with disagreements, they also wanted to learn more about the eating disorders. They raised questions from the first day of treatment that centered on how eating disorders come into being, their diagnoses, the role played by culture and biology in their development, and the medical toll they take on the patient.

Like other families, the Hamiltons were curious about the disorder and themselves. Yet even as they began treatment with a desire to do better, they also had a healthy skepticism. From a treater's perspective, they were a challenging but rewarding family to work with because they were "ready for treatment." That is to say, they were willing not only to learn about the many facets of eating disorders, but they were also willing to attempt the long-term process of changing themselves. In so doing, patients must search their own souls—and force their treaters to do likewise. Transformation also occurs in treaters, who learn so much every day about the illness from the experiences of their patients and families.

This book is written not only for patients and families like the Hamiltons, but out of gratitude to them. Over the years they have taught me much, not only about the eating disorders per se but also about how the human heart deals with suffering and tries to overcome it. Perhaps most importantly, their stories have encouraged me, as a therapist, to be open to learning more and to be hopeful about the possibilities in seeking treatment and changing one's life. In the words of the late Karl Menninger, each patient who engages in therapy comes to see the self "not as a mere spectator of cosmic events but as a prime mover; to regard himself not as a passive incident in the infinite universe but as one important unit possessing the power to influence great decisions by making small ones." With devotion and difficulty, patients and families learn to expand their personal choices.

The story of the Hamiltons, and those stories of other patients throughout this book, are a testament to the complexity of eating disorders and the many different avenues that one must take to understand and treat them. All the while, openness to new sources of treatment provides inspiration that only comes from working with bright and engaging patients. What begins for many as a disease of body and soul contains within it the seeds for physical and psychological renewal.

To see how an individual with a severe eating disorder can curtail her symptoms and transform her life, let's start by learning about the diagnoses and their treatments, much as the Hamiltons did when they came to the clinic. The book is really a series of stories about individuals who have valiantly—though often at first reluctantly—engaged in treatment. It is also about learning and growth. The chapters are really outlines of what patients who enter a comprehensive eating disorders program should encounter in treatment.

Emphasis is placed on education, because teaching patients and their families about these disorders is a cornerstone of recovery. My theoretical base is a psychodynamic one, although it obviously includes other important models of treatment, including family, cognitive, biological, and cultural perspectives. Each chapter will delve into some of these facets of treatment, both in the case examples that are described and in the more didactic portions of the book. Psychological growth occurs when all of these important treatment perspectives are interwoven correctly, depending on the individual needs of the patient. I hope to be able to demonstrate the value of each of these treatment modalities in particular cases, while remaining true to my experience that helping individuals understand their plight and their ultimate responsibility for self-cure is the heart of healing.

In this chapter, we began with the story of the Hamilton family and their initial anxieties and concerns at the start of the treatment process. Like most families, they had initial concerns that ran the gamut from what causes such distress to how one can be sure of diagnosis. The Hamiltons wondered what the outcome of Greer's condition would be and if specific treatments they had read about in newspapers and magazines might prove useful. But, like many families, they were also discouraged. Greer had already struggled with her illness for several years; she had made numerous treatment attempts without much progress. Let's look at what the Hamiltons and other families need to learn about the spectrum of eating disorders—their broad cultural context, how clinicians establish a definitive diagnosis, and, finally, the possibilities for recovery. These facts will help us appreciate why the treatment of an eating disorder is fraught with difficulties for a significant number of women.

## The Cultural Context

The questions raised by this family are very common, as the readers of this book can no doubt attest. Eating disorders are now recognized as major medical and psychiatric problems, affecting millions of women in the United States and Europe. Additionally, of late we seem to be immersed in a symptomatic sea of disordered eating among all women. Women's magazines tout the advantages of the latest fad diets side by side with pages of luscious recipes of America's nouvelle cuisine. The paradoxical message—to remain slender while still partaking of life's succulent smorgasbord—presents an immediate, albeit rather superficial, conflict: To indulge or to remain slender in the face of great abundance? How we wrestle with this conflict and finally resolve it depends on our individual values and beliefs. Of course, how we use food and what we use it for depends on a host of other issues as well that will be addressed throughout this book. Suffice it to say for now that we will learn why eating problems develop under a variety of stressors and situations. We will address the highly evocative and symbolic nature of food and how it helps people deal with intense feelings and periods of crisis.

We live in a society obsessed with size, weight, and image. This is readily apparent by merely observing the explosion of diet clinics, liquid fasting programs, advertisements for weight reduction vacations and spas, and the weight control pharmacopoeia at any local drugstore. What Christopher Lasch (1979) has deemed the narcissistic culture of our time is reflected in part by the quest for the perfect appearance, figure, and life-style. Meanwhile, psychiatrists, psychologists, social workers, and primary care physicians are flooded with complaints from patients that reflect disturbed body image and a plethora of symptoms that connote the diagnostic spectrum of eating disorders.

Our preoccupation with our bodies and beauty itself has supplanted other psychiatric conditions. Some mental health professionals even go so far as to wonder if the eating disorders are one of the late 20th century's primary mental health issues, much as hysteria was in Freud's time. This explanation leads clinicians to speculate about cause (etiology) and intervention. Yet time for philosophical discourse and historical critique runs short when the focus must be on providing immediate assistance to a patient with severe symptoms. For anorexia nervosa alone, the fatality rate is estimated to be between 5% and 20%; complications of obesity or bulimia can also lead to early death, often causing significant physical and psychological problems along the way. When family members and their loved ones become aware of these scary statistics, they worry all the more about what to do. Sometimes the patient herself has kept the problem secret for years or sought help, to no avail. No wonder that all concerned feel anxious and perplexed; sometimes the situation seems hopeless and overwhelming.

In reality, help is available and, over the long run, people can improve a great deal. But to begin directing the individual to the best resources to assist her, we must first answer some thorny questions: What really constitutes an "eating disorder"? How do the symptoms develop? What kinds of additional problems usually accompany an eating disorder and complicate getting well? Finally, what can be done to help?

## The Continuum of Eating Pathologies

Like mental illness, mental health is best viewed as a state or process occurring along a continuum that ranges from good or acceptable to bad or unacceptable. This conceptualization suggests that mental health and mental illness are not dichotomous entities but rather are dynamic patterns of change that occur in all individuals throughout the life cycle.

Like other diagnostic entities, the eating disorders should be viewed as falling along just such a spectrum. Thus any concern about weight, calories, diet, or figure can be viewed as extremely common—if not normative—among most adolescent and adult females. Likewise, an occasional pizza or ice cream splurge with friends does not necessarily make you bulimic. However, a patient's specific diagnosis of anorexia nervosa, bulimia nervosa, or atypical eating disorder must be rendered when the pursuit of thinness becomes more entrenched, ascetic restriction of food worsens, or when binge and purge cycles become more frequent and when the preoccupation with body image grows more distorted.

To make specific diagnoses, most mental health professionals make use of the American Psychiatric Association's *Diagnostic and Statistical Manual of Mental Disorders* (DSM; DSM-III-R, 1987; DSM-IV Draft Criteria 1993), as a guide. These diagnoses have been arrived at through extensive research and thorough review by practicing clinicians. This standard diagnostic guide enables clinicians to be reasonably secure when making an assessment or diagnosing a patient. The patient must have sufficient symptoms to fulfill a diagnostic category. This specificity allows patients to know when their condition is serious enough to warrant a formal psychiatric diagnosis. Clinicians also find it helpful as a kind of medical shorthand for communicating with other professionals. It thereby allows both patient and treater to be made aware of major areas of difficulty.

Diagnostic practices, even in psychiatry, change a great deal over the years. Research and clinical work with patients help clinicians refine what they do. In 1994, the fourth edition of DSM (DSM-IV) will be published for use by American psychiatrists. Because the proposed diagnostic conventions of this manual are the most up to date, I will follow them in describing the eating disorders. However, many of the research studies I refer to were based on earlier definitions (DSM-III [1980] or DSM-III-R [1987]) of anorexia nervosa and bulimia nervosa. The criteria from these manuals are included for reference in the Appendix. The reader can thus see the evolution of the diagnostic practices and how sophisticated research ensures that nothing will stay the same or remain concrete. This perspective is also crucial for clinicians, because it keeps us humble, remembering as we must that our most strongly held theories and ideas are subject to rapid change. In treating patients, as in refining diagnostic categories, one must always be open to broader vistas.

Naturally, DSM-IV tells only part of the story. No list of symptoms or diagnostic manual can ever convey the real pain of the patient and her family. Moreover, many people do not fulfill all of the specific criteria of a given disorder but nevertheless suffer a great deal. This contradiction is particularly true of the eating disorders, because a large number of individuals (especially women) do not manifest all the criteria but still have what in medical parlance is termed "subclinical pathology."

Before delving into this important area, I will list the criteria for the major eating disorders: anorexia nervosa, bulimia nervosa, and eating disorder not otherwise specified (NOS). Throughout the rest of this book, I will discuss how certain individuals with these diagnoses come into treatment in quite different—and often perplexing—ways. Their lives will illustrate how helpful a manual like DSM-IV may be in defining an illness; but they will also show how a diagnostic tool fails to convey each person's uniqueness and the heavy tolls exacted by the disorder. As we look at these fascinating case histories of women from a range of backgrounds and with different strengths, we might be prone to agree with psychoanalyst Elvin Semrad, who wrote that he gave up reading novels because he was so enthralled with the real lives of his patients.

The criteria for anorexia nervosa, bulimia nervosa, and eating disorder not otherwise specified from DSM-IV are condensed and summarized below.

### Anorexia Nervosa

A. Refusal to maintain body weight over a minimally normal weight for age and height.

B. Intense fear of gaining weight or becoming fat, even though underweight.

C. Undue influence of body weight or shape on self-evaluation, or denial of the seriousness of the current low body weight.

D. In females, absence of at least three consecutive menstrual cycles when otherwise expected to occur.

**Type:**

*Bulimic type:* During the episode of Anorexia Nervosa, the person engages in recurrent episodes of binge eating.

*Nonbulimic type:* During the episode of Anorexia Nervosa, the person does not engage in recurrent episodes of binge eating.

### Bulimia Nervosa

A.  Recurrent episodes of binge eating. An episode of binge eating is characterized by both of the following:
    (1)  eating, in a discrete period of time (e.g., within any 2-hour period), an amount of food that is definitely larger than most people would eat in a similar period of time.
    (2)  a sense of lack of control over eating during the episode (e.g., a feeling that one cannot stop eating or control what or how much one is eating).
    Option B1: Restrict to vomiting or use of laxatives.
    Option B2: No change from DSM-III-R criterion but with the addition of purging and nonpurging subtypes.
C.  A minimum average of two binge-eating episodes a week for at least 3 months.
D.  Self-evaluation is unduly influenced by body shape and weight.
E.  The disturbance does not occur exclusively during episodes of Anorexia Nervosa.

**Type:**

*Purging type:* The person regularly engages in self-induced vomiting or the use of laxatives or diuretics.

*Nonpurging type:* The person uses strict dieting, fasting, or vigorous exercise, but does not regularly engage in purging.

### Eating Disorder Not Otherwise Specified

1)  Subthreshold Anorexia Nervosa:
    a)  all of the criteria for Anorexia Nervosa are met except

the individual continues to have regular menses.
b) all of the criteria for Anorexia Nervosa are met except the abnormally low weight requirement.

2) Subthreshold Bulimia Nervosa:
a) Binge Eating Disorder: eating binges accompanied by significant distress, but without any regular compensatory behavior (e.g., vomiting, laxative abuse).
b) eating binges with atypical compensatory mechanisms (e.g., abuse of thyroid medication or diet pills, an individual with diabetes mellitus who intentionally reduces insulin dose).
c) eating binges at a frequency of less than twice a week for three months.
d) compensatory behavior in the absence of the consumption of sufficiently large amount of food to meet the criteria for a binge (e.g., self-induced vomiting after eating two cookies).
e) an individual who repeatedly chews, but does not swallow, large amounts of food (and instead spits it out).

Although patients with eating disorders whose diagnoses are confirmed by these descriptive criteria pose the greatest therapeutic challenge to clinicians, other individuals who may not be formally diagnosed also struggle with feelings about their bodies and eating. Their psychological struggle with food broadens the base of concern for this ubiquitous clinical problem. Moreover, as we come to appreciate more fully the struggles of persons with severe eating disorders, we cast additional light on others who are preoccupied with their eating and are commonly observed in clinical practice.

In this way, we find that the eating disorders actually occur on a spectrum and vary in severity in the general population. For example, some women may binge only once a month and not purge at all, yet can be very upset by their behavior; they may sense they indulge in bingeing to cope with underlying depression or fear of failing. Likewise, a woman may lose weight but never to the degree of having anorexia. She may also continue to menstruate and never binge or purge. Her weight loss may be based on the emphasis society has placed on thinness in addition to the general malaise she feels about life. She may be relentless in pursuit of thinness because her self-esteem is so poor in other areas. She may be blocked in achieving her life goals, including "the goal of anorexia," because her desired target weight never reaches a double-digit number.

As you can see, the eating disorder may be the one island of mastery and hope for an individual who otherwise is lost at sea, feeling less than adequate to engage life or other people. She is often lonely. She struggles to find herself because her life experiences seem so confusing. Her eating disorder may mask highly charged anger, frustration, sadness, or emptiness. When you look her in the face, however, she may look normal, even healthy. How often external appearance hides inner misery! So many people smile on the outside and cry within—the most common secret patients with eating disorders hide, in my clinical experience. Let us turn to a typical story from clinical practice to illustrate the impact of even subclinical eating problems and how bingeing can be an attempt at finding solace and soothing for loss and sadness.

❧ Karen A. was a 33-year-old moderately obese woman who worked as an artist and was divorced. She had made much progress in her relationships with men and in her creative productivity over the course of 3½ years of psychotherapy three times a week. A breakup with her boyfriend initiated a treatment phase where Karen focused on her body image, detailing her struggle with failed diets and exercise programs over the years.

One day, after the therapist's vacation had interrupted the therapy, Karen reported that her symptoms of binge eating had worsened during the therapist's absence. For the first time, Karen revealed that when she found herself anxious or lonely, she gorged on any food that she kept in the house. Although this behavior had been somewhat ameliorated during treatment, the recent interruption had caused her to lapse into dyscontrol. Karen had found herself grabbing handfuls of cake mix out of the box and stuffing it into her mouth with abandon, followed by remorse and embarrassment. The therapist wondered if Karen had to fill herself up with the cake mix because no one was available to console her or to fill her with self-understanding.

Over time Karen figured out that she not only missed her therapist or boyfriend but had been lonesome for many years. She had been able to hold this feeling at bay, however, by becoming a very successful artist.

Patients like Karen A. are common and perplexing to clinicians, but they do not usually provoke as much concern as those who fulfill all the DSM-IV criteria for anorexia nervosa or bulimia nervosa. Nevertheless, these persons suffer mightily. Problems like Karen's, which fall along the spectrum of eating-related symptoms, are pervasive in clinical practice. No physician or psychotherapist can avoid them. Of even more importance is the fact that these patients are burdened with such an overwhelming and shameful body self-hatred that often they are able to confide their symptoms only after months of therapy. It is thus essential for all who seek to understand and help themselves and others with eating disorders to learn more about the presentation and underlying meaning of the scope of these disorders' symptomatology. People learn they are not alone either in their struggles with eating or in the raw emotions that eating disorders help them hide. In this book, I hope to make others aware of the broad scope of the eating disorders and the heavy toll they take on patients and their families. I hope to demonstrate that these disorders are an attempt, albeit an ineffective one, at coping and self-cure.

By now you might be asking yourself why these difficulties deserve so much attention, even to the point of warranting publication of this book. After all, you might reasonably argue, true bulimic and anorexic patients make up a relatively small percentage of psychiatric and psychotherapeutic practice, especially compared to patients with other problems such as depression or anxiety. You might further suggest that health care costs have risen so high that, despite the distress these problems bring, we simply cannot afford to spend precious insurance dollars and personal funds treating them. No doubt, treatment is costly, both in terms of time and money spent; but the disorders are even more costly. Anorexia nervosa and bulimia nervosa are grave health problems of international magnitude. The case examples described throughout this book will highlight this more than any statistics I might cite. Yet percentages also make their point, as we recognize how common these disorders are and how they are currently on the rise.

When rigid diagnostic criteria are used, epidemiologic studies show that between 1% and 5% of the population has anorexia nervosa and that 2%–18% has bulimia nervosa. Granted, these statistics show that eating disorders are not nearly as common as affective or anxiety disorders; but they fail to take into account the diagnostic continuum of eating pathologies, those subclinical difficulties described earlier. Moreover, sociological studies have suggested that a range of eating problems may go unstudied and untreated—largely to the detriment of young women whose difficulties may become chronic but invisible. Although clinicians have been cognizant of these abnormal but undiagnosed eating patterns, they will need to pay more attention to them because of long-term medical and psychological effects of the disorders.

## The Spectrum of Prognosis

The eating disorders are variable in their outcome. Although many follow-up studies have shown a recovery rate as high as 60%–70% after 5 years, the psychiatric literature is just beginning to recognize the existence of a very large subgroup of eating disorder patients who do not get well easily or quickly. Their eating disorders may improve with treatment for a short period, but relapse is very high over the long run. Those who do regain their weight or stop bingeing and purging may still be plagued by poor interpersonal relationships, sexual concerns, limited independence, depression, anxiety, and impaired attitudes toward eating and weight. Those patients who remain ill over a prolonged period appear to develop a less satisfying life-style filled with social and psychological difficulties. With third-party payers placing more emphasis on limited treatment hours, the treatments to date have emphasized short-term, cost-effective strategies such as cognitive, psychoeducational, behavioral, and psychopharmacologic therapies. No doubt these treatment modalities have helped a wide variety of patients, but at least one-third of individual patients continue to remain ill despite these treatments.

These findings may at first seem disheartening and confounding, which is unfortunate, because psychiatry has more to offer its patients than ever before. Although this specialty is still young, people are being helped by a wide array of interventions. It is therefore important that therapists not relegate to the back burner the wise advice of Hilde Bruch and of those psychodynamically oriented clinicians who built on her work. These psychotherapeutic strategies, based on an appreciation of developmental concerns and the dynamic unconscious, add to what can be achieved by other approaches.

To provide a comprehensive view of what can now be done to treat eating disorders successfully, I will describe each important modality throughout this book. Unfortunately, despite treatment, some people will still not recover. However, these effective interventions may bring new hope to a significant number of patients with eating disorders whose symptoms have thus far been tenacious. Psychotherapeutic—especially psychodynamic—ideas must be integrated with other treatment modalities to provide patients with the best chance of full recovery.

Despite the real gains that have been made, patients and their families naturally wonder what the treatment follow-up studies tell us about what helps these patients. Relatives who are guardedly optimistic about their loved ones ask about who gets better quickly and who does not. They raise important questions that are difficult to answer in the abstract, because individuals have varying degrees of strength, motivation, and limitations that influence how and when they can make use of treatment. Moreover, research has still not been able to identify with any degree of certainty which patients will consistently benefit from treatment. Still, there are notable trends worth reporting. These sobering facts will show us the magnitude of problems confronting people with eating disorders. On the other hand, the case examples in this book will show much that statistical data fail to reveal—how and under what circumstances some individuals have truly been able to make strides in their lives, often despite a multitude of difficulties and tragic life events.

The psychiatric literature increasingly demonstrates that formally diagnosed patients with eating disorders find it very difficult to fully recover with brief and superficial treatment interventions. Psychoeducational, cognitive, behavioral, and psychopharmacologic treatments form the basis of most treatment plans and are of great help to 40%–50% of all diagnosed anorexic and bulimic patients. On the other hand, these treatment efforts fall short for a large subgroup of patients with significant symptomatology. Their lives have been seriously interrupted by a plethora of events and conflicts that impede their personal growth.

Garfinkel and Garner (1982) were among the first to bring this dilemma into bold relief when they summarized 25 follow-up studies. They found that at least 30% of the patients with anorexia nervosa were either dead as a consequence of their illness or were still chronically afflicted at follow-up. Even in those patients who had recovered their weight, only 17%–40% were symptom-free; most continued to have severe obsessive, compulsive, or depressive symptomatology. Clearly, many individuals were in need of more—or different—help than they had received or were receiving. Beresin and colleagues (1989) expanded on this early effort to describe the subgroup of patients with difficult-to-treat eating disorders. At follow-up, they found that among anorexic patients, 40% were totally recovered and 30% had improved; but at least 30% had either died or were chronically afflicted a few years after their initial evaluation and treatment. Moreover, 40%–55% of the sample had persistent family problems, while 40% had unsatisfactory sexual lives or poor interpersonal relationships. Halmi's 10-year follow-up study (Halmi et al. 1991) demonstrated that only 14% of patients were free of an eating disorder, but those who did well had participated in aggressive treatment the first year after discharge from the hospital. In addition to anorexia, a significant number of those patients in this longitudinal study had depression, anxiety, phobias, or obsessive-compulsive disorder.

Research on bulimia nervosa paints a similarly dismal picture. Because this disorder was not extensively studied until the 1970s, long-term follow-up reports are just beginning to appear in the literature. Bemporad and Herzog (1989) report that the short-term follow-up data for bulimic patients is encouraging. Indeed, studies from inpatient centers have consistently demonstrated rapid symptom control with strict behavioral methods. Throughout this book, I describe specific techniques that have been most helpful to patients and suggest the psychotherapeutic rationale behind such interventions. But for now, let me emphasize that therapists should not overestimate or overvalue symptom control alone for these patients. Studies conducted by my colleagues and me at the C. F. Menninger Memorial Hospital corroborate the findings of Bemporad and Herzog (1989). Our studies have shown that from one-third to one-half of those treated for bulimia are still ill at long-term follow-up. Bemporad and Herzog's work in a long-term study at Massachusetts General Hospital demonstrated that one-third of all bulimic patients are still in their index (initial) episode 35 to 42 months after evaluation.

Additional findings, captured in a different way, were reported at the University of Minnesota (Mitchell et al. 1989b). Observing that many current bulimic patients appeared psychologically sicker than those seen in the early 1980s, Mitchell wondered if the patient population was truly changing or if he and his research team simply saw a subpopulation of those who were "difficult to treat." The researchers concluded that this group was worse by several parameters, including poor interpersonal relationships, exacerbated laxative abuse, and increased work impairment. In two other reports (Mitchell et al. 1989a, 1989c), the Mitchell team showed that *one in every four bulimic patients was a treatment failure*. They concluded that the success rate may be even worse, because at least one person in the group committed suicide and several others refused to respond to the questionnaire, possibly indicating a worsening pattern of symptomatology.

These stark findings demonstrate that almost one-half of those diagnosed as having an eating disorder are plagued by more than the mere symptom of sporadic gluttony or food restriction alone. They suffer mightily in many areas of their lives. This concomitant dysfunctioning will come as no surprise to anyone who gets to know individuals with eating disorders. They are filled with unexplained anxieties and are unable to relieve their inner tension, yet they want to get close to others but are afraid to. Often they will cry out for (but simultaneously reject) interpersonal relationships, even with family members. This contradictory behavior makes it difficult for other people, including their therapist, to reach out to them consistently. Consequently, many clinicians are only too aware of how often their treatment efforts will fall short, often leading to personal feelings of inadequacy that are echoed by the patients themselves and their family members. Yet such findings are perhaps also paradoxically encouraging, because they reveal how much therapists would like to truly understand and support these patients and how much the patients also yearn to be understood.

It has become increasingly clear that the mere management of symptoms cannot be equated with definitive treatment. Patients want the quality of *all* aspects of their lives to improve, not simply their eating disorder. They know all too well that their eating disorder symptom is often the veritable tip of the iceberg of other pernicious and often interconnected psychiatric symptoms, as the case of Nicole B. shows.

❦  Nicole B. was a 20-year-old college sophomore when she was admitted for the second time to the eating disorders unit. Diabetic since age 5 and anorexic since age 16, she had made modest gains during her first stay in the structured inpatient program. She seemed to be collaborating well with personnel in the eating disorders clinic and with her individual psychotherapist. An insightful and engaging English major, Nicole became verbally abusive when she started to take steps away from her family of origin. During 2 years of outpatient therapy, she kept her weight stable but low.

Nicole finally required readmission to the hospital when her diabetes and anorexia nervosa became worse as she and the therapist discussed her concerns about her sexuality and her disappointment with her father. Nicole's eating disorder had placed her in grave medical jeopardy. Despite her intelligence, she would abjectly deny her plight as she raged at the treatment team for "making me fat and controlling me." Meanwhile, she insisted that she be allowed to return to college, even in the face of her deteriorating health. Nicole wanted to persist in her efforts to maintain academic placement on the dean's list and to edit the campus literary magazine.

Patients like Nicole can confuse and challenge their treaters. In the face of starvation and medical compromise they appear, superficially, to be doing well. So much of their lives seem intact, even idyllic, as they pose as "the most proper little girls in the world" and only belatedly blossom into womanhood. But a longitudinal and circumspect review of their illnesses reveals periods of exacerbation and remission of the eating disorder. Similarly, a detailed developmental history often reveals lags in psychological growth, family discord and divorce, death, physical or sexual abuse in the family, and a personal or family history of depression or other psychiatric disorders. Sometimes individuals with eating disorders also engage in unusual purgative behaviors or drug and alcohol abuse. To promote a thorough appreciation of the wide range of problems faced by people with eating disorders, the variety of these difficulties is addressed in subsequent chapters. We will review what the scientific literature says about the most important characteristics of eating disorders, while sharing clinical examples that illustrate the profound morbidity and personal cost of the developmental struggles that herald these illnesses.

However, because no statistical study will ever capture the inner struggles of a person, many patients who ostensibly do well may still be plagued with psychological problems and even the eating disorder itself. Such is the situation with both Karen A. and Nicole B., who function well in the outside world yet continue to suffer inside. Listening to another person describe her inner pain and anger is always difficult. Even clinicians, despite their professional training and experience, may unconsciously try to avoid hearing about what causes a manifest symptom, because it is most difficult to quickly alleviate and assuage. Sometimes it is even more disconcerting for concerned family members, who are well aware of their loved one's medical jeopardy and inner misery. They want so much to reach out and help, but they often don't know what to say or to do. As we study the cases that follow, we'll look at what gets in the way and how to overcome it.

## Of Psyche and Soma

For most of us, psyche and soma are essentially integrated. We use our bodies every day in many ways, but we really don't think about them very often. The opposite holds true when we become physically ill. Sometimes the illness is organically based, but sometimes it is caused by psychological factors or stress. Such an illness is called a "psychosomatic disorder."

Before we explore what might go wrong with the psyche to affect the soma, or body physiology, we must first think for a moment about what transpires every day as we go about our business, interacting in the world through our bodies. Medical writer Jonathan Miller describes the essential unity of psyche and soma—our body's importance to us:

> Of all the objects in the world, the human body has a peculiar status: It is not only possessed by the person who has it, it also possesses and constitutes him. Our body is quite different from all the other things we claim as our own. We can lose money, books, and even houses and still remain recognizably ourselves, but it is hard to give any intelligible sense to the idea of a disembodied person. . . . The body is the medium of experience and the instrument of action. Through its actions we shape and organize our experiences and distinguish our perceptions of the outside world from the sensations that arrive within the body itself. (1978, p. 14)

And so it is that we become concerned and perplexed when the body and spirit no longer reach out into the world with effective action. Growth experiences stop as the individual becomes focused on all of the sensations within her body, to the detriment of looking at the outside world and moving effectively into it. This disenfranchisement of the body constitutes the psychosomatic disorders of which anorexia nervosa and bulimia nervosa are an important part.

We might think of the eating disorders as stemming from impingements from the environment. Any one of a number of developmental factors we will look at may cause psyche and soma to disrupt their fragile but life-sustaining unity as they begin to wage war with one another. This very battle rages in anorexic and bulimic people, where the body is hated. These individuals attack rather than care for their bodies. For example, you are most likely familiar with the starving anorexic person who compulsively exercises to the point of causing bone fractures. No one can tell her how she is hurting herself, although she is consciously aware of suffering. Likewise, a bulimic person with medical complications will compulsively continue to binge and purge despite warnings and treatment. For many people, this self-injurious cycle is not easily broken, and we must look to the underlying causes to discover why this is so.

In essence, anorexic and bulimic people do not experience their minds, hearts, and bodies in unison, nor do they try to thrive and to grow. Instead, one part of the self wars against the other, as if within the body a hurtful relationship develops between the psyche and the soma. It is as if each part is trying to persecute another part. A patient will thus often say, "I hate the way my body looks and feels. I don't see any way out of the trap my body puts me in every day. The only thing I do that feels good is to not eat." This vicious cycle can create an intractable conflict for the individual, whose healthy striving toward integration of psyche and soma becomes blocked. The embattled self becomes enfeebled by the physiological effects of the eating disorder, as well as by a host of psychological conflicts and deficits. Let's begin to think about what might go wrong and cause individuals to relentlessly continue a hurtful eating pattern that interferes totally with their lives.

Sigmund Freud remarked that "the ego is first and foremost a bodily ego" (1923/1961, p. 26). By this, he meant that we are all interested in the integrity of our body and that our libido becomes invested in our body (Schilder 1950). In the earliest stages of life, libido is concentrated in parts of the body that have special significance—largely the mouth. The developing baby takes in or spits out with its mouth as it sensually enjoys its mother's expressions of tenderness through the skin. Thus, from our earliest days, there is a libidinal investment, or eroticism, in our mouths, our muscles, and our skin.

More than 40 years ago, the psychiatrist Rene Spitz (1959) studied a group of infants who had been separated since birth from their imprisoned mothers. The babies were kept at a prison nursery; all their physical needs (e.g., feeding, cleaning, changing) were methodically met. But loving contact (i.e., fondling, caressing, rocking, lulling, soothing) was totally absent. Despite the adequacy of their physical care, the children became depressed, withdrawn, and immobile. Their immune systems failed, and many of them died. They showed every evidence of having given up hope until Spitz brought back the mothers, instructing them to hold the infants, to feed them instead of propping bottles up on pillows, and to start touching, rocking, and, in effect, loving them. So treated, the children reversed their pattern of hopelessness and once again thrived. They required the somatic infusion of bodily tenderness to reawaken their infant psyches with life-sustaining hope and love.

Thus, the developmental voyage begins with the early interaction of psyche and soma under the loving eyes of one's parents. At this pre-verbal time, all communication occurs through the body without the "code of language" (McDougall 1989). A developing child gradually learns to have a clear representation of her own body image as distinct from that of her mother as the child develops the verbal skills to communicate with her. Yet it is not surprising that when the early developmental processes go astray, damage to the psyche and soma occurs. This malfunction leads to the disunity noted earlier and the internal battles that have no vent in words so early in life.

Such may be the roots of psychosomatic vulnerabilities (McDougall 1989), of which the eating disorders may be considered the quintessential example. The severe split between psyche and soma cuts off the patient from experiencing her body and her inner world. Such patients often have no way to express their feelings or to reduce inner tensions verbally (i.e., they are alexithymic), so any complex affective experiences are channeled instead through their bodies. They often "vomit up" their feeling states that they can't talk about in words (e.g., through bulimia); they also may seek to negate their body and their feelings altogether (e.g., through anorexia). These disorders tell us that development has been blocked and the individual must be helped to move forward on life's path. Because of the early origin of these disturbances, we might think of the problems as residing within the interior of the body that speaks for the patient in physical rather than verbal ways. No wonder anorexic and bulimic patients are often plagued by other psychosomatic complaints.

❦ Mandy C. was a 23-year-old secretary whose pixieish face and child-like mannerisms made her appear no older than 13. Plagued with life-threatening asthmatic attacks since childhood, Mandy also compulsively excoriated her skin and hair and then consumed these bodily vestiges. Severely anorexic for 10 years, she had proved resistant to behavioral, cognitive, and pharmacologic interventions. Meanwhile, Mandy defied school administrators and probation officers, developing a long history of truancy and of breaking and entering houses. However, Mandy never took anything when she entered a house illegally. She only wanted to "have a look around" and would solemnly shrug her shoulders whenever she was caught in the act by the homeowner, who was usually another woman.

Not surprisingly, Mandy's history revealed a dearth of maternal sustenance and care since birth. With the ministrations of nursing staff members and thoughtful interventions in psychotherapy, Mandy gradually realized that she was trying to nurture herself in the only way she knew how, without hope of maternal support from any quarter. She was, in effect, "tending her own garden" when she ate pieces of her own skin and hair (i.e., pica) and refused to allow others to feed her. She rejected other people because she herself had been rejected during the earliest period of her life. Meanwhile, she unconsciously sought succor in her attempts to be caught by "the woman of the house."

The continuum of eating pathologies also includes the semistarvation states related to or accompanying other major psychiatric disorders (e.g., schizophrenia or depression), as well as significant binge episodes associated with atypical depression or anxiety states. In addition, it encompasses the preoccupation and absorption with body image and shape that is indicative of major character pathology or neurosis. Scant attention has been paid to the unconscious meanings of eating pathologies as they relate to the major psychiatric disorders. Here, too, deeper insights into the individual can be gleaned by a more thorough pursuit of the psychodynamic significance of the symptoms and the link between psyche and soma.

❦ Jennifer D. was a 22-year-old woman with severe anorexia nervosa who was also severely depressed. Even after the usual efforts to renourish and gain weight in the hospital milieu, Jennifer maintained a distorted body image and the delusion that her male psychiatrist was attempting to poison her and disrupt her pseudoincestuous bond with her father. In an effort to return home to join her father, who lived in another state, Jennifer defied all attempts to arrest her disorder with medication, milieu therapy, and individual psychotherapy. Her eating disorder helped maintain a childlike dependence on her father, whom she simultaneously controlled with pleas to "rescue" her from her "malevolent" caretakers in the hospital.

Jennifer D.'s case demonstrates the importance of understanding and treating both diagnostic entities—that is, dual diagnosis—and of ferreting out the relative significance of each. The problem of comorbidity, which is observed with increasing frequency among people with eating disorders, influences psychotherapeutic strategy as well as diagnostic specificity and is more fully discussed in Chapter 2.

Examining complex cultural, biological, and interpersonal conflicts in patients like Mandy and Jennifer can shed much light on the treatment of those who have eating disorders. That is the focus of this book, which will go beyond the scope of the eating disorder per se into the earliest struggles and impingements on development. Like Mandy and Jennifer, many of these patients have life-threatening problems of the psychosoma that require a thorough appreciation of the roots of the eating disorder. As McDougall (1978, 1989) has explained, symptoms of an eating disorder are not only techniques for psychic survival but are also most difficult to master because they substitute for the patients' inability to express themselves through language, fantasies, or dreams. Indeed, the main tool that psychodynamic psychotherapy has to offer them—verbal expression—must confront their alexithymia.

However, over time, many of these patients are able to express themselves, and they often reveal tales of early trauma and betrayal: physical and sexual abuse, illicit substance use, and the burden of additional psychiatric disorders. As they become able to tell their difficult personal stories, we must *listen* and help them make sense of their distorted perceptions of themselves, their bodies, and their world. They tell us why they betray their bodies and how they often have been betrayed by the most important people in their lives—culminating in their disordered eating patterns and life-cycle predicaments. Theirs becomes the quintessential disorder of the soul and of the body. They challenge life in their raw battle between psyche and soma: their disease is most dangerous, because it pits soul against body.

# 2

# Comorbidity:
# The Dilemma of
# Dual Diagnoses

Many dishes, many diseases;
Many medicines, few cures.

Benjamin Franklin
*Poor Richard's Almanac*

Consider the plight of an ancient farmer, arduously attempting to water his thirsty crops in the midst of a summer drought. On each shoulder swings a large clay jar brimming with water, on his back rests a water-laden wineskin. His left hand grasps the lead of an ox laden with jars and pots. Each contains the life-giving liquid he needs to douse his shriveling plants. Surely each step he takes is more strained by the assorted loads he carries. Although he struggles to arrive at his final destination, he feels exhausted and beleaguered. All the more reason he might stumble and fall as he navigates toward his destination.

The eating disorder patient with other psychiatric problems is similarly taxed. Although anorexia nervosa and bulimia nervosa were once considered relatively simple problems of eating, mental health professionals are currently recognizing that these disorders are often the mere tip of an iceberg of other psychological disturbances. Thus, to pursue the analogy of our farmer friend, one jar of water—or one psychiatric problem—might well be the eating disorder itself. Another jug may be depression or bipolar (manic-depressive) disorder. Still another might be substance abuse, marital difficulties, or a personality disorder. The result of "juggling so many jugs" is that the patient, like the farmer, must cope with multiple burdens. They will ultimately have an impact on the kind of treatment measures employed. If these treatment measures are successful, help will be given for each problem. If not, life's spark will dim; the combined difficulties will prove too costly a load.

In her books about addiction, psychologist Claudia Black (1990) has called this important phenomenon "double duty." Black writes that the more we understand and accept the complex range of human experience, the more common it is to see people struggling simultaneously with more than one or two areas of difficulty. Symptoms such as depression, anxiety, hypochondria, self-mutilation, substance abuse, and obsessiveness find expression in a wide range of conditions and therefore often lead to complications in diagnosis and, consequently, treatment. Ultimately, however, the high cost of having more than one psychiatric problem is borne by the patient who, like the farmer, is understandably blocked from traversing straight, reasonably carefree paths to achieve her life goals.

Research studies over the past decade have shown how typical it is for eating disorders to be accompanied by other psychiatric problems such as depression, anxiety, obsessiveness, substance abuse, and borderline personality disorder. Although further research is needed to assess the extent to which these disorders influence the course of an eating disorder, the presence of any additional problems will of course complicate treatment. A wise consumer of psychiatric services will ask the clinician about specific diagnoses and their best treatments, including specialized individual therapy. For example, an uncomplicated eating disorder can usually be managed by working with a dietitian and learning to follow a tailored plan of healthy meals while also participating in psychotherapy. But this helpful prescription may prove inadequate for individuals who also have severe depression or an anxiety disorder. Medication, individual and group psychotherapy, and a careful look at social supports can be critical in working with the eating disorder patient who also has an associated disturbance of mood or problems in functioning at work or in school.

The case of Sophie E. exemplifies the high cost of comorbidity (the association of two or more psychiatric syndromes together). Because many dimensions of life are affected for the patient with a dual diagnosis, each domain must be assessed independently. Doing so ensures the most hopeful prognosis and most judicious interventions. Sophie's case demonstrates that if each problem is accurately diagnosed and treated effectively, life-enhancing change can and will occur. It also permits us to review some of the most pertinent information about eating disorders and their associated comorbidities.

## ❧ Sophie's "Choice"

When Sophie E., age 17, first appeared at her university's mental health clinic for intake, she appeared to be much like her fellow freshmen. Eager, alert, and challenging, she gravitated to a prelaw curriculum and adeptly made social contacts with both men and other women. But, unlike her peers, from the first week of school Sophie was also totally preoccupied with food. In her dormitory, it seemed as though food was everywhere. Away from home for the first time, she could now eat as she wished and do as she wished. Shocked and dismayed by the degree of anxiety she experienced in her solitude, Sophie sensed that college would be a greater challenge for her than she had ever thought. She had not anticipated her reaction to loneliness and to the intense competition of her peers "for grades." Downing a few extra candy bars and glasses of lemonade before attempting to study or going to a fraternity mixer initially helped allay Sophie's fears of social ineptitude and academic failure.

Over the first semester, Sophie noticed how the pounds began to add up, but it seemed like a small price to pay for feeling more confident and less lonely. Innocently, she believed that nobody noticed, but Sally and Wendy did. One evening they came to Sophie's room and told her she was about to be initiated into a special group. Sophie had totally avoided the sorority scene but was intrigued by what Sally and Wendy might be offering. That night, Sophie's initiation into the P.O. Club included stops at Dunkin' Donuts, Pizza Hut, and Baskin-Robbins, gorging on various treats along the way. Finally, Sophie shouted that she simply couldn't eat another bite and implored the others to drive her back to the dormitory.

Wendy reassured her that her discomfort could be handled, and so the two seniors took their new initiate to a dumpster, where they proceeded to ram their fingers down their throats and instruct Sophie on easy ways to purge. At first repelled by the technique, Sophie found that the vomitus began to pour out of her quickly and easily. Suddenly, she felt "as though I had found a miracle" because she could eat what she wanted without any guilt. Sharing the secret sisterhood with Wendy and Sally, she had become a successful pledge of the "Pig Out Club."

Over the rest of the semester, Sophie used the club's techniques to make the pounds melt away as easily as they had once been put on. Although Sophie enjoyed her evenings purging with her "sisters," she quickly found that she could use her new weight control method on her own. In addition, she felt relieved and calmed after a purge in a way she had never known before. Yet something inside told Sophie that her method of coping was dangerous and destructive. She found herself mysteriously drawn to the mental health clinic for help.

Bingeing and purging was one of the first secrets Sophie had kept from her parents, and now she would be opening that hidden part of herself up to someone new and unknown. As she courageously stepped inside the door of her therapist's office, she was plagued by a plethora of questions. Why had she begun this vicious binge-purge cycle in the first place? Why had she joined the Pig Out Club? Was she searching for friends and consolation at the transition point of beginning college or was she attempting to deal with more troublesome feelings? Would the therapist find her acceptable and likable, or would she be repelled by symptoms that Sophie herself felt repulsive? Even as these questions twirled in Sophie's mind, she suspected that her emotional pain went beyond her eating disorder itself and into the deeper recesses of her heart.

As much as she felt burdened by her pain, Sophie questioned her own capacity to explain it or explore it, let alone have it be acceptable and understood by someone she had never seen before.

The intake worker at the mental health clinic referred Sophie to a psychiatrist for an evaluation. Alarmed by what he thought was a deepening depression as well as an eating disorder, he believed that Sophie might be helped by the addition of antidepressant medication.[1]

When Sophie talked with the psychiatrist, she described herself as feeling intensely dysphoric. Moreover, she relayed how her own sexual drive had lessened and how life had begun to seem meaningless and hopeless. She slept fitfully and woke often. One night she even jumped from her bed after a nightmare she could not recall and began to sob uncontrollably.

After the diagnoses of bulimia nervosa and major depression are made, the psychiatrist is placed in an all-too-frequent dilemma of deciding whether a particular medication is helpful. Because of the physiological effects of the eating disorder (see Chapter 11), side effects of medication are hard to monitor. Moreover, the binge-purge cycle makes the therapeutic response to medication much more difficult to judge. When a patient is actively purging, drugs may not be adequately absorbed, so there is little benefit from the medication. However, when the binge-purge cycle is interrupted, antidepressant medication often can reverse depression. There is also growing evidence that binge-purge episodes may be reduced in frequency by some medications (e.g., fluoxetine [Prozac], imipramine [Tofranil]).

It would be pleasant for Sophie—and the optimistic reader—to

---

[1] Although numerous studies have reported a link between eating disorders and depression, it is as yet unconfirmed whether one condition actually stems from or is caused by the other. Clearly, the metabolic imbalances that can arise from either bulimia nervosa or anorexia nervosa may exacerbate a patient's underlying feeling of dysphoria. On the other hand, individuals who have had episodes of major depression describe the sensation as not only quantitatively but also qualitatively different from sadness itself.

learn that her saga ended when the correct medication was prescribed. Fortunately for many patients, both disorders can be corrected simultaneously with a combination of appropriate antidepressant medication and simple strategies for managing the eating disorder. But for others like Sophie, this point marks only the beginning of treatment. Their "choice" of symptom is predicated on deeper struggles (hinted at in Chapter 1) and necessitates a variety of psychotherapeutic techniques to uncover and intervene with the underlying problem. By the time Sophie completed her third interview, her journey was just beginning. The presumptive diagnoses had led to standard, acceptable treatment, but her therapist could not presage what was about to be uncovered.

## ❦ On a Tightrope

About 3 months after beginning therapy and taking the antidepressant (imipramine), Sophie awoke to a bright light streaming in her window. She believed it was the brightest light she had ever seen. She sat straight up in bed, then rushed over to fling aside the curtains as she heard a young bird chirping for its mother. Suddenly, the sounds of the bird enveloped her, becoming simultaneously loud and pounding while retaining their delicacy and innocence. She felt a rush of energy and giggled spontaneously for no reason. She then flung herself onto her bed, screaming out for her dormmates to come watch her as she attempted a rare balancing act on the rim of her headboard. Sophie later recalled that she had both wanted to fly and to demonstrate for her peers her nascent talent as a tightrope artist!

Unbeknownst to her at the time, Sophie was in the throes of a manic episode. All her sensations and perceptions were heightened and acute, and she felt an intensity of energy she had never known before. Colors appeared brighter and richer, sounds grew pulsating and loud, and she could sustain a high level of activity with only 3 hours of sleep each night. Because patients with mania or hypomania find their symptoms so syntonic, if not enthralling, Sophie refused to return to see her psychiatrist. She stopped eating altogether, believing herself to be beyond the need for food. She had previously disparaged her body to the point of grave distortion. Although attractive, she believed she was ugly. She now uncontrollably flaunted her body at young men on the campus while uncharacteristically provoking them with sexual innuendoes and suggestive taunts.

As Sophie's behavior grew more alarming, two of her dormmates contacted the hospital chaplain, a trusted friend on the campus. Chaplain D. accompanied Sophie to what was to be her first psychiatric hospitalization. He was able to provide enough history on the basis of what her friends reported that treatment for mania was begun. At this point Sophie's capacity to accurately report her life was totally impaired; she jumped from one subject to the next without any seeming connection between them (i.e., tangentiality).

From the psychiatrist's pharmacopoeia, agents designed to help control mania, although with very different mechanisms of action, were chosen (initially a benzodiazepine or antipsychotic, then lithium carbonate). Within a few weeks, Sophie was no longer as wild or irritable, but her mania had given way to feelings of depression and despair, the likes of which she had never experienced before. Feelings of guilt washed over her as she recalled her sexually outrageous behavior. As these reminded her of her earlier faults and failings, she felt compelled to punish herself. She became suicidal, and precautions were taken to keep her from harming herself. Meanwhile, Sophie began to restrict her intake of fluids and food to punish herself for the illness as well as her past "sins."

By now the list of Sophie's problems had quadrupled since the initial presentation of bulimia. After physical causes of her disturbance were ruled out (e.g., side effects of antidepressant medication, medical illness, or a tumor), her episode of mania mandated a formal diagnosis of bipolar illness. Yet after its remediation, her depression persisted. Like many bulimic patients, Sophie was now struggling with a period of food restriction, possibly indicative of an exacerbation of her eating disorder or of depression itself.

Although current studies in biological psychiatry point to a genetic and biochemical basis for some of Sophie's difficulties, they do not give us a window into her soul—that is, into the genuine human dilemmas with which she was struggling. Why had she chosen to binge to alleviate her anxiety to begin with? What was the deeper reason for her feelings of guilt and her need to show her dormmates that she was "larger than life?" But most important, how could her treaters begin to reach out and connect with a part of Sophie that she herself believed so unlikable and untouchable that she wanted to die?

These questions daunted both Sophie and her individual psychotherapist as they began to work together. At the beginning of the process, both of them seemed totally in the dark about how to answer the questions. But together, to lighten the self-hatred Sophie felt, they sought greater clarity about the array of difficulties she faced.

After a brief discussion of the concept of dual diagnosis, we will return to this case.

## Common Constellations of Comorbidity

Sophie's case, although quite dramatic, represents but a small subgroup of a large number of patients who carry the dual diagnosis of an eating disorder and another condition. In the 1980s, a number of reports began to surface in the psychiatric literature that suggested a relationship between bulimia and depression. Indeed, many investigations indicated that bulimia might actually be a variant of depression.

Although clinical studies of depression and bulimia have consistently linked the two conditions, researchers generally concede that bulimia is not a variant of depression. Moreover, the frequency of a full-blown manic episode (either bipolar disorder or bipolar disorder not otherwise specified) in combination with an eating disorder is much less common than pure depression and an eating disorder. Thus, early in Sophie's treatment, she appeared to be like many other women who carry a DSM-IV Axis I diagnosis of bulimia nervosa and major depression. Only as we followed her course did we, her therapists, see the manic symptoms erupt.

In Sophie's case, bipolar disorder was likely an innate condition, possibly familial, that typically made its appearance as she closed in on the third decade of life. Another possibility is that her antidepressant medication precipitated her mania iatrogenically (now classified in some psychiatric circles as either bipolar III or bipolar IV disorder). This categorization takes into account the potential side effects that affect some individuals: an antidepressant medication may precipitate mania. The combined experience of physicians at The Menninger Clinic suggests that depression and eating disorders are as commonly reported together as has been described in the psychiatric literature, but that manic depressive disorder and its variants occur with greater frequency than contemporary studies have heretofore led us to believe.

Depression itself is common among bulimic patients because of their accompanying feeling of demoralization about their behavior. The resulting low self-esteem exacerbates self-hatred to the point that these individuals may feel totally lost, disorganized, and fragmented. Meanwhile, those who binge often eat very poorly. Although they may appear of normal weight and in good health, they may in fact be starving in the face of plenitude. The foods they binge on are usually of the poorest nutritional values. Among anorexic patients, depression frequently results from starvation itself. Because bulimic people do not follow wise nutritional patterns, they can become starved as well, despite being at normal weight or a bit above.

Depression can also result from a failure of impulse control and impaired interpersonal relationships. Carole Edelstein and Joel Yager at the UCLA Medical Center report that social supports diminish as the eating disorder progresses, because the individual spends more and more time alone bingeing and vomiting instead of being with family and friends (Edelstein and Yager 1992). (The problem with impulse dyscontrol that manifests itself in personality disorders will be described elsewhere in this and other chapters; the specific problem of substance abuse is addressed in Chapter 10.)

Suffice it to say that any patient needs a thorough assessment to distinguish whether the depressive symptoms that she struggles with are manifestations of a prominent Axis I diagnosis of major depressive disorder or dysthymia or are related instead to the eating disorder alone.

Many times depressive symptoms will subside strikingly after a period of adequate nutrition. If depression persists after normal eating has been restored, some anorexic and bulimic patients may benefit from adequate doses of antidepressant medication. In addition, a family history of depression may indicate that the patient would benefit from pharmacotherapy. At other times, pharmacotherapy may be instituted to reduce mood symptoms and disordered eating. As treatment begins, it is impossible to predict whether the medication will affect the depression, the eating problem itself, or both.

Anorexia nervosa and bulimia nervosa can also be complicated by other Axis I conditions such as panic disorder, generalized anxiety disorder, schizophrenia, and posttraumatic stress disorder. A case vignette at the end of this chapter focuses on a patient with multiple personality disorder whose anorexia nervosa became life-threatening. Patients with anorexia nervosa may also be affected by obsessive-compulsive disorder. A large percentage of eating disorder patients will eventually be diagnosed with another Axis I condition as they forthrightly report all their symptoms to their treater. Still others may not fulfill all the highly specific criteria for a DSM-IV diagnosis yet may have what is commonly called subclinical pathology. It is important that everyone involved with the person with an eating disorder look carefully at *all* the symptoms, including irritability, poor sexual history, petty thievery, suicide attempts, or impaired social supports. Any of these may point the way toward a definitive diagnosis of a comorbid Axis I problem and lead toward more specific and more effective treatment.

An even larger body of evidence has been accumulating to support a high frequency of Axis II (or personality) difficulties among those who have eating disorders. At least one-third to one-half of all patients seeking treatment for eating disorders can also be diagnosed as having a personality disorder, most commonly borderline personality disorder.

To fulfill the DSM-IV criteria for borderline personality disorder (American Psychiatric Association 1993), a patient must exhibit at least five of these criteria:

A pervasive pattern of instability of mood, interpersonal relationships and self-image, beginning by early adulthood.

1. Frantic efforts to avoid real or imagined abandonment
2. A pattern of unstable and intense interpersonal relationships characterized by alternating between extremes of idealization and devaluation
3. Identity disturbance: persistent and markedly disturbed, distorted, or unstable self-image or sense of self
4. Impulsiveness in at least two areas that are potentially self-damaging (e.g., spending, sex, substance abuse, shoplifting, reckless driving, binge eating)
5. Recurrent suicidal threats, gestures, or behavior, or self-mutilating behavior
6. Affective instability: marked reactivity of mood (e.g., intense episodic dysphoria, irritability, or anxiety usually lasting a few hours and only rarely more than a few days)
7. Chronic feelings of emptiness
8. Inappropriate, intense anger, or lack of control of anger (e.g., frequent displays of temper, constant anger, recurrent physical fights)
9. Transient, stress-related severe dissociative symptoms or paranoid ideation

Still, some well-conducted research suggests that even the statistic of 30% is much too high and that, in fact, the impairment in social relationships, destructive behavior, chaotic life history, and difficulties with impulsivity usually found among people with borderline personality disorder are best understood as sequels to the eating disorder itself or to an undiagnosed Axis I problem. While the debate rages in scientific circles, clinicians continue to observe a wide range of behavioral problems and identity disturbances that are best subsumed under an Axis II diagnosis to point the way for treatment. As noted author, researcher, and clinician Craig Johnson has detailed in a variety of contexts, eating disorder patients with borderline personality disorder need more frequent therapeutic contacts because of their unsatisfying relationships, their higher degree of emotional distress, and their general pattern of self-destructive behavior. Borderline patients show a high degree of depression, somatization, anxiety, and hostility while acting out dysphoria through suicide attempts, self-mutilative behavior, and substance abuse. Interestingly, their eating disorders are not demonstratively different from those in the nonborderline population.

Throughout this book, we will study in great detail the life histories of many eating disorder patients who also had a personality disorder. At the outset, it is important to state not only that the exact relationship between personality disorders and eating disorders remains unknown, but also that there is general agreement that a clear relationship exists. Most patients with eating disorders will meet DSM-IV criteria for at least one personality disorder, be it borderline, histrionic, or obsessive-compulsive. As we learn more about these comorbid conditions, we will also learn more about their historical antecedents.

Much coalescing evidence indicates that disturbed family patterns, a history of physical and sexual abuse, and other major life traumas play a significant role in the later development of a personality disorder. Because patients who are dually diagnosed with both an eating disorder and a personality disorder demand more intensive treatment efforts, a team approach is indicated. Although little empirical evidence definitively supports how best to assist such patients, some solid treatment principles have emerged.

The case of Sophie illustrates how psychological guidelines can be applied in daily clinical work with a dually diagnosed eating disorder patient. The goal is to help such a patient become less burdened by her depression and her body so that she will ultimately betray it less, if at all. As a sizable number of studies have indicated, over time such an approach not only builds the self-structure of the individual, thus reducing self-defeating patterns and chaotic relationships, but it also interrupts the disturbed eating attitudes and behaviors as well.

## Choices Expand: Psychological Understanding

Psychological understanding of the eating disorder patient who has other psychiatric difficulties is often quite difficult. While maintaining the focus on behavioral control of the eating disorder and prescribing appropriate medication for any biological or medical illness, clinicians must still attend to the developmental causes and psychological cost of each of the diagnosed difficulties.

Marcel Proust wrote, "The only real voyage of discovery consists not in seeking new landscapes but in having new eyes." A fresh perspective for a patient like Sophie begins by helping her to avoid fleeing her difficulties, instead helping her learn how to focus on what they are so that she can begin to place them in proper perspective. Such patients are often poor caretakers of themselves. For example, they refuse to follow their meal plans or take necessary medications; they place themselves in jeopardy or spoil their successes at work. Although becoming a good caretaker to oneself must be stressed early in treatment, these patients must also learn good health practices without feeling selfish or deficient—often easier said than done.

People learn how to take care of themselves by having good role models at home. Personal growth is fostered by observing how family members structure their days, enjoy work, take time out for relaxation and fun, and rely on others for support and guidance when necessary. However, parents who are chronically anxious, depressed, or hurtful may be unable to soothe or comfort their child, let alone to provide healthy modeling of mature dependency and self-regulation.

As children grow up, they look for different ways to find an inner sense of calmness and relief from tension and anxiety. If this process fails, they enter adolescence and adulthood with impaired self-regulation, poor affect modulation, and weak impulse control. The individual psychotherapist is often the first person who can sit comfortably with the patient and help her learn new ways to develop self-soothing.

This capacity is crucial for control of the eating disorder and any other psychological problems that accompany it. Without the capacity to feel comfortable with oneself, the individual can never form meaningful relationships with others. Moreover, work itself is jeopardized. The individual becomes anxious with a new challenge or irritable at the slightest criticism from the boss. Binge-purge episodes may be the only times that seem tension free. As responsibilities increase, the eating disorder can take up more and more of the day to bring relief. The eating disorder also places the individual on a downward spiral metabolically and psychologically; depression, anxiety, and personality disorders make matters worse. Confusion, poor judgment and memory, and preoccupation with the illness interfere with getting any job done. Paperwork often piles up and appointments are missed; courses at school are not completed.

Friends, spouses, and parents believe that when they confront the person who has an eating disorder, they are helping that individual put her life on a better track. After all, the lay press currently touts the benefits of "tough love." But as much as the patient needs structure and firmness, untimely confrontations from others can often be disastrous and lead to even more difficulty with the symptoms. This reversal occurs because the individual must contain more anxiety and shame, and the only way to remedy either feeling is to engage in bingeing and purging. Treatment that stresses from the outset other coping mechanisms (see Chapter 14)—even those that may take time to develop and master—are often quite restorative and may be the first step in addressing multiple difficulties and rebuilding the self.

Sophie's psychotherapist finally reached her by explaining how in many ways Sophie must have always felt very grown up and how she even seemed quite grown up for her 17 years. However, in many other ways, she also seemed to experience herself as a small child. This explanation—that a small child exists within the body of an adult—is not a new one but may sound strange to someone unfamiliar with the psychological struggles of the eating disorder patient. The concept becomes more understandable as we learn about the personal dilemmas faced by many eating disorder patients within their own families of origin. For example, at the beginning of the case description of Sophie, nothing was mentioned about her early family background. When the treatment process first begins, neither the patient nor the mental health professional necessarily knows much about these crucially important years and determining experiences. Detailed questions bring to the surface invaluable information that may prove upsetting but enlightening for both participants in the clinical encounter.

As Sophie began to open up within the trusting relationship of psychotherapy, it became clear that her very successful parents, both law professors at an East Coast university, had given her every material advantage in life. Superficially, they had had the perfect home, and

Sophie had many pleasant memories of her earliest years. A good foundation was disrupted when her father decided to pursue advanced studies for 2 years in another state. At that point, Sophie's mother began to abuse alcohol—and then young Sophie as well. Mayhem resulted. The peaceful early years were soon forgotten. By the time Sophie was six, her mother had to be hospitalized for bipolar illness and her father was forced to return home to care for the family. Although life improved in some ways after his return, conflicts persisted until Sophie's parents eventually divorced when she was 13.

Trying desperately to please both her parents but caught in their unresolved conflict, Sophie listened carefully to determine what was expected of her. She hoped to be the academically gifted writer and lawyer her father longed for while also meeting her mother's expectations for her to be attractive, charming, and thin. The latter condition was simply impossible for Sophie, whose natural body shape was hardy and plump (see more on this topic in Chapter 7). Perhaps most crucially, the family home never again seemed like a safe haven. Long after her parents divorced, Sophie's home was the scene of frequent verbal tirades punctuated with dish-throwing episodes.

After Sophie was left alone with her mother, she grew accustomed to her continual harangues and angry outbursts. No wonder Sophie entered college feeling anxious and insecure. She had never internalized the image of a calm, soothing, involved mother who would care for her and understand her human problems and foibles. She had not developed the capacity to be alone, so it was impossible for her to weather the internal storms of anxiety and frustration.

Patients like Sophie who have had impoverished parental relationships, and consequently lack the capacity to soothe themselves, crave nurturance. If possible, they often require as many as two or three sessions per week of group or individual therapy. During times of stress, they profit from the opportunity to call the therapist and to use writing in a journal as a way to put their thoughts into words. Vacations or other interruptions in the treatment process may be particularly trying.

After Sophie and her therapist had worked together for some time, the therapist suggested that Sophie might benefit from the use of a transitional object—something to help her bridge the time between sessions. This technique is reminiscent of the toddler's early development, when the mother provides a blanket or cuddly toy to sustain the child in her absence, thus promoting independence. Mother is symbolically represented; to the baby, the toy is mother. In the past, any separation would overwhelm Sophie's capacity to stay emotionally connected. In this case, Sophie's therapist chose a small, furry bunny because one of Sophie's favorite books was *The Velveteen Rabbit*. During times of stress, Sophie could hold the stuffed animal and remember her therapist's concern for her.

Many patients have no need for a transitional object, but it is one modality that may foster reassurance. Other kinds of transitional objects that help patients maintain calmness and connection between sessions include tape recordings of the therapist's voice; journal writing that is later shared with the therapist; or an inanimate object that the therapist has in the office for loaning out during an absence, between sessions, or at times of stress.

The dually diagnosed eating disorder patient may feel so perplexed by many intense inner states and worries that self-soothing is particularly problematic. The theoretical position that informs the use of the transitional object here centers on providing the patient with another source of contact or attachment to the therapist between hours. Despite the multiple issues with which the patient struggles, the treater hopes and expects an eventual internalization of protective characteristics. Then she will be able to live without the need of an object—caring instead for the self in mature ways (e.g., responsible use of medication, age-appropriate friendships).

## Mourning the Past: Starting Anew

For patients like Sophie, having psychiatric difficulties defines the self. She felt safe within her group, the Pig Out Club. When she was bingeing and purging, she knew who she was. She was a person with an eating disorder. When other psychiatric problems reared their head, she simply tagged these illnesses onto this identity, disparagingly calling herself "the nut—a manic depressive bulimic with an IQ of 135." Meanwhile, her healthy friends, like so many peers of those who have eating disorders, were totally perplexed by Sophie's rigidly held, negative self-perceptions. Because she had so much potential for growth and professional achievement, they were angered by what they surmised was her laziness and lack of courage in giving up her role as an illness harbinger.

Whenever Sophie experienced the anger and frustration of her friends, she also became angry, feeling misunderstood and entitled to better treatment. She would quickly write them off, only to guiltily beg their forgiveness a few days after an angry letter or a fight. Beneath the surface, she believed her difficulties should be tolerated by others, and she felt entitled to their acceptance of her problem despite its cost to her and them.

In therapy, the personal cost of the eating disorder and other psychological problems must continually be pointed out to these patients. They must be made aware of how interpersonal relationships and the lack of a sense of self betray their manifest desire to improve. Unconsciously and unwittingly, the individual comes to rely on the eating disorder as if it is and will be forevermore her identity. Challenging this self-construct is extraordinarily difficult. Why? Because giving it up means that a new identity must be found; and the loss of anything or anyone elicits the difficult emotions of mourning.

In *Necessary Losses* (1986), Judith Viorst explained how we must all give up certain ideas, beliefs, and persons or objects in order to grow. Even for those who have internalized a basically good, benevolent parent, mourning is painful and takes time. In the Jewish faith, for example, the loss of a loved one mandates a mourning period of a year. It is assumed that all the important holidays, anniversaries, and birthdays must be traversed at least once before the mourner can adequately work through the loss of an important person. Of course, loss is probably never totally worked through for any of us. Even years after the loss of a loved one, you may find yourself spontaneously dreaming about the person or wondering what he or she might have said in a particular situation. The unconscious mind keeps that individual alive.

The mourning process is easier when our memories of the loved one are basically fond ones. They help balance the sad feelings and occasional tears over some memorable person or event long past. But eating disorder patients whose identity is steeped in food rituals may be devoid of a soothing internal parent or may have flagrantly harsh memories of a tumultuous past. As a result, the mourning process is made incredibly difficult. Yet these patients must mourn the symptom itself and what it means. To solidify a new identity, they must first give up the old. They must learn to see the many ways the eating disorder has helped or even saved their lives. Concomitantly, they must begin to build those very real islands of strength that will help them grapple with life more constructively.

To summarize, the eating disorder patient with multiple psychiatric problems has at her core a disturbance of her very identity. She may not be conscious of how she has categorized and derided herself. Surely she would eschew the blatant objectifying or stereotyping of another person on racial or gender grounds alone. But she is not thinking of another person—she is thinking of herself.

Ironically, we often harbor toward ourselves those very prejudices we would never tolerate about another. So it is that the eating disorder patient, sensing self-betrayal if she changes, steadfastly clings to what she knows. While others implore her to test new ground in treatment and life, we note how her investment in patienthood seems impoverished. Yet for her, that is all she has. A keystone of her treatment process involves giving up the eating disorder as a centerpiece of personal identity and gradually building the foundation for a new, mature, and richer sense of self. Neither the patient nor any of her loved ones savors the idea of the time it will take to build anew, but this endeavor will ultimately be the patient's only choice. Those involved might consider this extension of a clichéd aphorism: Rome was not built in a day, but it was built.

## Words, Work, and the Woodshop

Patients with eating disorders often struggle mightily to express their feelings in words. To develop their identity, they must learn to recognize and name these feeling states. Helping the patient create her own "menu of feelings" is one of the foremost tasks of therapy. Even though patients like Sophie are among the brightest as well as potentially the most creative and capable of women, their developmental impasses and cognitive distortions have interfered with their basic psychological functioning. Thus it is extraordinarily useful for them to learn to recognize their own anger and to develop the chutzpah in assertiveness training to engage others while they are upset. These individuals must also learn to recognize and express their sadness, fear, anguish, and nostalgia.

What happens when words are not available or forthcoming for verbal expression? The first forays into naming feelings often come not in verbal modes themselves but in other ways, such as through art, music, or movement. In most state-of-the-art treatment programs, music and art therapy are favorite activities of the patients. In art therapy, for example, people draw, finger paint, or make collages to express their hidden selves. Before Sophie was able to verbalize her own feeling states, she clipped pictures from magazines and pasted them on poster board to convey her sense of despair and confusion. In one of her first collages, she combined pictures of euphoric and despondent people interspersed with recipes and photos of foodstuffs. Thus she was able to convey the rigid identity of a manic-depressive patient with an eating disorder who was in turmoil.

With the help of her art therapist, Sophie began to express her feelings more clearly. After 6 months of treatment, she took a different approach to explaining who she was and where she was going. Again using cutouts from magazines, she divided her picture into two phases, one portrayed her old (false) self and one pictured the emerging new (true) self. In between was a rigid border, interpreted as Sophie's wish to avoid final integration of these two important aspects of her personality. The woman whom she hoped would emerge from treatment was one who traveled, ate well and appropriately, had a career, and was nurtured by strong, healthy relationships. With the support of the art therapist, Sophie was able not only to name her feelings but also to establish some new links between her two selves. Art became a conduit between the two despite Sophie's inability as yet to develop the capacity to trust others or to deal consistently with expressing her feelings in words.

Not all patients are as verbally stymied as Sophie. But as described in Chapter 1, these alexithymic individuals who must struggle to name their feelings often have eating disorders as well. Some studies suggest that as many as 30% of eating disorder patients are alexithymic. Although the therapist must focus on helping these patients develop their "menu of feelings" without suggesting what might be going on at a particular time with a given patient, it is also important to help patients express themselves in nonverbal ways, such as through art, music, and movement therapies. This emphasis on alternative means of expression also enables patients to employ their raw energies in a constructive activity via the defense mechanism of sublimation.

Sublimation—the capacity to channel one's aggressive energies into constructive, valued work—does not come easily for those individuals who may have grown up without a daily routine or hourly schedule. Family members and treaters unfamiliar with eating disorder patients often ask why their treatment takes so long. Yet the normal development of subliminatory channels typically takes the better part of childhood, adolescence, and early adulthood. Thus a daily schedule with planned meals and plenty of time for reflection helps the eating disorder patient deal with feelings and solidify a new identity.

Most of these patients have little idea what they like or do not like. They have never tested their capacities or talents in a variety of activities. Unusually focused on academic achievement and honors, they must come to terms with the value of having hobbies and using leisure time constructively. For example, because Sophie felt bitter toward both her parents, she needed to discharge her anger and aggression. She had spent many years avoiding her anger because it might have incited more of her mother's wrath. Sophie's therapist was not afraid to help Sophie give voice to her anger, and she often pointed out to Sophie that disappointments are a part of any relationship. The therapist also helped her recognize, name, and understand her angry feelings.

As Sophie began to see that her feelings did not harm her therapist, who, in fact, returned for another session, Sophie learned that her anger was not as dangerous as she had believed it might be. Talking is never enough by itself, however. Sophie was an energetic young woman who required other outlets for her energy. In the therapeutic woodshop activity, Sophie learned to work the lathe, something she had never considered doing prior to treatment. Whenever she became angry, she would turn to her wood projects and sand or oil a cabinet she built. She would also draw or put together a new collage and then discuss it with her treaters as a way of conveying her struggles and putting them in perspective. When Sophie became upset or agitated on the hospital unit, staff members would suggest that she take time out to write in her journal or simply to reflect on what she was feeling. The calm, quiet atmosphere of her room gave Sophie a sense of solace she had never known in her youth. Little by little, she formed a view of herself as someone with more to offer the world. Her eating symptoms came under control; her manic highs lessened with medication; and her periods of depression, although not totally eliminated, were substantially lessened.

## Multiple Personality Disorder

To date, most of the studies on comorbidity associated with the eating disorders have focused on clinical diagnoses such as the anxiety disorders, depression, and borderline personality disorder. In the past few years, we have also seen a number of patients who have various dissociative states, posttraumatic stress disorder, and multiple personality disorder. Frequently, the lives of these individuals have been punctuated with severe sexual and physical trauma, which will be discussed in detail in Chapter 9. The following case example highlights how multiple personality disorder and posttraumatic stress disorder often complicate the eating disorder.

❦ Faye F. was a 38-year-old homemaker and mother when she came to the clinic with a 6-month history of anorexia nervosa. Already under treatment for severe sexual and physical abuse, she acknowledged that she had had "the mentality of an anorexic" for years before developing a full restrictive pattern. Faye denied purging, diuretic and laxative abuse, and abuse of nonprescription medications. Although she had smoked marijuana heavily in her youth, over the past 15 years she said that she had neither experimented with drugs nor abused alcohol.

From Faye's perspective, her early life was filled with relentless torture on the part of both her parents. She alleged that her parents were actually part of a satanic cult, but these assertions could not be confirmed because both of them were deceased. Despite an early life of significant deprivation, Faye had been able to attach herself to various nurturing figures and acquire a college degree. Although her relationships were tumultuous, she managed to achieve some semblance of stability on the job. Finally, she met a man at work who was enamored of her attractiveness and skill. After a brief courtship, they married and settled into what seemed like a normal relationship. Immediately after the wedding, however, Faye became pregnant. Although she looked forward to the birth of her first child and later enjoyed the experience of mothering an infant, the expectations of maintaining a committed relationship and giving to others on a 24-hour basis proved too much for her. Faye sought therapy for worsening depression, lack of enjoyment in sex, preoccupation with her own early abuse, and a tendency to spoil relationships.

In therapy, as Faye began to recover memories of her childhood, it became clear that she had totally walled off certain aspects of her own life. Over several months, she revealed that she possessed various alter personalities, each distinctive and with its own name, who expressed different aspects of her own self. As Faye's trust in her therapist grew and they began to learn more about her past, her restrictive eating pattern grew worse. She lost 30 pounds in 5 weeks. Her various personalities were at war with each other, with some actively trying to kill her through starvation. The typical process of supervised eating that begins the treatment of those with anorexia nervosa was complicated by the fact that Faye seemed to be involved in a struggle to the end with certain alters who did not wish her to live to tell "the truth" about her past.

Besides being diagnosed with anorexia nervosa, Faye was also diagnosed as having major depression, posttraumatic stress disorder, multiple personality disorder, a history of substance abuse, and an underlying borderline personality organization. Although her treatment is beyond the scope of this chapter, her case demonstrates how eating disorder patients may often struggle with more than one comorbidity issue at a time. Despite Faye's genuine strengths, the real trauma she had undergone in her youth resulted in severe identity fragmentation. Greater expectations in life upped the ante, because she needed more care than others were able to provide. Fearing that people would never hear her inner despair and pain, Faye's psyche collapsed, leading to the formation of the alter personalities that attempted to sustain her as best they could.

Originally viewed as deriving from conflicts over separation from the mother, borderline personality disorder diagnoses are now reported with greater frequency among sexually and physically abused people. That is, recent findings suggest that childhood trauma, and specifically sexual and physical abuse, are significant precursors to borderline personality disorder. Like Faye, patients with borderline personality disorder perceive their mothers as attacking and abandoning and their fathers as hostile, neglectful, and controlling. The family environment itself is often categorized by conflict, hostility, or impoverishment. The support the borderline personality receives is thus minimal and may lead to affective instability and tenuous cognitive skills.

In her work with survivors of severe physical and sexual trauma, Judith Lewis Herman has come to believe that diagnoses such as the personality disorders might be unduly stigmatizing. In her comprehensive volume, *Trauma and Recovery* (1992), Herman suggests the need for a new diagnosis, which she calls "complex posttraumatic stress disorder" (p. 119). This disorder is being considered for inclusion in the forthcoming diagnostic manual DSM-IV. Herman believes that the concept of a complex traumatic syndrome would grant "those who have endured prolonged exploitation a measure of the recognition they deserve" (p. 122). Necessary to the diagnosis would be a history of subjection to totalitarian control and alterations in affect regulation, consciousness, self-perception, relationships with others, and system of meaning. Complex posttraumatic stress disorder captures "the protean symptomatic manifestations of prolonged, repeated trauma" (p. 119) better than any current diagnosis and is surely to be found among many anorexic and bulimic patients.

For our purposes, it becomes clear that we must look beyond the manifest symptoms of the eating disorder to gain a full appreciation of the myriad of problems with which any individual struggles. However, diagnosis takes us only part of the way. As we have seen in the cases of Sophie and Faye, our earliest relationships form the soil for the later flowering of personality. When these relationships are impaired, the individual will find it difficult to contain the fragments of her expanding personality. Never having the childhood she wants but voraciously desires, she enacts her yearning by developing alter personalities that represent "parts" of the whole self or by acquiring one or more psychiatric problems.

Unfortunately, much less is known about this "choice" of symptoms or diagnostic entities than about the early years themselves. In the next two chapters, we will review normative development as it is influenced by both mother and father and then suggest ways in which family life may go awry and lead to an eating disorder or any one of its common psychiatric concomitants.

# 3

# Daughters and Mothers

She named the infant "Pearl," as being of great price—purchased with
all she had—her mother's only treasure!

Nathaniel Hawthorne
*The Scarlet Letter*

Can you recall having a feisty argument or vociferous rift with your
mother? Most of us can easily remember several without much
effort. One day when I was an adolescent, I was quite piqued with my
mother—and she with me. Although the specific content of our argument is now long forgotten, my emotional reaction remains vivid in
memory.

Our conflict probably centered on typical parent-child battle-
grounds of peer relationships or school. My mother may have been
worried that my studies were suffering because of an infatuation or some
added investment in an extracurricular activity. She might also have
complained about the inordinate amount of time I spent talking on the
phone (again, to the detriment of my studies). Perhaps she was disappointed that I had chosen what she believed was a totally inappropriate
outfit to attend a dinner party she and my father were giving for their
friends.

Regardless of the circumstances, we each fervently argued our own
position until we both were sufficiently satisfied we had championed our

causes and won. Like most adolescents, I left the battle feeling both contrite and satisfied—only to quietly pine over the next few days because something had changed in our relationship. I was caught in another struggle typical of adolescence—how to stay close to my mother while maintaining my individuality. Upset that I had irritated my mother but bent on maintaining my own position, I turned for solace and support to my grandmother. She commented, "It is so sad that the relationship that starts out as the closest one on earth—mother and child—always ends so far apart."

I did not realize it at the time, but my grandmother had imparted a fundamental piece of psychoanalytic wisdom that was, indeed, a truism. By underscoring the intensity and meaningfulness of the mother-child dyad in infancy, while declaring the inevitable pain in separating from it during development, my grandmother addressed a central conflict of adolescent and adult women. She was attuned to the real emotional load carried by mothers and daughters that is predicated on a close and prolonged bond that is difficult—and in some ways impossible—for females to ever totally relinquish.

Daughters and mothers lock horns over many issues. They are caught in a struggle, with the daughter attempting to find out who she is so that she can establish her individuality yet maintain a bond with her mother. To grow, we must loosen some of the intense and powerful ties to our mothers, thus permitting a new kind of connection to form. Mothers must also permit this evolution to happen. This task is more easily said than done, and more easily written about than put into practice.

As Nathaniel Hawthorne's quote suggests, most mothers cherish their children, who are, indeed, their "pearls of great price." They sacrifice everything—often their own happiness, personal fulfillment, even life itself—to give birth to and to nurture their children. When a mother gives so much time, energy, and love to rear her child, she understandably becomes concerned with and invested in the product of such devotion. Every gaze and gesture she directs toward her infant will signal the unique bond being fostered, a bond that is beautifully depicted in the mother-and-child portraits of 19th-century artist Mary Cassatt. These paintings capture the attachment amply demonstrated by modern psychology through observation and clinical work with mothers and their children. Both parties thrive through such an intimate and life-enhancing connection.

Consequently, when the time comes for the child to move away from mother and establish new goals and relationships, both parties are sure to feel ambivalent. Mothers feel conflicted about loosening the connection with their daughters that has been so sustaining and comforting. Similarly, daughters must negotiate their own independence. They will voice their desire and need to individuate, only to find themselves turning back to their mothers at times of stress. Meanwhile, any mother whose life with her own mate is impaired will find it all the more difficult to allow her "pearl of great price" to launch her own life.

As family theorists have shown, some mothers find self-affirmation in relationships with their children, particularly their daughters, so they tenaciously hold onto them. Such a daughter then feels responsible for her mother's happiness; but the overly persistent connection, although signifying loyalty and devotion, can interfere with the daughter's ability to live her own life. To solve this thorny problem, the daughter will try many ways to establish independence. Developing an eating disorder is one possible outcome of the conflict.

Most mothers will assert that it is everyone's birthright, including their daughters', to live their own lives. They will nevertheless acknowledge that they miss the connection of early youth and yearn for the kind of affirmation they received from their infant daughters. Likewise, as daughters grow into adolescence and adulthood, they long for the comfort, safety, and sense of being known and ministered to that was inherent in the original mother-daughter bond. Although they protest their attachment to their mothers, they may have difficulty giving it up.

The autobiographical vignette at the beginning of this chapter illustrates the kind of dynamic struggles faced by most mothers and daughters. It also suggests some of the relational strain that affects mothers and daughters as the process of separation and individuation is carried forward. Naturally enough, by speaking to me plainly but privately about my mother and vice versa, my grandmother was fulfilling an important intergenerational role. As psychoanalyst Theresa Benedek has inferred, grandparents and grandchildren get along notoriously well because both have the same common enemy—the parent (1970, pp. 199–204).

More to the point, as my grandmother neared the end of her own life, she was able to counsel both my mother and me in a way that addressed our mutual needs for separateness and togetherness. This form of intergenerational bond between women, which has been disrupted in our current highly mobile and diversified society, has traditionally been a mainstay of support for mothers as they witness their children assume more adult responsibilities. By noting the example set by their mothers and grandmothers, women could see how they remain connected to their own mothers throughout adulthood. Having children grow up and live their own lives did not necessarily mean losing them. Ideally, fathers also supported the process. The father reassured the mother as the child individuated, then supported her as the child was encouraged to venture forth into the world.

Our current cultural climate seems quite ambivalent about the messages it gives women, specifically mothers, about the individuation of daughters. First, the intergenerational supports of the extended family are no longer as readily available. Second, despite the increasing involvement of men in parenting, they are still unable—for reasons of their own—to fully support the separation-individuation process. (This dilemma is discussed in more detail in Chapter 4.) In fact, many men are not involved in the lives of their children at all, instead leaving mothers to cope as best they can with strained (and few) resources, both financial and emotional. All these factors may sometimes strengthen the mother-daughter bond, but at other times may promote conflict within it.

However, despite these societal and familial patterns, the dilemmas faced by daughters and mothers in getting along with each other are timeless and relatively independent of culture. The central developmental questions center on how to become your own woman while still remaining connected to and receiving nurturance from your mother. The common denominator underlying many cases of anorexia nervosa and bulimia nervosa is the amount of maternal over- and underinvolvement that influences the child's ability to grow psychologically, establish personal boundaries, and regulate her own body. But before examining the eating disorders in depth, we must understand how the challenge of negotiating the mother-daughter relationship must be faced by all women. Then we will see that eating disorders can be understood, at least in part, as an exaggerated form of normal female developmental struggles.

## The Ties That Bind

Let's examine some of the questions that perplex each of us as mothers and daughters. How many times have you wondered whether you are being a dutiful daughter or are being too selfish in pursuing your own interests? As a parent, have you ever wrestled with guilt that you could have—or should have—given more to your child or, worse yet, that you have impaired her in some way? What sets us apart as individuals? How are we like our parents and yet different? How do we give our children nurturance without spoiling them? We may spend years and years educating ourselves to enter a profession, but how much time do we spend learning how to be a parent? How do we help ourselves and our children forge their autonomous personalities while assuring them that their needs for nurturance can be met?

Considering these questions makes us all the more aware of the knotty problem that the late psychiatrist Donald B. Rinsley called the individual's "ineluctable drive toward separation-individuation" (1980, p. 289). But everyone has mixed feelings about the process of separation. On the surface, we give lip service to wanting maturity for ourselves and others, especially our children. But letting our children grow up also involves loss—losing them to a career, a mate, friends, and other life interests. Successful parenthood requires us to allow our children to take their own place in the world so that they can lead their own lives. But the process is not easy for mothers or for daughters. In their hearts, they know they are leaving each other behind. As the English writer Elizabeth Gaskell wrote about separation, "All the earth, though it were full of kind hearts, is but a desolation and a desert place to a mother when her only child is absent" (1860/1991, p. 17). Both parties must withstand the loss and grow from the separation—that is, they must find new supports, if they are to permit their relationship to mature.

Mothers must also struggle with their jealousy and envy of talents that their children possess. Indeed, a daughter's youthful attractiveness and joie de vivre may produce great consternation in her mother. Although it may be exciting for a mother to see her daughter move out into the world to face new experiences and excitements, it also means that she herself is not as young as she once was. Thus not only has she lost her "baby" daughter who was once dependent on her and idealized her, but she must also now compete with yet champion her daughter as a vibrant, attractive, younger woman in her own right.

Caught up in typical adolescent preoccupations with self, the daughter is not much help to her mother. The daughter usually isn't even aware of her mother's internal struggles. Instead, she is primarily concerned with her own rather self-centered desires and simply wants to have it both ways. On the one hand, she would like a mother to be a constant, admiring audience for her talents, beauty, sexual intrigues, and successes, because this shores up her self-esteem and helps her feel womanly and adult. But on the other hand, the adolescent daughter will typically fly into a rage if her mother asks one question too many or makes a personal demand for more time and attention that seems to breach her privacy and space. She will declare that she has her own life to lead and knows what she is doing. However, if the daughter becomes ill, experiences a setback at school or at work, or finds herself pining for an unrequited love, she will more than likely seek the solace of her mother's shoulder.

If the attachment of infancy continued to flower smoothly and without disruptions, no person would ever grow up. There would be no reason to aspire to anything, because all needs would be taken care of by mother. It is our mothers' imperfections in caring that push us forward—for example, when they don't feed us on demand or omnisciently know what we need. Yet despite their faults, our mothers provide us with a form of consolation that we can never experience to the same extent with anyone else. This connection is exemplified by the way that elderly people, whose parents are long dead, cry out at the time of their own deaths for the comforting arms and soothing presence of their mothers.

Everyone must face the developmental issues between daughters and mothers that contribute to a continuum of concerns about nurturance, separation, and autonomy. The more we understand the struggles inherent in the mother-daughter relationship, the more we can see how they are, to some extent, merely exaggerated among individuals with eating disorders. As we begin to appreciate that *one aspect* of an eating disorder involves unresolved snags in the separation-individuation process, it helps us put the mother-daughter relationship on a better course. Ultimately, this evaluation has a significant impact on the treatment of the eating problem. It allows us to look more objectively into the real developmental pushes and pulls that inevitably affect both mothers and daughters, with the intent that each person will eventually develop a more realistic and tempered, if not necessarily empathic, view of the other's position.

Being a mother has never been easy. Modern psychiatry, if anything, has made it more difficult, because of the tendency to place the responsibility for a child's problems on the mother. Current psychodynamic theorists, informed by feminist thought and developmental studies, are trying to correct this tendency. Fortunately, psychoanalysts are becoming more attuned to how the responsibility for psychiatric problems has been inappropriately viewed as resting primarily and resolutely with the mother. As students of women's history can attest, this type of "mother bashing" has actually occurred for generations, and can be traced from the Judeo-Christian tradition to more contemporary political movements.

Because I wish to focus here on the personal, psychodynamic residual of the troubled mother-daughter relationship, I will simply refer in passing to those important works that trace the evolution of scientific thinking about the mother-daughter relationship. Readers who want additional information might wish to read broadly from the growing collection of works in women's literature, history, and psychology.

But my point of departure is the fact that the mother-child bond is crucial for both men and women. For an eating disorder to develop, some aspect or aspects of this relationship must have gone awry. In saying this, I may also be perceived, like other psychodynamically oriented clinicians before me, to be "mother bashing." But such is not my intent. Rather, I would hope to demonstrate, through case examples and citations from pertinent clinical literature, some of the perils of the mother-daughter relationship that will help readers gain an appreciation of how best to deal with them.

Such insights can help us reverse the common sequence of impeded growth. Furthermore, eating disorders are one of several mental health problems that represent a developmental snag that has temporarily but not irreversibly forced the individual off track. Emphasizing the developmental perspective "provides the impetus to restart emotional growth" (Levin 1992, p. 45) and helps make seemingly enigmatic and obscure eating rituals more comprehensible. Human beings ache for human understanding. They should never be regarded as mere containers of symptoms, something modern psychiatry has inadvertently perpetuated by its overreliance on symptom checklists found in diagnostic manuals such as the *DSM-IV Draft Criteria* (American Psychiatric Association 1993) and the *International Statistical Classification of Diseases and Related Health Problems* (ICD-10; 1992).

## The Mother in Psychoanalytic Circles: A Changing, Ambivalent Role

The primary role our mothers play in our lives—consistently recognized over the centuries in art, drama, fiction, and poetry—is currently being reexamined by students of anthropology and myth. Cultural portrayals have emphasized the ancient matriarchy and the role of the mother-godhead in religion. But this perspective, considered important by male and female intellectuals for centuries, was largely neglected by Freud. Although he actually fostered psychological treatment of women by taking the courageous and in some ways revolutionary step of listening to them (after being told by one woman patient to keep quiet and allow her to speak!), he emphasized the role of the father and minimized the role of the mother in the family. For Freud, the father was the primary parent who fostered the child's personal growth.

Freud generally ignored the long years that both little girls and little boys spend with their mothers. Although he acknowledged women's sexuality as a "dark continent" (Freud 1926/1966, p. 212) and viewed his own study of the psychology of women as incomplete, his followers have been reluctant to challenge and revise his theories about motherhood. Despite notable exceptions to this neglect, the limitations that affected the study of female psychology explain why psychoanalytic studies are just beginning to move forward to confirm the critical influence of mothers.

As research studies and clinical investigations in disparate disciplines have focused more on the mother-child relationship, contemporary psychoanalysts have begun to weave this information into a fabric of knowledge that has influenced the treatment of all patients. As a result, the role of the mother has been recast with an emphasis on the child's relationship to both parents. Nonclinicians must look to the entire parenting process as a pivotal point in the life cycle of the developing child. One then rethinks the issues less from the perspective of criticizing either parent overtly but recasting the dilemma in terms of how each parent might encourage growth or inadvertently block it.

New insights and questions about the mother-daughter relationship have arisen from the work of sociologist and psychoanalyst Nancy Chodorow (1978, 1989), the contributions from the Stone Center at Wellesley College (1991), and the other relatively sparse but significant contributions by analytic and lay writers. Although much is left unanswered, these new theoretical lenses help focus our daily work with individual patients.

Let's look at how evolving theories typically inform what we know intuitively about the world. It is common for most women to have at least one very close woman friend, whereas men do not as easily share their most intimate thoughts and feelings with other men. This observation has led investigators to wonder whether men's needs for nurturance are met by women while the men are providing women with erotic satisfaction. And although most women are erotically attracted to men, they get their emotional sustenance from other women. But what stirs this ongoing attachment to other women? Nancy Chodorow (1978) speculates that the girl never gives up her primary attachment to her mother. Unlike the little boy, who relinquishes his tie to the mother to establish his "differentness" and become a man, the little girl recognizes that she is the same sex and has the same genitals, so she does not feel compelled to be different. In some ways, she is; in other crucial ways, she is not. She thus maintains her bond to her mother, which causes the two to often feel fused or merged.

To become a woman herself, the girl must test out how she is alike, yet different, from her mother. Meanwhile, the mother experiences her little girl from the very beginning as "like me." Realizing that their genitals, if not their very psychological frameworks, are similar in comparison to a boy's, mothers and daughters must search out their differences. To some extent, a normal mother-daughter relationship connotes fusion and enmeshment, two very dirty words in contemporary psychology. They are used here to mean the highly intense, often charged, emotionally rich interconnection that is the sine qua non of the mother-daughter interaction.

The following chapter will focus on how the father helps the little girl separate from her mother by being an exciting, somewhat unknowable, but very different object in her emotional life. Available fathers and father substitutes support the little girl's femininity by their male presence and affirmation of her desirability and differentness. But any instinctual or biological mothering drive also seems nurtured by the connection with the mother. This connection fosters a desire to give birth and grow through relationships to other people.

As the little girl moves forward to attain mature sexuality in adult life, she must transfer her love for her mother to others. Her preference may be heterosexual or homosexual, but symbolically and realistically she is choosing a person outside of the world of her mother and often engendering as much conflict as joy. When mother and daughter are able to view each other as separate and whole, this transfer of affection never completely severs their tie. Instead, the woman maintains a primary attachment and identification with her mother, continuing to feel dependent on her in many ways. Mother also remains an important object of love, albeit an ambivalently held one. If the mother can accept the choice of partner of her daughter, the more harmonious and fulfilling will be their relationship. Permission for individuation and sexual expression paradoxically supports connection.

For the mother, the relationship with her daughter presents several possibilities for growth and love. No doubt she must be attuned to the one who is "like her," while allowing her daughter to grow. She must simultaneously acknowledge and buttress her own, and her daughter's, individuality. Because of her own developmental needs and struggles, the mother may subtly give the daughter the message, "You can grow, but only if you do it for me." This common intergenerational warning results from an unconscious obligatory loyalty oath the mother had with her own mother. She sacrificed herself to maintain connection and an ongoing fusion or enmeshment with her own mother.

In contrast, a sensitive, "good enough" mother also recognizes that her children are individuals with their own talents, potentialities, and problems. She will naturally want to hold on to their love but will nevertheless encourage their development, which necessarily takes them away from her. Thus, the major task for the mother involves incorporating new images of her growing child based on that child's realistic gifts and limitations. The most loving and helpful mother will enjoy her daughter's real growth and accomplishments, even as she mourns the developmental thrust that takes her daughter out of her own orbit. As this new mother-daughter relationship matures, it can never take the place of the symbiotic oneness the mother experienced when her child was an infant. The nirvana of early symbiosis always gives way to the more limited connections of everyday life.

It is difficult for all parents to accept that their children may know more about many matters of the world. In fact, as a child advances, no parent will know as much about that child's life as during the child's infancy. Here is still another loss to endure—the loss of total knowledge. Although the world expands for the child entering adolescence, the life cycle demands a shrinking of possibilities for the adult parent. Adults realize that they no longer have as many choices or opportunities open to them. Maturity thus involves giving up the sense that the world is one's oyster.

This transition may prove particularly difficult for mothers. Their self-esteem is lowered when they realize their daughters need them less. And mothers have often sacrificed so much of their own development for the good of their children. As the mother perceives the daughter as more grown up and emotionally distant, she may resent her daughter's new relationships or separate interests. To continue their relationship, the two must resolve this dilemma. On the one hand, they remain linked by their early bond, their gender, and the similarity of their genitals. But on the other, life no longer centers on the mother.

The mother may react with loneliness, bitterness, or depression if she is not happy with herself as a woman or with her mate. A common sequel to this all-too-frequent pattern is the overinvolvement of some mothers in the lives of their children and their children's spouses. These mothers may be attempting to reestablish a primary tie with their daughter as a way to allay their anxiety and depression on growing older. This desire becomes all the more pressing when the woman cannot turn to her husband for support and sustenance; such women truly lead lives of quiet desperation because of their impoverished interpersonal relationships. They look to their daughters for the kind of emotional support they should find instead with a peer. They may also be searching for the affirmation found in a gratifying relationship. This expectation sets up an impossible situation for both mother and daughter, because neither can meet all the adult needs of the other. They truly have different needs and need different people. Yet the mother may castigate the daughter for her lack of attentiveness and love, while the daughter launches a diatribe against a burdensome, never-satisfied mother.

## Too Much of a Good Thing

When taken to extremes, maternal overinvolvement may lead to anorexia nervosa. A number of writers, including Hilda Bruch (1973, 1978, 1988), Maria Selvini-Palazzoli (1978), and Craig Johnson (1991b), have described variations of this typical pattern. I would add that the anorexic patient's plight is an exacerbation of the developmental struggle all women face with their mothers.

The developmental challenge for women is to attain separateness and individuality while maintaining connection. This level of negotiation is impossible for the anorexic woman, who experiences her mother as too close and overwhelming. According to Selvini-Palazzoli, the more the child develops a womanly body, the more she experiences herself as exactly like her mother, therefore inhibiting her ability to be her own person. This terrifying experience may overcome some young women, who begin to starve themselves so that they can feel like a separate individual. It is "a desperate attempt to live" (Johnson 1991b, p. 169).

Yet the anorexic woman is doing all she can to assert herself and make known her own needs. Meanwhile, she sets up the situation so that caring figures must become attuned to her physical needs. The caretaking she exacts addresses the other side of the relational coin. The eating disorder brings the other person close by means of ministration and concern, even though these attempts are ultimately self-defeating. The individual must find new ways to assert her individuality while remaining connected, a central dilemma for all people regardless of gender, race, or class (Steiner-Adair 1991a, 1991b). This statement epitomizes much of our contemporary thought on the subject of anorexia nervosa. Johnson further explains, "The self-starvation is a desperate attempt to assert some autonomy, defend the fragile self against further internal intrusiveness, and protect the fragile ego from psychobiological demands of adulthood" (1991b, p. 170). The case of Aimee dramatically illustrates some of these points.

❦ Aimee G., age 18, was rushed to the eating disorders clinic for an emergency consultation. Both of Aimee's parents were physicians, but neither acknowledged their daughter's illness until her high school principal called their home for the third time, concerned about Aimee's third fainting episode in 6 months. At the time of the psychiatric consultation, Aimee had not menstruated for at least 4 years and weighed 27% below her estimated recovery weight. The psychiatrist insisted that she be admitted immediately to the hospital for nutritional support and further evaluation of depression.

On the unit, Aimee not only refused to eat but also continued to exercise compulsively. When the therapist explained to her parents that she needed to follow a protocol that would help her gain weight by eating balanced meals and curtailing physical exertion, both her parents reacted angrily. They told the hospital treatment team that Aimee's wishes should be respected. Despite the life-threatening nature of Aimee's illness, they believed the treatment structure was very foolish, if not harmful, to her because she complained belligerently about it.

In this case, both parents were unable to view their daughter's demands and complaints objectively enough to see how they were colluding with her destructiveness. Their intrusiveness in regard to the treatment structure reflected Aimee's experience of their intrusiveness at home. Much later in treatment, she was able to explain how her father and mother would go through her belongings at will, making her feel that she had "no space" of her own. The parents' attempt to rescue Aimee by devaluing the standard treatment for anorexia nervosa displayed their difficulty in allowing anyone else to care for or mean something to her. Aimee's eating disorder was, among other things, a last bastion of self-regulation and autonomy—a veritable Alamo around which she attempted to keep outside influences, including food, from invading her interior.

## But I Want More!

Thus far we have emphasized that the major conflict between mothers and daughters centers on how they attempt to remain connected to each other without surrendering their selfhood. Although this process often leads to a pattern of overinvolvement, that result is obviously not always the case. In bulimia nervosa, an opposite scenario seems to be the problem; these young women yearn for more maternal emotional involvement and nurturance than they received. Many bulimic patients tell how their early years were filled either with real emotional neglect or with the perceived need for a different kind of parenting. Their relationships to their mothers were frustrated. Despite seeking more nurturance from them, these daughters often felt lonely and found their mothers unavailable psychologically, if not physically. Sometimes these mothers were depressed or preoccupied with their own lives. Other mothers were simply unable to meet the needs of their children because of illness, divorce, career plans, or a lack of interest in parenting.

The young bulimic-to-be frenetically searches (often in vain) for a protective, available, ready response from her mother. As Bowlby (1969, 1973) has written from the standpoint of his research on animal relationships and his clinical work with patients, this type of absent caretaker experience sets up a dynamic that interferes with later attachments. If a mother is repeatedly unavailable or unable to meet the needs of her child, that child will anxiously cling to her mother. If the mother departs, the child will refrain from venturing out and exploring the world. The child's need for mothering will override any desire for age-appropriate explorations. However, if the mother is unlikely to fulfill the maternal role, a good, acceptable substitute can help launch the child along the appropriate developmental path.

Without a firm foundation, however, the child becomes insecure and tentative. She also looks for ways to self-soothe her inner state of restlessness, loneliness, and angst. When her mother is unable to fill the gap or the child is not provided with a stable human substitute (i.e., a consistent caretaker or nanny), the child will turn to food. Food not only symbolizes mother by its feeding function, but it also has the power to soothe. Eating thus becomes a reasonably consistent and available source of nurturance. It helps the child to regulate her needs and feelings when humans have failed her. She will look outside the relationship with her mother for her needs to be fulfilled; because food is easily available in our society, it is a ready alternative.

The next case study graphically demonstrates how this theoretical idea played itself out in the life of one very ill bulimic patient. Marcena H.'s situation illustrates the consequences of early maternal abandonment.

&#10087; At age 21 and mired in academic coursework beyond her capabilities, Marcena H. tried to please a harsh and demanding internalized image of her mother. That is, she was convinced her mother would care for her *only* if she were the brightest, most competent, and most gifted student in her class. Yet throughout Marcena's life, her mother had been "too busy" to be available to meet Marcena's strong dependency needs. Marcena sensed that her mother had almost no interest in her development as a person.

Marcena's internalized view of her mother seemed based on the unpropitious reality of her youth. The second of two children, Marcena had always been compared to her brother. His work with his chemistry set in their garage took first-place awards at science fairs and was extolled by Marcena's mother. In comparison to this academically inclined and scientifically gifted boy, Marcena always came second. Although Marcena was a talented violinist in her own right, her mother did not give her the same kind of attention she gave her son. Marcena recalled spending hours alone in front of the television set while her mother was actively involved in helping her brother plan his science experiments. Whenever Marcena practiced her violin or gave a public recital, her mother seemed aloof and critical. Sometimes she was too busy to go, all the while lavishing attention on Marcena's brother.

Marcena later told her therapist how she longed for the kind of companionship that her friends seemed to have with their mothers. Rather than risk being disappointed in other relationships, however, she coped with her loneliness by avoiding people and acting as if she did not care. Yet beneath her developing facade of intellectualization, superficial interactions, and haughty, aloof personality lay a frightened child who yearned for maternal attention and care.

Food became a tool that Marcena used to nurture herself. Bingeing was a way to calm herself whenever she was upset, because she had not learned how to turn to an adult for soothing. The restrictive patterns in Marcena's eating represented her tremendous fear of becoming vulnerable to anyone or anything. Because she experienced her mother's preoccupation with her brother as hurtful to her deepest self, she was terrified of taking in any nurturance lest she be disappointed or betrayed yet again.

She would show the world, by her driven violin playing and her power to avoid eating, that she needed no one; indeed, she needed nothing but herself. Like many other people, however, Marcena found this fasting state impossible to maintain. When she got hungry, she began eating, in part because of the biological need we all face when dieting; she also ate because she sought to fill her emptiness and quell her fears.

Of course, the stakes simply couldn't be higher. Although she compromised herself physically with her eating disorder (a combination of bulimia and anorexia), Marcena was attempting to meet her deep desire for nurturance. If she could not control or entice her mother toward more involvement, she could at least control what might come into her body. Believing that her mother favored her brother because he was a boy, Marcena found starvation to be a way to punish or attempt to kill off her feminine self.[1]

Marcena fantasized that if she were thin, she would look more masculine on the outside and thus win her mother's affection. Marcena did not consciously wish to be a boy; indeed, she rather liked being a girl. But her brother received what she believed was her due. Thus her masculine strivings, as manifested in her eating disorder, conveyed a number of messages to Marcena's mother about their failure to bond.

One of Freud's most helpful and enduring principles is that of overdetermination or multideterminism. Freud believed that a given behavior rarely has only one cause or meaning. Yet in considering the manifest behavior of an eating disorder patient, there is a great tendency on everybody's part to want to pin it all on a single cause. Hence we look to cultural values, biological deficits, or family factors to narrow, if not define, the cause. Life is rarely so simple.

Marcena's case illustrates how one narrow interpretation of the problem's source would not only be limiting but also ultimately incorrect. For although there were many aspects of her relationship with her mother that led to the eating disorder, she also needed to face other problems. For example, Marcena had many struggles and conflicts with her father and brother that contributed to her development of, and

---

[1]This tendency for the little girl without a close relationship with a woman to falter in becoming one herself is illustrated in the movie A *League of Their Own*. One of the women baseball players for the Rockford Peaches, who is inept at anything feminine because she has been raised without a mother, is transformed by the other women players. This athlete learned from her teammates what she couldn't learn from a man—how to act, dress, and woo a man of her own.

ongoing battle with, bulimia nervosa. Indeed, the eating disorder itself took on many symbolic meanings in Marcena's struggle for selfhood and feminine acceptance.

The most basic set of conflicts centered on Marcena's inability to have the secure bond with her mother that would make her feel worthy and worthwhile. When Marcena's early needs had not been met, she had to seek a form of self-caring. Some people might be able to meet this need on their own by finding other helpful relationships, such as with a teacher or other adult confidant, thereby permitting normal development.

Marcena was the type of individual who had the capacity to form relationships with substitute maternal figures but could not avail herself of them until she started therapy. Over time, her eating disorder was alleviated because she found the support she needed with different mentors in school and with therapists. Fortunately for Marcena, her parents were willing to look at themselves to try to help her. When Marcena began individual treatment, her parents accepted the therapist's recommendation to involve the whole family in a family therapy process as well.

In family therapy, Marcena's mother was able to address her own difficulties with mothering, which led her to change how she interacted with Marcena. This development ultimately led to a more nurturing relationship as well as to more give-and-take between the two. Over time, Marcena came to learn that her emotional needs could be met by people in ways that she had not believed possible. She began to give up her suspicious belief that those who would try to connect with her were only out to hurt, use, or abandon her.

The eating disorder patient improves as she learns that she can be a separate person yet still connected to other people. Both she and her mother must learn that forays into the outside world are not dangerous. Neither should they represent an all-or-none choice between having close relationships or none at all. Mothers in particular may be supported by their own individual or family therapy process, which permits them to express individual concerns as well as aspirations. Here they are inevitably helped by the daughter's father, who encourages both his mate and his children to experience and express their real selves. In this way, the daughter can remain her mother's real "pearl of great price," but she is not the only jewel in her mother's crown.

Let us examine how complex family interactions contribute to the development of eating disorders. We will see how treatment can help the woman achieve mature connectedness in the face of a greater autonomy, free of an eating disorder.

### ❦ The Price of Selflessness

Two years into her therapy process, Natalie I., age 25, ran to her session with a valuable new insight. Still experiencing great inner turmoil, she had struggled in treatment to uncover aspects of herself that had been buried for years. She was eager to find out why a 2-year bout of anorexia in her adolescence had evolved into a relentless cycle of binge-purge behavior. This typical evolution of the illness puzzled Natalie, and part of her desire to master her problem was through learning more about it.

Natalie was excited to share with her therapist an idea she had for further research on eating disorders. She wondered if anyone had studied whether mothers, aunts, and grandmothers of eating disorder patients tended to have a higher incidence of these difficulties themselves. Natalie explained that her curiosity had surfaced as she began to recollect that throughout her childhood her mother had been preoccupied by her own thinness as well as Natalie's. As a young girl, Natalie remembered her mother telling her that Natalie's grandmother was also concerned about her body size and shape. Interestingly enough, Natalie pointed out that at least three generations of women in her family had been obsessed with thinness. This obsessiveness had worsened over the years, and she wondered what that might mean for her and her family.

Natalie's insight was a most productive one that led to much therapeutic work for her and her family. It also casts light on some of the underlying causes of eating disorders. Because Natalie's mother had not had the chance to go to college and pursue a career despite her intellectual giftedness, Natalie felt great pressure to achieve for her mother's sake. In some ways, it seemed as if her mother were asking her to live the kind of life she had not had for herself.

Throughout treatment, Natalie had felt quite bitter toward her mother. In fact, their relationship had been marked by hostility and turmoil as long as Natalie could remember. But when Natalie began to acknowledge her mother's plight, she developed a deeper empathy for both of their struggles. She began to tolerate parts of herself that formerly made her uncomfortable. Because Natalie's mother had been held back by societal limits on achievement, she had projected her own wishes and desires onto her daughter, including her wish for Natalie to have a "perfect, thin body."

For Natalie, her mother's expectations posed an insurmountable burden. Being an innately competitive individual, Natalie faced the inevitable rivalry that arises between mother and daughter by developing a boundless desire to achieve scholastically. Unfortunately, her desire for success outstripped her innate endowment. Despite working extraordinarily hard, she usually received only mediocre grades. Anger on her mother's part would follow, only to be surpassed by Natalie's inner fury for not meeting the standard she herself had set.

Eating was another trap. No matter how much she attempted to lose weight by dieting, Natalie was never satisfied with her appearance. She was convinced that it never met her mother's standard. Yet her mother's desire for Natalie to achieve academically and socially (by having a slender figure) was derived from dictates passed down from her own mother. This intergenerational pattern intensified Natalie's eating disorder all the more.

Neither Natalie nor her mother was free to find her own self because each was so busy attempting to figure out exactly what other family members wanted for her. They adapted their interests, goals, and plans accordingly. The cost of following the path another sets for you rather than your own is always high. It produces what psychoanalyst D. W. Winnicott (1960/1965) described as a "false self."

Actually, as Winnicott observed, all of us are subject to self-deception; in certain situations, we embody falseness itself. For example, whenever we cover up a bad or depressed mood at work or attempt to smooth the ruffled feathers of an angry friend or spouse—despite our real disgruntlement with that person—we are behaving in a dishonest, contrived way (Zerbe 1993a). This functional pattern helps our society move on; it would be impossible to tolerate others if people said exactly what was on their minds at all times. However, the degree to which people mask their real feelings to please or to win favor with valued others can become a matter of some consequence. When we persistently hide our true feelings, we soon lose touch with how we really feel. Life is lived for someone else, not ourselves.

Despite extraordinary personal cost, Natalie tried to do exactly what she believed her mother wanted her to. So caught up was she in becoming attuned to her mother's desires while also attempting to exceed her, Natalie never had the opportunity to figure out what she wanted for herself. The day she arrived at her therapist's office so excited about her idea for research on eating disorders, she was not simply participating in an intellectual speculation that might have implications for her own treatment as well as that for others. For one of the first times in her life, she felt alive, because she had come up with an idea of her own. She risked sharing her excitement with her therapist, desperately hoping that she, too, would delight in Natalie's ability to have her own thoughts.

For Natalie, one important aspect of her eating disorder was the identity it had provided her (I starve, therefore I am). Never fully permitted to experience the joy and excitement of having her own ideas at home, she manifested what psychoanalyst Michael Balint (1951/1965, 1968) called "the basic fault." A defect within her personality kept her from believing that she had anything meaningful to say and certainly nothing meaningful to contribute to the lives of others.

The expectant note of pleasure that Natalie brought to treatment was a sign of progress. She believed her therapist would affirm her in ways that had been impossible at home, and in this sense she tried to repair the basic fault of childhood. The expression of her own true thoughts and feelings with her therapist was an important first step.

In this sense, treatment came close to providing Natalie with some of the maternal experiences she had lacked at home. It followed that, as she grew more assured, she no longer had to use food (an inanimate object) to provide what she hoped for and needed from a real person. That is, she wanted a soothing presence and supportive confirmation that could be controlled at will—something both malleable and available. She was also able to take in food on a more consistent basis, gradually reflecting a more trusting stance toward the world.

Food restriction in such a case may involve a furtive, paranoid view of the world as a place where no one can be trusted and, consequently, where anything taken in might "poison" the self. Some anorexic patients refrain from eating because they unconsciously equate nourishment with taking in a contaminating, controlling, evil maternal presence (introject). This persistence in starving reflects the unconscious belief that the person is saving her life instead of ruining it.

Johnson (1991b) has cogently summarized the role of mothers in eating disorders:

> Both maternal over- and underinvolvement can result in impairment in a child's ability to self-regulate . . . for the restricter, self-starvation may be an adaptive effort to defend against self-regulatory deficits resulting from maternal overinvolvement. In contrast, the bulimic chaotic eating behavior may reflect a desperate attempt to compensate for an "empty experience" resulting from maternal underinvolvement. In a sense *the fundamental difference between the restricting and bulimic mode could be thought of as the [bulimic patient's] search for something to take in, compared to the [restricting anorexic patient's] attempt to keep something out.* (p. 171; italics added).

## Patterns of Depersonification

Hoping others will accept our strengths and limitations, all of us want to be treated as the human beings we are. One of the real pitfalls of motherhood rests on the mother's dilemma of having understandable aspirations for her child while nevertheless helping that child to develop his or her raw talents to the fullest. Parents will sometimes unwittingly place their children in jeopardy by expecting them to be someone or something they are not. This pattern of interaction—depersonification or apersonification—involves the repeated placing of another human being in a role that fails to acknowledge the other person's uniqueness and value as a real individual (Rinsley 1980). Depersonification was evident in the actions of one mother in a waiting room; she either held her child so close as to disallow any exploration of the environment, or else moved the child rhythmically and erotically up and down and back and forth at will. Clearly, the child was being used to soothe the mother and probably to provide physical, if not sensual, arousal to her. The following is a more typical example of the depersonification that can erode a youngster's personality.

❦ Marian J. was 19 when she first sought treatment. As a beautiful but somewhat overweight child, Marian had been entered in beauty contests from the age of three. Her mother, a former beauty pageant winner, was enormously invested not only in Marian's weight but also in the entire concept of having her child be as much of a winner in the pageants as she had been.

Marian's innate proclivities lay in another direction, however. Although she was quite attractive, her tomboyish demeanor and her interest in mathematics led her to feel stifled and misunderstood by her mother. Chronically ill in her childhood, Marian seemed to use her ill health to avoid the beauty contests her mother attempted to place her in, as well as to receive nurturing or care from others. Nurses and physicians expressed genuine concern over Marian's physical plight, whereas her mother grew anxious and preoccupied whenever Marian could not participate in a pageant. Although Marian was continually angry with her mother for not allowing her to be her own person, she rarely found the courage to express her anger directly. As an adult, Marian not only struggled with bulimia and anorexia but she also engaged in self-mutilation. Her inability to tolerate bad feelings led her to deposit them in dissociated states that she later named. Unable to tolerate and modulate her own emotions, she got rid of them by placing them in a part of herself she could split off from awareness. Feeling guilty about her inability to please her mother, Marian believed she was so despicable that she wanted to die. Her mother had been unable to convey a belief that Marian was a beloved child regardless of whether she won beauty pageants.

When Marian's treaters began to focus on her eating behavior, it became apparent that Marian equated her slenderness with being young. She thus hoped to regain the childhood she had lost and, possibly, to find a parent who would allow her to be the person she was without inordinate or unrealistic expectations. Poorly equipped for independent living because she was totally confused about what she wanted as an adult, Marian found much satisfaction in the fantasy of bodily perfection through bony thinness. She was not only finally pleasing her mother but also finding a positive identity and self-image in at least one area. Her eating disorder served at least two important functions: 1) she maintained an important unconscious connection with her mother (I am finally the baby you want), and 2) she developed a sense of identity by clinging to the hope that childhood was not lost (I will be a thin child who does not have to worry about grown-up responsibilities).

## Having a Good Enough Mother Inside Oneself

In this chapter, we have begun to explore how difficulties in the parent-child relationship affect development and may lead to an eating disorder. Although mothers and daughters face problems in growing autonomously while remaining connected that can sometimes seem overwhelming, most mothers and daughters achieve a positive relationship. To be sure, the difficult balance of a warm and caring connection that also values separateness and other affirming relationships is not an easy one. What enables mutually affirming bonds to grow?

When mother and daughter are able to see themselves realistically, taking into account each other's real assets and limitations, they are truly appreciating each other's individuality. This capacity requires, of course, that the daughter respect her mother's own background, perspective on life events, and personal struggles. Just as clinicians must avoid "mother blaming," so must daughters. The daughter cannot fault her mother for some of her own difficulties, even though her mother may have played a role in them. The mother, meanwhile, must look inward and assess how she may inadvertently place unrealistic demands and expectations on her child. Mother and daughter then have the opportunity to form a lasting bond based on self-responsibility. Each avoids holding the other accountable for not meeting her own needs and desires.

In essence, mothers and daughters must cultivate an inner view of themselves that gives them permission to be who they are. In this way, they permit themselves and each other a more benevolent view of themselves. Mistakes are accepted; imperfections are acknowledged. The inevitable triumphs and tragedies of life are recognized. Meanwhile, neither mother nor daughter expects the other to resolve all her own life's dilemmas. Both allow each other full participation in the cycle of life, complete with all its mystery. Each has a "true self" as her core.

Clearly, daughters and mothers will continue to mend and amend their relationships as long as they are both alive. In psychotherapy, we learn that even women who have lost their mothers think about them long after they have died. Thus daughters reflect on their relationships with their mothers and rework their maternal image throughout life. Just as the mother's tie to her child is lifelong, so is the child's tie to her mother. This relationship can always be stretched to promote growth and a mature connectedness that is truly life affirming.

Having a good enough mother inside oneself means that the daughter must make peace with her mother and the memories of her. The mother then comes to be remembered and respected more as friend than as foe, despite previous strains and disappointments in the relationship. Not only is this model of an affirming relationship able to ease inner tension and promote growth, but it also truly sustains life. One young woman soldier serving in the Persian Gulf during Desert Storm was able to call up such an image of her mother as she faced battle. She said, "I wasn't anxious as I saw the first firefight around me. I didn't think much about it at the time, but I stayed calm, secure that I could do my job. Now that I look back on it, it was like knowing my mother was there with me all the time." This woman had been able to have a positive, soothing, benevolent image of her mother sustain her in a time of great stress. In treatment, patients learn that they too can rework memories and feelings about their mothers to approximate what this young woman was able to do.

A benign maternal presence can be cultivated by working on the relationship with one's mother in individual or family therapy. One may also search for suitable mother substitutes in life, such as mentors or teachers. Acquiring a positive inner image of one's mother is made easier if other persons are available, especially an involved and caring father. In the next chapter, we will look at how the father's presence influences a woman's development.

# 4

# Daughters and Fathers

She's full of education, and it's a delicate commodity.

Sir Thomas More in Robert Bolt's
*A Man for All Seasons*

An important subplot in the play *A Man for All Seasons* is the tender and mutually affirming relationship between Sir Thomas More and his daughter, Margaret, a Latin scholar. As the story unfolds, it becomes clear that More is not only a man of soundest principles, perspicacity, and decency, but he is also centuries ahead of his time in encouraging the educational pursuits of his daughter. Consequently, Margaret is able to converse with the likes of kings. Even more important, she intuits and supports the ideals and values of her father. But their extraordinary and heartfelt relationship, which obviously has promoted the talents of both and inspired the daughter's growth, has also created understandable envy in Sir Thomas's wife, Lady Alice. In a crucial scene, she acknowledges the affinity between father and daughter while subtly and lovingly conveying that it had threatened her position. Understandably, as his mate, she wished to be the premier object of his love.

The play depicts the father-daughter relationship at its best, even by contemporary standards. The father not only encourages his daughter's academic and personal pursuits but also champions her interests and sacrifices for them. He is, however, the keeper of appropriate inter-generational boundaries. First, he is steadfast in his love for his wife while permitting his daughter to choose her own love interest, albeit with proper paternal concern and questioning. Meanwhile, his daughter's ability to develop her own talents does not intimidate him. On the contrary, he delights in her virtuosity. Although their relationship is founded on an abstruse and mysterious understanding, the two share cerebral repartee. The daughter remains loyal and devoted, despite launching her own life with her own thoughts, values, and aspirations. And Sir Thomas, while still concerned, protective, and very much his own man, revels in her capacity to be her own woman.

Unfortunately, this appealing scenario occurs much less frequently in modern life than either daughters or fathers would like. Most fathers have usually not been as instrumental in the rearing and devoted support as mothers have been. In psychoanalytic circles, and as chronicled by the societal zeitgeist, the father remains known as "the forgotten parent." To some extent, current developmental studies are revamping this view. Studies of families underscore the paternal influence on the child from birth onward, yet show that the father usually remains in the background.

This finding is particularly interesting in view of Freud's original psychoanalytic stance, which was riveted on the centrality of paternity (1905/1953, 1909/1955, 1911/1958, 1925/1961, 1933/1964). No doubt Freud's own conflicts with his domineering mother and the societal impact of fin de siècle Vienna led him to neglect the mother's influence on the development of the child and to stress that of the father instead. He wrote, for example, how he hated to be seen as the "mother" in the therapeutic relationship (Fliegel 1986). He also based his entire theory of oedipal conflict on how children negotiate the critical relationship with their fathers. Yet, until recently, little has been said about the effect of the quality of the father-child relationship on the child in all areas of life. Fortunately, the tide is beginning to turn, which allows us to revise key concepts about the father's role in normal and abnormal development.

This acknowledged importance of fathers—and grandfathers—has direct implications for understanding some of the problems associated with eating disorders. The key is the quality of nurturance or the lack thereof. To nurture her offspring, the mother must also be nurtured, which is clearly one of the father's central roles. An "alliance of couplehood" must develop between the parents prior to the child's birth and then continue after it. If the father is unable to nurture the mother, she may in turn be less able to nurture her offspring, thus leading to demonstrable psychopathology.

The Tufts Family Support Program addresses this dilemma by providing preventive interventions for both mothers and fathers (Browne and Finkelhor 1986/1988; Tufts New England Medical Center Division of Child Psychiatry 1984). To further the parental alliance that promotes development of the child, this program provides prospective parents with therapeutic help in discussing their relationships with each other and with their own parents. They are taught how to resolve conflict and how to master the highly complex but crucial methods for supporting and nurturing each other as they face the strains of parenthood.

In addition to seeing the father's role as nurturer of the mother, contemporary analysts stress the positive, nurturant aspects of the father's identity in his own right. This perspective on fathering not only recognizes its difference from mothering but also notes that the father provides special and unique caring for the wife and child in addition to fulfilling his role as a representative of the outside world.

As a representative of the "nonmother" world, the father holds a special fascination for little children and draws them into the larger external world of new people and new challenges. The father's presence can thus be thought of as a benevolent disruption of the mother-child symbiosis. Of course, his capacity to father depends on the benevolence of the mother, who must overtly and noncompetitively give permission and support to his active participation and presence. If she does not or cannot, depending on her own struggles and conflicts, then the father may be denigrated and devalued, leading to what Joyce McDougall (1978) described as a view of men as insensitive, brutal, hoggish, and ineffectual. This disdainful image was conveyed by one young woman patient in psychoanalysis who, on reviewing her early years, said of her father, "He was never a hero to mother, my sisters, or me. He snorted around the house and had detestable manners. What an impotent slob! We had to take care of *him*!"

When a mother forbids a loving relationship between father and daughter, the child may view the father as dangerous, ugly, and despicable. He is not only lost as an object of potential love, but those affirming capacities and aspirations he harbors toward the outside world are also lost. The father's unique role in fostering and furthering autonomy can be waylaid by many forces—his own conflicts over paternity, his wife's struggles with greed and envy, our society's devaluation of his potential influence. As a result, a truncated paternal experience for the child—and for the father—will inevitably have a negative effect on the child's psychological well-being. Let's look now at how these principles apply to the development of eating disorders. In addition, we will also consider how the father's potential contributions might circumvent such dysfunctional coping mechanisms.

### ❦ The "Mystery Man"

Clarice K., was a 20-year-old philosophy major when she began therapy for severe bulimia. Bright and intuitive, she eagerly shared much about her early years. Like many young women, Clarice adored her father, albeit from a distance. Her parents had been divorced since she was four. Unlike many women in single-parent homes, where the mother unwittingly disrupts the burgeoning alliance between the daughter and father by making persistent reproachful comments about him, Clarice's mother tended to idealize her former spouse.

A popular documentary filmmaker and champion of liberal causes, Clarice's father showed élan and intelligence that assured him of both the interest and company of a variety of women. On first meeting him, his former wife had been immediately captivated but had always had to share him with what seemed like an ever-present coterie of admiring onlookers.

From early childhood, Clarice looked forward to whatever smattering of time she could spend with her father. She learned much during their visits together. Throughout her freshman year at college, she found herself defending his causes and interests, even bragging to her dormmates about her trips to see him. Despite noting a subtle display of envy on her friends' part, Clarice could not refrain from describing how her father had introduced her to Mikhail Baryshnikov at the Four Seasons in New York. This remembrance, among all others, seemed to encapsulate for Clarice her father's own charisma and elegance. Only a true star can bask in the light of another star.

Clinical and research evidence about the earliest relationship between father and daughter casts light on the origins of Clarice's intense tie to her father and its impact on her own development. Once regarded as almost peripheral to the development and psychological health of the little girl, the father is now taking his rightful place as a coequal partner in parenting the psychologically healthy female. Unfortunately, what we know to be of help and benefit from a psychiatric standpoint has outstripped how individuals actively behave or how courts adjudicate. More often than not, the father is eclipsed by the mother as the *parentus principalus*.

One outcome of this emphasis on mothering has been that psychological difficulties have been rigidly viewed in mental health circles as deriving from the mother's failed relationship with her child. In Chapter 1, I reviewed how this stereotype has been widely criticized as "mother bashing." Now we probe further to demonstrate how this perspective also lets father off the hook, even as we idealize him, his accomplishments, and his way of being in the world.

Fortunately, the developmental pendulum that swung in the direction of maternal primacy in the 1960s, 1970s, and early 1980s (partly as a result of the feminist critique) is now reversing itself with a notable recasting of the father's role. As women of all ages take stock of our lives, whether or not through a formal psychotherapeutic process, we must ask ourselves important questions about our fathers.

How did the presence or absence of our fathers affect us? How do we find ourselves assimilating his ideals and values, often in ways that are not readily apparent? Do we choose partners with the best—or worst— aspects of our own fathers? Or, more troublesome, do we find that when comparing our partners to our father, we have made choices that never quite lived up to that ideal mystery man of our childhood? After all, there is always another side to the glowing astral body within our sight and fantasies—the one that we know so little about, the ineffable "dark side" of the moon. We tend to deify him because we cannot unveil his mystery and learn his secrets, nor can we control him.

Clarice's pride in her father and her attachment to him is a common response of contemporary women. Yet as she began to explore the roots of her severe bulimia in individual psychotherapy, she found that her idealized view of her father was not her only reaction to him. Like a multifaceted, shimmering crystal, their relationship had many angles, some of which were veiled and sharper than Clarice could initially allow herself to explore. For example, she learned that when her parents divorced, she had felt much more responsible for taking care of her mother than she had remembered. In essence, it seemed as though her father had gone off to make his own mark in the world while leaving Clarice to mark time with her mother.

In more healthily functioning households, the adults nurture each other so that there will be sufficient emotional resources available to nourish the family's dependent younger members. One aftermath of divorce, death, or emotional abandonment is that only one parent is left with the principal caretaking responsibility for the children, and these tasks are often experienced as burdensome even by the most dutiful and giving of parents.

This theme is humorously illustrated in the movie *Three Men and a Baby*, in which it takes three grown men to equal one mother! Often exhausted from their caretaking responsibilities, the men badger and barter with each other. At one point, one of the men offers an exorbitant sum to another to change the baby's diaper.

Such fiduciary arrangements are, of course, not available in most homes. Characteristically, the principal caretaker must look for other ways to sustain the self. The parent without a partner whose other resources are sufficiently taxed may even turn to the children themselves for solace and sustenance.

This reversal of caretaking roles occurred between Clarice and her mother. After the divorce, Clarice's mother unwittingly turned to Clarice for emotional support. As a result, Clarice was placed in the role of the "parentified child" whose principal task was to care for her mother.

One determinant of Clarice's later symptoms of bulimia nervosa centered on this reversal. To nurture herself and to fill up the void she felt, she would rapidly ingest large amounts of food. Instead of receiving nurturance, however, she continued to provide it, and always felt depleted because of the constant drain on her own internal emotional supplies. But the loss of mothering was not the most crucial influence on Clarice. Instead, she felt the void of *both* her parents' absence. Food became a substitute for what she most wanted—parental love—and for what she most needed to secure age-appropriate, healthy functioning—parental structure.

When a little girl suffers the loss of her father, her psychological development will be impaired. Although her need for fathering may not be as crucial to development as it is for a boy, most authorities believe that the presence of a psychologically healthy adult male promotes the growth of both sexes. During a boy's first 2 years of life, father absence and enmeshment with the mother can irreversibly leave the child with a feminine core gender identity, which is often covered up in childhood by hypermasculinity. That is, boys who have lost a father very early may be more prone to a sexual disturbance or may exhibit more aggressive and competitive behavior than do other boys. When a boy loses his father between ages 2 and 4, his mechanical interests may be lessened, and he may be less competitive and more dependent than other boys. His spatial abilities may also suffer, even as his verbal abilities are strengthened.

On the other hand, girls with absent fathers develop a feminine core gender identity but seem to have more social inhibitions and troubled sexual relationships than do other girls. Core femininity itself may also suffer. A girl may feel less secure in her ability to compete with other women, to be womanly and sensual, and to display age-appropriate interests in her appearance and body image.

These global findings, though important, say nothing about other potential benefits of the child's relationship with the father. Our science is still rudimentary in its knowledge and understanding of how we internalize values such as courage, compassion, and fairness. In all likelihood, they are probably learned within the day-to-day workings and machinations of home life, with all its human errors and pitfalls. Nevertheless, it is increasingly clear that the perceived presence or absence of the father is a crucial variable in the psychic life and development of the little girl.

Mental health professionals who work with eating disorder patients must help them begin to ferret out the multiple meanings of their relationship—or lack thereof—with their fathers. We should not be surprised to learn that their feelings about their fathers are far stronger than we have ever imagined. The search for father often entails great pain, because it requires us to give up an idealized fantasy of him as being a brilliant star remote from earthly—and earthy—concerns. It may also involve a necessary search for male models and mentors to help the woman in ways that her father himself could not or was not available to do.

With female eating disorder patients at The Menninger Clinic, we have found that male treaters—whether psychiatrists, nurses, social workers, psychologists, group and individual therapists, or teachers—often serve pivotal roles in treatment. Perhaps these male caretakers provide these patients with (among other things) another chance to find a father, albeit in a more realistic and less idealistic form.

## The Emotional Underground of Loss

Although Clarice and Janiece did not know each other, they were, in a peculiar sense, soul mates. Both had developed intense attachments to their fathers, but each expressed that bond in a totally different way.

❦ When Janiece L., age 33, was admitted to the hospital, she was fighting a severe depressive illness. Over the previous 12-year period, she had also had bouts of anorexia nervosa. For months, Janiece had been unable to work as a physical therapist, an occupation she had once found most meaningful and sustaining. In addition to a recent loss of more than 20 pounds below her usual low normal body weight, she had felt no interest in going out with friends, had experienced early morning wakening and insomnia, and admitted to frequent suicidal feelings. Janiece also acknowledged making several serious suicide attempts. She believed that her plight was entirely hopeless.

Unfortunately, most of the medical professionals who had treated Janiece agreed with her. She showed no sustained improvement, despite taking adequate doses of antidepressants at satisfactory blood levels and despite several trials of electroconvulsive treatment. She felt better for brief periods, only to relapse as her initial improvement waned. Her widowed mother and favorite uncle insisted that she seek further evaluation and care that would help her learn about the psychological causes of her illness with the faith that her deteriorating condition could be reversed. Not wanting to relinquish her role as the dutiful, obedient daughter, Janiece reluctantly consented—at least on the surface.

The early weeks of therapy with Janiece were almost unbearable, not only for her hospital therapist but also for her peer group and other staff members. Everyone seemed drawn to Janiece, wanting desperately to help her out of her shell so that she could discuss her thoughts and feelings. But it was all to no avail. Even as the others sought to engage her, Janiece withdrew more and more.

The therapist changed approaches on noting this pattern of interaction, also common to many other eating disorder patients: the more one attempts to help, the more the eating disorder patient rebuffs that help. Working with Janiece was going to take time, so the therapist began a prolonged process of just sitting with her and overtly asking little of her. The therapist insisted that she was available to talk—if Janiece wanted to—but that she would not force the issue. She suggested instead that Janiece write about her life history as much as possible in autobiographical journal entries.

Occasionally, the therapist would discuss a banal aspect of life with Janiece to let her know that she was present and a real person. At no time, however, was there a "forced feeding" of interventions on the therapist's part, despite very real pressure from Janiece's insurance carrier to hasten her treatment. Quick fixes had already been tried without benefit.

Gradually, the tragic incidents of Janiece's life began to unfold in the notes she shared with her therapist. Janiece's weight had first dropped precipitantly on the sudden loss of her beloved 62-year-old father when she was 29. After he died, she began relinquishing her fragile hold on life. Janiece had always struggled with feeling that she was "too fat." She disliked the thought of sexuality and had never been involved in a significant relationship with a man. She also had few girlfriends. She exercised to the point of exhaustion, yet consumed fewer calories than concentration camp prisoners during World War II.

Despite priding herself on her professional work in physical therapy, Janiece believed that she was a complete failure because she could not "save" her father. After all, she had helped other people who meant so much less to her than he had. Not only did Janiece have to deal with the loss of a crucially important relationship, but she also had to cope with her guilt at being unable to fix or save whatever was destroying her. Although Janiece was opening up, there still remained much about her past that was hidden—even from her. As Janiece and her therapist began to talk about her feelings of guilt, her relationship with her father, and the need to let go of her feelings of guilt and pain, she began to engage a bit more with others. With difficulty, she shared her concerns for her fellow patients and made her therapist a gift in the hospital woodshop. Janiece seemed to be getting better, yet surprisingly, her therapist felt frustration and antipathy well up within herself during Janiece's sessions.

Friends and parents of persons with eating disorders frequently find themselves in the same position as Janiece's therapist. For seemingly no good reason, they experience an odd admixture of emotions toward the person. Yet whenever they are with that person, they cannot readily explain why they feel bored, frustrated, or hopeless.

This reaction is such a common finding in the practice of psychotherapy that it has become known as the important process of containment. By way of a technical mechanism called "projective identification," one individual comes to know the feeling state of another because it has been transmitted from one to the other. What seems like a magical process is, in reality, an invaluable experience of empathy and attunement. Through it, we are able to find a way to tune in and to come to understand what is really within the heart of another person.

In any case, Janiece's therapist was troubled by her own experience of antipathy and angst whenever she was alone with Janiece, and she soon realized that these troubling feelings occurred only when the two were together. First the therapist had to open her own heart and mind for personal struggles that might be occurring within herself but were unrelated to Janiece. On reflection, the therapist was able to sift out her own feelings that related to her own issues from those that were stirred by Janiece. Janiece seemed to have thoughts she desperately wanted to disavow that were being projected onto and contained within the therapist because Janiece could not yet deal with them herself.

One day Janiece was describing the last hours of her father's illness and her own ineptness in helping him. The therapist thought it timely to suggest to Janiece that, although strong love was one feeling she had for her father, strong hatred might be another. The therapist then suggested that hate is a legitimate emotion, particularly when directed at a person one wished to help who failed to respond as desired. In addition, some of her hatred toward her father might be due to his leaving her not only through death but also by failing to respond to her ministrations.

The therapist then indicated that she suspected Janiece had never been able to share much of her "true self" with her father and so had come to resent him for that as well. Janiece had repressed this and other painful feelings. The therapist suggested that there must have been many times in her life when Janiece felt angry at her father but had been unable to express it.

It would be heartening to write that this intervention led to an immediate and total transformation within Janiece. However, the real therapeutic work had just begun. Janiece was finally able to broach the true feelings of anger at her father that she had harbored throughout her life. Her feelings of loss, disappointment, and antipathy could only be acknowledged alongside her love for him.

Such a direct confrontation within oneself always takes time because it involves innumerable—and expected—steps backward along the way. Fortunately, Janiece was finally able to see how her suppressed negative feelings had held her back in many arenas and had even laid the groundwork for her eating disorder. Although her relationship with her father was not the only contributor to her dilemma, it was an important key to helping her understand both herself and her world. She could only begin to unlock the doors with the help of a trusted and knowledgeable other—her therapist. The therapy created an environment where Janiece's feelings of hate and despair could be safely contained until she could express them openly and learn to redirect them constructively.

## Toward Sexuality: The Exciting Object

In sparking the young woman's sexuality, the father plays a central role. This simple relationship seems self-evident, yet it belies the greater complexity behind what constitutes sexual evocation and fulfillment in our lives. The sexual concerns that plague eating disorder patients will be considered in depth later, and the important role of the mother as primary identificatory object was reviewed earlier. We must now consider the father's intrinsic role in encouraging his daughter's sexual receptivity while respecting appropriate intergenerational and familial boundaries.

The developmental pathway for girls has traditionally been deemed more difficult than the one for boys. Freud believed that, to achieve heterosexuality, the girl must shift her primary attachment from her mother to her father. If such a transition is waylaid, the girl's first love object (her mother) remains primary, and a homosexual orientation may ensue. Although a variety of factors are involved, when the parental relationship is solid, little girls are more able to make the transition to their fathers as principal love objects, and they have a greater chance of emerging to capable heterosexual gratification. This explication need not imply that heterosexuality is uniquely valued while all other modes of sexual expression are derided; instead, it outlines in a simplified form the little girl's normal traversing of developmental pathways to heterosexual expression. Sandra M.'s situation illustrates the complexity of the father's impact on the development of the sexual self.

❦ Sandra M., who is 26, came from a strict, fundamentalist family that shunned any type of sexual expression. Her older sister was so terrified of sexuality that even after marrying, she had numerous inhibitions that impaired her sexual functioning. In light of her sister's difficulties, Sandra worried that she, too, would never be able to enjoy a gratifying sexual life, or perhaps never even lose her virginity. What had happened to make her feel so restrictive about herself? Why did she deny herself access to one of life's most potentially beautiful and enhancing activities?

A cultural appraisal of Sandra's situation might point to her stern religious upbringing. Caught between a society that encourages acting on impulse and a doctrine that condemns any sexual thoughts whatsoever, Sandra internalized a conflict so invidious as to literally snuff out the life within her. If she permitted herself any conscious thought about a man, she would either bang her head on the wall until it bled or stand compulsively in the shower for hours to wash away her "sin."

When Sandra's therapist discussed the roots of the problem with her, Sandra was able to explain that there was more involved than just the messages from her religious community, although those were influential, too. Over and over, her father had made disparaging remarks about loose women and low morals, repeatedly telling her that young men were hedonistic devils intent only on sex. Sandra often cried herself to sleep at night, believing that her future (should she ever give in to a passionate embrace) would lead first to a sadistic traumatization by a would-be male captor, and then to eternal suffering and damnation. From her earliest years, her father's words had never conveyed the heretical thought that the union between a woman and a man could be a loving, joyful experience.

As might be expected, further investigation into the marital relationship between Sandra's parents unearthed some troublesome conflict that Sandra had internalized. Not only had Sandra heard her father's message that she should not be sexual, but also her only model of an adult relationship was her parents' aggressive marital union. The only version of adult intimacy she had experienced was her internalization of their unsatisfying bond.

On the surface, Sandra was an attractive, bright, compliant young woman; beneath that superficial exterior, however, she was a frightened, intense girl terrified of her awakening sexual rush. On one level, she was also furious with her parents for both their overt and covert messages that now pervaded her consciousness and cost her so much emotionally and physically.

Intense conflict between any two adults often only cements their relationship. As Sandra's parents remained bonded by anger to each other, so Sandra maintained an inordinate attachment to them, based on hostility. As witness to her parents' feuds, Sandra remained loyal to both by never deviating from their worldview and by avoiding any possibility of being totally and sadistically controlled if she loved a man. Thus she never moved out of her father's orbit by challenging his beliefs about the world, religion, or men. She stayed undifferentiated from him, even maintaining an unconscious libidinal bond between them. Sandra's own sexuality was sacrificed as she stayed "in love with" his views, his value systems, and in the end, him.

For a young woman to emerge into adulthood with a buoyant sense of her sexual self, her father must convey from his earliest interactions with her that she is beautiful—and loved—for who she is. A father's unconditional love and acceptance go much further and deeper than any cultural message that speaks to a woman's physical deficits. Societal values of the right weight, hair color, or size are more easily disregarded when a woman feels loved for more than her appearance alone.

The greatest challenge facing any father today is to somehow convey to his daughter that her physical, emotional, and intellectual self is more than merely tolerable—it is relished. Numerous researchers over the past two decades have shown that those women who achieve the highest career levels in various professions have had a particularly multi-dimensional father-daughter relationship. Successful women feel both accepted by and acceptable to their fathers on the deepest psychological level. Their fathers convey to them, perhaps on an unconscious as well as conscious level, that their talents and sensuality neither threaten nor tempt them, nor do they need to be snuffed out. In essence, a father proves himself to be a man who appreciates all aspects of his daughter, laying the groundwork for other men—who come later—to do so as well.

In their book *Success and Betrayal: The Crisis of Women in Corporate America* (1986), Sarah Hardesty and Nehama Jacobs describe how a few successful women within corporate America have been able to garner a life of extraordinary success both in work and in love. They are still far too few in number; but Hardesty and Jacobs believe that one of the key ingredients in nurturing women to be successful is an early, deeply held positive view from a father or significant male-parenting surrogate. By imparting a sense early on that his daughter is capable on all levels, the father plants the seeds for her flowering potential to sprout and bloom later.

Sandra's case also sheds light on the sexual conflicts underlying many eating disorders. In contrast to Hilda Bruch's (1973, 1974) groundbreaking work in the 1960s and 1970s, which stressed the central role of inhibited autonomous functioning in anorexia nervosa, we must now extend our focus to include the sexual conflicts that form another corner of the puzzle. Sandra's tendency to refrain from eating evolved from her wish to starve not simply herself (her self) but also her *sexual* self. She wanted to become as invisible sexually as she believed her father wanted her to be. Again, maintaining loyalty to him and to his value system was paramount.

Only when Sandra began to challenge her father's views under the aegis of a supportive male therapist could she begin to internalize other ideas of what it meant to be a woman and what men want from women. The process was not easy for her, because breaking unconscious loyalty oaths and looking at long-held, often unconscious belief systems are among the most difficult of life's hurdles. Few individuals try. Unwittingly, most people continue acting out the roles established by their internal parental introjects.

The development of parental introjects, which has been well described in psychotherapeutic textbooks, has been most recently commented on by philosopher Martha C. Nussbaum. In her book, *Love's Knowledge: Essays on Philosophy and Literature* (1990), she describes how one of Marcel Proust's characters finds out his lover is "not at a certain distance from me, but beside me" (Proust, *Sodome et Gomorrhe*, quoted in Nussbaum, p. 247). For Nussbaum, part of the mystery of the human soul yearning for love is the acknowledgment of the loved person's healthy entry into the internal world of the beloved. In the deepest pain or at the height of passion, a temporary and exciting fusion emerges. Therapy enables us to look at these inner objects and relationships that become a part of us.

Although Proust's character had an epiphany when he recognized that his lover's soul cohabited with his own and penetrated his heart to the depths of his being, few of us have the capacity to look so directly *at ourselves by ourselves*. As Sandra began to see how she was unconsciously repeating the lives of her parents by internalizing their bond to each other, she gained the opportunity to choose the life she wanted for herself. She also developed new insights into the early messages and took advantage of the opportunity to internalize new messages over time, which provided her with a different vision of what it meant to be a woman. Thus the all-too-common betrayal of the woman's sexual self can be reversed if she is able to passionately delve into both her past and her long-held suppositions. This process permits her to develop her own sexual expression and prepares her for life-enhancing intimate relationships.

## Father as Teacher

Psychoanalyst Heinz Kohut (1971, 1977) explained that all children imitate their parents, thereby developing particular skills and talents. The human desire for sameness or alikeness promotes our acquisition of knowledge, ultimately supporting our ambitions and ideals. This need for twinship comes into play in adulthood through our need for a strong mentor. Hardesty and Jacobs (1986) emphasize that mentoring has served a crucial function for many successful professional women and advise that a mentor may be essential at various points in a profession.

Of course, overreliance on a mentor can also be problematic. A woman's capacity to make good use of male mentoring relationships probably derives from an initially secure and libidinally invested relationship with her father. One female patient who was unusually mechanically inclined enjoyed learning the skills of plumbing and car maintenance from her talented father. Many other women are not so fortunate. They feel at some emotional distance from their fathers, as if the fathers disparaged their yearning to emulate their skills. More often than not, the father is perceived as being absent from the home, either emotionally or physically. Even when a father is physically present, his daughter might find herself having to enter his world rather than having him reach out to actively enter hers.

These deficits in fathering have led some young women to believe that their ambitions are wrong or unacceptable; although women are increasingly turning to other women as role models, the father-daughter relationship seems to provide a unique and important influence on the woman's development. When it is deficient, she feels out of sync with other human beings. Her capacity for relatedness falters as she shuns society. She is often lonely and lacks trust in her own abilities, no matter how much they have been affirmed by others.

Eating disorder patients in particular seem to have had a dearth of enriching twinship experiences. The dynamic just described above may come into play: the father is found particularly wanting in his desire to engage his daughter in activities and skill development that support her healthy ambitiousness. However, an eating disorder is also a taxing physiological phenomenon, leaving one with much less energy to make use of other bonds that might enhance learning. A vicious circle develops where opportunities are missed because the cost of the eating disorder leads to a reduction in opportunities based on skill. Hence, if the woman has all the more reason to cling to the eating disorder as a learned, highly skilled mode of relating, it is the one thing the individual believes she can do well! To move away from this cognitive position, she must have the opportunity—and the physical energy—to reintroduce herself to people who can provide the experiences she desperately needs to develop other talents.

Treatment modalities aimed at pushing the individual to experiment with new activities and classes under the aegis of an experienced mentor or teacher derive from this theoretical base. Treatment programs that have been most successful encourage using male and female treaters of various professional disciplines to perform as idealizable role models to patients. The same principle applies when individuals working in outpatient therapy are urged to stretch themselves by trying to do something they have never attempted before.

The original teacher in the home can be either father or mother, but mentoring is an experience one should avail oneself of throughout life. This point was brought home to me during a recent discussion with a close colleague, the head nurse of the Eating Disorders Program. The subject concerned two of the residents I was supervising. In my estimation, these two female residents were entirely different in terms of personality style, dress, and the way they engaged patients. One was married with two children; the other was single. One was rather flamboyant, the other shy. One tended to be on the thin side; the other was slightly overweight. When I remarked to the head nurse that these differences might prove confusing to our patients, she retorted, "The patients need as many different types of role models—male and female—as they can get!" Not only did I find myself agreeing with her but, in so doing, I also found that the nurse had served as an important role model for me as well. She was encouraging me to face the world with a broader view, much as we routinely encourage our patients to do, and stressing that we can all benefit from a fresh perspective.

## A Secret Sharer, A Separate Self

How is it that a father tends to assume a preeminent place as role model and mentor for his daughter? Although feminist scholars now contend that the mother—and other women—may be an equal if not superior model, humans seem to harbor an innate need to seek themselves through dialogue with someone totally different. The Tibetan religious leader, the Dalai Lama, has addressed this contradiction: "Our human mind always likes different approaches. There is a richness in the fact that there are so many different presentations of the way."

This spiritual truth may have a more pedestrian but essential developmental root. For both the little girl and the little boy, the father is the first "object" known to be different from the mother. As a different and separate person, he helps to wean the child from primary unity and dependency on the mother. Thus the daughter turns to him for confirmation of herself and to enhance her needed sense of separateness from her mother.

On the negative side, the father's distance from the mother and the family of origin may lead the child to idealize him even as, on the positive side, he facilitates separation from the mother and supports the child's burgeoning self. Fathers thus give birth to the psychological sense of their daughters as women in a way that mothers cannot. By virtue of the fact that father and daughter share a dyadic bond within a triangular pattern of relating to the wife-mother, they also participate in a "secret sharer" relationship against the mother. If not taken to pathological extremes, the father-daughter relationship can provide the daughter with a sense of specialness and lovableness. It also remains critically important for the daughter's ineluctable urge to separate from her mother.

When a father is unable to help his daughter move out of the maternal orbit, either because he is physically unavailable or not invested emotionally in her, the daughter may turn to food as a substitute. The very act of bingeing and purging occurs in secret. Mothers are often the last to know about these frequently blocked-out or minimized activities. Women with eating disorders keep their mothers out of the bathrooms they are using, much as they increasingly keep them out of their bedrooms as they get older. As Bruch and others have written, anorexia remains a quintessential way of saying "No" to mother (Bruch 1988; Sacksteder 1988; Steiner-Adair 1991a; Zerbe 1991, 1992a, 1992b, 1993a). The very act of refusing food cuts off the symbolic umbilical cord to the provider of food, that is, to the mother, and as such is an autonomous statement par excellence: "I don't need you. I don't need anything. I don't even need food to survive. I am totally independent."

Anorexia nervosa and bulimia nervosa have in common inadequate paternal responses for helping the daughter develop a less symbiotic relationship with her mother. When she must separate on her own, she may take on the pathological coping strategies embedded in eating disorders. Of course, there are other syndromal patterns that yield the same unconscious end. However, an eating disorder can be seen as a last stand for the beleaguered patient. She is trying—in the only way she knows how—to assert her autonomous strivings despite her father's less-than-optimal availability to foster her developing selfhood.

The cases of Clarice, Janiece, and Sandra reveal three very different patterns of fathering—and three very different manifestations of an eating disorder. However, all three women had had a dearth of parental functioning that led to psychological suffering condensed into an eating disorder. Behind each difficulty lay an inordinate inability to feel confident of being able to function effectively and independently in the world. None of these patients felt consistently good about her accomplishments or abilities. The patients needed to be treated over a sustained period of time in order to speak to their development difficulties with their fathers and mothers.

Each woman was helped to prepare to reenter the world by therapeutic modalities that encouraged age-appropriate investigation and adventuresomeness whenever ready. This approach reflects the therapists' deep belief that symptoms cannot simply be overcome, but that patients must instead be relaunched on important developmental pathways. Treatment on a continuum of care helps this push into the world so that patients may begin to experience skillfulness in work and interpersonal relationships. At its best, psychodynamically informed treatment inherently provides some functions that a father may not have been able to.

## Toward Growth

Erik Erikson (1963) used the term "generativity" to refer to the adult's desires and concerns for guiding the next generation. Clearly, fathers, mothers, and daughters have a vested interest in actively generating themselves and others in the universal quest to survive through children. Men want to continue the self by becoming fathers, and parenthood for both genders represents an opportunity to develop one's human potentialities in a new and essential direction. The paternal capacity of men may be inhibited because of their envy of the procreative ability of women, which may noxiously intrude into the father-daughter bond. When fathers are able to sublimate some of their urge to bear children into creating the most affirming and nourishing environmental nexus for them, they will actualize their own fathering potential as well. This position necessarily demands that fathers thrive in their new role yet recognize that it will take time and energy to fulfill it.

In writing about the costs of having a physician as a father, Martin Leichtman (1988), a senior psychologist at The Menninger Clinic, stresses that there is no substitute for the precious quality of time. Reading stories, going on walks and to movies, sharing a meal, and participating in childhood fantasy and play can help provide the backdrop of experience for children not only to learn about their father and his world but also to find their own interests and excitements shaped by his affirming presence. No one can know for certain the memory traces that build up over years of such seemingly inconsequential and innocent meanderings, but surely they give rise to enhanced feelings of self-esteem and to sustaining memories and experiences for times of disequilibrium and unhappiness. By giving their time and attention, fathers give of themselves, which helps to build their children's sense of self.

Jessica Benjamin, a therapist trained in object relations psychology, wrote in *The Bonds of Love* (1988) that women must reclaim their sexuality—and themselves—in relationship to both parents, who should make it clear that the development of autonomous desires, including sexual ones, are acceptable. In essence, according to Benjamin, both parents should convey a positive response to life and to growth:

> Girls should get what boys get from their father, and girls and boys should get it from their mothers as well—recognition of agency, curiosity, movement toward the outside. Consequently, I do not think that women should discount the world of phallic, symbolic functioning in order to celebrate their own sphere, nor do I think they should embrace the male world at the expense of denying the experiences that are part of the female world. (pp. 130–131)

Such a broad view has obvious implications for the prevention and treatment of eating disorders. As the father becomes less likely to be seen and to see himself as unattainable and ineffable—or only as the sole proprietor of his little girl's romantic and sexual wishes—then their felicitous relationship becomes much more paramount to her development. She is less likely to be stymied by a total preoccupation with physical appearance, because she has the benefit of his supportive and reinforcing view of herself as more than a mere vessel of beauty. His interest in her world demonstrates that she is loved for who she is, not just for her appearance, while simultaneously nurturing her and kindling her own capacity for self-nurturing. Consequently, she will have less need to turn to food for fulfillment. Other activities and interests, initially sparked by her father's exciting and adventuresome link to the outside world, will be cultivated within herself. She will also develop more resilience to the exigencies and difficulties of life—another not inconsequential benefit. Her capacity to love her own children, the arts, her work, and those within her entire relationship network will become a source of replenishment that the concretization of food through an eating disorder could never provide. Moreover, she will learn to nurture rather than deny herself, because she saw her father take his rightful place in the cycle of her life, welcoming her capacity to sow and reap her own unique fruits.

In a scene in *A Man For All Seasons*, Sir Thomas More touches on some of these points as he talks to a young man about his future. He does not believe that this young man is particularly suited for the practice of law but instead would make a fine teacher. He challenges the young man to think about his choice and direction in life by saying that having one's family, one's students, and God to serve as one's audience is a noble and sanctified aspiration. The young man wonders, "Who will know?" More reassures him, "You will know." By emphasizing what is worthwhile and essential through encouraging one's unique talents and gifts and by recasting the problem of worldly praise and acclaim into more self-directed and self-affirming (albeit humble) goals, the fathering figure necessarily but compassionately instills attainable goals, stalwart values, and noble ideals. For the woman, the father's generosity of spirit, belief in her potential, and refusal to enviously attack her abilities can shape both her being and her talents. A father who is a man for all seasons certainly wants his daughter to become a woman for all seasons as well.

# 5

# When Self Meets Society: The Interplay of Cultural and Psychological Factors

Reality is something you rise above.

Liza Minnelli

Living life to the fullest is never easy. Instead, we meet with a variety of entanglements. Some of the biggest hurdles are those posed by our society whose doctrines make us choose between mind and heart, dogma and self-direction.

Every day, each of us makes innumerable decisions—some minor, some much more significant—that map the paths of our lives. These decisions are almost always difficult, because they demand that we select one alternative out of many, leaving behind equally intriguing possibilities along the way.

Philosophers and theologians have traditionally been sensitive to the burdens individuals face in making choices. In the 19th century, Kierkegaard concluded in his masterpiece Either/Or (1844/1971) that one root of all human misery and anxiety is the dilemma we confront when we must choose. As patients and treaters alike reflect on their life paths, we are struck by the inherent wisdom in Kierkegaard's assessment.

Consequently we look for practical guides or principles to help us contend with personal choices that are rarely made without regret or worry.

A well-known line from Shakespeare helps illustrate how we need to establish priorities and make choices based on our deepest desires and self-knowledge: "To thine own self be true." In *Hamlet,* Polonius, the father of Ophelia and Laertes, speaks these words to his son as the young man is about to depart on a journey; the old courtier precedes this advice by emphasizing "This above all else . . . " The idea of being true to oneself is frequently summoned up by women drawn together for mutual support and affirmation in confronting life's challenges. But what does being true to the self mean? Don't societal roadblocks often impede the full blossoming of this true self? Why is it that most of us can easily acknowledge the value of making clear and self-determined decisions, yet nonetheless fear the fallout of mistakes, feel plagued with indecision, and (once a choice is made) pine for other equally plausible alternatives we might have picked or acted on?

Posing these rather philosophical queries at the beginning of a discussion of the cultural understanding of eating disorders may appear totally off the mark. However, as we investigate the conflicting currents of cultural history and contemporary research that tell us much about the societal influences contributing to eating disorders, we will see how difficult it is for women to make good decisions about their bodies and remain true to their deepest needs and selves. Although aware of the fads promoted by the multibillion-dollar diet industry, women persist in placing themselves and their daughters at risk by fasting regimes that lead to and perpetuate eating disorders. Growing evidence supports the notion that the value society places on slimness and dieting behavior is crucially important to the formation of eating disorders. Concerned men and women are thus asking apt but perplexing questions: Why do we ignore the potential health hazards imposed by misapplied and unsafe dieting practices? What forces lead us away from the knowledge we have, and thus from our true selves, to acquiesce to a cultural stereotype? What compulsions force us to abandon our deeper ideals and values, finally even betraying our body to follow the crowd?

I hope to explain how our culture's impact on eating problems coalesces with individual psychology and societal attitudes. We can begin to address these questions only by soberly assessing all aspects of the enigma—how they intertwine to create both the epidemic of eating disorders and the rampant interest in dieting. Without the fertile ground of societal standards, individual concerns are less likely to flower. Without individual susceptibility, liabilities imposed by society are less likely to take root.

A fascinating study by Furnham and Alibhai (1983) illustrates the complexity of this problem. Recognizing that fatness has traditionally been a greater preoccupation in Western than in Third World countries, these investigators explored the body image concerns of immigrants from Africa to Great Britain. African women in general enjoy their fuller figures, and they lovingly adorn themselves in brightly colored robes and headdresses. Not surprisingly, traditional Kenyan women perceive a larger female size more favorably than do their white British counterparts. But Kenyan immigrants who have resided in Britain for only 4 years will have adopted the British viewpoint with respect to size and shape. These immigrants tend to desire a smaller physique than their African peers. The study also found that British women favored an almost anorexic body size.

Another study that focused on Hispanic women yielded similar results (Pumariega 1986). According to this report, as a particular Hispanic woman acculturated, she began adopting the more stringent eating attitudes of the prevailing culture. Like the Furnham and Alibhai study, this one demonstrated how easy it is to acquire a society's predominant values about weight.

Even though women may overtly subscribe to the deeply held value that we must be true to ourselves, cultural ideals about beauty will shape our attitudes about appearance. These studies show how, to be appealing and conventional, women tend to turn their backs on a long heritage that they hold dear. To fit the given cultural stereotype of attractiveness, women may try to overcome a natural proclivity toward a fuller figure. It is apparently hard to "just say no" to society.

Nowhere can the interplay between the powerful influences of culture and individual psychology be seen more starkly than in the development and maintenance of eating disorders. Unfortunately, it has become commonplace to frame the debate about the ultimate cause of anorexia and bulimia—society versus psychology—into two disparate camps, with little converging or blending of positions. Hence, those who favor a cultural cause of eating disorders look primarily at the prevalence of the problem in an affluent, 20th-century society that idealizes slimness. They note the classic study by Garner, Garfinkel, and colleagues (1980) that compared the shapes and weights of two standards of beauty—the *Playboy* centerfold and winners of the Miss America Pageant—from the 1950s to the 1970s. By demonstrating how the weights and measurements of these beauties were consistently being lowered and the favored shape was being shifted from more of an hourglass to a cylindrical form, these researchers underscored society's growing penchant for thinness.

To buttress their argument, proponents of a cultural cause also look to the rash of diets and dieting clinics, the numerous studies that demonstrate how dissatisfied women are with their weight, and the number of Twiggy-like fashion models occupying the pages of *Vogue* and *Mademoiselle*. Small wonder many researchers and lay people agree that society's idealization of thinness has resulted in the epidemic of eating disorders. In 1968, the average fashion model was 8% thinner than the average woman. Today, models are 23% thinner, perpetrating unrealistic ideals of beauty and attractiveness. Although somewhat useful, these cultural studies fail to shed light on why individual women place such primacy on what society believes they should be—particularly if that ideal causes suffering, costs money, and ultimately jeopardizes their health. In my view, eating disorders must also speak to the difficulties individual women have in regulating their self-esteem. A woman may be inclined to follow a cultural prescription for what she should be, because it helps maintain her self-worth. If she is thwarted in following her own goals, at least she can receive powerful positive reinforcement for attaining and maintaining society's goals. In essence—like men and women of previous eras who conformed to widely held societal values to feel whole, adequate, contrite, or simply to survive—women preoccupied with attaining thinness take refuge in what society believes they "should do" or "must be." This accommodation shores up a shaky sense of self-esteem, which has not been strengthened by any other means. In any case, one can be proud of one's body.

On the other hand, caving in and conforming shows a lack of forti-tude for going against the grain. The following case histories illustrate how these cultural issues impinge on particular women and intertwine with their complex psychological makeup. They will also enable us to explore some of the important data that have been collected about the cultural aspects of eating and body weight. Our purpose is not to propa-gandize any particular point of view or perspective, but rather to encour-age reflection about the complex roots of eating disorders. An argument can be made that the likelihood of women's betraying our bodies by any means increases when we find it difficult to be true to ourselves because we have not had the resources to develop a sense of self. We thrash about to form a self that meets the multiple demands of society, loved ones, and our own ideals.

Before turning to the case histories and the evolving literature about cultural influences on eating disorders, let us briefly consider Dostoyevski's "The Grand Inquisitor" to illustrate this point. In this challenging segment of The Brothers Karamazov (1880/1945), Dostoyevski tells the story of a family tragedy that illuminates the roles of suffering, evil, social injustice, and individual freedom in life. The story places Jesus back on earth at the time of the Spanish Inquisition. After performing a miracle and drawing people to him by the force of his compassion and personality, Jesus meets the Inquisitor, a Catholic Cardi-nal. The Cardinal insists that most people are weak and cowardly; they therefore cannot comprehend the message of Jesus's spirituality and free-dom to love. The Inquisitor then implores Christ to return to heaven, leaving the church and its worshipers undisturbed. He reasons that peo-ple are really like sheep who need to follow the dictates of a high secular authority (in this case the church) rather than Jesus's spiritual authority. In essence, to follow Christ's teachings would make them anxious, be-cause they would have to think and live without immediate answers.

The freedom to think requires us to make independent choices be-tween good and evil, choices that most of us would prefer be made by others, because we cannot bear to assume the responsibility of our ac-tions. The Cardinal explains to Christ that most people prefer simple rules and regulations to enduring "the freedom which they have found so dreadful." He asks Christ to return to heaven rather than to encourage human beings to believe in a hard and disconcerting theology of freedom and choice that they cannot accept because "they are only pitiful children . . . weak and helpless, and [allowed] to sin" (p. 39).

The lessons of "The Grand Inquisitor" apply to the study of eating disorders as well as to many other subjects. For we must also be ready to eschew easy answers, realizing all the while our natural proclivity to want them. Particularly in studying how cultural and individual psychology interdigitate, we must avoid adherence to any single theory or system. Simplification can be temporarily satisfying but ultimately dangerous. Only freedom to entertain a variety of perspectives and possibilities will give us a reasonable panorama of the current landscape. Our hope is that we will instead be able to achieve, at least in part, a biopsychosocial integration. Thus we are all investigators and inquisitors, because so much of the puzzle remains unsolved.

# Eating For One

One generally conceded risk factor in the development of eating disorders is the dissolution of family mealtime and group dining experiences such as those in the sorority houses and dormitories of the 1950s and 1960s. By the 1970s, many colleges began to do away with formalized meal plans as more and more specialized food services became available to students. Nowadays it is possible for young people to eat 24 hours a day from fast-food chains, vending machines, and minishops at gas stations near campus and home.

Readily available food sets the stage for "vagabond" or "promiscuous" eating. But this activity actually begins in childhood. When children are left to fend for themselves at mealtime, the responsibility proves too great for most of them. Alone, many children will not only eat beyond their physiological needs but will also tend to make up for psychological deprivation by eating too much. Any of us who don't sit down for regular meals may fall into a pattern of continual snacking or "grazing"—eating small amounts of food, usually high in calories and fats, throughout the day.

The continual availability of food for grazing, of course, rests on the financial resources of an affluent society. At times when food was scarce, people had no choice but to sit down together and share their food. But dining together also promoted interpersonal ties, a source of support through good times and bad. The current patterns of irregular meals, nonstop eating throughout the day, lack of socialization during mealtime, and the resulting need to fill one's psychological hunger with food all paves the way for eating disorders.

Reversing these patterns can help curtail the problem. For example, one young woman who was a first-rate ballerina developed severe bulimia to maintain a low weight so she could dance professionally. She binged and purged with the alarming frequency of 14 episodes per day. Despite the progress she made in therapy in understanding herself, her binge-purge frequency persisted until her career forced her to relocate in another state. At this point, for financial reasons, she moved in with a distant cousin and his wife. The couple, although not impoverished, could not afford to support the patient's habit; the three were forced to eat rather Spartan meals three times daily. The patient wrote to her former therapist that this financially enforced restriction of available food was the only intervention that had significantly affected her bulimia. She no longer had unlimited amounts of food available for binges. One unexpected but additional benefit was seeing her cousin and his wife actually converse at mealtime and cement their partnership by a kind of emotional feeding. They truly valued what they had in life, although to outsiders it did not seem like much. As a result of their influence and her respect for them, this patient sought to bring her own value system into harmony with theirs; her cousins inadvertently served as good role models for her in regard to moderation and respectful interaction.

Eating for one has other social connotations as well. The mere idea of someone eating alone conveys a sense of disconnection, loneliness, and alienation, just as sharing a meal communicates the opposite. Festivities such as Passover suppers, wedding feasts, Christmas brunches, and Fourth of July picnics all convey attachment to other people in the context of eating a meal. As psychologist Sara Gilbert writes,

> Meals have less to do with the need to fuel the body than with the practice of long-held traditions and the symbolic representation of

special relationships. In the same way, to eat too much or too little often conveys a message to other people—consider for example the emotional impact of the hunger strike. (1986, p. 4)

In any society that does not take advantage of everyday and ceremonious food rituals, a tendency toward eating disorders may be perpetuated by the lack of self-sustaining attachments inherent in meals. Not surprisingly, the family therapist Salvador Minuchin also understood that mealtimes punctuated by fighting and antagonism will exacerbate eating disorders (Minuchin and Fishman 1981; Minuchin et al. 1978). So, too, eating for one or by oneself helps us sidestep noxious family conflict.

As people have drifted more toward solitary eating, there have also been some fundamental shifts in what they choose to eat. For example, grazing contributes to the currently observed change in eating habits that involves the consumption of more fat and animal protein at the expense of carbohydrates. A close scrutiny of binge foods themselves, commonly thought of as rich in carbohydrates, also reveals their high percentages of fat content. These nutritionally poor foods set the stage for purging. People who binge like to gulp chips, cookies, ice cream, doughnuts, and cupcakes that taste good, are easily swallowed, and are even more readily evacuated.

In a less extreme manner, our changing food preferences may also pave the way for a greater proclivity toward diseases such as diabetes and coronary artery disease. None of these facts should be startling, because they have been widely reported in women's magazines, in bestselling books about eating disorders, and on television talk shows. The question then becomes why both men and women persist in holding on to dangerous patterns of behavior despite knowing better.

Writing from the vantage point of a historian of the 19th and 20th centuries, Joan Jacobs Brumberg reveals in her book *Fasting Girls* (1988) the devotion with which women in particular have pursued a more beautiful body over the past 150 years. Brumberg's nonclinical perspective explains how women have "internalized the notion that the size and shape of the body was a measure of self-worth," with those even in the Victorian period having "believed that the process of losing weight would bring spiritual as well as physical transformation" (1988, p. 248).

Brumberg's historical view faults modern dieting for most eating disorders, a view endorsed by current psychiatric opinion that ties the problem to the rash of dieting interventions. But this historical analysis also shows that women—struggling in a nonaffirming society and within themselves for security, personal freedom, sexual fulfillment, and a firmer place in the political and economic circle of the world—still find self-enhancement through the body beautiful. Hence the rush to perfect the body at all costs; to do so means to elevate and sustain the self.

Some important statistics provide still another perspective that emphasizes the cultural contribution to the dissatisfaction contemporary women have with their bodies. Fallon and Rosen (1985) studied the importance of being thin to upper-middle-class white women. These investigators asked over 400 men and women undergraduates to rate their ideal figure by looking at a set of figure drawings. Among the men, "current," "ideal," and "most attractive" figures were about identical. For women, however, the ideal figure was almost always much more slender than their current figures. Surveys among high school students in the 1960s showed that 65%–80% of females wanted to weigh less than they did and 60% reported actively dieting. There is good evidence to indicate that this last figure has now jumped to as high as 80%, and regrettably this preoccupation is occurring at earlier and earlier ages. One recent study completed at the University of South Carolina (ANRED Alert 1993) looked at body weight and weight attitudes among 3,100 grade-school children. Researchers found that 40% of boys and girls believe they are fat. Of these 40%, 30% had dieted, 10% had fasted, and 5% had vomited to lose weight!

Youngsters only seven or eight years old are as preoccupied with slimness and dieting as are adolescents. Alarmingly, in my experience, their parents often concur with them. They mistake baby fat that will likely be outgrown with real body fat that will not; they put their children's health at risk by untimely diets when food is needed for growth. These parents may also risk their children's psychological health by emphasizing thinness, thereby setting the stage for eating disorders.

The following case example depicts a wiser solution to the dilemma our children face when they learn about society's views that they should be slender to be a part of the crowd.

❦ Fortunately, Natasha N., age six, has a mother who is not preoccupied with how her daughter fits the cultural standard. One evening when taking a bath, Natasha looked down and complained to her mother that her thighs were too fat. This striking statement by a six-year-old occurred after Natasha had been teased by a friend at school about her weight. Slightly plump, Natasha worried that she had disappointed her parents and had not lived up to their expectations of what she should be. She asked solemnly why her mother's legs were more slender than her own.

One could infer that Natasha was trying to identify with her mother and perhaps compete with her a bit, too. Natasha's mother was attuned to these and other issues at hand: she recognized the growing preoccupation of young children, like her daughter, with the cultural stereotype and with the shape of their own bodies. She reassured Natasha that as she grew to womanhood her figure would change: the "fat" that she was seeing would be redistributed on her body and used to feed her own children. This sensitive mother then empathetically explained, "Someday you will need some fat to feed your little ones just as I fed you. It's not bad for little girls or women to have fat on their bodies. They need this fat because it will later be put to very good use and keep them healthy."

Natasha was unconvinced. For quite some time, she continued to complain to her mother about her "fat legs." Because of what Natasha had seen in the media and heard discussed by her friends, her mother had to spend a great deal of time educating and reassuring her daughter about what was normal. Peer attitudes, originating and reinforced by the cultural view, were not easily overcome even by this sympathetic and involved parent.

# Women of Color

Women of color in Western society have a lower incidence of eating disorders. However, this trend appears to be reversing itself, as more Hispanic and African American women feel the impact of media stereotypes and move into the middle and higher socioeconomic brackets that

reward slender physiques. Although scientific data support the low incidence of eating disorders among these women, clinicians see eating
disorders in all socioeconomic groups, races, and ethnic backgrounds.

Because eating disorders have been reported much less among African Americans, Asian Americans, and American Indians, clinicians
sometimes fail to diagnose them in the nonwhite population. This over-
sight reflects a cultural bias and unintended yet prevalent bigotry. In
addition, when an eating disorder is formally diagnosed in a nonwhite
patient, inadvertent treatment problems may arise. Despite the best
intentions of all involved, unconscious tinges of prejudice can undermine treatment. To move the treatment forward, mistrust and discomfort on the part of both the treater and the patient must be openly
addressed. Because any of us may be unaware of some of our own prejudices, we must continually scrutinize our attitudes. This self-examination is especially necessary when two people from significantly different
backgrounds work together.

❧ Rose O., a 31-year-old African American woman with two school-
age children, was brought to the hospital by her mother, who was a
teacher. Having felt the pressure to become thinner at her job,
Rose, a moderately obese young woman, had turned to bulimia and
consequently had had several brief inpatient treatments for various
related conditions. At least three times every year for the past 10
years, Rose had been admitted to hospitals for dehydration, fainting,
and other residual effects of electrolyte imbalance. She was initially
so ashamed of her weight problem that she would do anything to
control it. As she began using up to 40 laxatives and diuretics a day,
Rose also became "addicted" to the syrup of ipecac she used to
induce vomiting.

Rose's husband had been less than supportive of her problems.
He physically abused her on numerous occasions and often derided
her mothering skills. Fortunately, Rose had the support of an involved mother and several good friends. They had encouraged her
to attend local support groups, such as Overeaters Anonymous,
which she initially had attended quite conscientiously.

But nothing seemed to help Rose overcome her eating difficulties, and eventually she added shoplifting to her repertoire of self-defeating behavior. She even admitted to stealing different diuretics, laxatives, and ipecac in a final effort to lose weight by purging. The mental health professionals who worked with Rose in several settings suspected that her difficulties had deeper roots than she could acknowledge but found they could not seem to help her elaborate on her problems.

The fifth of 11 children, Rose reported growing up in a very happy family. She was glad to have many brothers and sisters, and she categorically denied having been abused either physically or sexually. Like her teacher mother, her father was a devoted parent. This hard-working couple was able to provide emotional and financial support for all their children. After graduating from high school, Rose received a scholarship to a major Southern university. She moved away from home and completed a degree in political science.

Rose's ambition to become a patent attorney was waylaid by her eating disorder. Despite her high LSAT scores, her obesity and race may have contributed to her rejection from admission into professional school. This possibility enraged Rose; and although some treaters who worked with her suspected that her belief was unfounded, eventual investigation proved otherwise. Rose had been subjected to three types of bigotry that had gone unacknowledged: she was a woman, she was African American, and she was overweight. Despite her aptitude, Rose was prevented from engaging in her chosen career. At first the rejections clearly lowered her self-esteem; later she decided she would do anything, including forceful efforts to lower her weight, so that she could pursue her goals.

Rose revealed this history only over a long period and with great difficulty. She acknowledged forthrightly that she did not trust her white treaters. Brought up to be egalitarian and fair, she found herself turning away from her family values that eschewed demagoguery because of her own experiences in the workplace. Her only joy seemed to be her two children, for whom she would sacrifice anything. Their welfare had pushed her to initially involve herself in treatment, only to later reject it before completion so she could return home to care for them.

Rose's difficulty with trusting anyone was so intense that she tended to turn treaters into persecutors. At one point she even refused to eat or to drink, requiring her treaters to become more forceful in their attempts to care for her. Her actions clearly conveyed her lack of trust and symbolized her primary need to make others restrain her and force her into changing despite her own ambivalence. Previously Rose had met rejection involving her highest career aspirations with passivity; now she actively rejected those who attempted to assist her. Indeed, the more anyone attempted to motivate her to accept treatment, the more resolutely she avoided it. She was determined this time to be the ultimate victor in the fight for control over her life.

Rose's resistance also included avoiding having to share how badly she felt about herself vis-à-vis her color, her body, and the early impediments to her career. One could easily understand how difficult it would be for her to trust anyone she equated with those who had betrayed her out of hatred and intolerance. As a result, members of the interdisciplinary treatment team working with Rose often questioned their own value judgments that might be based on cultural and racial differences that would impede treatment. As we attempted to place ourselves in Rose's unfavorable position, we could see why she distrusted us. Sadly, her Pyrrhic victory over treatment was won by her own long-standing struggles with self-worth and reluctance to accept help.

When Rose decided to leave treatment, those who worked with her were notably perplexed and sad. Why must it be, we asked, that differences like color or religion keep people apart when humans have so many basic similarities? We reflected on an observation Freud (1921/1955) had made in the early 20th century about the composition of groups: small differences, and not the large ones as we might suspect, are what keep people apart. Thus we tend to emphasize differences like race and ethnic background that may unwittingly impede deeper communication and understanding among people rather than underscoring the similitude of all humans. As psychoanalyst Harry Stack Sullivan put it, "We are all much more human simply than otherwise" (Fromm-

Reichman 1950, p. 45), thus reminding us of the basic alikeness of all people. Even the conflicts of the emotionally troubled are not dissimilar from the "normal."

Recalling the words of T. H. White in *The Once and Future King* (1939/1958), who recommended learning as a solace for loss and disappointment, we attempted to turn our inability to help Rose into a search for more knowledge about cultural factors and eating disorders. The results were startling, and make White's advice worth recounting. In White's novel, Merlin tells the young King Arthur:

> The best thing for being sad is to learn something. That is the only thing that never fails. You may grow old and trembling in your anatomies, you may lie awake at night listening to the disorder of your veins, you may miss your only love, you may see the world about you devastated by evil lunatics, or know your honor trampled in the sewers of baser minds. There is only one thing for it then—to learn. Learn why the world wags and what wags it. (p. 173)

Our staff members learned that because eating disorders have principally been recognized in the white female population, issues of culture, race, and ethnicity may be overlooked. Still, a number of case reports have described the occurrence of anorexia nervosa and bulimia nervosa in women of other races. Because all case reports are subject to methodological difficulties, they may actually underestimate the prevalence of these disorders in the nonwhite population. Service availability and usage may also factor into what disorders get reported and to whom. In England, women of black African descent have been quite vocal in complaining that psychiatric and medical services are less available to them than to the general population. Consequently, nonwhites who are underserved may have a higher incidence of eating disorders than reported. They are not receiving the help they need. This inference has significant implications for the health delivery system that must develop ways to help minorities acquire necessary treatment.

Traditionally, epidemiologic surveys carry more weight than single case reports. However, because they usually involve questionnaires, their results may also underestimate difficulties. Most surveys are conducted in easily accessible student populations, so the findings do not necessarily apply to divergent cultural groups where data are more difficult to retrieve. Surveys are also less reliable than information gained from personal interviews. Despite these caveats, some important information is nonetheless available.

In the United States, two surveys (Dolan 1991) have examined the eating attitudes and behavior of African American women. Applying strict diagnostic criteria, one group of researchers found that African American women had fewer eating difficulties than their white counterparts. A second study corroborated these results. Three percent of African American women met DSM-III (American Psychiatric Association 1980) criteria for bulimia, which was significantly less than a comparable group of white students (13%). Interestingly, African American and white subjects binged with about the same degree of frequency, but African American women reported less self-induced vomiting, laxative abuse, and diuretic use. Although more work must be done to understand why eating disorders are currently uncommon among African American students, the available studies incontrovertibly show that the prevalence of eating disorders is higher for whites than for African Americans.

A fascinating study by Nasser (1986) compared the eating attitudes of female Arab students studying at the University of London and Cairo University. She found that 22% of the students in London had impaired eating attitudes, in contrast to only 12% of those based in Cairo. Diagnostic interviews revealed that 12% of the London group met full criteria for bulimia, whereas none of the Cairo group exhibited bulimic symptoms. Westernization was also apparent in how the groups dressed. The London group of Arab students dressed like Europeans, in contrast to the more traditionally attired Cairo group. Although far-reaching conclusions cannot be drawn from this study alone, it supports the general impression that Westernization may push individuals along a continuum from dieting behavior to full-blown eating disorders.

Westernization has also affected Japan, where eating disorders are now well recognized and clinically prevalent. In densely populated urban areas, anorexia nervosa is reported to have an incidence of 1 in 500. However, bulimia in Japan is less frequently reported in research studies. One distinct binge-eating syndrome called *kibarashi* has also been identified. As a result, Japanese psychiatrists have established eating disorder units in hospitals that are now quite busy; anorexia and bulimia are reportedly becoming more common than Japanese scientific literature has indicated to date.

Two case reports describing anorexia in Africa point to the social and psychological conflicts engendered by cultural changes as leading to anorexia. How cultural tensions may signal the development of eating disorders was suggested by studies performed by Mumford and Whitehouse (1988) and Lee (1991), who studied British, Asian, and Hong Kong schoolgirls. These investigators found that the subjects who developed eating disorders maintained traditional practices and views and were not necessarily as concerned with body shape as were Westerners. Those individuals who had eating disorders held onto their traditional ways of living and knowing, despite the great social shifts apparent in their environment.

In a paper examining the influence of acculturation on young women, Bulik (1987b) described two cases of eating disorders in Eastern European immigrants to the United States. One subject met DSM-III criteria for bulimia, and another met the criteria for anorexia nervosa. When facing pressure in adapting to a new culture, reorganization of traditional family goals and values may be crucial elements in the development of eating disorders in these women. Bulik has suggested that attempting to become a part of the new culture may encourage one to overidentify with certain aspects of it. In this case, overvaluation of slimness probably led to the eating disorders.

Studies of the Hispanic population in the United States have also been meager. The one available report suggests no difference in treatment outcome between Hispanic and white patients (Dolan 1991). However, it is difficult to infer much from a single study or a small population. More cross-cultural studies will help us better understand how changing attitudes of beauty and female roles foster eating disorders. The entire area merits much more investigation because of the information it will reap and the methodological flaws in the studies we currently rely upon (Davis and Yager 1992).

Suffice it to say that there is mounting evidence that cases of anorexia nervosa and bulimia nervosa are on the rise outside the Western world. Case reports of these disorders among many races are beginning to appear. In a letter to the *British Journal of Psychiatry*, Gandhi and colleagues (1991) noted that anorexia does occur on the Indian subcontinent; 5 new cases out of 2,500 referrals were presented to their clinic over a period of 4 years. Although one hypothesis about these trends might be that thinness was becoming more laudable in certain societies than it had been, an equally attractive idea might center on eating disorders as a cultural change syndrome. That is, eating disorders might appear in different cultures at various times because of enormous changes that society is undergoing.

By pulling these cultural and psychodynamic perspectives together, we might gain a clearer view of the overall situation. As indicated, eating is such a basic human activity that it carries many psychological meanings. Even tiny disruptions can easily get a person's eating off track. One might tend to react to cultural turmoil at times of transition by "choosing" an activity that is ubiquitous and symbolic, but also related to socialization and physiological integrity.

In the 1990s, transcultural studies are demonstrating how some societies undergoing rapid economic and sociocultural change may become more prone to eating disorders. This idea is an adjunct to the commonly touted culture-bound syndrome hypothesis, which posits that an emphasis on thinness and the body beautiful explains the female preponderance of eating disorders. However, a look at the history of anorexia nervosa reveals that eating disorders are not a modern disease, nor do they present themselves in the same way in all populations. Consequently, we know that the disorder can surface in disparate societies at various transitional times with quite dissimilar political, biological, and psychological meanings ascribed to it.

## Fasting Saints

The historian Robert M. Bell (1985) gave an account of the lives of several saints and pious women from the 13th to 16th centuries who developed a syndrome that looked much like present-day anorexia. Bell coined the illness "holy anorexia" (e.g., *anorexia mirabilis*) and described how women like St. Catherine of Siena and St. Mary Magdalen De' Pazzi exemplified the disorder. Leading lives of asceticism to garner spiritual fulfillment, these women partook of diets that were barely subsistent in both quantity and quality. St. Catherine eventually died of starvation, willingly taking in only the communion supper and abstaining from other food and drink to expiate sin. In contrast, St. Mary Magdalen De' Pazzi struggled with cravings for food but existed on a depleted diet of bread and water. Believing that the devil was either tempting or impersonating her, other nuns reported that she sometimes gobbled food in secret. Bell speculated whether her actions might be tantamount to the current binge-purge pattern of bulimia nervosa.

In any case, his scholarship elucidates that eating disorders are not new phenomena at all but probably occurred in other societies for different reasons than in our own. Bell (1985) explores how this "holy anorexia" is both similar to and yet different from today's anorexia nervosa. He points out that the cultures in which these young women mystics lived valued spiritual health, fasting, and self-denial much as our own values thinness, self-control, and athleticism.

By pursuing what she believes her parents and the society at large want her to be, the holy or nervous anorexic woman emerges from a frightened, insecure, psychic world superficially hailed by her own outwardly pleasant disposition to become a champion in the race for (bodily-spiritual) perfection. Her newly won self-esteem and confidence initially receive the approbation of those she depends upon "causing her to deepen her self-denial pattern until it takes over as the only source of her sense of self" (Bell 1985, p. 20).

Like medieval women ascetics, the contemporary woman may "choose" anorexia to express her cultural dissatisfaction, as a way "to gain control of her life" (p. 20). Thus, according to Bell, both holy and nervous anorexic women have at their core a deficit in the sense of self that leads to an impaired identity. Their pattern of self-starvation addresses their insecurity, albeit self-destructively. For the medieval anorexic woman, fasting enabled her to become saintly and draw close to God, exchanging a devastating form of self-hatred for one of narcissistic grandiosity. Union with God supplanted other relationships, testified to extraordinary holiness, and signaled to the society at large that fasting was a way not only to follow society's dictates for a godly life but also to achieve saintliness itself.

In a commentary on Bell's work, psychoanalyst William Davis (1985) recognized how self-starvation waned when medieval women were permitted self-actualization and affirmation through the work they did in their society. "Holy anorexia" provided women with a highly valued status in both church and society. When this "definition of holiness was altered, so eventually was the incidence of holy anorexia" (p. 190). That is, when other sources of achievement and gratification became available to Catholic women, their identity and self-esteem were shored up through those outlets instead. The women found other ways to feel affirmed and valued, which alleviated their legislated quest for saintliness.

The medievalist Caroline Bynum has argued for an even broader interpretation of *anorexia mirabilis* than the one offered by Bell. In her book, *Holy Feast and Holy Fast: The Religious Significance of Food to Medieval Women* (1987), Bynum shows how medieval culture associated women with food. Although female spirituality was expressed by fasting and other eating practices, the ultimate goal was always service to others.

Certain mystical women supposedly had the capacities to lactate, although they were virgins, or to cure disease through their saliva. But this was a truly rare and anointed subgroup. However, the majority of women were also spiritually preoccupied with religious zeal to alleviate suffering through service. Their curtailment of eating became a way to express that religiosity. Concomitantly, doing so increased their sense of individuality and self-affirmation.

According to the revisionist viewpoint of Joan Jacob Brumberg in *Fasting Girls*, contemporary anorexia nervosa and medieval *anorexia mirabilis* cannot be reduced by identifying them as the same illness. Because the cultural contexts of the two disorders differ greatly, "From a historical perspective, it becomes evident that certain social and cultural systems, at different points in time, encourage or promote control of appetite in women but for different reasons and purposes" (p. 46).

Although the differences between the medieval and modern cultures are obviously great, one overarching concept attests to similarities between the two illnesses. Self-abnegation, the primacy placed on control of appetite, and the willingness to surrender oneself to the attainment of an ideal, whether it be godliness or thinness, are all attempts to feel more assured and self-reliant. Control of appetite by any means engenders respect from families, men, and the society at large; it shores up any type of flagging self-esteem. Eating disorders thus express more than a quest for spiritual ascension or individualism. They become a way to keep vibrant the very lifeblood of the self. In effect, woman takes ownership of her body by taking in or keeping out what *she desires* and believes important for survival.

Brumberg bridged the gap between the 13th and 20th centuries by pointing out that, "In the earlier era (13th to 16th centuries), control of appetite is linked to piety and belief . . . the modern anorexic strives for perfection in terms of society's ideal of physical, rather than spiritual beauty" (1988, p. 46). Yet each culture also speaks to a desire for a "narcissistic pursuit of perfection" (Rothstein 1984) whereby individuals attempt to recapture a sense of specialness and adulation from childhood that they cannot find in other human interactions or achievements.

Women who find themselves held back by a society that will not grant them reasonable, measurable successes may be more prone to an illness, such as an eating disorder, that offers the illusion of bodily perfection and is clearly measurable on a scale. The pursuit of thinness seeks to restore in concrete form the notion of transcending limits of both body and spirit.

Life for all of us is limited, and mourning its finiteness must occur throughout the life cycle. For those who fear dependence on others but whose self-esteem otherwise requires constant buttressing and affirmation based on beauty, a secret terror erupts when this ideal is not possible. Our narcissistic culture's (Lasch 1979) emphasis on youth and beauty perpetuates eating disorders in two paramount ways. First, this narcissistic outlook implies that beauty and thinness can be achieved and that the ravages of age can be avoided. Second, it seduces the individual by proselytizing that surface appearances are more important than underlying substance. Beauty is ensconced in value and reinforced by a belief system espousing that thinness means you will win and be secure. Life itself becomes impoverished because intellectual curiosity is stymied, artistic and ethical values are decried, and ambivalently held but warm relationships provide little solace. In summary, eating disorders can be understood as part of our "culture of narcissism." Although there are, of course, other important reasons for the occurrence of eating disorders, which are explored in detail throughout this book, our society's emphasis on superficiality in relationships and its idealization of the body beautiful promote self-esteem regulation by modalities that are neither substantive nor enduring. At some point we all must deal with illness, aging, and the finiteness of life itself. To prepare for this confrontation with life's vicissitudes, we must find meaning and purpose that transcend the acquisition of thinness and beauty.

In a family and societal environment that does not challenge a developing child's sense of what is important, eating disorders are bound to flourish. In addition, family members who appear disinterested, self-involved, or excessively critical will reinforce the fragile sense of self in the developing child who needs an understanding, secure parent to help her overcome shame and doubt.

The child may blame herself for her inability to consistently engage her parents, even as she needs them to challenge society's reign. If her insecurity goes unchecked, she will progressively internalize a view of herself as incompetent and defective. She will long all the more for stability. Choosing a deeply held societal value, like thinness, may provide her with "the magic" of temporary safety and worth.

As the culture clings to an image of an ideal body self, seeking it becomes an entrenched way of life. Small children come into the world believing they are perfect; Kohut (1971, 1977) called this self-image the grandiose self. He asserted that only with the help of available parents who permit mistakes do children gradually become able to see themselves as whole and good but not necessarily flawless. *If, on the other hand, an ambiance exists at home and is fostered by society that we must continue to pursue our original quest for perfectionism, then we will feel compelled to seek the unattainable ideal.*

As a result, demoralization and disappointment will become rife, pushing girls to solve their dilemma by other means. Indeed, this despair and helplessness are the most common complaints among both anorexic and bulimic women who may lament: "I am flawed. I am defective. I can never live up to my parents' or somebody else's vision of what I should be and, consequently, I am damned."

Society becomes a shaming other that is always unempathic, critical, and harsh. One can never be "thin enough." The more the ideal of the perfect body goes unmet, the more vulnerable is self-esteem and the tendency to internalize humiliating experiences of shame. In reality, this "failure" is but one of a "pursuit of illusions of perfection" (Rothstein, p. 284), which can never be met by anyone, but which lead to the rampant quest to fulfill an impossible dream—a perfect body.

## Conclusion: The Double Standard of the 1990s

For centuries women have been aware of the cultural double standard applied to sexual behavior. Although parents guarded the virginity of their daughters, they encouraged sons to "sow their wild oats" to gain sexual experience before marriage. Women have always been appalled by this double standard, more than their open discussions might indicate. Concerned grandmothers and mothers alike would advise their daughters: "You must be a virgin when you marry, but don't expect it from your husband. Nine times out of 10 he won't be."

In the past 20 years, this cultural double standard has shifted from its focus on sex to beauty and weight. For better or worse, the sexual revolution opened the way for greater freedom in sensual expression for women. Now, by the time most girls graduate from high school, 70% are no longer virgins. By the time they begin college or a job after high school, the majority of young women have had at least two sexual relationships. But these statistics are only part of the story. Informed by feminism and influenced by female role models, young women are demanding more sexual fulfillment in their relationships with men than did their mothers or grandmothers.

In light of the toll exacted by eating disorders, few would argue that the same freedom should also apply to beauty, body image, and weight. Central to this analysis of the sociocultural factors that place women at greater risk than men for eating disorders is the inherent and inexorable value our society places on attractiveness and thinness. In an extensive *Glamour* (1984) magazine poll, 63% of the respondents reported that weight *often* affected how they felt about themselves, and another 33% reported that weight *sometimes* affected how they felt about themselves.

Numerous other studies have reported that a woman's body image satisfaction is more highly correlated with self-esteem than is a man's, which should be apparent to any reader of this book. Interestingly, not all research has confirmed this view. But one interpretation of the conflicting data is that men, for the most part, view their bodies as primarily functional and active. A man therefore tends to feel satisfied as long as his body is healthy and working well. In contrast, women are prone to feel good about their bodies *only* if they are aesthetically pleasing to themselves and others. Consequently, if a woman feels less attractive than her male counterpart, her sense of self-worth will be lower.

Just look at any art history textbook or series of reproductions of sculpture or painting from the Renaissance to the present era. You will confirm what you already know intuitively: the ideal of feminine beauty has varied considerably over the centuries. Although women have used makeup and dress to try to alter their bodies to conform to a given historical period's ideal, a woman who was considered a magnificent model for Rubens, Rembrandt, or Renoir would consider herself fat by contemporary standards.

The effort to have a figure that conforms to what is culturally pleasing, however, has not been restricted to women alone. As detailed in Hillel Schwartz's survey *Never Satisfied: A Cultural History of Diets, Fantasies, and Fat* (1986), elections have been won and lost in the United States by touting a slender versus a rotund build. For example, Schwartz examines the election of William Henry Harrison, throwing new light on his defeat of Martin Van Buren in 1840. Van Buren's corpulent body made him appear a glutton, the supporters of the lanky Harrison exclaimed; they promulgated a kind of "diet politics" that won the day. Concerned with a government that was simply "too fat" and indulgent, Harrison supporters decried plump politicians who had an "unrelenting tyranny of appetite" that would necessarily influence their decision making and add to government waste. These social concerns are so familiar that they almost sound funny, but what is less known is how the physical appearance of male politicians served as leverage for votes.

Schwartz's scholarship shows how dieting wars and strategies have influenced American culture over the past 200 years. All purported to help men and women acquire balanced, measured, buoyant bodies for health and sex appeal. Over the course of time, fashions and methods of dieting have changed, but their significance has not. Both sexes continue to be affected by whatever is in vogue as the cultural ideal.

However, more often than otherwise, women have been both the focus of and proselytizers for various healing dietary regimens. As Schwartz details, women of the 19th and early 20th centuries sought knowledge about the newest dietary practices, not only to promote health and beauty but also to acquire feelings of expertise and power that they did not have or could not attain in other arenas. Unable to pursue vocational or professional education, they avidly listened to stump speeches by physicians and nutritionists who preached specific dietary regimens with evangelical fervor and took the women's desire to learn seriously. Women were drawn to "cures" that would supposedly help them feel, look, and act better. In an effort to promote their businesses, these vendors had to respect women and their concerns. No doubt, women were drawn to such efforts to provide them with knowledge and the hope that they could take better care and control of their own and their loved ones' bodies.

In the current climate, other parallels have been drawn between eating behavior and femininity. In one study, women who ate smaller meals while on a date were rated as significantly more feminine, less masculine, and more attractive than women who ate large ones. In contrast, meal size had absolutely no effect on how attractive the women perceived the men to be. Another study suggested that contemporary women actually restrict their food intake in the service of making a favorable impression on men. How often do we hear women friends and ourselves complain how we eat a small English muffin and tea on a date while coveting the man's thick steak and beer? Such are the restrictions we place on ourselves to fulfill this image. Physically attractive women are perceived as more feminine, whereas less comely ones are viewed as more masculine. These data support what we intuitively know all too well: physical appearance counts heavily in the workplace and in dating relationships, and much more for women than men.

Feminist researcher Ruth Striegel-Moore has ascertained that bulimic patients are prone to accept without question these sociocultural mores about attractiveness (Striegel-Moore et al. 1986). Striegel-Moore found that bulimic women believe that "what is fat is bad, what is thin is beautiful, and what is beautiful is good" (p. 247) and that their professional success depends on thinness. Her research also shows how social norms are applied more stringently to women than men. Obesity thus becomes a highly stigmatized condition for women in our society, but not for men. The risk for eating disorders is bound to increase in a climate where the value of attractiveness and thinness are such important codifiers of success and self-worth.

Even women who are highly regarded in terms of their occupational success may worry about weight. These women set high personal goals and standards. They know that thinness is not only a symbol of personal accomplishment but that it also gives a woman a real competitive edge (Brownmiller 1984). According to Striegel-Moore and colleagues,

> [It] may be difficult for women to abandon femininity wholesale—and looking feminine, even while displaying "unfeminine" ambition and power, may serve an important function in a woman's sense of self as well as in how she appears, literally, to others. (1986, p. 249)

In Chapter 6, we will see how selected populations of eating disorder patients are particularly affected by these sociocultural expectations. We will examine further those aspects of female development that predispose some women to eating disorders. We will also pursue our critique of the sociocultural ideal of thinness, questioning why some groups of women might be more vulnerable than others to anorexia and bulimia. As we become more aware of the societal values that impinge on women's self-images, we should begin to rise above current cultural reality and move forward to discover our "truer selves." That true self can then be based on a reality of goals and values deeper than a quest for the perfect figure or personal approbation alone and stronger than the temporary glow of approval mustered by our narcissistic culture.

# 6

# Special People in the Life Cycle: Eating Disorders in Infants, Children, Athletes, and Older Women

You grow up the day you have your first real laugh at yourself.

Ethel Barrymore

So far, this book has focused on the largest group of people with eating disorders (i.e., adolescent and adult women). We now turn our attention briefly to those individuals with eating disorders who are often forgotten but who pose special issues in diagnosis and treatment—infants, children, athletes, and older women. Although about 10% of eating disorder patients in Western society are men (Andersen 1990), their difficulties are beyond the scope of this text, and the reader is referred to other comprehensive reviews. However, like the other special subgroups of those with eating disorders, the male population has been understudied and not well understood. Likewise, these men often tend to "fall through the cracks," because clinicians fail to consider the eating disorder diagnoses when evaluating them for medical or psychiatric reasons.

There appear to be a growing number of eating disorder cases among each of the special populations I review in this chapter. As with the more typical presentations of eating disorders, the exact cause of the difficulty remains unclear but seems best understood as a complex interaction of genetic, biological, personality, and family factors. As we focus on the specific difficulties of infants, children, athletes, and older people, some fascinating commonalities must be kept in mind. Each impediment presents a potentially serious illness with major physical complications secondary to weight loss. Once weight is restored, the individual begins to thrive again. Assessment should focus on multiple areas of biological and psychological functioning but also must emphasize involvement of family members for treatment to proceed. The first step is a full medical examination and evaluation to rule out primary medical diseases and physical complications. Treatment begins with a focus both on normalizing eating and weight, but it also addresses the psychological problems that have created the difficulty to begin with.

In these populations, the cultural preoccupations described in Chapter 5 are particularly apparent. The value of thinness and having a perfect body uniquely mesh with the psyche's need to control one's parents, one's body, and even one's own aging process, to the detriment of good health. Eventually, these interconnected preoccupations and arenas for conflict find expression in the final common pathway of disordered eating. The regulation of eating is central to life, as the study of food in these special populations again underscores. Struggles around eating can quickly become life-and-death issues from infancy to the end of the life cycle.

## Anorexia Nervosa in Infancy

Anorexia nervosa occurs in infancy. It develops between 6 months and 3 years of age, having been first described in the 1980s as part of the "failure to thrive" syndrome that afflicts infants and children. A current best understanding hypothesizes a rupture in the mother-infant bond. As children begin to separate and individuate, they begin to assert themselves in the feeding relationship with their caretakers as well.

Some are bold and willful and do not give in to their mother's sense of timing or her way of initiating feeding. Perhaps an innate, temperamental endowment typified by vigor and testiness leads these children, from their earliest days, to pronounce that they are going to do things their own way.

Consequently, the mother becomes frustrated, self-attacking, and angry when the infant refuses to eat. It seems as if the child actively pushes away the mother's vain attempts to engage and feed the child. She finds herself in a great predicament, because the child she wants desperately to nurture is rapidly losing weight. She searches for ways "to be a better mother." But no amount of coaxing, cajoling, bargaining, distracting, or "forcing food" (Chatoor 1989) will get these infants to eat.

Sometimes the mother has difficulty recognizing the child's efforts to eat autonomously. For example, the child may want to feed itself by taking the spoon, but the mother does not interpret the child's desires correctly and inadvertently thwarts an early striving for independence. Mother may decide to give the infant a bottle or feed it herself; she may also start to play with the child and divert its attention from eating. We surmise that the willful infant reacts by oppositionally refusing food; this impedes the infant's development of the capacity to differentiate a variety of body feelings such as hunger, anger, and satiety. It cannot learn when or how much to eat, and the desire to take in food may shut down altogether. In a real sense, the infant engages in a hunger strike.

Although there may be many causes of the problem, some of the difficulty may lie in the mother's own unresolved struggles with her own mother around independence. Studies of mothers whose infants had infantile anorexia nervosa showed that they had the best of intentions as mothers but extraordinarily high expectations of themselves as well. According to their own high ideals of mothering, they felt quite guilty at becoming angry or irritated at their infants for not eating. They also could not recognize the normal, healthy ambivalence that all mothers have about their infants, especially those who are sometimes draining and difficult.

Often these women remember that their relationships with their own mothers were conflictual, and they naturally want to do a better job of mothering their own children. For the first few months after birth, these mothers are delighted by the innate passivity of newborns who "drink in" mother's goodness and good feedings. All mothers are pleased to see their child respond; but once the child begins to assert itself, the mother must receive gratification from the child's independence and forward movement out into the world. Those mothers of infants with anorexia seem unable to sense when their children need or want to eat on their own, which would give them greater autonomy.

🐛 Melody P., age 16 months, posed such problems. Her beautiful young mother, a striving interior designer, was stymied whenever Melody shoved her food away. Watching mother and baby together clearly revealed that this mother adored her child. When the parents were interviewed in joint sessions, they appeared to have no conflicts. Melody was nonetheless losing weight and refusing to eat anything, despite her precocious explorations and verbal expression.

After Melody's pediatrician completed a full medical workup for organic disease, he advised her mother to allow Melody to eat only at mealtime. Because the mother had taken her baby with her when she visited clients' homes for appointments, snacks had become a normal and necessary part of the child's day. Structuring mealtime helped Melody learn when she was hungry. Because she was so bright, her treaters also suggested that she be allowed to feed herself as much as possible. Little dishes of baby food, bits of finger food, and spoons were introduced, all to the delight of the youngster. Mealtimes were also limited to a 30-minute maximum and, if Melody did not eat, food was put away. Within 2 weeks, Melody's pattern had reversed. She began eating with relish, to the surprise and delight of her mother, whose self-esteem had been bolstered by the suggested interventions. When followed up at age 4½, Melody had no more food difficulties at all. She was doing well in a preschool for gifted children.

Sometimes babies appear thin and always hungry. Interviews of the mothers reveal a history of an ongoing struggle with an eating disorder. In an effort to avoid having "a fat baby," mothers who are preoccupied with thinness and their own body image will try to restrict the intake of their actively growing infants. Women with a history of anorexia nervosa, bulimia nervosa, or other restrictive patterns of eating must be careful not to impose their food preoccupations on their infants or children. Athletic, body-conscious men have also insisted their chubby youngsters be placed on diets to lose baby fat out of the fathers' own preoccupation with fitness and appearance. Instead, they must remember that most children, unless emotionally distressed, will eat only as much as they need to satisfy their innate biological needs. To limit an infant's food source endangers health.

Parents sometimes have religious or philosophical beliefs about food that also threaten the livelihood of their children. In one case that received national attention in the press, a year-old baby weighed only 10 pounds. She was fed only milk by her parents, who argued that their religious beliefs forbade them to feed the child a more diverse and age-appropriate diet of fruits, vegetables, and meat products. Most jurisdictions will implement child-protective services in such a scenario and remove the child to foster care. Concerned citizens may be called on to alert authorities to such cases. The medical practitioner will then need to rule out malnutrition based on an organic disease, infantile anorexia nervosa, or deprivation of food and nutrients causing failure to thrive based on parental neglect.

## Eating Disorders in Childhood

There appears to be increasing evidence that eating disorders among children are on the rise. One need only turn on the television some Saturday morning to see how youngsters are indoctrinated with the desire to be thin and attractive from an early age. Impressionable children take these values to heart, believing them to be the quintessential ingredients of a happy life and fulfilling personhood. Advertisements teach children how to look, what size to be, and what to eat; stereotypical patterns of what constitutes the well-proportioned child and adult even find their way into cartoons and plays. Children beg their parents for the latest designer clothes, then diet at earlier and earlier ages to fit into them. In fact, concern about recognized and unrecognized eating disorders in children has grown to the point that a structured assessment method has been developed to test for them. The Children's Eating Attitude Test (ChEAT; Lask and Bryant-Waugh 1992; Maloney et al. 1988) measures feelings about eating, body dissatisfaction, and interpersonal concerns among children. In one study, 7% of 318 children scored within the anorexic range on the ChEAT, a figure that parallels the results of standard assessments given to adults.

Among children, anorexia nervosa has been found much more frequently than bulimia nervosa. In fact, until recently, researchers believed that bulimia did not occur in children, because they had not been exposed to the condition nor had they acquired knowledge about the disorder on their own. Children also had not developed the cognitive skills to learn how to purge. Maturational fears that lead to eating disorders among adolescents had not yet been sparked among children. But some cases of bulimia have been reported. They share commonalities with the larger group of childhood anorexic patients: inappropriate parental pressure, sexual abuse, rebellion, and a history of obesity have all been implicated in the etiology.

Sociocultural attitudes, as stated earlier, play a distinct role. Little girls learn from an early age that appearance is—and will continue to be—important in their lives. According to sociologist Ruth A. Striegel-Moore, little girls learn that being attractive will please others, help secure love, and be a way to receive positive feedback (Striegel-Moore et al. 1986). In fact, whereas boys receive compliments for their intellectual performance, girls are more often praised for "intellectually irrelevant aspects such as neatness" (p. 249), which implies that appearance is more important than substance.

Children's books also emphasize the little girl's appearance. According to Striegel-Moore, surveys reveal that children's books and television programs frequently comment on how little girls look, but rarely do so for boys. Children's media have tended to project that "attending to one's appearance was a major activity for the girl characters, whereas the boys were more likely to solve problems and play hard" (Striegel-Moore et al. 1986, p. 249). Developmental studies have documented that as girls internalize these societal messages, they become much more preoccupied than boys with looking attractive.

Readers shouldn't be surprised to learn that children are preoccupied with dieting, fear of fatness, and their figures. A survey of schoolchildren completed in 1988 revealed that many 11- to 13-year-olds were worried about the shape of their stomachs and thighs (Salmons et al. 1988). Another study examining the diet and body shape concerns of youngsters reported that about half the young girls in the study wanted to lose weight (Davies and Furnham 1986). Of these, only 4% were actually overweight, but more than 40% considered themselves so. In this age group, dieting and size concerns may be less sex-specific. But in one report, 45% of the girls wanted to be thinner (37% had already tried dieting), and the boys did not lag far behind. Sadly, the subjects in this study were only 7 to 13 years of age (Maloney et al. 1989).

Until recently, research on body dissatisfaction and low self-esteem among children with eating disorders was virtually nonexistent, and clearly more must be done to reveal the concerns and attitudes of school-age children. We are currently undertaking such a study at The Menninger Clinic. However, measures of body build and self-esteem among fourth, fifth, and sixth graders have been correlated in one major study. Girls believe that the thinner they are, the more likely they are to succeed academically and socially. Like adult women, these girls are less satisfied and more preoccupied with body image than are their male counterparts, because they link it to success and happiness (Lask and Bryant-Waugh 1992; Satter 1986, 1991).

As significant as these societal trends may be, the parental relationship has also been shown to play a pivotal role in some cases. Based on intensive work with families of anorexic patients, writers such as Minuchin (Minuchin et al. 1978), Selvini-Palazzoli (1978), and Crisp (1980; Crisp et al. 1974) have demonstrated the special role that the anorexic child and adolescent may play in diverting family conflict and tension away from the parents. These families are seldom able to address conflictual issues directly, but instead "detour" them through the symptomatic individual. Thus it is necessary to examine the relationship *between* the parents and not focus solely on the individual issues and conflicts of the child or both adults.

The parents of the anorexic person are often preoccupied with themselves but overtly appear worried or concerned about other family members. On the surface, the mother may seem quite generous and solicitous to all; but beneath this facade, she may be quite insecure about her own worth and talents. Her "giving" is not so much to develop the child's real potential as it is to control the child. The mother appears to be engaged and connected with the child, but she is really unable to empathize deeply or to encourage growth in their relationship. As much as she tries to mother lovingly, she is really trying to meet her own needs rather than those of the child. This unconsciously duplicitous form of mothering leads the anorexic child to feel perpetually discounted. To receive anything offered by the self-sacrificing mother, the child must always be good; hence a desire for perfectionism is fueled. But the child also senses that her mother's "gifts" are not from the heart, so she learns to distrust the world and herself. In a way, the mother's love comes with a heavy "tax" on it; to secure her portion of care, the child must be compliant and well-behaved, and she must follow her mother's admonitions. Unconditional love is anathema.

Within the family, the dilemma of the anorexic child is heightened by an authoritarian, entitled father who secretly devalues his wife and all females. On the surface, he may seem like the paragon of success, beloved in his work or profession, and the possessor of many (albeit superficial) friendships. Underneath, however, he is unable to give his wife much of anything except material satisfaction. The wife's fragile sense of self-esteem is eroded because her husband subtly devalues her capabilities. He is secretly terrified of the power of women, especially in his wife. The resulting corrosive parental union keeps both partners from being able to grow. The parents do not sustain each other in a mutually supportive, enhancing bond. They are not happy for each other's successes. For the daughter, their relationship is the poorest form of role modeling. Closeness seems terrifying. To her, "dependency will equal slavery; intimacy will mean surrendering integrity; sexuality will mean a loss of control over her own appetites and a man's appetites" (Gordon et al. 1989, p. 39).

Anorexia is much more likely to develop in little girls than in little boys because girls are more sensitive to the mother's empathic failures. Because the woman's identity flourishes as a "self in relation" (a term developed by the Stone Center in Wellesley, Massachusetts, to high-light women's connection to other people such as their children, friends, and mates), a mother who has trouble connecting with other people will be unable to model for her daughter the joys derived from relationships. Consequently, to be with men will be equated with being subjugated. To be close to women will mean being controlled.

As a result, the anorexic girl will become an island unto herself. No wonder she forsakes food as much as people. She is deeply perplexed by what it means to need anything or anyone. The little girl faces the dilemma of wanting to idealize her mother, love her father, and see the two in a union that is safe and mutually supportive. When this fantasy does not become real,

> Anorexia may be seen as an attempt by the child to awaken her mother, to contact her, and to break her out of her own vicious cycle of self-sacrifice and self-denial, but without any appearance of rejecting the mother herself. The anorexic daughter can be viewed as a caricature of the mother's version of womanhood. The illness is a desperate attempt to comply with the mother's standards and, at the same time, to question their very foundation. (Gordon et al. 1989, p. 40)

Not surprisingly, there is a high incidence of depression among children with early onset anorexia. In one study, 56% of these children were clinically depressed (Fosson et al. 1987). The significance of depression and childhood anorexia is yet to be totally elucidated, but clinically it is of great concern. Treatment centers have been struck by the poor outcome of children who develop an eating disorder at an early age. For childhood anorexic patients, early intervention must focus on interrupting family discord, establishing sound, healthy nutrition, and dealing with underlying depression as well.

In addition, pediatricians and other medical personnel must be educated about the fact that eating disorders do occur in young children. Anorexia is still perceived to be a disorder that begins only in adolescence and that can be diagnosed only after extensive medical tests. Although a thorough medical workup is always warranted to rule out physical causes of malnourishment, family members must be educated consumers who can talk to their physician about the possibility of an eating disorder. The combined experience of our Menninger staff with that of other clinicians around the country demonstrates that an alarming number of cases have been missed for a long time, leading to costly but inappropriate medical workups and delayed, ineffective treatment interventions. Thus, parents and doctors must be alert to the possibility that a child who suddenly loses or gains an inordinate amount of weight may have an eating disorder. The current poor prognosis that accompanies childhood eating disorders can only be remedied by greater awareness and insight into the illness on the part of physicians and parents.

## Pica and Rumination

Pica and rumination are two uncommon eating disorders that usually occur in childhood. Pica is defined as a pathological craving for a substance not commonly regarded as food. The medical complications of pica can be serious; inner-city children who eat lead-based paint may end up with severe intellectual and physical impairment as a result of lead intoxication. In pregnancy, at least 50% of women describe cravings for various kinds of foods. Some impoverished African American women in the South eat starch and clay, an adult form of pica.

Pica seems to be a complex behavior with multiple determinants. Although based to some extent on the individual's sociocultural context, pica may be a response to neurobiological mechanisms still poorly understood. Numerous studies have associated pica with iron deficiency and starch eating; in these cases, nutritional supplementation with iron has produced a reversal of iron deficiency anemia and has curtailed the craving for starch or paint. However, even in cases of pica caused by iron deficiency anemia, psychosocial stressors such as maternal deprivation, parental neglect, child beating, and impoverished parent-child interactions have been implicated as contributing to the ingestion of pathological substances for food. Learning more about pica can help us appreciate the intricate roles of sociocultural influences, the significance of appetite and neuropsychiatric disorders, and the psychobiology of human food selection.

Rumination is an eating disorder that can occur from infancy throughout adulthood but is most common among children and young adolescents. Derived from the Latin *ruminare*, rumination literally means "to chew the cud." It is the act of bringing ingested foods back into the mouth; in essence, food is regurgitated after being chewed and swallowed. This rather unsavory disorder has been associated with a variety of medical complications, from aspiration pneumonia to dehydration and failure to thrive. Most recently, it has been associated with bulimia, anorexia, and depression.

As with other psychiatric disorders, rumination has been linked to an impaired mother-child attunement that stems from maternal depression and anxiety. But this theory of its origin may unduly emphasize mother-child interactions. Other factors at play may include medical disorders such as gastroesophageal reflux, which has been found more frequently in ruminating children. Impaired regulation of neuropeptide and opioid activity has also been suggested as a cause (see Chapter 12). Hypothetically, conflicts centering on parental attachment could diminish endogenous opioid activity, provoking rumination behavior in infancy. Rumination is a highly reinforcing eating behavior that is thus chronically perpetuated in the individual sufferer.

In all likelihood, rumination is probably underreported and, consequently, undertreated. Various treatment approaches—inpatient hospitalization, pharmacotherapy, and behavioral therapy—all claim acceptable positive results. However, when rumination becomes severe enough to cause a failure to thrive, there may be no choice but to hospitalize the patient and proceed with supportive family interventions and a thorough diagnostic assessment.

As with other eating disorders and psychiatric problems in general, most parents will feel guilty or ashamed about having a child who ruminates. Parents need reassurance that they are the experts with their own children and are important to the entire treatment effort. Their children can overcome the problem. Professionals can sometimes help diagnose and then interrupt a rumination pattern with specific treatment interventions. Relaxation techniques such as guided imagery, biofeed-

back, and hypnosis are particularly useful with older children and adolescents.

🍂 One patient with rumination who entered treatment did so in the
midst of a deep crisis. Mindy Q., age 12, had known severe parental
neglect and family upheaval. Placed in at least seven different foster
homes since age three, Mindy had never known the meaning or
experience of consistency or love. Her biological mother visited her
only infrequently; her mother's series of angry and abusive par-
amours had frightened Mindy. Her father had seen her only 3 times
in 12 years.

Mindy was clearly enraged by what she had been through but,
like most 12-year-olds, she found it difficult to express her feelings
in words. Brought to the hospital under a child protective custody
action, Mindy did her best from the first to defy treatment. Despite
the vigilance of the nursing staff, which included supervision in the
bathroom and at mealtimes, Mindy continued to vomit. She refused
suggestions to relax after meals by talking with her peers. She ignored her therapist's encouragement to begin to think about her
situation and try to put it into words. Mindy's feelings of abandonment ran so deep she could not allow herself to trust anyone. All
adults were the enemy.

Even while sitting next to a staff member and talking about her
day, Mindy would regurgitate her meal. Her rumination had become
a learned behavior that she could not escape, but it also demonstrated her anger at staff members by vomiting on them. If left
unsupervised for even a moment, she would vomit into her clothes,
under her mattress, in the shower drain, and in other concealed
spots on the unit. Mindy's creativity manifested itself by the unique
hiding places she found, such as the live plants on the unit and
the used medication cups of other patients. She even pulled up a
section of new carpet and poured her vomit between it and the
protective pad.

From a diagnostic point of view, Mindy's disturbance appeared to
be a mixture of rumination and bulimia. But this diagnosis revealed
little about her underlying misery. Psychologically, her difficulties

obviously represented a way to express anger and get back at adults for the injustices of her life. She made sure that others now gave her the attention that had not been forthcoming when she was a young child. For Mindy, rumination had become a fight to the finish. At several junctures in her life, her nutrition was so poor that she was actually close to death. But rather than cooperate with efforts to help her find a more fruitful form of self-expression, she persisted in her behavior out of anger and spitefulness.

# Athletes

Sports that emphasize maintaining a lean body appearance predispose athletes to an increased risk of eating disorders. Yet coaches and trainers seem perplexed by the growing number of eating disorders in the people they work with. Nevertheless, they find themselves on the front lines of those who usually spot the problem. Other people may begin a healthy fitness program with moderate exercise as a goal, only to develop a frenzied, compulsive exercise routine. Training for a sport or exercising compulsively can dominate the lives of these athletes.

Champions like tennis star Zina Garrison and former Olympic gymnasts Cathy Rigby, Nadia Comaneci, and Kathy Johnson have come forward to tell about their battles with anorexia and bulimia. Their courageousness and openness have helped others become more aware of the magnitude of the problem among athletes and nonathletes alike.

As Zina Garrison testified, "It's something a lot of women and a lot of girls have a problem with and a lot of them are afraid to tell about it. I believe the way to correct something is to hit it head on and talk about it" ("Battle with bulimia prevents Garrison from reaching No. 1" 1992, p. C3).

Increasing the public's awareness of eating disorders is an important first step. Because eating disorders are manifested by the pursuit of thinness and the denial of hunger and fatigue, an athlete may not at first perceive her eating preoccupation as abnormal or unusual. She will shun the advice of coaches and other athletes who urge her to maintain good nutrition. Even after she begins to look emaciated or to perform poorly because of the eating disorder, she will most likely hold on to the belief that she can become a better athlete by losing more weight. Sometimes her fellow athletes will confront her about a recurrent, pungent smell of vomit in the locker room. Despite repeated confrontation, the bulimic athlete will deny her secret for the longest time (Zerbe 1987). This unpleasant telltale tip-off indicates how important weight control has become for her.

The usual life-threatening complications of electrolyte disturbance and cardiac arrhythmias are even more dangerous for the individual undergoing strenuous physical training. Because she is taxing her body physically and struggling with an eating disorder at the same time, she is more prone to sudden death. Before reaching this point, she may acknowledge her faltering performance and listlessness. As Zina Garrison commented in regard to her own struggles with bulimia, "You can't control it. You're very depressed and you don't know why you're depressed. Your fingernails are very soft; your hair starts to fall out; your skin is bad." Even after marrying and winning the U.S. Open in 1989, Garrison failed to take the Grand Slam title. She sees her bulimia as the culprit. "I lost to someone ranked 350th in the world and I lost because I didn't have any energy. That had never happened to me before," she explained ("Battle with bulimia prevents Garrison from reaching No. 1" 1992, p. C3).

Sports that require leanness—figure skating, diving, synchronized swimming, gymnastics, cheerleading, ballet, and rowing, among others—are more frequently associated with eating disorders than sports that tolerate a greater range of body build. For sports like skating that require performance evaluations, William G. Johnson and David Schlundt have found that successful competition is based on the appearance of the body. They write, "If one's body is short and squatty, even if it does not have a high body-fat percentage, judges may cut the score down as opposed to someone long, slender, and tiny" (1991, p. 7). Women who participate in sports such as basketball, field hockey, track and field, swimming, skiing, and volleyball may exhibit less pathological eating behavior, because winning is not predicated on body shape, and these sports encourage participants with a greater range of body build.

For sports that do emphasize leanness, approximately 50%–60% of the participants have some form of pathological dieting. A range of well-conducted studies shows that as many as 25% of participants in these sports actually have an eating disorder. In those sports that do not emphasize physique, 40% still relied on pathological dieting behavior, and 10% had true eating disorders. Johnson and Schlundt explain what this prevalence of maladaptive eating behavior means.

> When you look at female athletes in sports that will tolerate a little bit more range of body build, you are going to find a distribution of eating or dieting disorders that is very similar to the rest of the population of that age. When you get into these particular sports that promote leanness or require thinness as part of the criteria for performance, you will find perhaps a doubling of the rates of these behaviors and problems. (1991, p. 7)

This view has been confirmed by another noted study. When Anthony and colleagues (1982) assessed 245 female college students who studied exercise, physical conditioning, and body image, they found significantly higher scores of body preoccupation and abnormal eating among dance and drama students than among those majoring in physical and health education. Alarmed by the role played by sports and fitness in eating disorders, Canadian educators Mary and Dick Moriarty (1991) have launched a national effort to address the problem. They cite the findings in the Anthony study as an indication that those at risk for eating disorders will gravitate toward areas of study emphasizing body image rather than to physical exercise itself. The Moriartys' efforts to alert the public to the incidence of eating disorders among athletes and aerobic exercisers should be heeded in all Western countries. As the Moriartys observed, it is all too common for a reasonable fitness plan to start out as a "solution to stress and problems of life" (p. 1) only to become the problem in its own right.

In her book *The Woman Runner* (1984), Gloria Averbuch writes firsthand about her own running and thinness compulsion. Although Averbuch never met all the criteria for anorexia nervosa, she noted some anorexic tendencies in herself. In her poignant recollection of her own self-destructiveness toward her body, she reveals that she insisted on working out at least 2 hours a day and maintaining a dress size 4, despite her 5-ft. 6-in. height. Averbuch felt a stronger sense of self-esteem as she grew slimmer and as her speed and grace at running increased. Her story is typical of anorexic persons who thrive on the confirmation of others when their thinness is applauded. They are proud of their physical achievement, including thinness, and believe that their athletic identity is their true, total self. If weighing more than they want, they "know" their true self is merely hiding beneath a temporarily bigger one. Sports and thinness promote their ownership of their bodies.

Even while these athletes ostensibly exercise for weight control and health, those with insight recognize their compulsiveness and their inner discord. Averbuch writes,

> Yet, I suspect that something wasn't right about my instincts: curbing my appetite with carrot sticks, rinsing butter or oil from my food, and making sure not to go to bed on a "full stomach." I didn't feel unhappy, hungry, or without strength; I was just careful. I liked my thinner self and my eating habits, which were far from starvation, but spare enough to give me a sense of asceticism. Even if I were physically longing for food to gain the weight back, I never felt it. Something far deeper than my own conscious effort was controlling my appetite. It wasn't self-loathing; it was part of my desire to be a disciplined athlete. (1984, p. 105)

Averbuch's dilemma raises several questions that are still debated among athletes, coaches, and health professionals today: when does the healthy discipline and sense of purpose found in exercising turn into an extreme compulsion and anorexia?

Anyone can turn to the diagnostic criteria used by professionals, but doing so seems to beg the question of the real emotional and physical toll exacted on people's lives by eating disorders. When anyone, including the athlete, is so driven by the desire to be thin and to succeed that other life goals go unacknowledged, then she is clearly hurting herself and in need of help and redirection. Her athleticism and her pursuit of thinness may be painful cries for help.

Some women athletes become the object of envy and jealousy because they truly seem able to "have it all." In the 1988 and 1992 Summer Olympics, Jackie Joyner-Kersee displayed those attributes of a strikingly attractive, happily married, and emotionally secure woman absorbed in her sport. However, her dedication to the heptathlon never took her away from other life pursuits. Most of us are not so innately endowed and thus will have to accept less than the ideal projected by Joyner-Kersee.

Accepting less than the ideal is not easy for anyone in our culture, let alone a highly competitive and resourceful athlete. One former Olympic gold medalist confided that she had struggled with severe bulimia for years despite resounding athletic success. Unhappy in many areas of her life, she complained of feeling "torn because I can't maintain a relationship and practice every day. Throwing up helps me throw up some of the pain. After I work out, I can eat what I want then get rid of it, knowing it won't affect me. It helps me forget what I don't have in life." Yet a superficial appraisal seemed to show that this bright woman, who was so sad about what she could not accomplish outside her sport, was inordinately successful. The honors bestowed on her would stir envy in any of us, but we would not be aware of her inner struggles. Below a veneer of success lay fresh pain, wounded personal desires, and unfulfilled ambitions. Athleticism was just one way she could try to fill up her emptiness and appear whole.

Indeed, within the past decade a number of reports have linked sports (especially running) with underlying depression. The hypothesis rests on how naturally occurring endorphins, the neurochemicals that may be implicated in depression, become elevated during intense physical workouts. This "endorphin high" remedies any underlying dysphoria and sadness and, after a short period, can make exercise addictive (Yates 1991; Yates et al. 1983).

In one study of women runners, a high percentage became severely dysfunctional (Gadpaille et al. 1987). When unable to run, they exhibited symptoms of depression and agitation. This group encompassed a subset of runners who were also amenorrheic and had anorexia nervosa or a major affective disorder. Thus there may be a spectrum of illness that includes athletic amenorrhea, eating disorders, and major affective disorders. The related disturbances in endocrine functioning and neuro-

transmitter metabolites point toward a biologically and genetically me-
diated illness in this susceptible population. Clearly, it behooves us to
try to understand the links between exercise, eating disorders, and depression more thoroughly. A significant percentage of women athletes
may be training intensely—not only out of a manifest desire to acquire
skill, improve self-image, and enhance physical control, but also to stave
off deep, overwhelming depression.

Finally, it is important to acknowledge those family members who
have turned to this chapter because they are aware that a loved one is
using excessive exercise as a way to cope—and purge her body of
weight. Just as laxatives and vomiting prevent the absorption of calories,
exercise increases energy expenditure and promotes weight loss. Indeed,
nationwide, study after study has shown that a majority of women exercise to promote weight loss, not because it is an especially healthy thing
to do. Although common sense dictates that regular exercise promotes
physical health, an individual with an eating disorder will engage in
prolonged exercise to burn off excessive calories. Thus *exercise can be
used and often is used as a form of purging.* Typically, running is the
preferred method of purging through exercise, although weight lifting,
swimming, and race-walking are becoming more popular methods
among women. Concern is warranted when the individual exceeds the
recommended 20–60 minutes of intense aerobic exercise 3 times a week.
As with other modes of purging, family members may be the last to
learn about their loved one's compulsive exercise. The addiction can be
so consuming that the individual will lock her door, turn out the lights,
and keep the activity up even in bed. She will keep arms, fingers, and
legs moving to continue generating weight loss.

The best available data indicate that 64% of bulimic patients engage in excessive exercise as a way to control weight. Clearly, the relationship between exercise, athletics, and eating disorders is not simple.
Some authorities now even believe that excessive exercise, rather than
dieting, may be the main route to anorexia nervosa for a majority of
patients. If this proves true, it will be essential for women to consider
the degree and extent of their exercise and their reasons for doing it. In
one poll of 33,000 women readers of *Glamour* magazine (1984), 95% of
the respondents remarked that they exercised to control their weight,

not for reasons of improving their health (Krejci et al. 1992; Striegel-Moore 1986; White 1993a, 1993b; Yates 1991). For unknown reasons, anorexic persons are able to keep exercising despite very low body weight. Normal persons who had lost this much weight would be too ill to carry on a daily routine. Thus what may appear as true dedication to a sport may, in fact, be compulsive physical activity masking anorexic behavior.

Because of the large number of athletes who struggle with eating disorders, coaches and health professionals at some universities are insisting that vulnerable competitors avail themselves of counseling. As coaches, trainers, and athletes stress a wide variety of treatment options for the athlete with an eating disorder, they are educating themselves about this health issue. Becoming educated and sensitized to the problems posed by eating disorders will help compulsive exercisers and women athletes overcome them. First, however, they must be helped to feel safe in coming forward to share their dilemmas, and then encouraged to develop techniques so that they can participate in their chosen sport without risk of bodily harm. Good health and a reasonable lifestyle must also be hailed as a mark of the successful athlete.

## Older Women

Both anorexia nervosa and bulimia nervosa can surface for the first time in midlife (ages 40–60) and later life (age 60+). Although these disorders tend to occur in adolescents and younger adults, women at midlife and beyond face similar struggles with attractiveness, thinness, self-worth, and body dissatisfaction. In addition, they are confronted with what Susan Sontag dubbed "the double standard of aging" (1972, p. 29) in our society. That is, as men grow older, they are perceived as more attractive, whereas women are considered to be less attractive and desirable. This is all the more reason some women become fixated on their bodies as a way to stay alluring and appealing.

Sometimes women at midlife seek treatment for the first time after struggling for years with a full-blown or subclinical eating disorder. They have kept the disorder secret from their loved ones while they have suffered in silence. Often a daughter or niece is herself trying to cope with an eating problem and intuits the difficulty in her relative. The younger family member may even seek treatment. Both scenarios lead the middle-aged woman to reconsider her circumstances, particularly as knowledge about the life-threatening nature of eating disorders has found its way into television documentaries, movies, dramas, magazine and newspaper articles, and novels. This generational problem of eating disorders is portrayed beautifully in Henry Jaglom's 1990 film *Eating*. This movie, billed as a "very serious comedy about women and food," is a must-see for anyone interested in how preoccupied our culture has become with food. Although sex and food are clearly linked as a group of women at a party discuss their adventures (one character even mentions that she has never found a man as satisfying as a baked potato), daughters and mothers also discuss their food concerns from their differing vantage points. A hidden truth emerges: sometimes a person's struggles with food may be as downplayed as an adulterous affair was years ago, by turning away from the obvious. At other times, food issues are as dramatic and apparent as walking into a bathroom and seeing your best friend purge while she begs you, "Don't tell Mother." Older women deny their own and their daughters' food-related concerns, only to confess when they cannot be avoided any longer—much like the aging process itself.

Sometimes culture is not the culprit. Those cases of anorexia that develop in later life usually reveal a strong affective component. However, before a definite diagnosis can be made, the patient must undergo an extensive medical workup. For example, there may be an underlying tumor or endocrine problem that is causing weight loss and depression. Many authorities believe that at least 40% of cancer patients initially complain of a depressed mood before they have any other indication of illness. Therefore, when symptoms of an eating disorder (particularly malnutrition and weight loss) appear in later life, organic illness must be ruled out first.

When the diagnosis of either anorexia nervosa or bulimia nervosa in an older woman can confidently be made, depressive symptoms so frequently found in this population must also be assessed and (if present) treated. Nutritional management alone will sometimes improve the patient's low energy level, general weakness, sad mood, and social incapacity. Sometimes an antidepressant will also be needed. With elderly patients, a lower dosage than is generally prescribed for adults is indicated as both patient and physician judge improvement in strength, stamina, and engagement in life.

Older people must also be reminded of the dangers of taking too many laxatives and diuretics. A number of recent studies suggest that being underweight and malnourished is a major health risk among elderly people (Hall and Beresford 1989; Morley et al. 1988; Price et al. 1986; Wilson et al. 1991). Nutritional impairment may also increase the likelihood of osteoporosis. Women at midlife and beyond, particularly those with eating disorders, need to take calcium supplements to prevent fractures. A therapeutic vitamin can combat deficiencies that might exacerbate an underlying depression (e.g., vitamin $B_{12}$ deficiency, zinc deficiency, iron deficiency anemia).

Addressing these medical concerns combats only part of the problem. Realizing that loss is part of the aging process, older women need to seek support groups and therapists who will help them review their lives with particular attention to loss. At times, as in the following case, unresolved feelings about loss can precipitate an eating disorder. In addition, women will find it helpful to recognize how they may base their self-concept on a cultural stereotype. Some older women may have difficulty embracing feminist concepts, although certain research done on women at midlife clearly demonstrates that they struggle with the same concerns as younger women. For example, in one longitudinal study of people over age 62, the second greatest personal concern expressed by women was change in body weight (memory loss was listed first; Rodin et al. 1985). In the same sample, men rarely expressed concern about their weight. Yet this concern flies in the face of a biological given: both sexes are inclined to put on weight in midlife. Women have a lower resting metabolic rate than men and a higher fat-to-lean tissue ratio. With aging, women's lean body mass decreases, with a concomitant increase in fatty tissue as compared to men. This predisposes women whose self-esteem is based on body satisfaction to go on diets that are rarely successful over the long term and may further predispose them to developing an eating disorder.

❦ Marjorie R., a 70-year-old grandmother of three who was a hospital volunteer, sought treatment for a 20-year history of caloric restriction and depression. According to Marjorie, she had struggled with a lifelong preoccupation with constipation and a fear of gaining weight. These concerns had escalated after the death of her only daughter in a car accident. At that time, her husband, a successful financier and city council representative, dealt with his grief by having an affair, which also injured Marjorie's self-esteem.

By the time Marjorie entered treatment, she had lost more than 30 pounds and appeared frail, emaciated, anxious, and depressed. She tended to express her emotional struggles by displacing them onto her body. As a result, she had developed numerous psychosomatic complaints, including breathing difficulty, chronic constipation, abdominal bloating, low back pain, tension headaches, and blurred vision. Despite repeated reassurances that multiple medical workups had revealed no organic illness whatsoever, she continued to have physical problems, including anorexia. These symptoms clearly served to help her cope with the loss of her daughter and with her husband's affair. Marjorie's anorexia was also a way for her to acquire nurturance; being ill was a socially acceptable way to get others to take care of her. Finally, her husband's affair signaled that the relationship had been strained for years.

Marjorie's underlying self-concept was chronically poor. Just as many younger women do, she found success in weight loss that initially reaffirmed her flagging sense of self-worth. At least temporarily, she began to believe that she was adequate in one centrally important domain.

Marjorie's case demonstrates a number of central issues for women at midlife and beyond. Although she first sought help at age 70, her eating disorder had actually begun 20 years earlier. Like many women, Marjorie valued her physical appearance, and she blamed herself for having a body that was too inadequate to entice her husband. Several losses that were unresolved and unmourned for years contributed to her psychological pain, while ongoing depression and anxiety exacerbated her low self-esteem. Malnutrition probably augmented her dysphoria. Finally, she expressed her problems in a way that is much more socially acceptable than having an emotional illness: she compressed them into a physiological metaphor. Her emotional aches and pains found expression more easily in physical symptoms. As Marjorie's therapist began to help her acknowledge and express her resentment, anger, and losses, her somatic preoccupations diminished. Although her nutritional state improved and she addressed her internal misery in other ways, her concerns did not quickly abate. She voiced a lifetime of unexpressed worry and disappointment in ways that were not hypochondriacal, and she began to deal more effectively with her somatic preoccupations. Marjorie began to see how to address her losses and discord more effectively and how to get more gratification from relationships and activities for the rest of her life.

## Conclusion

This chapter has focused on how eating disorders may affect several different but often neglected special populations. Infants, children, athletes, and older women all exhibit unique constellations of eating disorder symptoms and struggles. In each group, early intervention can help assess the difficulty and prevent it from worsening. These special populations are linked by a variety of psychological issues and stressors that predispose individuals to eating disorders. Although their specific conflicts and aspirations are all different, their final expression is similar. It appears that the battles an individual wages with respect to weight and self-esteem exacerbate tendencies for abnormal eating and exercise. Thus, the onset of anorexia and bulimia can occur at any time. As women's health becomes a greater concern for our society as a whole, and as more research focuses on health-related areas, we will begin to learn how to better address these crucial issues that affect both women and men over the life span.

# 7

# Chasing the Ideal:
# The Quest for a Perfect
# Body Image

> What was capable of changing Agnes' relation to the body? Only a
> moment of excitement. Excitement: fleeting redemption of the body.
>
> Milan Kundera
> *Immortality*

In Mexican mythology the canine monster-creator Xolotl (pronounced sho'lot') is honored for bringing a giant bone from the un-
derworld. This bone provides the raw substance from which men and
women are made. As the story unfolds, Xolotl stumbles on his return
from hell, and the bone falls out of his arms and shatters. The many
broken pieces are the raw material of human substance; their various
sizes result in the wide variety of human shapes and forms.

As we stroll through a shopping mall, spend a day in a busy mu-
seum, attend a political rally, or simply enjoy the sport of "people
watching," we are usually impressed by the outcome of Xolotl's act. The
array of human body forms and proportions seems even broader than
their polyglot, multiracial, and religious ancestry.

Why is it then that so many individuals are dissatisfied with their physical appearance? In the fascinating book *Inside America* (1987), pollster Louis Harris reveals the secret worries and personal desires of Americans. Harris's study uncovered the fact that preoccupation with changing one's body size or parts is a major focus for most adults. Seventy-five percent of women and 54% of men say that they often think about their physical appearance and would prefer that their bodies were different. Among women, 78% are dissatisfied with their weight, 35% want to lose 25 pounds or more, 37% want to change their teeth, 32% would like a bigger bust, and 34% want better legs. Although there is a gender gap in the specific corporal areas men would like to change, they too are surprisingly dissatisfied with their physique; 56% would like more hair, and 34% would like to be taller. Both men and women are preoccupied with getting older; 48% of women and 27% of men try to conceal signs of aging.

From plastic surgery clinics to cosmetic counters, we keep ourselves and others busy battling nature's inevitable course. Nowhere is this fact brought home more than by television and cartoons or comic strips. The comics "Cathy" and "The Far Side" illustrate the human tendency to seek physical change.

Year after year, poor Cathy searches for a swimsuit that will not only cover her plump figure but also make her look ravishing. She is always frustrated and never satisfied while we, the readers, are amused because we recognize her plight as our own. We are left to wonder if she is really as pudgy as she thinks she is, or if she is struggling with a body image problem and just believes she looks worse than she does.

Meanwhile, in "The Far Side," cows are taken to liposuction clinics, and birds console each other for their lack of lips. Their creator Gary Larson has made a fortune by showing us how ridiculous animals would seem if they had the same body image preoccupations as humans. To underscore the perplexities of the human heart, we must look to humor as well as the Harris statistics.

Harris's poll provides data for something that we all know intuitively about our cultural obsession with external standards and image. Meanwhile, the immense amount of time, attention, money, and energy spent on appearance necessarily means that we shift away from discovering inner beauty and developing personal and sustaining values. For so many, this inner beauty—character—seems like an admonition from one's mother to accept second best, but one rarely stops to think about the absurdity inherent in chasing the physical ideal.

The pursuit of a more perfect body and physical demeanor may reflect a deeper personal and societal preoccupation with narcissism. In his bestseller *The Culture of Narcissism*, Christopher Lasch spells out our difficulty in acknowledging constraints in terms of money, power, and standing. Unwilling to accept traditional limits inherent in the human condition, we strive to have more and more—including a perfect body. Of our narcissistic society, he writes,

> The beautiful people—to use this revealing expression to include not merely wealthy globe trotters, but all those who bask, however briefly, in the full glare of the cameras—live out the fantasy of narcissistic success, which consists of nothing more substantial than a wish to be vastly admired, not for one's accomplishments but simply for one's self, uncritically and without reservation. (Lasch 1979, p. 390)

When the individual places so much primacy on her body image, she has less energy for and investment in developing unique competence as a worker, parent, spouse, or friend. Yet this investment in the body may also mask a deeper dread of looking at the self starkly and honestly. After all, building one's life around the quest for a perfect body avoids the vital existential (if not personal) issues of life that are probably never completely answered. These anxieties are diverted into the pursuit of a perfect body in a way that tends to encapsulate the self in a protective veneer that avoids self-scrutiny and personal and spiritual development.

If we assume that a tendency toward growth is inherent in humans—even as we accept the limitations of our intellectual endowments or financial situations and the appeal of our own bodies—how do we become snagged by the pursuit of such an elusive ideal? Why are our bodies so endowed with personal meaning from the beginning? What is body image to begin with? And how does it become distorted, in particular, in people with eating disorders? Finally, how do we begin to address people's immense investment in their body images—whether or not they have been formally diagnosed with an eating disorder—so that we as a society can rethink the value we place on external appearance rather than internal growth and development?

To look at these questions, we must first focus on what body image is and why it becomes important in our development. We will then trace what happens to body image in those with eating disorders in particular, and how these problems might be worked with psychologically to help transform illness into health.

## Through the Looking Glass

In 1950, psychoanalyst Paul Schilder wrote a book that was destined to become a classic in psychoanalytic circles. *The Image and Appearance of the Human Body* still has much to teach us about how we form a mental picture of our body, why we value our body the way we do, and what can go wrong with our body image in certain psychological and neurological states. Schilder wrote that the caresses we receive as babies and the interest that others take in our bodies will have enormous influence on our developing body image and how we feel about ourselves. Quoting Freud, who said that the ego is first and foremost a bodily ego, Schilder made sense of why we place so much narcissistic value—or love of one's self—in our body.

First, the body lets us experience the world. Our hands enable us to move outside ourselves into the world, as do our body openings, such as the eyes. Our eyes take in and our arms reach out; we test our limits and we react. Through our body, we extend our world, while the world "wanders into ourselves" (Schilder 1950/1970, p. 125). Hence we place enormous importance on all the body openings, because they enable us to "come in closest contact with the world."

Clothes can change our body images and our attitudes. Witness the amazing success of books written for both genders touting the "power suit" as a way to enhance one's image and effectiveness on the job. We become transformed by the clothes we wear. As they enhance our body image, our narcissistic power increases. Every change of dress and every physical action equally affects changes in our bodies. As Schilder writes, "We live constantly with the knowledge of our body. The body image is one of the basic experiences in everyday life" (1950/1970, p. 201).

Schilder's definition of the body image is still helpful today as we think about the mental images we have of our bodies and the psychological importance they have in our lives. Schilder believed that we all carry in our minds a picture that we have formed of our own bodies. This image is built up from many different types of sensations, such as pain, touch, and heat. We are constantly comparing our mental image of what we believe our body is or should be with an ideal human body or figure. Meanwhile, we feel tied down by our bodies and bound to the earth through them. Hence, performing in dance or watching a sporting event helps us break through the boundaries of our own bodies as we suspend ourselves, however briefly, in time and space.

Think for a moment about two people in your life—one whom you love and one whom you hate. Experience the truth in Schilder's comment even as you reflect on changes in your own body image as you read these words:

> Every emotion changes the body image. The body contracts when we hate, it becomes firmer, and its outlines towards the world are more strongly marked . . . we expand the body when we feel friendly and loving. We open our arms, we would like to enclose humanity in them. (1950/1970, p. 210)

There is a plasticity about our own body image such that through every action—whether it be a touch, a change of clothes, or a movement—we magically transform our bodies. Yet our focus does not stay within ourselves. We yearn to know the bodies of others and to expose our bodies to them. Natural curiosity propels us to discover the other—first with our eyes, then through touch, and then to penetrate more deeply. Schilder believed that the continual interchange between our own body image and the body image of others helps us to learn about ourselves through what we take in by the expressions and caresses of others. We then revise our sensations unconsciously and apply them to the other person. Thus social exchange is founded on the subtle perceptual interchange of body images. As Schilder writes,

> It is obvious that interest in particular parts of one's own body provokes interest in the corresponding parts of the bodies of others. Between one's own body and the body of others there exists a connection . . . it is remarkable that interest in others and interest in one's self run in some parallel way to each other. (1950/1970, p. 225)

Schilder's work obviously provides a number of insights that aid our understanding of body attitudes and feelings. However, his was not the only approach to the problem. Alfred Adler (1917, 1929) developed the concept of organ inferiority. He observed that individuals who have difficulty with one organ may attempt to compensate for the defect either by using another organ or by intensifying the use of the inferior one. Thus a celebrated pianist, born with a noticeable club foot that could not be corrected surgically, compensated for it by developing an increased ability to use her hands. But she also drew attention to her misshapen foot by wearing odd shoes and alluding to it in everyday speech, conveying unconscious conflicts she held about her feet. She also tended to have a very poor body image. Following Adler, when an individual perceives one aspect of the body as inferior, the person tends to generalize this inferiority to the entire body concept or self-concept (Fisher and Cleveland 1968). Another individual struggled for years with subclinical anorexia nervosa and the maintenance of a lifesaving colostomy. Although she had won a victory over rectal cancer, she emphasized the importance of being "the thinnest" in her social set and spent long hours tending to the colostomy. She believed her bag gave off noxious odors, even though there was no objective evidence for this.

One's body also serves the crucial function of a protective enclosure. People find refuge in their bodies and fend off attack with them. In scriptural passages, the body is referred to as our home or temple; we are commanded to respect and cherish it, because it is our physical and spiritual safeguard. As the medical writer and television producer Jonathan Miller has described it, "our body is where we can always be contacted, but our continued presence in it is more than a radical form of being a stick in the mud. Our body is not, in short, something we have; it is a large part of what we actually are" (1978, p. 14).

In contrast, eating disorder patients often talk about their bodies as hideous receptacles or as harboring parts that attack or are otherwise persecutory. One patient complained, "My big stomach will make me explode," even though she was 25 pounds under her recovery weight. Another exclaimed that her body was "a gift for everybody else's enjoyment" but not her own. She vomited profusely after every visit to her family, because they would comment on her body; she wanted to stay a little girl because this was how she received attention. She wished to get rid of her maturing body symbolically through the act of purging and was fearful her female therapist would "turn [her] into a woman" against her will. She sensed the love she got would be lost as she grew up and "my family wouldn't hold or cuddle me. I must be a dependent child to get what I need and haven't gotten yet." Thus people with eating disorders tend to believe that others are trying to attack them (e.g., get them to eat or lose weight), and they find little refuge in their own bodies. Their sense of the body as a good or worthwhile container is impaired.

It is not uncommon for individuals with an eating disorder to believe that their bodies are malevolent. They describe their bodies as "monsters" or "vampires." As a protective container, the body harbors our experiences of our feelings. Again, the person with an eating disorder tends to get rid of feelings by purging or by not filling the body with food. The sense is that the body as a container, if developed at all, has been punctured, which leads the individual to feel an imperfect or ruptured sense of bodily self.

The idea of how a person experiences her feelings and protects herself within her body necessarily leads us to the concept of body boundaries. This idea, originally postulated by psychoanalysts Paul Federn (1926, 1952) and Wilhelm Reich (1945/1972), helps us understand why some individuals with a poorly functioning body boundary experience the world as strange and depersonalized. Federn believed that a strong "ego boundary" was essential for normal psychological functioning, but fluctuated in sleep, psychosis, and other states of consciousness.

We are aware that ego boundaries are eroded or taxed in those with eating disorders. For example, an anorexic patient may avoid interpersonal contact with her parents or peers, because she must maintain a rigid wall lest others fuse with her and "take over" her thoughts. Her state of emaciation is a fortress for an enfeebled body boundary that protects her from the perceived threat of invasion by another person. For example, one perceptive patient explained that if she gained weight, she knew she would have to relate more maturely with men. She felt that her anorexia helped keep them at bay and hence protected her from "sexual invasion." Her refusal to eat also seemed to convey "I take nothing in, therefore I am separate and safe."

The binge-purge cycle may be understood in some individuals as an attempt to feel one's own body more fully. Bingeing is an attempt to experience containing by exerting control over what goes in; purging defines the body boundary by explicitly keeping certain contents out. For the bulimic person, what is outside or inside the body is often quite confusing; therefore, there is a problem in establishing and maintaining normal body boundaries. One patient said, "I like to see what I had put in when I throw up. I need to *see every piece*. I know exactly what I've eaten and that I can control whatever I take in because I can get it out when I want to."

It is not uncommon to see bulimic persons struggle with addictions, sexual promiscuity, and stealing. All these activities may be, among other things, attempts to define and reestablish the body boundary. The quest to feel alive and full by taking in exciting substances, having sex, or stealing an object is fueled by experiencing one's self—and one's body—as inherently empty or dead. Such behavior often has an intoxicating and sedating impact, which perhaps eradicates a feeling of bodily inferiority while paradoxically and magically promoting a momentary feeling of strength and wholeness. In this scenario, the binge is also a surrender of control—a merging with food and a quest for nurturance. Aloneness and death are avoided by these other efforts to define the self.

As I indicated earlier, it is also not uncommon for individuals with eating disorders to experience episodes of dissociation or multiple personality disorder. In these disturbances, the person feels most disenfranchised from her own body—walled off in another state of awareness altogether or taken over by an alter personality, often of a different age and gender. One's bodily self thus becomes totally abrogated and denied. Usually there is also the illusion that more than one bodily self exists (i.e., alter personalities). One patient went so far as to "prove" she had more than one body by slicing open her arms and legs. In effect she said, "I cut one body but feel no pain in my other body." She totally resisted her therapist's attempt to convince her that she had only "one body."

Reich believed that conflict necessarily affected one's body and body boundaries, resulting in abnormal muscle tone. Conflict does affect the individual's experience of self and others. Whenever you are tense or upset from a hectic day at work, you may notice a cascading effect in your own muscles that causes you to be much less likely to give or receive affection until the tension has been discharged. In fact, many individuals who do not have eating disorders have found respite from daily stressors in regular exercise or massage therapy. Their intuitive awareness of the price they pay as individuals and in their relationships has led them to use physical touch and workouts to dissipate some of the inner turmoil.

Stress and strife do have an impact on body boundaries. Chronic conflicts may lead people to develop rigid personality styles, often causing habitually rigid body postures and expressions. Reich called this tendency "character armor" and believed that parents who emphasized inhibition and self-control raised children who tended to have an armor-hard body boundary. As adults, these children had great difficulty not only with relaxation and tension relief but also with allowing others to be close to them. This is dramatically observed among anorexic individuals who walk as if they wore a back brace; their upright posture conveys immobility of body and psyche. They maintain rigid control of each aspect of their physical selves and what they put into their bodies.

In psychoanalytic circles, people with anorexia nervosa have been pejoratively described as "anally retentive." They are the individuals who must maintain such firm control over themselves—and others—that they cannot give an inch. Inflexible and resolute, they reveal little, even to those who have known them for years. They are impenetrable and often secretive. The task of therapy for them is to loosen and dissolve their armor, but their terror of interpersonal closeness nearly always prevents them from seeking out the relationships where they might safely shed protection. Instead, they tend to live life as if in a fortress, keeping their own feelings and those of others chained in the dungeon.

## Body Dissatisfaction and the Eating Disorders

In Erica Jong's novel *Fear of Flying* (1973), she extolled in detail the erotic acrobatics of her Asian lover. She playfully nicknamed him "the perfect hairless body." Women were fascinated with the identity of this oriental Lothario, only in part because of his bedroom machismo. Because the masculine ideal is usually portrayed as hirsute, the charms of a perfect hairless body bespoke an enigma about what constituted an adroit partner.

Many American women, on the other hand, define their femininity by having a hairless body. A major study by Susan Basow (1991) examined why women actually engage in the almost "universal" behavior of hair removal. She found that the ideal of hairlessness among her cohort of women rests on concerns regarding attractiveness and social propriety. Beginning in adolescence as "the thing to do," women continue to shave because it is the norm, believing that hairlessness is more appealing to men. The seemingly trivial behavior of shaving is difficult to give up because of the social norm and women's desire to avoid social disapproval. (The study did not address other cultures such as in Europe, where shaving is less common.) Basow found hairlessness as a norm to be so pervasive that it is surprising that about 20% of all American women do not conform to it and refuse to remove leg or underarm hair even occasionally.

What does Basow's study about women and their body hair tell us about body dissatisfaction in general? First, it illustrates that so many of our ideas about our body are conditioned or habitual. Many of us shave our legs whether or not we think about doing so, much as we value a thin body size without taking into account its potential consequences. Second, if women emphasize the importance of removing body hair (much of which is unseen), how much more emphasis are they likely to assign thinness, a condition that is evident to any observer? Third, we are all subject to cultural stereotyping and unquestioned beliefs about what we deem attractive or unattractive. Men are supposed to be hairy and women are supposed to be hairless. Likewise, women are supposed to be thin—and if they are not, the culture assumes that they are unhappy, dissatisfied, lazy, slovenly, and ugly and that they need to do whatever is necessary to rectify their condition. The end result is to be more appealing and noticeable.

How much value we place on appearance and external validation, whether or not we consciously acknowledge it! In Basow's study, hair removal was a must even among strongly feminist women—those whom we likely credit with a perhaps more enlightened perspective. Because we fantasize that these women refuse to do what other more traditional women feel compelled to do, we place them above ourselves as models of courage. Most of us—no matter how much we tout feminist or liberal principles—cannot avoid the cultural imprint of what is acceptable and beautiful. Thus it is much more likely that those who struggle with an eating disorder are even more prone to be dissatisfied with their bodies. The first step in rectifying the problem is to question what we do and why we do it vis-à-vis our bodies. As women, we must start by challenging our belief in the necessity of a "perfect hairless body" as we must question the relative value of slenderness.

Evidence suggests that women with eating disorders and body image disturbance have had personal experiences with social rejection in connection with appearance. From their poll of 33,000 women, Susan Wooley and Ann Kearney-Cooke (1986) found that women with a negative body image were more likely to have had mothers who were critical of their appearance. Another large-scale survey of body image attitudes reported that childhood teasing about appearance led to a negative body image and a tendency to develop an eating disorder (Fabian and Thompson 1979). Numerous studies have shown that a high proportion of bulimic persons were overweight prior to the onset of their disorder, which suggests that they received negative feedback about their appearance as children and adolescents (Ben-Tovin and Walker 1992; Casper 1992; Steiner-Adair 1991b; Zakin 1989).

Racial differences in body image may explain the lower rate of bulimia nervosa in African American women. In comparison to white girls, fewer African American girls report trying to lose weight. In cultures where plumpness is valued, eating disorders are rare. Although social factors by themselves cannot explain the development of a negative body image in a person with an eating disorder, the cultural pressure to be thin and the negative feedback experienced when one is overweight may be predisposing social factors for other difficulties.

Body dissatisfaction in those with an eating disorder is best viewed as a multidimensional phenomenon that involves perceptual, attitudinal, and behavioral features. Hilde Bruch (1973, 1982) first observed the body image disturbance among her adolescent patients. She reported that despite their often grotesque, emaciated appearance, they showed no concern for their condition. Rather, they maintained that they were "fat." A gap had developed between the reality of their appearance and their perception of it. Bruch saw that the emphasis these women placed on their body image had reached delusional proportions, which she argued was the key to a diagnosis of anorexia nervosa.

This view was followed up by A. H. Crisp (1980), who saw anorexia nervosa as a kind of weight phobia. Experimental studies in the 1970s were undertaken to see if anorexic persons overestimate their own body size in comparison with those who are not anorexic. Studies have not confirmed these early views, however. That is, there are no consistent findings that anorexic persons markedly overestimate their body size in comparison with control subjects without eating disorders. However, it may be that in a culture with ubiquitous concern with weight, both nonanorexic and anorexic women overestimate their size (Brown 1985; Cash and Pruzinsky 1990). Clinically, treaters often observe that most patients with anorexia nervosa have some body size distortion (Rogers 1990). It is common for patients to focus on one part of their bodies as being too fat, even though any other person might deem them to be emaciated. Moreover, they show great disdain for their overall body shape, which may prove to be of greater clinical significance than any perceptual disturbance.

Many investigators and lay writers have noted how investment of self-worth in a person with an eating disorder centers on her appearance. When a woman believes that others evaluate her mainly on her appearance alone, she may have an overt or subclinical eating disorder. Often such individuals catch our attention because their statements about themselves seem so hyperbolized. Believing themselves to be of value "only when on a man's arm," they experience themselves as adornments only, and not for what they do or who they are. They will not give up their quest for the ideal even though family members will tell them over and over again, "Those hips are just in the family, sweetie." These women may seek an outpatient evaluation with their chief complaint being that they are grotesque looking, bad, greedy, lazy, or unlovable. Further investigation reveals that they may not meet all the diagnostic criteria for anorexia or bulimia nervosa per se, but they have invested their bodies with such importance that they believe they are worthless unless they lose weight.

Overall, with respect to body image disturbance, people with bulimia have not been studied as much as people with anorexia. Yet the completed studies show that bulimic individuals are inordinately concerned about shape and weight (Cooper and Taylor 1988). Patients with bulimia nervosa or subclinical bulimia nervosa frequently report that they feel fat. As a result, some researchers have argued that a negative attitude toward body shape may be of greater clinical significance than body size overestimation per se (Slade 1988; Wardle and Foley 1989; Whitehouse et al. 1988). Many of these individuals with an eating disorder describe their bodies as loathsome and repulsive, and they frequently overestimate their body weight, even though they are not obese (Strauman et al. 1991).

Both anorexic and bulimic patients who place a high personal value on body shape may exhibit depressed mood and low self-esteem manifested in a more general state of self-depreciation. They describe the terror of being touched lest someone see their cellulite; even when they are attractive, they believe they are ugly and unacceptable. Not only are they plagued by a negative body image and subsequent self-consciousness in many social situations, but they also tend to avoid any activity that would make them more aware of their physical appearance. Consequently, they may decline to participate in social outings, prefer baggy clothes to more tight-fitting ones, and avoid sexual intimacy altogether.

These individuals may confide that they feel extremely anxious about their appearance and will do anything to avoid situations that could trigger disquieting feelings. As a result, the more such women feel fat or undesirable because of a negative body image, the more likely they are to want to change their physical appearance. They are inclined to be drawn into a relentless binge-purge cycle or even to perpetuate greater restrictions to accomplish their aims. Yet they are never pleased with their body image, which Schilder called "the picture of our body that we have in our mind" (1950/1970, p. 11).

This overestimation of body dimensions is also found in other conditions. Furthermore, overestimating one's body size does not really explain why a person believes she is fat. The exact relationship between body disparagement and fear of fatness remains unclear, because the two may occur independently. The new edition of the *Diagnostic and Statistical Manual* (DSM-IV; American Psychiatric Association 1993) will correct some of this lack of clarity. To fulfill the criteria for anorexia nervosa and bulimia nervosa, *one's self-evaluation must be unduly influenced* by body shape and weight. This qualifying statement contrasts with the earlier DSM-III-R (American Psychiatric Association 1987) criteria, which describes body image distortion only as a "disturbance in the way one's body, weight, size, or shape is experienced" (p. 67).

This nuance is as important for patients as it is for clinicians and researchers. The new criteria have a less pejorative and condemnatory connotation. As a result, they help both the struggling individual and the clinician pinpoint where the source of difficulty rests—in the inordinate role that body weight and shape play in establishing how one feels about oneself.

## 🐛 Alexis's Dilemma

Alexis S., a 21-year-old Mexican American college student, assured me that she would be the worst patient I had ever worked with. When I first saw her in consultation on the East Coast at the request of two colleagues, she talked about her problem as if it were a "red badge of courage."

Born to successful first-generation immigrants from Mexico,

Alexis had inherited their dark hair and darker skin. Even though she envied her mother's beauty, she found herself wishing that she could be blonde and blue-eyed. She seemed totally obsessed with her appearance and with pleasing people and was particularly sensitive about her mother's wish for her to have "the perfect figure."

Alexis seemed driven to be the best in everything she did. In fact, the high points of her life were when she heard she was accepted into a highly prestigious university and had won her school's athletic achievement award. She explained that a rush of excitement had coursed through her when she heard the applause of the crowd. I sensed that she desperately wanted to obtain the approval from others that she wished were more forthcoming from her own parents.

Alexis began every day by looking in the mirror. She would stare at her deltoid muscles and cast her gaze downward to her thighs. If she found them to be the proper proportions, she knew she would have a good day. If she assessed them to be larger than her ideal, she castigated herself relentlessly. One would never know, from looking at Alexis on the outside, how much she struggled on the inside with self-hatred. Her facade was of a highly self-enamored young woman who described herself as "sensitive, sexy, outrageous, bubbly—and fat and stupid."

Despite Alexis's inherent abilities, she seemed increasingly preoccupied with her body image, hating what she saw. Rather insightfully, she observed that if she had to focus on anything other than her body, it might become apparent that she lacked inner substance. She believed that she had fooled her teachers into believing she was more intelligent and knew more than she really did. She also ardently believed that other people had little if anything to offer her. She hated her classes because "others simply can't tell me anything I don't already know. They are ugly and stupid, so why should I listen to anything they have to say?"

Alexis was aware that she had a severe image problem and a distorted sense of self-worth. When I commented that she seemed to be feeling a great deal of pain because of the emphasis both she and her family members had placed on her body (e.g., hating their

Mexican origin), she replied that she had a constant and persistent need to be validated. Her pursuit of center stage created a feeling inside that she could never get off the merry-go-round. She had to do more and more to feel that she had anything worthwhile to offer. Quite capable of easily charming young men, she had been unable to establish any long-lasting relationships. She found herself envious of anyone who had anything she did not.

Alexis's family constellation was similar to that of many patients with eating disorders. Her parents placed enormous emphasis on looking good at the expense of recognizing true but often unpleasant feelings. Alexis's mother had difficulty supporting her daughter emotionally and tended instead to emphasize superficial concerns. Her father, on the other hand, conveyed a powerful masculine image as he attempted to control other people. What emerged over-all was a core lack of appreciation for Alexis as a whole person. No wonder she hated her heritage; her parents had hated their own. Their attempts to emphasize ideal physical attributes had been tragically identified by Alexis as the only way to be an acceptable member of the family.

One might say that the family lacked empathy for Alexis as the person she really was. She had been pushed and prodded to be something she was not. As a result, she had become a highly inse-cure and sad young woman who outwardly appeared cocky, preoccu-pied with herself, and totally focused on her own body.

Investment in one's body to the exclusion of other concerns serves the defensive purpose of avoiding connection or dependency on others. In attempting to attune herself to what would please her parents, Alexis had to avoid or deny her own dependency needs for them. If she be-lieved her body was, indeed, the perfect container and not inferior to anyone else's in any way, then she wouldn't need her parents. However, the reality of life is that we all need other people, particularly in times of stress or change. One of the most critical periods of need is the transi-tional time, such as leaving home for college. This transition frequently marks the point at which people with body image problems begin to have real difficulty.

As Alexis did, some people will encounter demands that are beyond their emotional ability to handle alone, and they cannot continue to rely on family members or friends for emotional support. On a conscious level, both of Alexis's parents wanted to help her, but the groundwork for a relationship built on shared vulnerabilities had not been laid in her youth. When her efforts fell short, she felt belittled. In addition, an inordinate amount of attention had been centered on successful achievement of a physical image. For Alexis, her eating disorder represented a compromise against feelings of failure and inner fragmentation; to buttress her poor self-esteem, she strove to be a popular and desirable woman.

## Body Dysmorphic Disorder (Dysmorphophobia)

Body dysmorphic disorder, or the preoccupation with an imagined defect in physical appearance, is usually not associated with the eating disorders per se. However, it pertains to a different kind of profound disturbance in body image. This disorder has been described more frequently in Europe than in the United States, but it is probably more common here than generally realized. Affected individuals sometimes appear totally normal, although a slight physical anomaly may be present. The individual's reaction to the misperceived flaw is always intense.

Some of the more common features that affected persons become preoccupied with include large ears, buck teeth, a prominent nose, small genitals, and tiny breasts. It is usually difficult to persuade patients with body dysmorphic disorder to involve themselves in psychiatric treatment. This avoidance is unfortunate, because the subjective feeling that one is ugly or has a profound physical defect can lead to social withdrawal. Like an eating disorder, body dysmorphic disorder is often kept secret because the person feels humiliated and embarrassed by the obsession with ugliness. DSM-III-R precludes diagnosis of anorexia nervosa and dysmorphophobia at the same time, but both have been noted in the same person at different points in time. Both reflect a disturbed body image, but anorexia involves negative feelings about the whole body, whereas body dysmorphic disorder concerns isolated body parts.

Body dysmorphic disorder is an interesting condition because it also leads us to wonder about the point at which normal concern with physical appearance broadens to become more pathological. In psychiatry, the continuum from health to pathology arises in other areas, such as in differentiating normal grieving from deep depression. However, as we have seen, concern with physical appearance in our culture is nearly universal. In addition, cultural factors dictate how much concern should be placed on imperfection. With these caveats in mind, it is still important to note that there are individuals who are excessively preoccupied with and give undo attention to one part of their bodies. Their preoccupation should be distinguished from normal concern. Treatment may help them to give up their deeply held belief that they are deformed, thus necessarily improving their quality of life.

## At War With One's Own Body

Most of us know individuals who stay in very painful life situations despite adverse consequences. On the surface they will complain of poor relationships or recount travails that lead them to fail repeatedly at work or in love. Sometimes these individuals will participate in sexual encounters where they are physically assaulted and humiliated (sexual sadomasochism). Others may come close to establishing a goal such as graduation from a doctoral program, only to find themselves the perpetual student who is never able to complete the final dissertation.

Although many different psychological roots can lead to the final common pathway of self-sabotage (which is explored in depth in Chapter 14 on coping styles), I am emphasizing here how eating disorders express aspects of body hatred and masochism. The disorder comes to embody the quest for pleasure in pain (masochism), while the individual consciously denies this aspect of the disorder. Freud believed that masochistic issues were psychologically mysterious because they defied the pleasure principle. He wondered why people would hang on to relationships, symptoms, and sexual practices that produced such overt misery. In essence, these persons defy the pleasure principle by derailing the obligatory search to gain pleasurable sensations and avoid painful ones.

The root of masochistic conflict probably stems from the earliest time in development when the establishment of a body self is disrupted. As a result, the individual may be prone to psychosomatic reactions, eating disorders, or self-defeating patterns of behavior. In my clinical experience, it is all too common for this triad to occur together, manifesting itself in various ways. When the individual has an eating disorder, she speaks of being at war with her body and has a plethora of other physical complaints. Meanwhile, her entire life plan goes off track. The exhausting preoccupation with what can and cannot go into the body leaves less time for other pursuits. These developmental struggles, which lead to self-sabotage, are apparently based on deficits that must be repaired to put life on a better track—to stop self-defeating and masochistic patterns.

Patients who have anorexia and bulimia describe a dreaded state of being with their own bodies. As portrayed by Meredith Baxter Birney in the television movie *Kate's Secret,* this lack of an internal cohesiveness compelled lonely Kate to eat voraciously. It was as if she had no understanding of when to eat or how much to consume. Her eating disorder was an attempt to solve a severe interpersonal problem with her friends and family, but it also grew out of a state of impaired or inadequate body boundaries and deficient self-regulation. Like Agnes in the Milan Kundera quotation that opened this chapter, Kate used bingeing to make her feel alive and excited momentarily, only to have this sensation fade away as soon as she purged. She ate as if overwhelmed by an external force that later caused her great shame and pushed her into a vicious cycle of self-reproach. Likewise, patients with eating disorders seem impervious to body sensations and may even sense an estrangement from their body. They simultaneously try to feel soothed and energetic—Kundera's "fleeting redemption of the body." In dreams or in the waking state, such a patient may feel "as if my skin is being pulled off" or as if she would explode when fed. For treatment to be effective, these individuals must address aspects of the body self and integrate them along with aspects of the psychological self.

In a peculiar way, eating disorders may be an attempt to self-cure a very early developmental disturbance. Consider the infant whose cranky temperament might overwhelm a highly sensitive mother. At the other extreme is an anxious and self-involved mother who cannot adequately respond to her infant's specific needs for comforting, feeding, and so forth. In both scenarios, the end result is a baby whose development may go awry. Neither gets the necessary environmental feedback for developing an affirmed and confident sense of self. One sequel may be a false or distorted body image because of environmental or parental failure to console the child. Most likely, this disturbance occurs during the preverbal period (the first year) of life. This timing is significant because the lack of language keeps the individual from being able to talk about feelings in words but instead forces her to express them somatically or physically. Interestingly, research studies show more than 50% of eating disorder patients struggle with alexithymia, which is defined as difficulty in putting feelings and fantasies into words. We believe that this difficulty in using words or symbols causes the individual to engage in a body-oriented activity to communicate inner distress.

The somatic sensations of eating, feeling the pangs of starvation, experiencing the muscle aches of overexercise, or enduring the twinge of delicate self-cutting (self-mutilation) can all help the self to feel alive within the body as well as to regulate feeling states. In addition, these sensations preserve the individual's need for self-definition. The person with an eating disorder may be importuning us with pleas such as, "I can take in what I want and be myself. I am not my mother." To begin to separate from one's mother is always a lonely experience; while becoming autonomous, the child hopes to preserve a connection to the mother. Because food may be the first bridge between mother and infant, a problem with the regulation of eating may connote a struggle with how close or how far away one can comfortably be from one's mother.

In summary, the struggle with body image faced by patients with eating disorders derives from their difficulty with expressing feelings and in developing a full emotional life. Although researchers have debated and will continue to debate whether having a body image distortion is a necessary parameter or criterion for an eating disorder, body image problems are often noted clinically, and the concept is quite useful for developing a psychological understanding of what goes on inside these patients.

❦ Jeri T. was a 40-year-old former airline pilot and beauty queen.
Despite her obvious proficiency in a number of areas of life, she was
totally obsessed with her body image. The only time she had felt
appealing was when she had won beauty pageants (she had been a
finalist for a major international contest). When others believed she
looked attractive or sexy, she felt "fat and ugly" and had an almost
delusional belief that her long, blonde, naturally wavy hair was brit-
tle and wild.

Jeri repeatedly confided to her therapist that "I feel like I lost
20 years performing in a show because I have been so preoccupied
with how others think I should look." Her notable exhibitionistic
tendency, as conveyed by her participation in beauty pageants, was
also a way for her to hide from her feelings. She saw her fellow
contestants as individuals who were totally preoccupied with themselves, as if a title provided them with an identity. She explained
that "a lot comes from the praise I see in other people's faces. What
I feel I want are their goals, not my own."

Underlying Jeri's body preoccupation was a continual fear that
she would be humiliated. Despite the obvious intellect and skill
that enabled her to become a pilot, she was terrified of real success
when doing anything other than displaying her body. Yet even in
this area she felt pervasive shame, as if she never lived up to the
ideal that she, herself, or others had established for attractiveness—
witness how, despite her beautiful face and hair, she persisted in
believing she was unattractive. Her anorexia was actually an attempt to resolve an inner feeling of a basic defectiveness: to finally
feel whole or good about her body "if I only became thin enough."
Of course, her self-starvation was a singularly life-threatening mode
of adapting.

However, like patients who struggle with psychosomatic illness,
eating disorder patients who feel the pain of self-starvation may
actually feel more alive. In Jeri's case, starving herself meant, among
other things, that she was doing everything she could to maintain
a very fragile sense of identity. It was therefore not surprising for
Jeri to uncover in her treatment process that she had never felt
accepted by either of her parents, for whom she was nothing more

than a beauty queen. For reasons of their own, her parents were unable to provide Jeri with the kind of affirmation that helped her believe in herself. Hence she continued to seek affirmation in her body self, yet she always came up short.

Jeri had to become aware of how her emotional life had been completely cut off by her preoccupation with her body. This time-consuming task was not an easy one. Prognostically, individuals like Jeri who have a very distorted body image for a prolonged period tend also to have a high relapse rate with their eating disorder. This likelihood can be explained by the fact that many years are spent denying one's emotional life while attempting to save the autonomous self by focusing totally on one's body. As Jeri worked on the early issues in her family of origin that had contributed to her eating disorder, she had to learn a whole new repertoire of words to describe her feelings.

Finally, she had to do the hard work of mourning the loss of the perfect body image that she had so long desired. This became possible only when she saw that perfection was an illusion. She would never receive the parental approval she yearned for by achievements with her body alone. Jeri, who had become her own worst critic, had to learn that less than the ideal was acceptable—if not welcome.

Further exploration of Jeri's difficulties revealed another commonly held idea among eating disorder patients who tend to abuse their bodies with relentless self-starvation or gorging and purging. She kept alive inside herself a "bad object" who always punishes. Psychoanalyst Ronald Fairbairn (1943/1952), who called this concept "loyalty to the bad object," explained how we are unwittingly subservient to it often without even being aware of it. This focus on the self as bad may be a final commonality not only among eating disorder problems but also among psychosomatic ones. If, during development, we experienced someone on whom we profoundly depended as being rejecting—particularly when we began to launch ourselves as autonomous, self-directed individuals—then we might develop the fantasy that having anything good or developing further means loss and revenge. Thus we might unconsciously hold onto the only relationship we know—the bad object relationship.

In Jeri's case, both her parents had died when she was in her early teens. She had no way to go back and rediscover what they had really wanted from her, but in her mind she had always thought that she disappointed them by not living up to their ideals. She had not been able to fully mourn or grieve the loss of her parents, but her earliest memories of both of them were that they were entirely dissatisfied with her. The objective reality of Jeri's life will never be known, but Jeri herself firmly believed that she was a worthless and disappointing daughter. The only way she could maintain any link to her memory of her parents was to stay in her defeated position, thereby remaining loyal to them even as they unconsciously punished her for not living up to their ideals. Her attempt to control her body by taking in very little food was also a way for her to control the dissatisfied inner parents, whom she viewed as being abusive. She could listen to their admonitions to be beautiful whatever the cost, but she could not listen to her own feelings.

## Conclusion

Body image difficulties are likely to continue to play a prominent role in the symptomatology of people with eating disorders. These difficulties stem from the earliest times of life and often reflect failures in the individual process of separating from the family of origin in an age-appropriate way and thereby attaining autonomous functioning. Because these separation problems occur so early, individuals may lack the ability and words to express their feelings. Nevertheless, those feelings become concretely expressed through the body.

Despite prompting and urging from concerned people in the patient's life, the body may be used in a highly self-destructive fashion. The eating disorder is a failed solution—but nonetheless an attempt—to correct these very early deficits in self-esteem and strivings for independent functioning. The body is abused in part to engage the caretaking person, albeit often unconsciously. The aim is to finally control or master the most noxious influences from one's early life. In a sense, both the self and the most important persons in the individual's life are punished. An eating disorder is a painful and self-abusive way to attain self-definition and independence, perhaps only in part—but always at great cost.

In the treatment process, these individuals must learn that they are using the eating disorder to make significant statements about their need to suffer. They must be helped to voice their concerns about control, their struggles for autonomy, and their memories of deprivation. One can view the eating disorder as a way for the body to speak about issues of concern that were raised very early on, when words were not available. We may never know precisely what happened in childhood, but we must take what these patients believe happened to them as children seriously and as a crucial component of their reality. Only then will they begin to trust enough to take the risk of revealing their desperate but unmet needs in treatment.

Eating disorder patients must learn to respect the inner messages from their bodies that have been neglected for the longest time. The physical sensations created by self-starvation, gorging, and purging may be physically and psychologically discomforting. But they are also a way to feel alive and to thereby preserve the body from a potentially greater demise—psychological death.

How the psyche and the soma interrelate remains an enigma. It is quite unlikely that any medication or short-term treatment process will ever cure the most severe eating disorder because of the deep and unconscious way that the illness preserves body limits and boundaries. In essence we are asking patients to learn to speak with a new language—the language of words—instead of their body language, and this process is likely to take a good deal of time. They must learn to master rather than avoid whatever it is that their eating disorder has protected them from. They must convert the pleasure and pain of their eating disorder to a more constructive use, so that they can experience the pleasurable fatigue after a full day's work, the pursuit of high personal goals, and the joys of long-term commitment in relationships. Finding the words to express the pain helps these individuals define themselves in a way that can allow them to begin filling an emotional hunger formerly expressed by the eating disorder. More recently, experiential therapies (e.g., massage, biofeedback, movement therapy) have been used in treating people with eating disorders. These modalities may be particularly helpful because they help define the body boundaries in less destructive ways. They help develop the individual's capacity for an inner image of the body without having to resort to excruciating and dangerous means of experiencing it. These treatment modalities also help the individual to feel purged or rid of the "bad object" and to find affirming and life-enhancing "good objects" in treaters.

Ultimately, the need to control one's body through the eating disorder must be reframed so that the individual learns there are other ways to self-regulate, soothe, and affect the body. The tendency to stay enmeshed with a bad internal object must be replaced by relying on others for more positive, affirming bonds. Gradually the patient learns that greater control of her body comes not from denying it but rather from affirming it, which results in a firmer sense of psychological self and improved body image. This step toward separation involves giving up the old modes of coping, which will need to be mourned. But the individual should become enabled through good treatment to vent the tears and pain in words instead of food rituals, asceticism, and other psychosomatic problems.

# 8

# Fasting on Love: Concerns About Sexuality and Pregnancy

I paint myself because I am so often alone.

Frida Kahlo

Like many women today who struggle with eating disorders, the Depression-era Mexican painter Frida Kahlo was a charismatic, vibrant personality with the power to attract men and women. Married to the Mexican muralist Diego Rivera, Kahlo indulged in her own affairs of the heart, although she herself was often devastated by her husband's well-known and compulsive infidelity. Despite the fact that she was a rare beauty, a mesmerizing companion, and an excellent artist (who recently has been "rediscovered"), Kahlo remained resolutely insecure about her femininity and sexual power. Continually worrying about maintaining a slender figure, she wore long skirts in an effort to appear thinner. She eschewed the size of her portly mother and plump sisters. The time she spent adorning herself in native Mexican costumes and making her appearance meticulous and alluring hid her deeper insecurities. Still, they became manifest in her discussions with friends and physicians, with whom she found it much easier to speak of life and love than to actually enjoy living.

Kahlo's penchant for painting, however, led her to convey the depth of her misery and obsession in oils, particularly in self-portraits of disfigured and distorted bodies, all of which still retained her strikingly magnetic face (e.g., *A Few Small Nips*, 1935; *My Nurse and I*, 1937; *The Two Fridas*, 1939). Just as one would never suspect the range of sexual concerns and conflicts that perplex persons with eating disorders, one would never know by looking at many of Kahlo's paintings that she was similarly troubled throughout her life. Her fascinating but haunting biography also exemplifies a truism of psychotherapeutic practice, if not of life itself: what often appears on the surface is but a mirage masking deeper preoccupations and conflicts. Just as Kahlo often found herself to be alone, so it is with eating disorder patients who feel isolated as they rivet their attention on their bodies instead of those closest to them.

Two of life's most basic activities—sex and eating—are commonly linked. Traditionally, eating together communally occurs after any type of festive gathering—weddings, funerals, graduations, and birthdays. In the biblical account of the marriage at Cana, for example, Jesus turned the water into wine as part of the feast celebrating the couple's union.

Rollicking jokes often associate eating and sexuality, particularly by addressing the ravenous feelings that occur after a lively but exhausting night of lovemaking. Indeed, any intense sensation may seem heightened after a passionate encounter. Witness the literary allusions to the unusual tastiness of a cheese omelet or pancakes after a night of amore. Not surprisingly, courtship, from time immemorial, has occurred over tea and cookies or a good meal. As the cliché says, the way to a man's heart is through his stomach! This traditional way of wooing one's beloved speaks to the unconscious equation of love and food but also alters that equation to make it a bit more precise. Just as the original feeding relationship between a mother and child stimulates and molds their bond, so too can a couple build their relationship around food. Imagine a new couple sharing a romantic evening over a candlelight dinner with wine, music, and succulent food. As they gaze into each other's eyes and talk of their love for each other, are they not "making love" in their minds?

The kitchen is the central site of activity in most homes. As we take in food, we also take in the experience of our family members who share their helpful, altruistic concern for us and our lives together. In addition to this early mode of nurturance, partners who give willingly of themselves are reexperienced by their lovers as able ultimately to provide more than a filling repast. By offering to give what is most needed and necessary for their loved ones' bodily sustenance, they revive earlier modes of comfort while paving the way for adult gratifications.

It follows that the mere presence of an eating disorder suggests an inability to receive the same gratification of love and bring it to fruition in the form of life-enhancing sexuality. Clinical experience reveals that patients with eating disorders may have a range of sexual problems. Although they insist to their loved ones how much they deplore these difficulties, their problems nevertheless remain inscrutable to themselves and to others. Meanwhile, they may seek treatment for their sexual dysfunction, only to befuddle those who try to help them get well.

Hilda Bruch's contribution to our current understanding of anorexic persons neglected the host of sexual problems that also befell them, although she emphasized their need to establish a secure sense of self and to separate emotionally from their mothers (1974, 1982, 1988). Still, patients with eating disorders have many questions, concerns, and shameful past experiences and ideas about sex that lead them to hide their suffering from others. They tend to restrict their sexual interest and pleasure much as they do adequate and normal eating.

Let's examine some of the specific issues with respect to sexuality that trouble patients with eating disorders. Learning some facts about commonly asked questions can help us address speculation about their underlying issues. Not all women will want or need to make sexuality a major part of their lives; their direction will take them to other places. For those that do, the more we grasp what impedes their sexual expression, the more we can overcome those blocks, ultimately making sex more vibrant and fulfilling for the person with an eating disorder.

## ❧ Sexual Issues in Anorexia Nervosa

Lori Ann U., a 23-year-old married secretary who was also completing a cosmetology program, had restricted her eating since eighth grade. Her sexual difficulties paralleled those of other patients treated over the years in an outpatient clinic. Although Lori Ann's weight was low for her height, she was able to avoid hospitalization. However, she was unable to avoid the tenseness she continually felt about her own sexuality.

Married at age 19½, Lori Ann had felt no real desire for sex since high school. She had always been afraid of intercourse and was a virgin when she married. Her first attempt at intercourse was quite painful, and she avoided consummating her marriage for 9 months. Her main complaint now centered on her lack of desire for any kind of sexual activity. She insisted that she "never really liked it."

With the exception of a few episodes of coitus after her marriage, Lori Ann had been unwilling and unable to engage in sex. Her natural lubrication was scant, her vagina tight, and she experienced such intense pain that she was actively considering divorce when she sought an evaluation. This possibility frightened her deeply, because she also depended on her husband for her sense of security.

Lori Ann's dearth of sexual functioning was in sharp contrast with her earlier achievement in school and at work. In high school, she had been elected homecoming queen twice and had been voted "best dressed" of her senior class. Always able to secure good jobs and high pay as a secretary for several entrepreneurs, her aspirations and natural appeal led her to pursue additional training in cosmetology. The youngest in a close-knit family, Lori Ann had four older brothers who had all married and settled near their parents' home. She found it difficult to disagree with her parents, and they seldom discussed even typical adolescence conflicts such as how late to stay out and what job to take. She had serious questions about her future and wanted to become more independent. The main theme that surfaced in her evaluation was her conscious wish to be lovingly cared for and adored by others, versus a deep desire to be bolder, more independent, and self-directed.

Because Lori Ann derived pleasure from making others happy, she believed she could not speak up for herself and so hid her genuine feelings under a veneer of congeniality. When the psychologist asked, as part of her evaluation, what Lori Ann would most like to be if she were anything other than human, she answered that she would like to be an expensive brooch, because then she would be taken care of and would not have to worry. That response reflected her wish to be valuable and to stand out in the crowd even while she was also being protected from life's dangers. Her fantasy to be a brooch also signified her desire to be held and admired but not penetrated.

Lori Ann emphasized control in her life. Whether it involved suppressing her feelings and behavior, or conflicts about whether she or others would assume dominance in a particular interaction, her desire for power was an organizing factor in her life. Beneath that wish for total control, she experienced an inner mayhem of intense feelings that intruded persistently into her life. Anorexia had actually been a rather creative (albeit self-destructive) way for her to master these feelings and worries.

In her interpersonal relationships, Lori Ann seemed to be battling over who would win and who would lose. Her sexuality represented a loss of control, and as such it evoked deep resentment and rage. Although Lori Ann loved her husband, giving in to her sexual desires made her feel dominated when, in fact, she wished to assert control over others. In individual psychotherapy, she explored what life experiences had placed her in such a bind that she desired, yet was blocked from finding, life's most fulfilling experiences. In essence, she had no awareness of genuine sexual needs, just as she had little appreciation for genuine hunger. She offered her sexuality in exchange for nurturance but did not own her own body.

Not surprisingly, as Lori Ann began to trust her treaters, she confided that she had always been perplexed and wounded by what she perceived as her parents' very troubled marriage. She could not remember ever having observed any loving interactions or meaningful relatedness between them. She lamented the fact that she also had an unsatisfactory marriage. Like many people, Lori Ann found it impossible to have something better than what her own mother had, although she was not fully aware of all the reasons why she could not permit herself to have full sexual expression and loving interaction.

Lori Ann's case demonstrates how the conflictual areas of sexuality, feminine identity, and love relationships can all impinge on the developing adolescent and help create the final common pathway to anorexia nervosa. After anorexia develops, normal sexual interest and participation wane all the more. The well-known manifestation of amenorrhea results from prepubertal or pubertal levels of hormones in up to 90% of anorexic individuals. Thus both physiological and psychological factors are likely to cause the sexual blocks.

Whether a specific physical or psychological factor leads to the problem of anorexia nervosa remains a question still open to scientific debate. But as we see in Lori Ann's case, the seeds for her eating disorder were planted in the childhood experience of a difficult parental relationship and came to fruition in her adolescence, when she was confronted with sexual feelings brought on by physical maturation. Most likely, both biology and family history played a role in Lori Ann's anorexia. All personal disruptions ultimately affect the brain and its intricate neurochemical workings, which then go on to influence behavior in enigmatic but fundamental ways.

In Lori Ann's case, having four brothers may also have affected her sense of femininity. Tight control over herself helped her maintain appropriate boundaries with the boys but precluded a deeper awareness of her own female genitals. For Lori Ann, being a woman was "only skin deep."

Lori Ann's feelings of guilt about going far enough in life to surpass her own mother are a common but often unconscious concern. Girls also tend to feel more guilty about touching and knowing their physical bodies than do boys. The woman-to-be views herself, particularly her sexual self, as "dirty." Of course, this negative view is reinforced by our culture, which gives a multitude of conflicting messages to girls. On the one hand, we should stay pristine and pure while our male peers may acquiesce to the all-too-human wish to be dirty, wild, active, and passionate. Yet, when they marry, women should be ready, willing, and able to express their passion in the marital boudoir.

This admixture of competing cultural messages, which are then transcribed and translated by parents, teachers, and friends, underscore for the woman that her sexual instincts or drives are not as acceptable as those of men. Her dirtiness is further inculcated by messages about menstrual staining and the booming business of feminine hygiene products (e.g., deodorant sanitary pads, douches). Indeed, until recently, even female sexual fantasies—let alone actions—have been vehemently discouraged. One result is that as the woman-to-be reaches adolescence, she feels punishment for any breakthrough of her sexual drive. She seeks to control her sexuality to the greatest degree possible, lest she be rejected or punished for becoming out of hand. For some, sexuality is more to be "put up with" for the sake of the man rather than to be enjoyed. Many women still take to heart the wedding night advice once given by Victorian mothers to their daughters: Close your eyes, hold your breath, and think of England.

Lori Ann was therefore struggling with the double burden of betraying her mother by outdoing her and of giving in to impulses that both she and her mother found despicable in women. By trying so hard to control herself—and others—Lori Ann was thus being completely loyal not only to the cultural stereotype of what a woman should be, but also to what she believed her mother wanted her to be. The tragedy was that Lori Ann was prohibited from any pleasurable bodily experience, whether eating or sex. Yet triumphing over her impulses to such a finely tuned degree made her feel strong and secure in other ways. It reinforced her belief that she was an independent, competent person who could master her passions, even at great personal cost.

Treatment helps by clarifying the individual psychological struggles that underlie concerns about sexuality. However, if the person is dealing with underlying issues of guilt about doing better than the parents or struggling with what happens on losing control, therapy is bound to take some time. The mechanism can be explained, but it takes persistence and motivation to work through and incorporate new insights. It is like learning any new skill. Some of the basics are taught relatively quickly, but to master their intricacies and derive pleasure from them takes patience and practice.

Along the way, reading books about sexuality can help the individual to feel more self-accepting. I recommend Nancy Friday's books about female sexual fantasy: *My Secret Garden* (1973); *Forbidden Flowers: More Women's Sexual Fantasies* (1975). In addition, Ruth Westheimer's *Guide to Good Sex* (1983) and Lonnie Barbach's *For Yourself: The Fulfillment of Female Sexuality* (1976) are excellent resources for more general information about sex. Because these books can also stir questions and anxieties about conflictual areas, it is best to review these slowly and patiently, perhaps also talking about the material with a trusted friend or therapist.

Discussing sex in support groups or psychotherapy groups can help patients acquire a wealth of information from their peers. Skilled therapists should be involved in such meetings so they can answer questions and clarify misconceptions and "old wives' tales." Misinformation about sex is literally boundless. But through education and discussion, patients learn that they are not losing control, behaving badly, or being "whorish" or disappointing by becoming more aware of their sexual responses. They also learn about the connections between their sexuality and eating disorders. For example, one patient who had been sexually abused by her uncle equated eating with sluttishness. Because she ate to give up sexual desire, her moderate obesity was an obvious sign of her sexual sinfulness. Talking with others about sex permits acceptance of one's drives, fears, and attitudes. It also confronts the notion that the woman is the passive recipient of the man's wishes, with no ability of her own to initiate or terminate an encounter. Learning to experience and to love one's own body often feels safer than exploring it first with a partner. Healthy self-direction of feelings is thus asserted by making sexual desire more welcome and gratifying.

## Sexual Issues in Bulimia Nervosa

Although more research must address the difference between anorexia nervosa and bulimia in regard to psychosexual functioning, some major differences play a role in treatment. In contrast to anorexic patients, who restrict both their caloric intake and their sexual activity, bulimic patients tend to have more past and current sexual involvements. In addition, bulimic patients tend to be more sexually active than individuals who do not have eating disorders. In our experience, some bulimic patients use sex to find comfort and connection with an available partner. Although their behavior may be overtly sexual, it masks a form of childlike relatedness that is a plea for nurturance.

In essence, sexuality is one way to draw a mother figure or mother substitute closer. The partner may be either male or female, because the individual is not looking so much for a compatible and complementary partner as she is attempting to experience herself as more whole and alive. Sex, like bingeing, is an attempt to fill a void. The physical aspect of the relationship alleviates terrifying anxiety and brings the other person close through the union of bodies. Such fusion is often experienced to such a degree that the patient loses sight of any boundaries between herself and her partner. Although it is sought after, this merger can also be a paradoxically terrifying experience that leads to a temporary loss of identity—that is, the patient loses her sense of who she is and where her body ends and her partner's begins.

Some bulimic patients have multiple sex partners but do not really enjoy their sexual relationships. Yet their ardent, compulsive search for partners serves to stymie their inner fragmentation while providing a soothing, caring presence. Such patients will do anything and risk anything—even AIDS—to avoid this inner experience of abandonment. What appears a ploy for sexual fulfillment and experience is really not sexual at all. Instead, it is an attempt to pull out all the stops so as to feel excited and alive while anchored to another person.

❦ Janie V., age 22, had bulimia as well as a problem with compulsive shopping. Despite a college degree from a prestigious university on the West Coast, stylish clothes, and a winning way with people, she was a frightened and lonely woman. She told her therapist that she never felt nurtured by her highly self-involved, depressed mother. Janie had always been popular with boys and often willingly gave in to their sexual advances. Yet when she was questioned in psychotherapy about the meaning of her sexual proclivities, Janie confided that she seldom felt sexually aroused. She was not particularly inhibited or ashamed of her body. On the contrary, when involved in foreplay or sexual intercourse, she experienced a hitherto unknown sense of nurturance and emotional connection to her partner. For the same reason, she compulsively sought out food and material possessions. Like sex, either could quell the overwhelming loneliness and angst she had grown to despise and shun at all costs.

Janie herself realized that her sexual liaisons seemed to give her a form of parenting she had sought but not attained at home. Janie's therapist suggested that she attempt to fulfill her legitimate needs for physical holding in a less dangerous way than by sexual acting-out behavior. She might benefit, for example, from getting regular massages and continuing to verbalize her needs in therapy. (Professional masseurs and masseuses provide safe touching while also helping the individual experience deep relaxation.) Although the therapist maintained appropriate professional boundaries with Janie by not touching and holding her, this emphasis on touch permitted Janie to understand her needs for caretaking and to get them met realistically.

Janie gradually began to be able to meet her needs in ways other than by finding almost interchangeable sexual partners. The supportive contact of therapy, the use of medication, massage, and exercise therapy, and the availability of nursing staff members all helped Janie calm the storms of intense anxiety she felt because she had not been appropriately soothed as an infant. Not surprisingly, these techniques also added to the greater command she felt over her bulimia and compulsive shopping, the other coping devices she had used to experience self-soothing.

### ❦ Dampening the Fire

Some bulimic patients completely stifle their sexuality. For Sally W., the roots of her inhibited sexual response were established early in childhood. When Sally was only 7 years old, her mother died after a prolonged illness (systemic lupus erythematosus). Reared by her father, Sally had often felt lonely because he worked long hours and had little time to spend with her, although he devotedly provided for her financial needs.

Sally's father refused to allow her to talk about her deceased mother, however, because the loss continued to pain him. Consequently, Sally had never been able to fully mourn her mother's death. It is difficult enough for young children to express their feelings about loss in words. But since Sally was not allowed to talk about her mother, she never dealt with her intense feelings about her mother's illness and death.

Sally's arrested sexuality signified a psychological compromise. Her denial of her own sexuality permitted her to believe that she could always be a little girl who might recover her lost mother. Her inability to develop a relationship with a man was not the only aspect of her life that hindered her happiness, but it contributed to her feelings of loneliness and ineptness.

On the other hand, Sally's sexual restraint also kept her close to her father. She had already lost one parent and could not bear to lose another. If she became sexually functional, she might have to give up her close (albeit ambivalent) tie to her father.

For Sally, both the eating disorder and impaired sexuality clearly represented a compromise between her dependent childlike self and her potential for independent adulthood. She never fully challenged or went beyond either parent. Remaining ill ensured her the closeness and parenting she had missed early in life from her mother.[1]

In Sally's case, the death of her mother had various meanings for her father. By not allowing Sally to talk about her mother and by not talking about her himself, he failed to convey to her the genuine love he had held for his wife. Sally also felt guilty that she was alive while her mother had died—and because she had "taken" her father away from her mother.

Because her mother was dead, Sally could not see how her wishes

---

[1] The little girl needs for her father to awaken and accept her sexuality in an appropriate (and boundaried) fashion. In expressing love for the mother, the father shows that he finds her sexuality pleasing. If, however, he devalues his wife or conveys that she has been an inadequate mate in any one of a number of ways, he implies to the daughter that her own feminine self should not blossom in full form in front of him.

toward union with her father, and eventually other men, would not "undo" her mother or invite rejection from her. In suppressing her sexuality as an adult woman, Sally was in essence saying to her mother, "I will remain loyal to you and never challenge you, even after death. I am innocent. I would never want my father or any other man for myself. I know you cannot have a man now, so I will not have one either."

Children who have lost a parent often have difficulty feeling that it is acceptable and natural for them to succeed in love and in work. Many patients with eating disorders must deal with unresolved grief from childhood, adolescence, and adulthood. In Sally's case, her eating disorder and inhibited sexuality could be worked through only when she recognized that she had been unable to address her loss of her mother. As she began to do so in treatment, she felt freer to try to achieve more in her life.

First, though, Sally had to recognize that she was not permitting herself to have more in life because she had not given up either the fantasy that her mother would return or her strong childlike loyalty to her mother. Therapy helped Sally understand that she could live only her own life, not her mother's life. Having a female treater who was married and had children of her own provided Sally with a new "object of identification"—a person whom Sally could model herself after who would be able to survive Sally's forward movement in life.

To facilitate a child's development, parents need to take pleasure in and accept their own sexual identities as male and female. If both parents enjoy their own sexuality as well as the sexuality of their mate, they will convey to their children their respect for the complementarity of the sexes. The mother affirms her daughter's sexuality not only by valuing her own femaleness, but also by championing her husband's maleness as separate but also worthwhile and gratifying. In so doing, she imbues her daughter with the sense that what a man has to offer, including his penis, is valuable and enjoyable.

On the father's part, he should adore rather than envy the competence and attractiveness of his wife. He should also permit the full flowering of his daughter's attachment to him without violating intergenerational boundaries. He thus presents himself as a secure object to be loved and who can handle the passionate forays of the female. If the parents cannot provide this type of nurturing climate, the daughter's feminine self will not flourish, and she may develop an eating disorder as well as other difficulties.

## Eating Disorders and Pregnancy

Many women with eating disorders have been able to become pregnant and carry their babies successfully to term. These women may question the effect of their eating disorder on the fetus, even while hoping that pregnancy will lessen if not produce total remission of their symptoms. Because pregnancy is a time of many psychological shifts as the woman reflects on the responsibilities of motherhood, it can herald the development of an eating disorder. The fact that an eating disorder can surface during pregnancy and continue afterwards is arguably stronger evidence that these disorders stem from individual psychological conflicts. Still, most of the research on pregnancy and eating disorders is based on studies of women who became pregnant after developing an eating disorder. The major concern for most women centers on whether their eating disorder will cause a fetal abnormality. One study reported that infants born to bulimic mothers may run a higher incidence of cleft lip and cleft palate. Nevertheless, most women can rest assured that major birth defects do not accompany anorexia nervosa or bulimia nervosa. Some women also worry that psychotropic medication for depression and eating disorders might be harmful to the fetus. These mothers-to-be are preoccupied with their desire to be good parents, and they want to do whatever is necessary to avoid hurting their unborn children.

Patients under the care of a knowledgeable psychiatrist should feel reassured that tricyclic antidepressants can be used, although some medications (such as monoamine oxidase inhibitors) should be avoided. The risk of fetal abnormality subsequent to eating disorders has not yet been fully substantiated and may be linked to other factors such as heredity or concomitant drug and alcohol abuse. In fact, a large percentage of women will experience remission of their bulimic symptoms during pregnancy. These mothers-to-be refrain from bulimia because while pregnant they experience their bodies as belonging to their babies, not themselves. Although a number of patients will revert to their old coping patterns under the stress of motherhood, others will experience for the first time the feelings of mastery over and success with normal eating after the birth of their babies. Pregnancy may not inoculate against bulimic or anorexic symptoms, but it can produce at least one positive outcome—greater control over the eating disorder.

Pregnancy stresses not only the body but also the psyche. Most women intuitively know, as they confront the new joys and challenges of prospective motherhood, that their lives will change dramatically. The resulting stress means that, even under the most beneficent of conditions such as a supportive spouse and an extended nurturing family, most women will find themselves worrying about the outcome of their pregnancy: Will the baby be healthy? Will she (the mother) be a good parent? How much will the eating disorder affect the capacity to mother? Like any great opportunity for positive good, pregnancy invariably carries with it great risk as well.

In bringing new life into the world, women must necessarily put their own lives into perspective. Mothers-to-be realize that they touch future generations in concrete ways, so they should deal with their own issues of mortality and immortality. Even the dreams of pregnant women highlight such themes. Dream images of dense jungle growth, the ebb and flow of moving waters, the conjoining and eventual separation of bodies of water vivify the psychological concerns the pregnant woman has about the growth occurring in her own body. She also first engages in a struggle she will negotiate over a lifetime: How will she remain emotionally close to her child while allowing appropriate experiences of separation?

Women with eating disorders or other psychological problems would be wise to resist the temptation to terminate treatment during pregnancy because of convenience, other commitments, or financial strain. Ongoing therapy can help the pregnant woman sort out her legitimate concerns and gain a sense of command over them. At this time, more than any other, she may benefit from discussing her hopes, fears, and dreams for her child and herself. A concerned therapist can also provide important education about pregnancy. For example, a support group at UCLA for bulimic pregnant mothers encouraged openness about any and all questions that came up regarding pregnancy (Edelstein and King 1992). Many of the members believed that mother and baby share a common stomach and that purging would evacuate the stomach contents of both, which would lead to compromised nutrition for the fetus. The women in the group experienced great relief when they learned that both mother and baby have separate stomach contents and that purging will not necessarily damage the baby.

Women with eating disorders also struggle with how to feed their children appropriately. Restrictive eating behavior in mothers has occasionally been linked to restrictive feeding practices that are inappropriate or unhealthy for infants or small children. Because they themselves are preoccupied with their weight, the mothers fear that their children will become fat. They refuse to feed them carbohydrates and protein, both of which are necessary for growth and development. This dilemma is beautifully illustrated by a scene in the Japanese film *Tampopo*, in which a young Japanese boy carries a sign from his mother that he should not be fed anything sweet. A passerby stops and feeds him an ice-cream cone, which the youngster naturally and defiantly relishes.

Women with eating disorders can benefit from nutritional counseling that stresses the different needs of adults and children. They should also be reminded that, beyond early infancy, they will not be able to control much of what their children will taste or experience in the world. This reality is all the more reason for women who struggle with issues of control to stay in treatment or support groups that can help them deal with their intense reactions when their children assert age-appropriate independence and challenge them.

Birth will also reawaken conflicts the mother had with her own mother. She may be especially preoccupied with concerns about autonomy and separateness. New mothers are prone to wonder: Who am I? Where do I belong? Am I still attractive? Can I be sexual or a wife and mother only? As these questions come to the fore, eating disorder symptoms may return.

Through it all, the mother-to-be should remember that she will occasionally feel very stressed in her multiple roles. She may not have had the ideal nurturance in her own early life. Consequently, she may worry about her ability to give adequately to her child. Being able to take advantage of parenting support groups, discussions with other women, and treatment itself will allay some of these concerns. But pregnancy also provides a time to "fall in love" in a new way. After all, the eating disorder has often so preoccupied the individual that she has not been able to take full advantage of her relationships. Having a baby allows her not only to experience anew her capacity to love but also to expand her own capacity to be loved.

## A Treatment that Failed

As noted earlier, sometimes pregnancy stimulates anorexia nervosa or bulimia nervosa for the first time. In view of all the conflicts produced by sexuality, femininity, and the responsibility of childbearing, it is understandable that pregnancy will tax any psychological system.

❦ For Miranda Y., an elegant 35-year-old divorced woman of Basque descent, motherhood seemed closely linked to her eating disorder. Before becoming pregnant, Miranda had functioned well despite her early years of abject poverty and physical and emotional abuse.

Miranda's father had renounced his paternity of her, angrily accusing his wife of having had an affair while he participated actively in the Basque separatist conflict. Both her parents often used the most vile language to curse her, and they also slapped her and refused to support her in any positive endeavor. Despite always feeling demeaned and rejected, Miranda was able to finish her college degree in economics and landed a successful job in New York after immigrating to the United States.

Beauty was important to Miranda. Her own physical attractiveness no doubt helped her find employment at the United Nations, where she met her future husband. After their whirlwind courtship and marriage, however, he later betrayed her by engaging in multiple infidelities. Perhaps more tragically, Miranda found that he kept many financial secrets from her. They eventually had to declare bankruptcy because of his failed financial ventures.

Soon after marrying, Miranda became pregnant. But her marriage quickly deteriorated because of her husband's lying and their numerous separations after bitter arguments. Although Miranda accepted responsibility for herself and her child after the divorce, she found motherhood extremely taxing. She continued to work but often forced herself to exist on a restrictive diet or else would engage in purging after eating. She developed physical complaints in several body systems, although various physicians could find nothing physically wrong with her. By the time Miranda's daughter was 4 years old, it was clear that their parental roles had been reversed. Years sooner than most would be able to, Miranda's daughter could relate her mother's life history to her treatment team in the eating disorders program. She also urged Miranda to accept responsibility for herself and to find a way of curtailing her eating disorder.

From the first, it was clear that Miranda struggled with very serious psychopathology. She had grown up under the most horrendous circumstances, oppressed by economic deprivation and severe psychological and physical abuse. Despite her impoverished background, she had pulled herself up by her bootstraps and had been able to function competently until the birth of her daughter overburdened her.

One interpretation of Miranda's dilemma focused on her difficulty in mothering when she herself had had such poor mothering. To her credit, she had been able to give her daughter some appropriate mothering, and they both considered their relationship to be more positive than negative. Yet Miranda wished that both her treaters and her daughter could provide her with the nurturance she had never had. Miranda's eating disorder and her many somatic complaints served partly as maneuvers to gain the guidance and nurturance hitherto lacking in her life. Highly attuned to recognizing what others wanted from her, Miranda thought that by pleasing them she would find the warmth, soothing, and sense of peace she desperately needed. This pursuit, manifested in numerous psychiatric complaints and conditions, left her with little time or energy to spare for appropriately parenting her daughter.

Miranda's situation demonstrates how pregnancy itself can overload an already compromised individual whose life has been disrupted and derailed by trauma. Only after being appropriately cared for, which enables us to accept appropriate caretaking, can we give to others. Miranda wanted to be a good mother, but she lacked internal resources that would allow her to be such. Instead, like many other survivors of trauma, she tended to find herself in abusive relationships, because no friend met all her needs. She also provocatively attempted to get others to abuse her. No therapist or supportive friend was ever "enough" to give Miranda all that she wanted. In each therapeutic relationship, she would start out believing that at last she had found the perfect treater to understand and soothe her. But Miranda would quickly find her idealization of the therapist fading whenever perfect understanding and a reversal of fortune were not immediately forthcoming. She would then devalue the treatment and leave it.

Of course, this process paralleled Miranda's own internal state. Although she felt good about some aspects of herself and her accomplishments, she had also internalized her parents' early view of herself as someone who should be mistreated and hated. Feeling so desperate and needy inside herself, Miranda had little nurturance to give anyone else, let alone much ability to use her innate resourcefulness in fulfilling the special needs of a young child. Thus her eating disorder, which began after her daughter's birth, was a cry for help—a way of saying she had nothing left to give and needed to be fed herself.

One of Frida Kahlo's paintings depicts just the kind of dilemma Miranda must have felt she faced. In *My Nurse and I* (1937), Kahlo depicts herself in the arms of a Mexican Indian wet nurse; she has the body of an infant but the head of herself as an adult woman. She is suckling the wet nurse's breast. Like Miranda, Kahlo knows she is an adult, but her unmet needs and desires make her wish to be the small infant that suckles.

Rather than be a mother herself, Miranda wanted and needed to be mothered. Before her pregnancy, she could hold these desires at bay. But after her daughter was born, life took too much out of her. All of us may, in times of stress, feel temporarily like a raging infant inside that must be given attention and caretaking. Most of the time, this fleeting feeling can be satisfied when a supportive significant other, friend, parent, or therapist steps into the role of caretaker. But it requires us to allow ourselves to depend on another person without feeling either threatened or burdensome. Such brief returns to more childlike behavior are part and parcel of the course and expectations of everyone's life.

For someone whose past is as full of deprivation and abuse as Miranda's, a regression of this nature is not temporary. Those who have not had consistently loving parents to allow them to grow up will continue to search relentlessly for the experience. Like the infant-adult in Kahlo's painting, they recognize their babylike desires for nurturance, even though their bodies are grown up. For these people, an eating disorder can signal a return to a more childlike mode of adaptation in search of someone who will finally have the right "milk" to restore them to life.

## Conclusion

Mature sexuality and pregnancy pose unique challenges for individuals who struggle with anorexia nervosa or bulimia nervosa. Early sexual and physical abuse may trigger feelings of being unclean or unworthy because of the innate sexual drive. These individuals may also feel empty and demoralized, with a full response to sexuality engendering an even greater feeling of self-fragmentation. By inhibiting their sexual response, these people may feel greater control over themselves and their partners. This control may be especially important if they feel a lack of competence in other areas of their lives.

In addition, such individuals may feel guilty about being happy and fulfilled whenever they respond sexually. This feeling of guilt can be linked to an experience of competitiveness with one's parents, with the guilt occurring whenever one does better. Individuals with an eating disorder should therefore learn new ways of nurturing themselves, especially—but not exclusively—in the realm of sexuality. Only when they feel free to have more success or satisfaction in every sector of their lives will they be able to truly say they have overcome their eating disorder. To establish this degree of self-acceptance requires the individual who has an eating disorder to address how she might unwittingly reenact old patterns of abuse or restraint. She can then avoid such reenacting and live her own life to the fullest—doing better in the process than her own mother did.

This unconscious burden of guilt may affect not only what is taken in as food, but also what is experienced as the sensual side of life. This sensuality may manifest itself in love of music, art, one's significant other, and even one's own baby. It requires the eating disorder patient to relinquish her earlier adaptational mode of having less for herself so that she can find new ways to permit herself to have more.

# 9

# Swallowing Anger and Despair: The Impact of Physical and Sexual Abuse

There was a time when men were kind
When their voices were soft
And their words inviting
There was a time when love was blind
And the world was a song
And the song was exciting

Then it all went wrong.

I dreamed a dream in time gone by
When hope was high
And life worth living.
I dreamed that love would never die
I dreamed that God would be forgiving
There I was young and unafraid
And dreams were made and used
And wasted

There was no ransom to be paid
No song unsung
No wine untasted
But the tigers come at night
With their voices soft as thunder
As they tear your hope apart
As they turn your dream to shame.

I had a dream my life would be
So different from this hell I'm living
So different now from what it seemed
Now life has killed
The dream I dreamed.

"I Dreamed a Dream"
*Les Misérables*
(Lyrics by Herbert Kretzmer)

In the musical *Les Misérables*, Fantine's opening solo laments lost innocence. In her lyrical reminiscence, she recounts how the buoyancy and enthusiasm of her youth were spoiled by the betrayal, and eventual abandonment, of some unseen man. Who was he and what did he do? We quickly learn that he was Fantine's lover in adolescence, leaving her pregnant and with a legacy of poverty and, eventually, prostitution. He has also left her in a state where she experiences some of the common sequelae found in those with posttraumatic stress disorder (PTSD), which sometimes arises from the devastating traumas of childhood physical and sexual abuse.

Like others who have also lost their innocence very young and are left with enormous residual psychological pain, Fantine decries her impaired sleep and nightmares, intrusive thoughts and unusual physiological stimuli, despair and psychic numbing, and feelings of existential malcontent and futility. Unlike many survivors of trauma, Fantine does *not* describe any manifest problems she may be having with her sexuality, her capacity to parent, or her eating. However, severe trauma often fractures not only one's sense of meaning and order in life but also one's appreciation of the most fulfilling activities, including those that give physical and psychological pleasure. One area of disturbance is the pattern of abstention, or disordered intake, of food.

Since the 1980s, self-destructive behavior in adulthood, including eating disorders, has been increasingly correlated with any history of childhood physical and sexual abuse. Acute and chronic trauma such as prolonged separation from caregivers and parental neglect have been shown to play a major role in impaired interpersonal functioning, memory storage, and normal behavior. This seemingly new emphasis on the causes of psychological pain is actually an elaboration of discoveries made over a century ago. The clinical occurrence of dissociation was first described in the 1890s by the French psychologist Pierre Janet. He stressed that eating disorders consisted of conscious but concealed fixed ideas linked to split-off unacceptable memories. In an early form of cognitive retraining and restructuring that is still helpful in overcoming food refusal, Janet used hypnosis to manipulate these dissociated ideas. Perhaps most important, he developed a comprehensive formulation about the effects of trauma and traumatic memories. He explained that the traumatic events left "indelible and distressing memories—memories to which the sufferer was continually returning, and by which he was tormented by day and by night" (Janet 1919/1976, p. 589, quoted in Van der Kolk and Van der Hart 1991, p. 425). Modern-day psychiatrists are rediscovering Janet's early assertions and finding his treatment techniques helpful for traumatized individuals who come forward to tell their stories. In so doing, treaters broaden their view beyond seeing the individual as a mere bag of interactive neurochemicals or symptoms pressing for discharge. Instead, they begin to take into account the patient's *memories*, as well as any forbidden wishes, fantasies, and conflicts.

Let us trace this different and more encompassing view of people, particularly as it applies to people struggling with eating disorders. It will help us see how the field of psychiatry is always changing, partly at the behest of patients, and it will underscore how an understanding of childhood trauma may also influence the care of individuals in psychotherapy. Nowhere does verbal psychotherapy play a stronger role than in the treatment of physically traumatized people. A review of the changes in theory, as illustrated by a few clinical cases, will help us see why.

## The Impact of Trauma

In the 1980s, the mental health world underwent a radical shift that had an inevitable impact on treatment. This change was not the result of the discovery of either a new drug or an innovative psychotherapeutic technique. As much as clinicians and patients alike may yearn for such panaceas, they are not readily forthcoming. No pill can help us solve all of life's daily dilemmas and challenges. Paradoxes and mysteries that often defy simple, straightforward answers compose the bulk of the practice of medicine, especially psychiatry. As in life itself, we must learn to navigate as best we can through what novelist Chaim Potok has called the "grayish sea of ambiguity" (1981, p. 359).

Nowhere has this cloud of ambiguity settled more stubbornly than in the revelation and understanding of how sexual trauma often affects adult women. As a psychiatrist who trained in the late 1970s, I recall a few passing mentions in didactic classes and assigned readings on the subjects of incest and rape. The sequelae of those phenomena, currently best diagnosed under the rubric "posttraumatic stress disorder" in the proposed DSM-IV criteria (American Psychiatric Association 1993), were observed clinically in veterans of the Vietnam conflict. Like most of my resident colleagues, I spent many months training at a Veterans Administration hospital, where I learned to recognize the symptoms and to treat this condition in our war-ravaged citizens. Little did I or my colleagues know then that what we observed and learned from treating these veterans would later be helpful in developing treatment strategies for a great number of women clients. These women, seemingly emerging from the woodwork after generations of cultural and self-imposed silence, are survivors of childhood physical and sexual trauma.

In the current women's literature, the term "victim" has been aptly and positively supplanted by the term "incest survivor." Although this understandable and acceptable modification applauds those patients who have truly triumphed over an inexpressibly arduous and damaging childhood, it is essential that its positive connotations not whitewash the subject in any way or lead writers and mental health professionals alike to deny its impact. To listen to the often horrific details of sexual abuse and explore the grave personal toll it exacts, clinicians must depart from established psychiatric theory. Instead of giving short shrift to the basic details of the client's past while emphasizing the role of unconscious fantasy, therapists in psychodynamic psychotherapy and psychoanalysis must now seriously consider how both fact and fantasy influence psychotherapeutic treatment. Neither the patient nor the therapist may ever be certain of the exact nature or sequence of events; in this way, an intertwining of fact and mental elaboration will form the lapidarian context of daily psychological work. Yet valuing both aspects of the human condition is made difficult by the individual's own desire to simplify her task and arrive at one incontrovertible truth about her existence.

The therapist would also like to simplify. To gainsay imagination, unconscious factors, and fantasy requires one to find a culprit, a common pathway, a reason, or some concrete factor that might be more easily remediated, if not understood. On the other hand, bearing witness to the childhood recollections of abuse and acknowledging the reality of the accompanying terror may go against more recently held psychoanalytic postulates. Although Freud himself never abrogated the influence of trauma in psychopathology, most of his followers emphasized that fantasies and unconscious conflicts stemmed from the preoedipal and oedipal family environment. Thus, the impact of ideas, dreams, family, romance, and early attachment—but not trauma—has been the thrust of traditional psychodynamic thought, and thus of daily clinical practice in therapy. Contemporary therapists working with survivors of trauma must seek out new methods of working and listening. They must de-idealize their intellectual heroes and heroines as they approach each treatment hour without guru or theoretical security blanket. To genuinely hear the individual, they must tailor the treatment to the patient. They may find that what is useful for some may not be helpful others. Some people will benefit more from hypnosis, others from movement or psychodrama techniques, and still others from psychoanalysis or psychodynamically informed therapy.

Tailoring the treatment to the patient's needs first and foremost demands what psychoanalyst Wilfred Bion extolled as entering each therapy hour without "memory or desire" (1967/1981, p. 260). This approach tacitly gives individual patients permission to say exactly what is on their minds, with minimal moves to categorize them according to a given theory. This tack is particularly crucial for patients who have been abused.

Incest survivors must be reassured repeatedly that they can express and face the painful and previously buried facts without qualm or question. The therapist must trust the client's veracity and ability to accept and rely on her own memories and self-experience. More and more evidence shows sexual abuse to be on the rise in our society, although its prevalence has probably always been considerably higher than acknowledged in statistical reports. The data accumulating from many refined studies emphasize that sexual abuse has affected as many as one of every two adult women living in the United States. (This statistic does not differentiate among the specific forms of misconduct, from incest to sexual harassment. Common sense dictates that frequency and type of abuse will have bearing on the amount of psychological effects the woman experiences.)

In addition, 50%–65% of all eating disorder patients report a history of physical or sexual assault (Bulik et al. 1989; Jacobson and Herald 1990; Palmer et al. 1990; Shure 1989; Tice et al. 1989). Although a few reports suggest that the frequency of such abuse is only 4%–25% among eating disorder patients, these findings may be particularly low. Clinical experience confirms the high incidence found in most research studies. All women, especially those who have eating disorders, find it difficult to confide whatever they deem to be shameful and despicable about their pasts.

Clinicians themselves are often aghast to learn a year or more into an otherwise solidly based and helpful therapy process that their patient has begun, for the first time, to recollect repugnant details of physical and/or sexual abuse. It is now generally conceded that this material is sometimes repressed or temporarily forgotten, or more frequently split off or dissociated, only to emerge in the context of a trusting and established psychotherapeutic relationship. Indeed, most people will not open their deeper selves easily but will benefit from the continual presence of a concerned other who reassures them that what seems unspeakable can be put into words. What must be mastered and transformed is, at its core, a distrust in basic benevolence and respect for other people. The case of Sarah Z. illustrates how supportive psychotherapy can result in a gradual attenuation of the emotional and psychological scars from the abuse.

🍂 Sarah Z. had been in twice-weekly individual psychotherapy for 3 years. She had difficulty in maintaining intimate relationships with boyfriends and a tendency to distance from connectedness with her women friends. Although Sarah did not meet all the specific criteria for bulimia nervosa, she binged and induced vomiting at least three times a month. However, she did not seem caught up in the wish for the cultural stereotype of a perfect figure but seemed content instead with being a few pounds overweight. For her, the bulimic symptoms seemed a diversion from the more anxiety-provoking situations of dealing with conflicts in relationships.

Early in therapy, Sarah assessed how her family of origin had dealt poorly with strong emotions such as frustration and anger. As a result, she had not developed the ability either to perceive or express the words to connote her feelings in emotional situations. For Sarah, any response was better than experiencing anger or irritation. As she began to remember important scenes from her childhood, she also began to recall incidents of physical abuse, later confirmed by her mother. Mrs. Z. acknowledged in a family therapy session that she had used severe corporal punishment when Sarah was a girl. At the time, Mrs. Z. had been severely depressed, after losing both of her own parents. Fearfully, Sarah had learned to obey her mother at all costs or else risk a severe beating. In an effort to appease her mother, she swallowed any discomfort or anger. Thus, in a technical sense, memories were temporarily forgotten—or repressed—and her ego had to work overtime to keep them buried.

Although this process had helped Sarah function when she was young, in adulthood it cut off from her conscious awareness part of her vital inner life. She stayed emotionally distant from other people, in part because she did not recognize or trust that she or others had the ability to deal with her deeper feelings. To risk exposure meant inviting the very abuse she had gone to great lengths to avoid. For Sarah, friends and boyfriends were potential victimizers to be kept at a manageable emotional distance so as to avoid unwittingly provoking rage or her own unmanageable tension.

Early in their work together, Sarah's therapist was caught up in a typical bind faced by therapists of eating disorder patients. She suspected that Sarah might be having relationship struggles because of earlier traumas and memories that were not easily recalled because they had been repressed. However, to push Sarah at too rapid a pace might provoke in her what should be avoided—a retraumatization involving psychological rather than physical assault. Instead, Sarah's therapist chose to quietly speculate about what might have happened during Sarah's childhood and to listen attentively for the material to emerge in the process.

The therapist was then able to help Sarah learn more about her own feelings by naming them with her and by helping her link them up with what she could remember about her past. Aware that all memories may be condensed, colored, and confusing, Sarah's therapist was less concerned about the actual veracity of the recollections than about the meaning and feeling with which Sarah endowed them. This matter-of-fact approach gave Sarah the greatest freedom of expression she had ever known. The therapist patiently waited for Sarah's revelations and did not force her own ideas, truth, or theory on to her. As Sarah worked less hard to hold her memories in abeyance, her eating difficulties noticeably and predictably lessened.

Realizing that we as individuals will see different meanings in any play we attend, any story we read, or any situation we encounter, therapists and patients must concur that no one person has a corner on absolute truth. This open-mindedness allows a blending of what psychoanalysts have called narrative and historical truth. Simply put, this process involves the welding of actual corroborated past (historical truth) and psychical emotional reality (narrative truth). The latter includes all the feelings, fantasies, magical ideas, dreams, and misrepresentations that are part and parcel of our imperfect memory system. The fact that memories are malleable, constantly reworked, and recategorized (Van der Kolk 1987; Van der Kolk and Saporta 1991; Van der Kolk and Van der Hart 1991) means that each of us *constructs* our life history to some degree. This fact has fortunate implications for treatment, because it also means that we can reshape and master past trauma. New experiences, including (but not exclusively) therapeutic ones, help us see that the present and future may be—and should be—different and better than the past.

## Into the Wall

Many patients are not as fortunate as Sarah. In contrast to having stored or buried memories that can be retrieved later in psychotherapy because they are well integrated into ordinary memory stores, some may have memories that are actively dissociated as a way to cope with traumatic experiences ("traumatic memory"). To deal with abuse, individuals develop dissociative phenomena that occur along a continuum—from conscious efforts, such as floating near the ceiling or becoming part of a wall (Gelinas 1983), to multiple personality disorder (Kluft 1990). The dissociative phenomena are the psyche's attempts to deal with the symptoms of posttraumatic stress disorder. Awaking from nightmares, experiencing recurrent visual or auditory hallucinations of the abuser, struggling with recurrent obsessive thoughts, and experiencing spontaneous weeping episodes or anxiety attacks are only a few of the behaviors with which these patients struggle. Secondary problems include chronic depression, poor self-esteem, feelings of powerlessness and hopelessness, and the inability to achieve professionally or interpersonally.

Years often pass between the termination of the actual abuse and the emergence of the posttraumatic neurosis, and this delay precludes early treatment and exacerbates negative consequences. Because food and eating have such highly symbolic, multidetermined meanings, clinicians are increasingly aware that eating disorders and dissociative states may accompany each other. Indeed, bulimia and anorexia may sometimes be thought of as dissociative phenomena par excellence. The eating disorder is often referred to as "the monster" or "the dark side," as if it were a separate, hideous aspect of the self (Zerbe 1993b). Like dissociation, the symptom has been used as a mode of survival and is not easily given up. The individual must be helped to see how the eating disorder has become a reliable identity ("I'm a bulimic") that has buffered her against the storms of her own overwhelming anxiety and rage. Determining the focus of treatment is complicated because both the eating disorder and the dissociative pathology seem to threaten the quality of life—if not life itself.

❦ Jill A., age 24, was an emaciated woman with anorexia who arrived at the hospital after being physically assaulted while shopping at a local mall. Jill denied any part in provoking the attack, although it was later learned that she had been teasing several gang members in the parking lot. On the hospital unit, the primary nurse observed that Jill would fall spontaneously into trancelike states, similar to those her roommate had observed for months.

As her treatment progressed, Jill began to describe a complex history of sexual and physical abuse at the hands of her father. What she told her nurse and psychotherapist was later corroborated by her older sister. However, this proof of her inner reality was small solace to a woman who had totally split off from conscious awareness any memories of her father's use of a whip and hairbrush while she was in the bathtub. These physical assaults had been preceded or followed almost daily by paternal rapes.

Jill believed there was no safe retreat from her father's abuse. Her dissociative states began in childhood, with her feeling as if she had left her body and entered the bedroom wall whenever her father beat or sexually assaulted her. As Jill "observed" herself from a position high above the actual incident, she became immune to her father's attacks by entering her own fantasy world. As a result, she was able to blunt the effects of any physical pain.

Most noxious to Jill had been her father's demand for oral sex. Her abhorrence of fellatio later manifested itself in the concrete symptom of her purging. It was nearly impossible for her to ingest any food without vomiting afterward as a way of controlling what had previously been beyond her control. Moreover, she associated any aspect of her body, including her mouth, with sex and as therefore abhorrent. Years of overstimulation were manifested in her eating disorder, whereby consuming a meal repeated the trauma. Her father had forced her to "eat meat," so she found this staple particularly intolerable.

Not only does Jill's case demonstrate the classic problem of dissociation, combined with an eating disorder, but it also brings to light the need for bodily control, which these individuals yearn for. In lieu of having had their own needs and wishes respected by parental figures, they develop defensive structures and symptoms that speak to the urge to control strong feeling states of anxiety, hatred, and victimization. Psychoanalyst Karen Horney (1950) theorized that it is difficult for anyone to bear hostility because of the fear that in the future those we are hostile toward may turn against or abandon us. The abused person may fear for her very survival, yet often depends on those who hurt her, which leads her to disavow her anger at all costs. Gaining precise control over bodily functions by refusing food or evacuating it on demand are unfortunate but lifesaving compromises to counteract the fear that annihilation from a malevolent persecutor is around the corner.

Thus, it should not be surprising that so many psychologically impaired women who were sexually abused also have an eating disorder; likewise, those women with a primary struggle around eating are often found to have been sexually abused. Both conditions speak to the deep despair and hidden aggression encapsulated in the symptoms. Slowly, these individuals can be taught that their lives can become meaningful despite the pain they have endured and that they can discover appropriate ways of dealing with aggressive energies.

Parents, friends, and treaters often sense the unspoken aggression when the patients reject help and support on the one hand while talking nonstop about the details of their bingeing and purging on the other. If not totally repellent, such descriptions are usually off-putting at best. By describing their behavior, these women keep others at a distance and induce in them feelings of disgust, malaise, nausea, hopelessness, and helplessness (Zerbe 1991, 1992b). Maintaining emotional closeness to a person with an eating disorder requires a high level of tolerance for feeling states such as anger that are often ignored for the longest time. Similarly, incredible patience is a prerequisite to learning to recognize and accept one's own split-off hatred and denial, but it is more easily developed by acknowledging that very real traumas precipitated the patient's difficulties.

## On Becoming Your Own Best Parent

A popular self-help book written in the 1970s, *How To Be Your Own Best Friend* (Newman et al. 1971), gave pertinent advice about how to legitimately care for oneself. Defining your needs and having the chutzpah to make your goals a reality are defining characteristics of the mentally healthy person. During childhood we usually come to recognize our needs under the aegis of our parents. They structure our days, praise our successes, challenge our views, and impose necessary limits, thereby launching us into life.

As young adults planning our day-by-day existence, we may seldom think consciously of our parents' guiding hands and presence, but we have derived from them the capacity to organize thoughts, plan our activities, and confidently set forth to achieve our personal vision. In the best of circumstances, our parents are our champions. For although they must accept our foibles and limitations, they also take delight in our growth and employ judicious limits to help us build a healthy sense of self. Through it all, we internalize the process itself and some of our parents' attributes, eventually generating a vital and flexible internal structure (in psychodynamic terms, the ego or self).

Of course, any memory of childhood also brings to mind disappointments, failures, unwarranted punishments, and disagreements that foster our ability to come to grips with imperfections in our parents. In moving toward maturity, a 3-year-old's normal, idealized view of perfect parents gives way to a more leavened but realistic view. An appropriate, optimistic resolution, hoped for by most parents, is that their children will forgive them of their weaknesses and mistakes when they themselves become parents. Our adult sensibilities enable us to accept that our parents actually did the very best they could with all of their human frailties and limitations.

This supposition fulfills Voltaire's vision from *Candide* that our world is truly "the best of all possible worlds" (1760/1959, p. 31), embodying enough gratification and happiness to make life fulfilling and worthwhile, although far from perfect. But when these expectable parental functions, taken for granted by most of us, are not forthcoming, what are the consequences? What occurs when the usual intergenerational boundaries within a family break down and the youngster is left to shift for herself, emotionally and physically?

For example, when a parent is either impaired from drugs or alcohol or has a deep emotional disturbance, the child may be called on to care for that parent. Who then cares for the child? Inevitably, the child must take full responsibility for herself, her parents, and also often for household tasks and the care of younger children. The usual supports and boundaries between the generations are diminished, and the child learns to forsake her own needs for those of others. In the home of the incestuously abused child, the parentified daughter also assumes the role of sexual caretaker, and a collusive role reversal deepens at grave psychological cost to her.

❦ Laurie B. sought outpatient consultation for symptoms of severe bulimia. Already ill for more than 7 years, she had undergone several hospitalizations for heart irregularities caused by electrolyte imbalances. As Laurie recounted her past in expressive psychotherapy, it became clear that she was a highly parentified child, as well as the survivor of fraternal incest. No one would have guessed Laurie's plight from a superficial look at her "perfect" family. Her father, an international businessman of some renown, had married Laurie's mother when she was a highly successful industrial engineer. While he traversed Europe, investing in several summer cottages and châteaux for his family and solidifying an already impressive financial empire, his wife reared their children.

After Laurie's two younger sisters were born, her mother became overwhelmed with the tasks of parenting and found her own career easier to manage than parenthood. She succumbed to heavy bouts of drinking and drug abuse, often leaving Laurie as the sole caretaker of her sisters and brother. On these occasions the brother would take advantage of the lack of available parenting and force Laurie to perform fellatio. Later, he urged his friends to do the same. Whenever her mother returned home late at night intoxicated, she would scream and beat Laurie. If Laurie gave an indication of any pain whatsoever, her mother became even more violent. As a result, Laurie quickly learned to silence herself—and her pain—by "numbing" her body and by vomiting. For her, vomiting became a secret, symbolic way of crying, while simultaneously venting her hurt or disappointment.

Even after she formed a trusting relationship with her psychotherapist, Laurie manifested behavior that conveyed a need to protect her parents. She refused to acknowledge any anger toward them or toward her treaters, because she believed rage would push others into abandoning her. Her eating disorder persisted as a safe expression of her sad feelings and tearfulness.

Within the context of a parentified home and a paucity of genuine caretaking, Laurie's eating disorder takes on the aura of receiving nurturance. Although she did not relish the medical interventions she received for the complications of her illness, she no doubt benefited from the secondary gain provided by the ministrations of the nursing and medical staff. Laurie's eating disorder also seemed to be her entrée into a therapeutic relationship where she sought direct guidance and support. In fact, over the several years of intensive outpatient work, she actually flourished. However, whenever Laurie made positive moves ahead, she worried that her therapist would abandon her out of envy and rivalry.

The parentified child often believes that her success is predicated on the ruin of another. Love itself has been so highly coveted that her psychological legacy is an entrenched belief that there is never enough to go around. A difficult but crucial lesson occurs in life as the patient begins to take risks in relationships and learns that love begets love. She slowly realizes that her successes will not destroy or ruin another. (These lessons are typically learned at home when parents rejoice at success but do not demand it to buttress their own enfeebled egos.) Therapists should thus be attuned to their own issues of envy and should be genuinely pleased for the patient who makes progress. Commendations and compliments may not be an active part of the therapy process, but the patient will sense genuine recognition and pleasure on the therapist's part.

Along the way, both therapist and patient will face many obstacles. Specifically, the patient will have to recognize and mourn the loss of her childhood. She may tenaciously hold on to the belief that the therapist can magically become the mother or father she never had. She may implore the therapist to hold her or provide other gratifications outside the therapy hours. For example, one patient would show up at her therapist's house on Saturday mornings, hoping she would be invited in for breakfast and to play with the therapist's children.

The neglect faced by these patients may lead the therapists to feel guilty for establishing boundaries. Yet this tack usually should guide the process. The patient must learn to mourn in her adult life the fantasy childhood years she can never reclaim. The therapist who gives in to demands for extra contacts will become resentful over time, may neglect other patients, and will be doing the patient a grave injustice. Adults can never be totally satisfied by mother's milk (Giovacchini 1978; Kohut 1984).

Most helpful is the ambience that permits patients to speak about their childlike inner yearnings. Until recognized and appreciated, these needs will linger, unsatisfied. Helping the patient's adult self tolerate and care for the demands of the lonely and angry child within is a pivotal point in treatment that often takes time. The adult patient emerges with a stronger sense of the many aspects of herself as a person and is able to make appropriate life choices, albeit with difficulty. The parentified child has developed antennae highly sensitive to what others want her to do and to be. As she repeatedly denies her own needs, she sacrifices so that others may benefit, eventually developing a mode of adaptation that is not easily given up. As an adult she unconsciously perpetuates her own victimhood by choosing disastrous partners in relationships, harboring deep anger and resentment, sabotaging her own career, and inconsistently mothering any children she has. In therapy she can begin to understand the reasons behind her tendency to abet her own self-destruction, freeing her to make healthier, life-enhancing choices.

Changing such a long-held life script is exceedingly difficult, and both therapist and patient must approach their work together as an extensive, difficult adventure. Making mistakes along the way and resisting change are inevitable. Making any choice can be a sad process, because it means giving up other choices. Individuals faced with change may be haunted by insistent worry about making the wrong choice.

The quest for perfectionism that accompanies an eating disorder makes choice all the more difficult and anxiety provoking. In this regard I remind my own patients (and myself) that all of us sometimes make poor choices and decisions, but we can often reverse our decisions or overcome their consequences. Recall the climax of the movie version of *The Wizard of Oz*. Glenda, the Good Witch of the North, reminds Dorothy that she is wearing the magic ruby slippers. Indeed, she has had them on her feet during her entire stay in Oz but has simply not been aware of their power! By clicking her heels, Dorothy can return home at any point. Similarly, we all carry more power within ourselves to effect change and survive tumult than we give ourselves credit for having. Like Dorothy, we must all remember that we wear our own pair of ruby slippers—as do our friends and loved ones. Poor choices should not be encouraged, but they can be survived. The eating disorder patient who can accept that mistakes are an inevitable companion of maturity and personal growth benefits greatly from that knowledge. If sexual abuse has been a part of her history, she won't be able to change her past; but, with knowledge and acceptance, she can influence her present and her future.

## Unconsummated Incest

Not all incestuous activities are overtly sexual acts. A variety of seductive behaviors, often made unconsciously by parents, constitute "unconsummated incest." These frequently contribute to the development of eating disorders and other psychological problems, particularly sexual deviation. Unwittingly, parents may make sexual gestures, encourage age-inappropriate cuddling or hugging, smile seductively, or repeatedly invite the child to share their bed. The latter occurs particularly in the homes of divorced parents such as when a lonely mother may consciously seek to comfort her anxious and worried child but actually is seeking solace and warmth for herself. As a result, a mother may overly stimulate her daughter's genitals, anus, or breasts by activities disguised as cleaning, medicating, and inspecting. Yet the same mother may castigate her child for any masturbatory activity. This inconsistency sends mixed messages to the child, who eventually becomes subject to what psychoanalyst Selma Kramer (1983) has described as "object-coercive doubting." By this Kramer means that children must distort their own reality, because they want to believe what their mother says but must also defend themselves against their knowledge that what she does is inappropriate.

🍒 Ellen C., age 22, entered individual psychotherapy because she was struggling with her sexual orientation and an eating disorder. For years Ellen had complained of unexplained abdominal pain and had self-medicated for chronic constipation. When Ellen began her first dating relationship with a man, her mother seemed to withdraw emotionally from her. Meanwhile, her mother asked many inappropriate and intrusive questions about Ellen's sexual experience. Ellen's eating disorder worsened, and she lost a considerable amount of weight.

In psychotherapy, Ellen traced the development of her highly involved relationship with her mother. Divorced when Ellen was 13, her mother would crawl into bed with Ellen at night and disregard any need she had for privacy. Mrs. C. would often throw open the bathroom doors and waltz in, casually inspecting Ellen's body while she bathed or used the toilet. Although her mother denied her behavior by explaining that she was just "making sure the bathroom was in working order," she also rationalized her intrusion as "checking to make sure you are well and pure." Her behavior enraged Ellen, who "swallowed her feelings" because of her incapacity to handle anger. Ellen's mother was extremely jealous of anyone who visited her daughter and frequently went to great lengths to discourage Ellen from developing relationships. The conflict between them surfaced when Ellen's mother sensed her daughter's attraction to both men and women and demanded that Ellen confide her sexual thoughts and feelings to her.

Ellen's conflict over her choice of sexual partner was a red herring for the deeper issue within her family of origin. Ellen's mother had made her daughter the object of her own unconscious, unconsummated incestuous acting-out behavior. In many ways, her boundary violations were more subtle than those inflicted on someone coerced into an incestuous liaison, but they were nevertheless damaging to Ellen's psychological health. After her divorce, Ellen's mother, for unknown reasons, had been unable to find solace in other activities or in adult relationships. Her loneliness was temporarily ameliorated by her intense affection for her daughter. Awareness of her mother's isolation made it impossible for Ellen to deny the intense suggestiveness of her mother's behavior even though it cost her her own independence.

Similarly, eating disorder patients often place their own needs below those of others but still manage to find some semblance of autonomy in their eating disorder. Not surprisingly, Ellen never mentioned a word to her mother about her bouts of bingeing and purging! Further exploration in treatment revealed that Ellen's mother may have felt unconsciously attracted to her own women friends and so had displaced her feelings onto Ellen through her inappropriate attentions. Ellen unconsciously identified with her mother's latent homosexuality but could not acknowledge this possible dynamic for the longest time. Because of object-coercive doubting, Ellen wanted to believe that her mother's actions were based only on affection rather than on misdirected sexual wishes.

Ellen's eating disorder also represented a compromise wherein she swallowed the anger she felt toward her mother for not helping her become more autonomous. Her enmeshed relationship with her mother left her unable to explore relationships with men or women, which perpetuated a childlike state for both Ellen and her mother. Meanwhile, Ellen struggled to trust herself in many areas of life and doubted every choice and decision she made. For affirmation, she turned to her mother instead of to an age-appropriate partner or career plan. Ultimately, her life lay fallow because she doubted every aspect of her being.

## What the Research Does—and Doesn't—Show

The clinical examples provided in this chapter describe some of the difficulties faced by sexually abused people. They are by no means all-encompassing. What remains an enigma for mental health professionals and the public at large is the fact that sexual abuse may or may not harm the individual. Some people who have had highly traumatic pasts not only survive but flourish. In the mental health literature, these individuals are sometimes referred to as "invincibles" because of their fascinating ability to absorb emotional nourishment despite very poor emotional soil. On the other hand, many other individuals seem severely affected by relatively minor traumata. Thus, a genuine controversy rages in psychiatry as to the nature of the impact of sexual abuse on children, and future research will be necessary to help treaters understand more about the population of survivors.

With this caveat in mind, let's examine some notable trends in the plethora of research conducted over the past two decades. Of paramount importance are the intense emotional reactions among survivors—fear, anxiety, depression, anger, and hostility, as well as the poor self-esteem and difficulty in handling aggressive and assertive feelings already described. Inappropriate sexual behavior in child survivors is not uncommon. For example, in one study conducted at Tufts University, 27% of the 4- to 6-year-old survivors scored significantly above the norm on a measure of inappropriate sexual activity (Tufts New England Medical Center Division of Child Psychiatry 1984). These children were prone to open masturbation, excessive sexual curiosity, frequent exposure of their genitals, and acknowledged sexual relations.

Sexually abused children and adolescents are more likely to be truant, to experience difficulties in school, to run away from home, and to marry early. A landmark study by Judith Herman (1981) found that incest survivors were six times as likely to run away from home in adolescence. Herman also determined that 60% of the incest survivors in her clinical sample had a negative self-image and experienced major depressive symptomatology. A variety of researchers have linked feelings of isolation and alienation to sexual abuse, with those individuals who have experienced father-daughter incest having particularly tenacious feelings of being branded or stigmatized (Chandarana and Malla 1989; Demitrack et al. 1990; Finkelhor 1984; Torem and Curdue 1986, 1988). Not surprisingly, a high incidence of suicide attempts is also commonly found among these individuals.

A preponderance of evidence reviewed by Angela Browne and David Finkelhor of the University of New Hampshire (1988) now suggests that abuse by fathers or stepfathers has a greater negative impact than abuse by other perpetrators. Being forced rather than seduced into participating in a sexual act makes for a more devastating long-term outcome. The survivor's relationship to the offender also seems relevant. For example, Browne and Finkelhor's review of the data suggests that abuse at the hands of a trusted neighbor or relative produces more devastating effects than that by a distant relative because it involves actual betrayal by a valued confidant. In addition, the effects are usually worse when the explicit sexual contact involves vaginal, anal, or oral penetration or genital manipulation. Finally, the effects of sexual abuse are more long lasting when the perpetrator is male rather than female and an adult rather than a teenager.

Clinical experience has repeatedly shown that the survivors of many incestuous acts have parents who tacitly permit the abuse or deny its occurrence, even when confronted with reality. This collusion is particularly damaging to the survivors. The prognosis for overcoming sexual trauma is worse for those whose families are unsupportive or who are forcibly removed from the home. Although these findings have been confirmed in only two studies (Anderson et al. 1981; Tufts New England Medical Center Division of Child Psychiatry 1984), they nevertheless point to the need for clinicians and concerned friends and family members to deal forthrightly with any evidence of abuse and to support the survivor throughout disclosure and treatment.

Fortunately, a number of thorough self-help books are available for women survivors, their partners, and families. Although such material can provide support through education that leads to mastery, no book can take the place of the beneficial human interactions available in individual, family, and group psychotherapy. The professional literature continues to enhance our understanding of how to work with incest survivors within the clinical encounter, as well as demonstrating that experienced professional care has a positive impact on outcome.

One recent focus of both professional and lay literature is the influence of early sexual abuse on later sexual functioning. Famous people such as Sandra Dee (1991) and Oprah Winfrey, who have come forward to share their own history of sexual abuse and eating disorders have helped others acknowledge personal difficulties, including sexual abuse's profound impact on sexual relationships. Excellent self-help books, such as Ellen Bass and Laura Davis's *The Courage to Heal: A Guide for Women Survivors of Child Sexual Abuse* (1988), wisely advise women that sexual problems can be worked through and often resolved in a loving relationship. Harriet Lerner's three volumes *The Dance of Anger* (1985), *The Dance of Intimacy* (1989), and *The Dance of Deception* (1993) are other useful guides in helping one develop and maintain relationships. Although they do not exclusively deal with the effects of sexual and physical abuse, they provide thoughtful perspectives on the topic and other personal dilemmas.

Of paramount importance are timing, individual desire, and feeling in control. This sage advice—to proceed slowly and avoid placing sex at the center of life—is grounded in studies that demonstrate how a variety of sexual problems common to abuse survivors can be overcome. Sexual anxiety, increased feelings of guilt about sex, and greater dissatisfaction in sexual relationships all occur at higher rates among incest survivors than in matched control subjects. Because as many as 80% of those who have been survivors of incest find it difficult to relax and enjoy sexual encounters, they avoid sex or try to master it through compulsivity.

According to Herman, survivors of incest may use promiscuity and "sexually stylized behavior" (1981, p. 40) to garner affection and attention. However, there is little empirical confirmation that sexual abuse leads to a higher incidence of homosexuality. Many abused individuals choose to reclaim their sexuality slowly, if at all. Because they experience orgasm less often, they report being less sexually responsive, and they find less satisfaction overall in their sexual relationships. Periods of celibacy may, in fact, be necessary so that a woman who has been sexually abused can learn to establish other types of intimate bonds and feelings of empowerment. The self-help literature wisely recommends proceeding slowly in reclaiming one's sexuality, but it can be done over time, often resulting in a full sexual life.

In fact, the most heartening research cited by Browne and Finkelhor (1988) reports that only one-fifth of incest survivors experience any serious psychopathology. This comforting fact raises more questions than it answers, however. We know relatively little about the factors in life that enable some people to emerge from serious trauma relatively unscathed while others bear lifelong effects. Moreover, apparent psychological health may mask underlying struggles and conflicts. Browne and Finkelhor warn that the effects of childhood trauma should never be flippantly dismissed because of the absence of demonstrable long-term side effects. Painful and confusing life events should always be taken seriously, especially when dealing with survivors of childhood sexual abuse.

Bonnie Buchele of The Menninger Clinic, an expert in treating incest survivors and perpetrators, believes the effects of abuse are always lifelong (Ganzarain and Buchele 1988). Buchele has worked with many survivors who fortunately improve greatly with treatment, but she reports a minority are riddled with guilt for their perceived transgressions. They fail to improve despite multiple efforts in therapy.

## The Biology of Sexual Abuse

The psychotropic drug fluoxetine (Prozac) is being shown to have positive and selective impact on posttraumatic stress disorder. In addition to relieving symptoms of depression, Prozac alleviates sleep difficulties, nightmares, flashbacks, and intrusive reliving of trauma in this group of patients. Even hyperarousal seems to be ameliorated with this medication. However, unlike individuals who have depression, survivors of incest who benefit from medication for posttraumatic stress disorder find it essential to also continue with their verbal therapy to work through the psychological effects of their trauma. The medication helps readjust an "internal thermostat" that enables these patients to experience intrusive thoughts less intensely, which facilitates their ability to engage in psychotherapy and other forms of human interaction.

Posttraumatic stress disorder apparently involves biological mechanisms. Alterations in norepinephrine, dopamine, serotonin, endogenous opioids, and hormones have all been linked to trauma. A number of animal studies help explain the human physiological response in posttraumatic stress disorder (Van der Kolk and Saporta 1991). Noradrenergic stimulation of the brain's locus ceruleus–hippocampal pathways at the time of trauma may actually mark the beginning of impaired memory tracks that predispose the individual to repetitive intrusive reliving of trauma. Autonomic arousal may be associated with flashback experiences, a common clinical phenomenon in this patient group (Van der Kolk and Saporta 1991). Whenever a survivor encounters a scene reminiscent of the original trauma, even in mild form, an intrusive reexperiencing of the event may occur.

Similarly, brief separations from the maternal figure may affect neurotransmitter systems in animals and humans. Infants who are separated from their mothers show changes in hypothalamic serotonin, adrenal gland catecholamines, cortisol, and immunoresistance. These findings suggest that the psychological effects of early separation noted by Bowlby (1960a, 1960b, 1961, 1963, 1969, 1973) probably have a neuro-biological base. Although any understanding that we would now bring to bear on these phenomena is probably an oversimplification, Fields (1981) has suggested that the mother's role as principal soother and arouser of the child can lead to physiological instability if there is any failure in the development of their relationship. As a result, the child may become unable to assimilate and accommodate new information, which sets the stage for PTSD later on under certain circumstances.

Although not associated directly with eating disorder behavior per se, biochemical alterations secondary to trauma may play a role, as do depression, poor tolerance of affect, and fixation on the trauma. Both trauma and eating disorders have been linked to low serotonin levels, but whether this connection is a specific and real phenomenon or is related to a much more complex neurochemical event remains un-known.

Children are much more likely than adults to react to trauma, per-haps because they do not have the capacity to give voice to what they see and feel. Although persons with particular cognitive capacities are buffered against overwhelming stress, children may be more vulnerable to the effects of abuse because the hippocampus, an area of the brain involved in memory, does not mature until the third or fourth year of life. Children may therefore remember the quality of an event rather than its content or details. Hence, they do not have the skill to process associated effects. Stress can disrupt the functioning of different parts of the brain, perhaps leading to a lack of development and resulting in impaired cognitive appraisal. Thus children may not be able to recall or describe specific events or their context, even as adults, because of the immaturity of their brains at the time of the experience and the disrup-tion in development created by the trauma.

No wonder then, as Freud observed as early as 1920, that traumatic memories gain only partial representation (Freud 1920/1955). The anxi-ety anyone feels when recapturing a painful event is only partially re-lieved by the accompanying emotional response. A developmental deficit originating in the brain may impair the historical context, its essential symbolic representation, and the words needed to process the ideas. Understandably, primitive defensive maneuvers are thus called into play, perhaps including an eating disorder. It is not unusual for traumatized adults to regress to earlier patterns of behavior, including obsessive-compulsive behavior and aggressive outbursts, which reflect the immature organization of the young brain. Traumatic experiences are stored in memory, but without the benefit of the central processing ability of language. The ultimate outcome may be anxiety attacks, panic disorders, eating disorders, and a general lack of capacity to make calm and rational assessments. Thus, the typical symptoms of trauma (including dissociative phenomena and emotional constriction) may have a highly complex but important brain-based etiology, which eventually should enable us to develop additional specific medications to aid the sufferer.

Finally, in some societies or isolated regions, fathers have routinely used their oldest daughters for sexual gratification. Anthropologists speculate that incestuous behavior in primitive societies may provide a type of birth control by having prepubescent girls engage in sexual intercourse rather than their still-fertile mothers. Yet the girls do not emerge psychologically scarred. However, the cultural meaning of any act must be taken into consideration, and what is acceptable in one society may of course be anathema in another.

## More About Treatment

The person who has an eating disorder must be asked about her personal history and, if sexually traumatized, encouraged to give voice to her past. Like other survivors of trauma, these persons must feel believed in and understood, both by family members and treaters. In my experience, this acceptance is often a difficult first step, because we feel uncomfortable listening to painfully intimate details and stories that often seem hyperbolized and unbelievable. It is important to reassure survivors that only one-fifth of those who have been sexually abused experience major emotional side effects, although little is known about why some survivors of actual trauma apparently experience few or no aftereffects, whereas others with more limited trauma have greater difficulties.

Interestingly, a person who has been assaulted by her father will often direct more rage at her mother than at her father. Helping these individuals express their suppressed rage at both parents, with special emphasis on the mother, can be helpful. However, because this rage is often split off from consciousness or detoured into eating disorder symptomatology, much time and patience is needed to get the patient to experience and work it through. Buchele also stresses that survivors feel guilty about the boundary breakage in the family and frequently attempt to make amends for their guilt by an overly solicitous concern for family members, friends, or partners (Buchele 1993; Ganzarain and Buchele 1988). Self-respect in the form of legitimate "saying no" to demands must be garnered for self-healing.

The process of working through the effects of sexual abuse in clinical situations often leads to an exacerbation of the eating disorder, because reexamining the sexual trauma stirs up intense feelings. During the most intense times in therapy, a patient may need additional support with dietary plans, pharmacotherapy, and even hospitalization. Traumatized individuals tend to see their future as severely limited and without hope, so they must be confronted at this stage. Trauma exacts a very real toll in damaging what Erikson (1963) termed "basic trust," which can only be reestablished over time with a treater who respects limits and boundaries. The symbolic meaning behind particular types of abuse and the understandable tendency to feel betrayed by the abuser often make it even more difficult for a patient to "take in" insights and reassurance from her therapist. This skepticism on the part of the patient often leaves both treater and patient feeling frustrated. However, experience bears out that, if both can keep working on the treatment relationship, progress can be made both in mastering the traumatic situations and in controlling the eating disorder.

❦ Lindsey D., age 31, was an active participant in her twice-weekly group psychotherapy sessions. Struggling with subclinical bulimia since her college days, Lindsey had gained control over her symptoms through the insights and support of her group. As she began to recover memories of sexual abuse, members of the group expressed natural curiosity about the specific episodes and behaviors that had been foisted on Lindsey. However, she reacted haughtily to the suggestion that she reveal more detail than she was ready to provide. Meanwhile, Lindsey also began focusing on the sexual abuse as the principal cause of her eating disorder and troubled life. No doubt, the abuse had taken a significant psychological toll, but Lindsey shortchanged herself by temporarily narrowing her focus down to the sexual abuse alone.

Lindsey's case demonstrates our tendency as individuals to pin our difficulties solely on one aspect of our lives when, in fact, the past is much more complex. Lindsey would not be helped by pinning all her problems on one event or even solely on a series of events.

Lindsey's case also demonstrates the necessity for allowing individuals to reveal themselves only at the speed each person can handle. If peers or professionals push too quickly for details, a person in treatment may begin to feel revictimized. The potential for revictimizing the survivor requires family, friends, and treaters to be sensitive in supporting the individual's selection of her own pace. Parents and siblings who are willing to help support the survivor and repair past errors are greatly aided by ancillary family treatment.

Denial, psychic numbing, self-hypnosis, and dissociation are classic symptoms of prolonged trauma and posttraumatic stress syndrome. Bingeing, purging, and periods of self-starvation may be expressions of these defense mechanisms. Bulimic patients will describe how calm they feel after an episode, as if they are encased in a cocoon. A binge is often preceded by a trancelike state, or a period of self-hypnosis occurs during the binge so that the individual has little recollection of the event itself.

Most dramatically, in cases of multiple personality disorder combined with bulimia nervosa, one distinct personality emerges to do the bingeing and purging totally unbeknownst to the other alter personalities. This spectrum of dissociative pathology complicates diagnosis and treatment of the eating disorder per se, because the episodes may be forgotten, split off, or temporarily buried in the unconscious. Treatment begins by establishing a descriptive diagnosis of the phenomena that emerge in therapy, with a linking of the events, feelings, and memories that are at first blush isolated by the experience of numbness in the binge-purge cycle. As therapy proceeds, traumatic memories may emerge that initially bring out much pain but eventually lead to a greater integration of the memories themselves and ultimately to control over the disturbed eating patterns.

Fortunately, verbal therapy is quite helpful for individuals who struggle with posttraumatic anxiety and eating disorders. Verbalizing the contextual elements of the trauma is the essence of the treatment. Sometimes hypnosis itself may be the treatment of choice. But even if it is not the sole modality, hypnotic suggestion may add to the patient's ability to overcome traumatic anxiety and memories. For example, Pierre Janet (1919/1976) suggested to one of his patients that she replace the images of her dead children with those of flowers. After making the children fade away in trance, he asked the patient to emphasize the future. Helping the survivor focus on a positive or comforting image in the traumatic experience may be crucial. Similarly, Van der Kolk and Van der Hart (1991) cited the case of a Holocaust survivor whose therapist suggested that a flower be imaged at Auschwitz, providing much comfort. Fantasizing about having power over the perpetrator in a trance state or in fantasy that can be dwelt on at will may also be quite helpful. Hurtful memories can be softened when the original scenario is imagined as less noxious, more controllable, and ultimately less damaging.

Another key to successful resolution of both posttraumatic stress disorder and eating disorders involves clarifying how stresses in the individual's current life bring back—in full force and bold relief—past traumata. Once the individual can see that current experience can and must be disengaged from past trauma, the impact of the original trauma will lessen. With eating disorder symptomatology in particular, it is essential to find new ways of expressing whatever the eating disorder stands for, as well as to learn more about which aspects of the self-experience it has encapsulated. Because many people must struggle to put their feelings into words, I encourage patients to keep a daily journal and to read novels, biographies, and poetry. A familiarity with literature can develop a language for feelings and give patients an opportunity to find role models or new coping strategies.

The eating disorder takes the pain away temporarily, but it can never serve to master the pain or build a new identity. Instead, these women are able to consolidate their new identities when they are en-couraged to learn how others have found themselves—through involve-ment in peer groups and by reading the life stories of other survivors. The central thesis of this approach rests on the fact that the eating disorder has been at once both self-affirming and self-destructive. The goal of treatment is to enhance the self-affirming activities with the knowledge that deep, safe, interpersonal bonds can be formed and main-tained. As Van der Kolk (1987) explains, "Traumatized patients are frequently very difficult to engage in psychotherapy. This probably is related both to a fear of attachment, which reawakens the fear of aban-donment, and to the reluctance to remember the trauma itself" (p. 187).

Yet experience has proven these patients can be some of the most gratifying people to treat, because they *do* respond to the beneficial effects of the therapeutic relationship, which they can then transmute into their personal lives. Each of the women described in this chapter has made significant progress, not only in terms of controlling the eating disorder but also in establishing mature connectedness and in develop-ing give-and-take relationships. Their lives bear witness to the potential for forgiveness—and to the mastery sung in one of the last stanzas of *Les Misérables*: to love another person is to see the face of God.

# 10

# Drowning Sorrow: Chemical Dependency and Eating Disorders

People who drink to drown their sorrow should be told that sorrow knows how to swim.

Ann Landers

A solitary woman sits next to a rumpled bohemian man in a Paris cafe. With a glass of an intoxicating substance in front of her, she stares dejectedly into space.

Focusing on her gaunt demeanor and disheveled appearance, we imagine that she is troubled by years of drunkenness and loneliness. As our minds elaborate her story, we fantasize that she has become disenchanted with life through many personal tragedies unknown to us. She appears to be literally drowning her sorrows in absinthe, a bitter, anise-flavored liquor frequently imbibed in fin de siècle France.

Whatever the particular nuances of this woman's story, those who view her immediately feel a sense of compassion, if not pity. Her tragic plight leaves us wondering what has caused her solemn expression and obvious withdrawal from the world. All her natural vibrancy and color seem to have been transformed into tawny or grayish hues.

This is a description of the famous painting *Absinthe*. It hangs in the Musée D'Orsay in Paris, evocatively conveying the plight of a lonely, inebriated woman. When it was exhibited in London in 1893 by its creator, the French Impressionist Edgar Degas, a scandal erupted. Despite Degas's skill in producing a powerful psychological portrait of the ravages of alcoholism, his contemporaries shunned such an apparently somber—if not pessimistic—portrayal of Parisian life. As many people still do today, there were those who wished to dwell on pleasantries and to avoid the seamy, darker side of human existence.

Like the people who struggle with the problems of chemical dependency and alcoholism by using the defense mechanism of denial, our society also denies the impact of both problems. An increasing number of women are thus beset with a multitude of side effects derived from their drug dependence and alcoholism. They find it difficult to openly reveal their desperation and sense of personal failure and futility. Like the woman in *Absinthe*, who conveys the painful isolation imposed by her addiction by sitting next to but being totally disconnected from her compatriot, the women today who abuse addictive substances often find it difficult (if not impossible) to engage in helpful, mutually fulfilling relationships. One function of their chemical dependency rests on a substance's easy availability and usefulness as "a friend." Users turn to these substances for solace and care and to avoid dealing with pain and disappointment in life.

Increasing evidence shows that a large number of women with eating disorders also have problems with alcoholism and chemical dependency (Bulik 1987a). The number of research reports in the literature about this important connection has skyrocketed over the past 3 years. Although a few well-conducted studies argue that there is no connection between addictive behaviors and eating disorders, most studies have found that at least 30% and perhaps as many as 50% of patients with bulimia nervosa also have a history of current or prior substance abuse (Mitchell et al. 1992). The problem of alcohol and drug abuse among people with anorexia is less clear. However, investigation of food restricters who also binge (a bulimic subtype) reveals that they have an increased prevalence of alcoholism and drug abuse.

The family members of the dually diagnosed patient who struggles with both an eating disorder and chemical dependency have been shown in at least one report to have a higher incidence of depression and chemical dependency themselves (Strober et al. 1982). Dually diagnosed patients and their family members tend to struggle also with personality disorders and impaired interpersonal functioning. Thus, despite the lack of a clear-cut relationship between eating disorders and substance abuse, most researchers believe that the two addictions are somehow linked. Most troubling are the conclusions from some reports that indicate a poorer outcome for bulimic patients with a history of alcohol abuse or chemical dependency, compared to those whose sole addiction is to food. Understanding the link between both disorders as fully as possible is therefore extremely important.

The suggestion that alcoholism and drug dependence are observed more often in people with bulimia than in those with anorexia rests on the hypothesis of impaired impulse control. Giving in to impulses of any kind is anathema to the anorexic individual. To maintain a fasting state, anorexic people must exert extraordinary self-control. On the other hand, bulimic people and people who abuse various chemical substances are alike in that they lose voluntary control over the substances they use. They also frequently engage in repetitive and highly destructive activities, despite adverse consequences. Their strong impulse to consume the substances that are hurtful to them persists despite repeated admonitions to avoid them.

About 24% of all people with bulimia also struggle with compulsive shoplifting, or kleptomania. Thus a great controversy rages about whether eating disorders are real addictions, best understood by an addiction model, or whether the two syndromes (anorexia and bulimia) are not different enough to warrant contrasting conceptualizations and treatments.

In addition to the descriptive resemblance of the two conditions, both carry psychological similarities. For example, both chemical addiction and food preoccupation help individuals deal with uncomfortable feelings, albeit in a self-destructive way. Because of the shame associated with both disorders, people will go to great lengths to deny and hide the intensity of their involvement. They might be able to keep their disorder secret for years. Even though patients are aware from what they see in the media that eating disorders and addictions are hurtful, their involvement with both gives them a sense of security. From a psychodynamic perspective, case examples can help us understand why this feeling of security might develop.

Addictions are characterized by preoccupation with the substance being abused; this manifest behavior simultaneously keeps the person from engaging in meaningful life activities that might evoke overwhelming anxiety. After all, taking a chance on becoming involved in work, a new relationship, or life itself increases the potential risk of failure.

Many times, the individual who is addicted and who also has an eating disorder has experienced multiple psychological losses and physical problems. The addiction helps avoid life's difficulties because of the preoccupation—or obsession—with food, alcohol, or drugs. This notion may explain why 12-step programs are helpful for some groups of patients with either disorder. Although the merits and deficits of programs such as Overeaters Anonymous (OA), Alcoholics Anonymous (AA), and Narcotics Anonymous (NA) are subject to debate, such organizations do provide a sense of healthy belonging and group identity for the addicted person. They combat the kind of loneliness exemplified in Degas's picture by providing social support in meetings; caretaking and interest in the form of individual sponsors; and a homelike atmosphere where thoughts, worries, and anxieties can be not only shared but also heard, accepted, and understood. These functions theoretically replace some of what the participants do not now have—or may never have had—within their family of origin: a place where they are treated with respect for individual differences and where they are encouraged to speak their own minds and to act in their own best interests.

Researchers now generally concede that there are many causes for alcoholism and chemical dependency (polysubstance abuse), just as there are for eating disorders themselves. However, the disorders all converge on the difficulty that troubled people have with maintaining self-esteem and caring for themselves. Someone who seeks treatment for both an eating disorder and alcoholism or substance abuse represents a highly complex interaction of genetic, cultural, family, and personality variables that have contributed to an often highly entrenched and diffi-cult-to-treat problem.

Current psychodynamic therapy emphasizes that there is probably no single personality characteristic that predisposes anyone to these disorders, but the intoxicant effect itself can enhance the vulnerable person's desire to feel temporarily stronger, less tense, and happy. People who lack the internal resources to soothe themselves can remedy their inadequacy by using mood-altering substances such as drugs, alcohol, or food—or a combination of these. Studies also indicate that individuals with an eating disorder who are prone to use such substances will also tend to have more than one "chemical of choice." One hypothesis about this dangerous tack of multiple abuse derives from knowledge of the deficit in self-esteem and self-care that lead to the problem in the first place: individuals who feel so ill at ease, lonely, ashamed, and desperate will turn to a variety of substances despite any adverse consequences. This inability to avoid self-destructive behavior is a defining character-istic of the addictive process.

In this chapter I allude to the fact that the drug or food itself may be used to fill up the individual or as a replacement for other people or friendship. Actually, this is an oversimplification used to highlight an issue, but it is not meant to imply that there is a simple substitution of drugs and food for failed relationships with people. As Kohut (1971) has described, "The drug serves not as a substitute for loved or loving ob-jects, or for a relationship with them, but as a replacement for the deficit in the psychological structure" (p. 46). This distinction is import-ant in understanding how people who struggle with eating disorders and substance abuse disorders actually have deficits in their capacity to self-regulate. As E. J. Khantzian (in press), an addictions specialist and psy-choanalyst, describes it,

> Suffering is at the heart of addictive disorders . . . addiction is a solution to life's problems . . . individuals are not apt to become drug dependent if they are more or less in touch with and able to bear and express their feelings, if they feel good about themselves, if they have reasonably healthy relationships with others, and if they have an adequate capacity for self-care.

The tendency toward addictions thus reflects the deficit in the ability to relate to others and to deal with life's pain constructively. When I speak of the multiple roles that substances play for some people, I am alluding to the personal vulnerabilities people attempt to repair and recover from by turning to substances.

The subject of substance abuse naturally brings to mind illegal drugs such as cocaine, heroin, marijuana, and amphetamines. Yet individuals with an eating disorder also abuse other substances that are more easily obtainable—diet pills, laxatives, diuretics (water pills), thyroid hormone, and insulin. Because these latter drugs do not cause the same "high" as the physically addictive substances do, their psychologically addictive capacity is less well known. However, diet pills, laxatives, diuretics, and the like can reinforce the individual's craving for other substances or the desire to lose weight.

Misusing purgatives and diet pills can cause severe physical consequences, including death. As a result, the parents of some anorexic and bulimic individuals have petitioned the U.S. Food and Drug Administration to legislate greater control of over-the-counter laxatives and diet pills because of deaths linked to their misuse. Just as with other drugs of abuse, a person should be under medical supervision when attempting to discontinue using these substances, because rapid withdrawal from them can lead to medical complications.

## Dangerous Liaisons

We have seen how people who abuse multiple substances and food yearn for greater control over their feelings. One of the most striking pitfalls of such an adaptation to life is the ultimate loss of control over the disturbed eating pattern or psychoactive substance use. As the disorder progresses, a person's degree of control diminishes, and the obsession with food or the substance grows. Finally, a pattern of obsessional thinking may interfere with daily life to the extent that work or enjoyable activities are neglected.

Naturally, a simple yearning for control is not all that is involved. Rather, the individual willingly trades known consequences (albeit very harmful ones) for some measure of mastery of underlying pain. One aspect of the compromise may be the desire to change an original, passively experienced event into one that is actively mastered, thereby helping the person to feel not only more in control but also more alive.

Meanwhile, these individuals usually deny or keep secret their behavior. One hallmark of a combined eating disorder and psychoactive drug abuse problem is a degree of denial or secretiveness so extensive that some mental health professionals describe it as nearly "delusional." People with such a dual diagnosis want to avoid acknowledging the toll exacted by their eating disorder and substance abuse, lest they be forced to acknowledge the problem and work with it directly. Even those individuals with more self-awareness tend to hide their complications from loved ones and treaters, to protect both themselves and others.

Patients with the dual problem of chemical dependency and eating disorders confide to their treaters that drugs and alcohol often lessen their inhibitions. This can precipitate a relapse of the eating disorder. Moreover, because they may feel guilty about the eating disorder to begin with, they drink to relieve painful self-recrimination. That is to say, "falling off the wagon" with one illness prompts them to give into the other with a laissez-faire attitude about both conditions. One patient told her concerned, experienced therapist that she used alcohol to make herself vomit. In this case, alcohol was used as destructively as syrup of ipecac to institute purging.

Clinical experience has repeatedly demonstrated that even after several months of treatment, patients will often finally confess to a much greater involvement with addictive substances or to their misuse of food than they had originally shared. These patients, perhaps out of shame and despair, conceal the extent of their problems for the longest time despite being urged by treaters to be honest. Unfortunately, treatment without honest acknowledgment of the problem goes nowhere. Nevertheless, family and friends need to be aware of this common defensive style on the part of their loved ones. For example, anorexic patients will often merely push their food around on the plate to pretend that they are eating, just as alcoholic individuals who acknowledge taking a drink or two occasionally may in actuality be getting drunk every night.

Despite these significant commonalities, there is one important difference between psychoactive substance abuse and the eating disorders. While it is possible, with treatment, to become totally abstinent from drugs of abuse, it is not possible to ever abstain totally from food. People who struggle with both types of disorders will be asked to learn to modulate their food intake while totally refraining from their chemical of choice. To deal with this paradox, these complex patients need a great deal of emotional support and education.

It is also essential to keep in mind that eating disorders and chemical addiction cause clear physiological changes. The starvation state may create an increase in the endorphin level that leads to a high in the initial stages of the illness and leads an individual to excessive dieting, exercising, and possibly addiction to chemicals. This has sometimes been described as an "autoaddiction" that makes the anorexic person susceptible to craving opioid substances. The endogenous opioid system may also play a role in the development of bulimia, and certain foods can be used to compensate for a decrease in important neurotransmitters. Anorexic and bulimic patients may thus have cravings that may be based on biological vulnerabilities that they attempt to make up for with their eating disorders and substance abuse. The role of eating disorders and substance abuse in close relation with one other must be remembered. One anorexic patient became addicted to Xanax (a commonly prescribed benzodiazepine) because her eating disorder gave her substantial insomnia, and she insisted that her physician prescribe a sleeping pill.

The prescription of different treatments for each of these problems leads to complications for both patient and treaters. One benefit of the psychologically focused approach is that it helps patients gain control over emotion and learn healthy ways to cope so that they feel less inclined to turn inappropriately to food or chemicals for solace.

An unfortunate link between eating disorders and substance abuse disorders is the high relapse rate after treatment. The high risk of poor outcome and the medical consequences of each disorder have led conservative clinical practitioners to begin treatment with an inpatient phase. The patient might then be followed less intensively, such as through living in a halfway house, going to psychotherapy, and participating in alcohol and eating disorders programs. After a thorough assessment of the severity of the patient's problem, the patient needs sustained efforts to confront the extent of her denial and secrecy. Clinicians are often surprised to find that the patient's illness is more complex and severe than originally thought.

However, successful treatment is more likely to result when it integrates an eating disorders protocol with standard alcohol and drug rehabilitation methods. This integrated approach is illustrated by the case of Heather E., which posed an extraordinary treatment challenge because of the heritage of alcohol abuse in her family of origin as well as the personality difficulties of both Heather and her parents. When patients are considered on an individual basis and their treatment needs are assessed one by one, it is not uncommon to find a severity of problems as great as those faced by Heather. Yet both professionals and laypeople tend to simplify by focusing on one aspect of the overall problem, perhaps because we would prefer an easy answer to even the most difficult dilemmas. Nevertheless, focusing on one part of the whole might lead us to miss what is crucially important in beginning an effective treatment process for the patient and her loved ones.

## ❦ A Family at War: A Treatment Divided

For years, Heather E.'s parents seemed unable to agree on anything. Even before their divorce when Heather was 13, Heather could remember only their pervasive discord and frequent fights. In some ways, Mr. and Mrs. E. seemed caught in a sadomasochistic solution to their conflicts. Pleasurable sexuality was never a part of their marital relationship. They both demanded an unrealistic amount of affirmation and gratification, and each often responded with childlike expressions of rage and sulking. They spent 5 years finalizing their divorce because of their bitter disagreement about visitation rights and child support. They displayed an intense need to remain durably but unhappily tied to each other, despite trials of family intervention and divorce mediation.

Because both her parents drank heavily, Heather frequently found herself in the role of family caretaker. She saw no way to avoid the frequent alcoholic outbursts of her mother or the cunning, manipulative behavior of her father. (Only after years of treatment did Heather finally reveal that her father had frequently engaged her in seductive behavior during his own drinking bouts.) Heather felt disconnected from her parents and staved off any real feelings about her dilemma by turning to food and alcohol herself.

Despite her gift for languages and her empathy for the plight of others, Heather avoided any semblance of mature responsibility by following in her parents' footsteps; in her final years of high school, she drank to excess nightly and became highly self-destructive. A suicide attempt led to an inpatient evaluation, and Heather felt ambivalence about the support and treatment she received. On the one hand, the hospital was a safe haven from which she could eventually launch herself; but on the other hand, it raised the threat of exposing the problems of her struggling family.

On the surface, Heather appeared cooperative and agreeable to treatment, only to reject it a few days later by becoming frightened and apprehensive. Various attempts at inpatient diagnostic evaluations only led her to feel more confused about her problems: Should she focus on her drug abuse or her eating disorder? Was the primary issue the subtle sexual abuse inflicted on her, or had the family discord caused her plight? At first Heather's struggle to determine what avenue to pursue was paralleled by the staff as well. Such confusion staves off the real pain any patient must address, which must be understood, interpreted, and contained by her treaters.

At first blush, of course, a patient like Heather presents treaters with the dilemma of how best to focus the treatment. Which problem should be selected, assuming that the patient will participate fully in a comprehensive evaluation? In essence, family members and clinicians have three choices. First, they can admit the individual to a substance abuse program for detoxification and primary treatment of the substance abuse. Or, if the eating disorder is considered life-threatening or more severe than the chemical problem, they can seek treatment for the patient's eating disorder in a specialty program. Finally, they can look for a program that treats dually diagnosed individuals with a systematic integration of an eating disorders protocol with standard alcohol or drug rehabilitation activities. The most sophisticated services now willingly draw on the expertise of all subspecialties to help make the proper selection of treatment techniques for the patient's benefit. They should have a range of supports available—from full inpatient hospitalization to partial hospitalization and therapy.

When the family relationships are as complex and dramatic as in Heather's case, intensive family therapy must be undertaken from the outset. Such therapy obviously assumes a willingness on the part of both the patient and her family to look at and try to change maladaptive aspects of their own behavior. Not unexpectedly, such willingness is not present in many individuals—nor was it for Heather. This is especially tragic when all of the people involved are in so much pain and could benefit from understanding. They require suggestions about how to improve communication and directness without blaming each other.

Despite our own program's usual policy that both parents be present at the admission of their child, Heather's parents simply packed her up and flew her halfway across the country to meet with the preadmission team of our eating disorders unit. In the early stage of her treatment, neither of them showed much interest or emotional investment in Heather's treatment. Lacking so much guidance and care in her youth, Heather immediately and predictably latched on to our staff with childlike abandon.

With our standard treatment protocol, Heather's eating disorder came quickly under control, because her "false self" was activated in an attempt to please the staff. She was so hungry for acceptance that she banished from thought any hint of disagreement with her treaters. Usually, patients with both an eating disorder and a substance abuse problem can be treated by adding the typical structure of a 12-step program, drug and alcohol counseling, and education about chemical dependency to the daily regime of the eating disorders program. In Heather's case, however, a consultant found her addictive behavior severe enough to warrant a 2-month stay on the substance abuse unit.

This fortuitous recommendation led us to diagnose a relationship repetition that was crucial in helping Heather overcome both her eating disorder and her substance abuse problem. What transpired after her transfer represented the terrible bind Heather felt in vis-à-vis both her parents. Once she was moved to the substance abuse unit, her eating disorder flared as she mourned the loss of her favorite nursing staff members and psychiatrist. She implored the staff of the eating disorders unit to take her back, and she made two suicide attempts to try to manipulate them into doing so. Our attempts to help Heather work through her feelings about the transfer were foiled until she began to understand that she was repeating the struggles she had felt for years: whenever she was with her father, she felt totally disloyal to her mother, and vice versa. To deal with the tension caused by her seemingly insoluble predicament and to ease the pain of witnessing her parents' continual battles, she binged, purged, and drank.

Not even the helpful presence of an outpatient psychotherapist and the 12-step AA program provided Heather with the support she needed, so inpatient treatment was her only option. Her life-threatening difficulties had become entrenched because she had internalized an aspect of both her parents that she was using to abuse herself. Although her biological predisposition to alcoholism was certainly a contributing factor, she benefited over time by understanding how she was attacking herself—just as each of her parents attacked themselves by drinking and engaging in impulsive behavior toward each other. In lieu of taking care of herself, Heather was launching a violent assault on herself and others.

Because Heather had never learned the basics of self-care in her family of origin, a treatment program that focused heavily on education around the substance abuse and the eating disorder was not enough. Staff members also had to instruct Heather in daily tasks that people usually learn growing up. For example she was given an hour-by-hour schedule and practiced doing her laundry, learning to cook, and participating in leisure pursuits. Some of Heather's fondest memories of treatment were the times she spent with an older female staff member who firmly but lovingly taught her how to sort, wash, and iron clothes.

During these seemingly banal routine tasks, Heather—like any child in a loving home—not only learned the duties at hand but also absorbed much from her interactions with the staff member. How much this particular treatment intervention helped Heather's later sobriety and freedom from her eating disorder is unknown; but she certainly looked back with pride on what she had learned, as well as on the staff member's praise of her. Like a small child who yearns to please her parents and be acknowledged for her good efforts, Heather felt her self-esteem and, consequently, her capacity for self-care increase as she learned fundamental aspects of day-to-day living.

Pathological behavior can only be given up when healthier behavior is put in its place. Of course, Heather also had to let go of her tendency to wish that her parents would be different than they were in reality. Part of the hard work of treatment involves mourning what is hoped for but will never be. Heather's growing capacity to do so on her own meant that she no longer needed to binge or drink to handle painful feelings.

## An Integrated Treatment Approach

The first goal in treating a patient who has both an eating disorder and a substance abuse problem is to complete a thorough medical and psychiatric evaluation. Both illnesses can severely compromise nutrition, so nutritional rehabilitation and maintenance become cornerstones of any good program. To facilitate good eating habits as well as to deal definitively with the underlying psychological issues, treaters must stop both the patient's binge-and-purge behavior and any substance abuse. Specialty units for eating disorders usually implement a high level of structure around eating, often using a relapse prevention model similar to that found in a substance abuse program. From the outset, patients are also encouraged to attend specific group meetings for chemical dependency, such as NA or AA. To encourage and maintain the interruption of binge-purge and addiction cycles, treaters should develop a tailored relapse prevention plan.

One treatment modality that is often underemphasized with substance abuse patients is that of psychotherapy. As Dodes (1988) has pointed out, some patients benefit from psychotherapy alone, whereas others will profit most from AA. Still others profit from a combination of the two approaches. Clearly, patient and treater must work together to decide what is best. Focusing on only one aspect of the overall picture (just the eating disorder or just the substance abuse) may cause the other to be neglected. Patient and treater must both try to maintain a global viewpoint that allows both aspects of the issue to be worked on simultaneously.

Individual, family, and group psychotherapy may prove useful with these patients. In one study of abstinent alcoholic subjects, 90% of those in AA who also sought psychotherapy found the latter helpful (S. Brown 1985). Just as most of us benefit from having more than one caring, supportive figure in our lives at any given time, so too do those who are burdened by these multiple problems benefit from a variety of ongoing multiple treatment modalities. Individual therapists, group therapists and other members of the group, and participants in AA or NA groups converge to encourage these individual patients to take better care of themselves.

AA promotes self-esteem by awarding coins after a given period of sobriety, and group members often praise fellow members for a new accomplishment or courageous behavior. The AA group also offers opportunities to help other people, which virtually assures improved self-worth. How can you not feel good about yourself when you know you can offer something beneficial to another person?

Finally, each treatment modality provides the opportunity to learn about one's illness and oneself. Although insight alone will never produce the behavioral change necessary for stopping an eating disorder or a chemical problem, it can enhance a sense of mastery by focusing on individual strengths and weaknesses. In turn, such mastery helps the patient weather the storm of self-defeating behaviors and thoughts and past neglect. Group and individual psychotherapy also provide new ideas about how to use leisure time and cultivate new types of friendships—both crucial areas for growth when a person is attempting to overcome outdated modes of adaptation such as bingeing or imbibing.

## In Search of Nirvana

Freud (1897/1966) provided the insight that alcohol and drugs can sometimes replace love objects in the unconscious mind. In describing the psychological struggles of the adolescent who drinks, Conroy (1988) suggested that addictions may be a kind of substitute lover. And when Karl Menninger looked at the range of self-destructive behaviors in his classic work *Man Against Himself* (1938), he saw alcoholism as one of a myriad of self-destructive behaviors. In his view, alcoholism is a dangerous and potentially disastrous attempt at self-cure of inner conflict.

Vaillant (1983) found that people who abuse more than one substance are more likely than alcoholic people to have had unstable childhoods and, consequently, to use mood-altering substances more often as a form of "self-medication." Particularly in adolescence, such individuals may use marijuana to ease an underlying depression. But their emphasis on obtaining the drugs can keep them from moving into other life-enhancing activities that might help alleviate poor self-image and ennui. Most contemporary psychoanalytic clinicians emphasize how internalizing good parental figures can help people avoid addiction. Individuals without adequate protection may seek an alternative way to regulate their intense feelings and impulses. One feeling in particular that may need to be modulated concerns the level of closeness or distance with which a person feels comfortable in interpersonal relationships. Some individuals may turn to addictive substances as a way to contain their aggressive feelings, while others yearn for an experience of oneness with a maternal figure who might compensate for the lack of such a relationship in infancy.

Many readers will understandably believe that this rationale gives addicted individuals an "out" for their pathology. One might also surmise that the joint problem of eating disorders and chemical addiction results from some as-yet-undetermined biochemical process, which may indeed be the case for some people. Still others will argue that the stress or underlying causes and meanings of the disorder lets these individuals off the hook and helps them avoid taking ultimate responsibility for their difficulties. Yet clinical experience has shown that patients who understand some of the meanings behind their addiction will be able to keep their treatment on a better track.

❦ Hilary F. was an attractive, 26-year-old doctoral candidate in engineering when she came for treatment of severe bulimia nervosa and addiction to nitrous oxide. Her boyfriend, a young dentist, had introduced her to her drug of choice when she had some minor dental surgery performed in his office. Hilary, who had always felt put down by her parents despite her outstanding academic accomplishment, believed that the nitrous oxide helped her recapture feelings of an infantile nirvana. After a temporary high, she would continue her flirtation with oblivion by gorging on boxes of glazed doughnuts and pound cake.

Soon Hilary was caught up in a vicious circle, able to experience total, unremitting pleasure and gratification—unless she stopped using or bingeing. Because all her impulses were gratified, she felt as if she had stumbled on a source of unending love. Nevertheless, she still feared losing what little autonomy she had gained for herself.

Hilary gained consistent control over her behavior only as she began to see, in therapy, how her addictions had helped her deal with overwhelming anxiety. Castigated by her family for years, she had developed an image of herself as so bad that it could only be made good by her temporary and unsuccessful addictive pursuits. For such individuals, treatment must center on consistency and help to build an internal structure devoid of addictive patterns. Hilary came to recognize that her disorders worsened whenever she wished to regain a feeling of oneness with a maternal object who would view her as decent and good. Her addictive behavior allowed her to stay childlike and dependent, while the substance became the mother she had always longed for.

Even her boyfriend's procurement of nitrous oxide for her (albeit self-destructive in the long run) was equated in Hilary's unconscious mind with her desire to feel special. Following a purge or after inhaling nitrous oxide, she was able to negotiate interpersonal relationships without feeling as worthless or ashamed. Like the life histories of many other dually addicted individuals, Hilary's showed that a variety of factors contributed to her bulimia and drug addiction. These were remediated only as she came to understand—and then replace—her quest for infantile oneness with more age-appropriate, mature gratifications.

# Relapse and Recovery

As I already mentioned, both eating disorders and psychoactive substance abuse have a high rate of relapse. To be effective, treatment must emphasize how to avoid relapse. Not only do cravings for the misused substance lead an individual to seek it out and backslide, but a resurgence of previous behavior associated with the addiction can precipitate deterioration. Many authorities believe that relapse occurs when the person even begins to think about using a substance that has been abused or about returning to a behavior that has been hurtful.

People with eating disorders often feel extremely guilty when they do relapse. Their sense of shame and disappointment about their failure initiates a compromise pattern wherein they persist in abusing food to lessen the pain they feel about regressing. This inner turmoil causes more complications with bingeing and purging. Moreover, because these people often believe that others will be as punitive with them as they are with themselves, they are especially vigilant about keeping their relapse secret. Better to struggle with the emotional pain of failure alone than to risk the anger and disappointment of a loved one or therapist! This tendency to feel guilty and ashamed about relapsing can lead to its perpetuation. The quickest way to interrupt the cycle is to consider it a "working relapse." The individual is encouraged to take a hard look at whatever brought on the relapse to begin with.

To facilitate the process of regaining healthy control, these patients might add some new structure to their lives and avoid thinking patterns or places where they feel tempted to engage in maladaptive behavior. When individuals are encouraged to place the relapse in perspective and follow Scarlett O'Hara's guidepost, "Tomorrow is another day," they can see that all is not lost. Their self-esteem is enhanced, particularly when it is possible for them to honestly assess the denial as being weaker than in the past or the relapse as being shorter than before. Such assessments fight the guilt-fueled tendency to develop a prolonged relapse.

In the area of relapse prevention, cognitive therapy is joining forces with long-held psychodynamic principles. Making healthy decisions and avoiding situations where alcohol and food have been misused in the past are encouraged by both cognitive and psychodynamic therapists.

Enhanced coping skills (e.g., meditation, hobbies) help redirect the individual who may be on the verge of a relapse and gradually help build the ego's capacity to do other tasks. Patients are also taught to refrain from making relapse or other errors into a catastrophe. By stressing the need for rational thought and the opportunity to regain control quickly, people also gain in self-mastery while diminishing the tendency to be self-critical. Consequently, the propensity to see the worst in a situation and in themselves is reframed as a potential avenue for mastery, growth, and decision making. Often these principles quickly enable patients to turn untoward events around to their benefit. They begin to think and to act differently—and ultimately more compassionately toward themselves (Brownell et al. 1986; Schlundt and Johnson 1990).

But just when things seem to be going well, temptation can lure these patients off track and unconsciously defeat their growing sense of self. An alcoholic person, for example, may want to be able to drink socially even though doing so is an unrealistic expectation because of the high tendency toward relapse with alcoholism. Although the physiological craving for certain food substances is addressed in Chapter 12, it is important to note here that most eating disorder patients can list at least one food that can trigger an entire binge. To indulge themselves with even a taste of the desired substance (which is usually something sweet) is to tempt fate. Yet many do just this before they are able to cope with the consequences, thus setting off a whole cycle of relapse.

One of Freud's most brilliant insights came from observing the general tendency of certain people to undermine their own success. In his paper "The 'Exceptions': Those Wrecked by Success" (1914), he argued that people feel guilty for the very success they have tried hard to achieve. Often this conflict, which is almost always rooted in the infantile situation, occurs because of an unconscious belief that our parents will be angry or envious if we do better than they did. Those who are "wrecked by success" are able to snatch defeat from the jaws of victory.

This self-destructive tendency is illustrated by the case of a successful physician who, after years of struggling with subclinical pathology, was nearing completion of her residency training. At that point, she began drinking heavily, had an affair, and developed an eating disorder. With her career goal well within reach, she ended up defeating herself—perhaps because she sensed her mother's long-standing envy of her. Although this physician had chosen and grown in her professional sphere because it was not an apparent source of rivalry with her mother, she could not permit herself to challenge her mother on other grounds, such as in the areas of romantic relationships or physical attractiveness.

Treatment can help people with self-destructive tendencies learn how to avoid repeatedly and unconsciously creating patterns of failure that let them undermine themselves. In addition to encouraging sobriety, groups such as NA and AA challenge the addict's automatic minimization or dismissal of good feelings such as pride in accomplishments and commitment to relationships. Group therapies also help individual members identify and enjoy their own talents and successes without inflicting guilty self-punishment. The individual must come to recognize that it is she herself who wrecks success or the prospect of her success.

This formulation can augment the commonly held feminist view that tends to hold society in general—and men in particular—responsible for the difficulties confronting women. No doubt society's and men's preferences have influenced the apparent increase in the incidence of these disorders. But social considerations must be emphasized along with individual perspectives. Ultimately, any avoidance of self-responsibility perpetuates the fantasy that society wrecks the individual rather than that the individual is responsible for hurting herself. If a woman avoids seeing the part she actively plays in perpetuating her difficulties, it hinders her engagement in the therapeutic process. In reality, one can only change oneself. Women must be helped to see how we have accepted the status quo. For centuries, we have played our assigned roles. In so doing, we may not have achieved in the areas we purport to want to, but we have warded off the envy of others, maintained a sense of personal coherence by having established roles, guaranteed our own security, inflicted our own guilty self-punishment, and stayed loyal to the unconscious admonitions of our own mothers. In essence, these unconscious strategies have served important functions for self-regulation.

Society has been an important stifler of women's ambitions; but as we as women begin to challenge long-held values and ourselves, we will not have the sense of safety that we once did. The more women can acknowledge our own quest for security and the change incumbent in shifting political ideals, the more free we will be to change ourselves and to live fully.

A single or dual addiction helps people avoid the challenges of looking at themselves more deeply by filling up time and space. One unpalatable but nonetheless important reason for addiction is that it helps people avoid the unconscious psychological pitfall of having a more successful future. As Schafer (1988) has written about this tendency to sabotage one's own success, "It is a model of unconscious activity disguised manifestly as passivity, and it is a model of unconsciously gaining pleasure or security through manifest unhappiness" (p. 90).

### ❦  Avoiding Painful Separation

Tanya G., age 18, started drinking when she was in second grade. Her first encounter with alcohol occurred when she stayed overnight with a school friend. Her use of alcohol remained consistent until she was in sixth grade, when she also began overeating. She reported that she was able to keep her behavior secret because her parents seemed to take little interest in her, rather appearing more preoccupied with their own lives.

By the ninth grade, Tanya was drinking daily ("three to four beers") during her school lunch hours and enjoyed getting drunk on weekends. Despite her high intelligence, she began to skip school frequently. By the time she was a junior, a friend had introduced her to cocaine, which she loved instantly. Tanya's use quickly escalated from ½ gram to 1 gram of cocaine per episode. Finally, she began to use methamphetamine as a cheaper alternative to cocaine.

Because her family was relatively well off, Tanya never lacked money for her "supplies" but nevertheless enjoyed shoplifting regularly. Meanwhile, her bulimia grew steadily worse. Her personal drug portfolio was also beginning to look like a pharmacy. Tanya frequently used cocaine and methamphetamine to achieve highs and to diet, but she varied her usage by smoking cocaine, swallowing LSD, popping diazepam (Valium) to sleep, and experimenting with a variety of other psychostimulants.

During one of many episodes of intoxication, Tanya was date raped. She became pregnant and had an abortion. She managed to avoid any type of treatment until she was hospitalized in a university drug abuse program while in the throes of a suicidal crisis. By this time Tanya's daily consumption of cocaine was 7–8 grams. In addition, she was consuming a case of beer a day, an occasional bottle of NyQuil, and any prescribed addictive medications she could get through her highly manipulative and seductive personality. The university treatment team was at a loss about how to understand the difficulties of this otherwise talented and engaging young woman.

One central problem for Tanya was her failure to separate and individuate from her parents. As was discussed previously, the substance-abusing individual—like the person with an eating disorder—may yearn for a strong, overly close (symbiotic) relationship with a maternal figure, supposedly based on lack of such in infancy. Tanya's mother had always been preoccupied with her own life as a fashion designer; not surprisingly, Tanya turned to her father for comfort and support. However, he was also emotionally uninvolved with his daughter. Consequently, as Tanya grew up, she did not have the firm foundation of loving, giving parents. To cope with her sadness about this lack, she used her eating disorder and drug abuse to alleviate her underlying depression. Without a sure base to be launched from, she could never feel appropriately independent and autonomous, nor had she developed normal ways to care for herself.

Drugs helped Tanya compensate for a deep-seated feeling of inadequacy. Her insecurity stemmed from her feeling that she did not have, as she put it, "the right stuff" to engage her mother. Tanya's impoverished and unstable childhood led her to use food and addictive substances as a desperate attempt at self-care and, consequently, self-cure. On the surface, her behavior seemed very unhealthy, which of course it was. However, her therapist chose to try to connect with Tanya from the first by suggesting that both drugs and food had been her way of coping with life.

As long as Tanya engaged in her symptomatic behavior, she was able to hold her deep feelings of sadness and unworthiness at bay. Even as her symptoms kept her from using her talents in life, they also served the important function of making her feel more human and soothed. In a peculiar and paradoxical way, the symptoms provided her with a sense of being mothered or cared for that she had not known before. Only when she began to understand the function of her apparent self-destructiveness could she begin to replace drugs with human interactions.

Then Tanya had to face the difficult task of mourning the loss of her symptoms. Because any addiction becomes a highly valued part of one's identity (despite its destructive potential), it must be replaced with a new internal structure. Without becoming transformed and feeling more whole, the individual faces inevitable relapse. Tanya's therapist therefore tried to encourage her not only to abstain from her eating disorder and drugs of abuse but also to begin building a self by going to school, making new friends, participating in sports, and so forth.

Tanya's therapist also helped her patient say good-bye to the symptoms. For Tanya, both her eating disorder and her addictive behavior seemed like old friends—understandably so, because they had been more reliable figures of soothing than her parents. They had been a solution to the life problems of dealing with intense feelings and providing self-care, albeit ineffectively. As with any loss, Tanya had to face anger, denial, and eventual acceptance of her changed life as she buried her bulimia and chemical dependency.

In the first century C.E., the Roman poet Caladusa wrote that grief must be shared to be endured. Tanya's therapist had the wisdom to insist that her patient not only attend NA and AA, but that she also talk in individual therapy about how giving up drugs felt. It is crucial for those who struggle with addiction to find a therapist and a group or groups with whom they feel comfortable and at ease, and who in turn can tolerate their most painful feelings. A therapist who seems aloof, controlling, or unable to hear sadness and rage will never help the patient through the difficult but central treatment issue of mourning her symptoms.

# Kleptomania

In addition to the addictions described earlier, people with eating disorders sometimes also have problems with compulsive stealing (kleptomania) and compulsive shopping (oniomania). Usually they do not need the objects they steal and could well afford to buy them. Intensive psychotherapy can help these individuals understand and work through their compulsions for shoplifting, food, and chemical substances.

Schwartz (1992) believes that those who struggle with kleptomania are often devoid of affectionate relationships. So, fearing betrayal and wanting to avoid abandonment, they reduce people to things. They treat other people as if they were puppets, quickly becoming angry at those they cannot easily control. Because stolen objects cannot abandon or betray them, these individuals remain in control and feel excited by the act itself. Patients with kleptomania and oniomania confide that they are out of touch with what they really want and need. They often use objects very concretely, because they have little ability to use symbolic language. Taking from other people is also a handy way to express aggression for perceived attacks without dealing with the feelings and destructive impulses in words. Therapy can help these women name their feelings and become better at speaking about what actually bothers them, thus reducing their need to fill themselves up—literally—with tangible food or stolen objects.

These women often complain that they feel little capacity for love. Playful, intimate exchanges are lacking in their lives. Frequently anorgasmic, they commonly express feelings of monotony and deadness. They sense that their significant others are bored with and disconnected from them.

Sometimes the serotonergic antidepressants (e.g., fluoxetine [Prozac], sertraline [Zoloft], paroxetine [Paxil]) may help these patients reduce their impulsiveness. However, medicine is not a panacea and may

only bring about a temporary improvement. They can sometimes provide enough of a jump start, though, to give a person an opportunity to
find enough motivation to work on a deeper understanding of her feelings in therapy.

The patient must come to understand that all addictions may have
an intoxicating and sedating quality. Sometimes kleptomanic behavior
is so dissociated from a patient's conscious awareness that great pains
must be taken to call it up in treatment. At least one successful legal
case has stressed how unconscious motives and the dissociated experience of stealing can launch a defense against the criminal charges that
had been filed for theft (Ziolko 1988).

The danger in treating any one of these impulse problems is simply
that if one symptom goes into remission, another symptom may take its
place. Thus kleptomania might be replaced by bulimia or drug abuse, or
vice versa. Furthermore, psychosomatic symptoms such as asthma may
also take the place of impulsiveness. The underlying problem is the
inability to express emotion directly or use symbolic processes. To remedy the situation, these patients must work through their unconscious
issues of guilt, which they try to undo by vomiting or taking drugs. Even
then, whenever they undergo a separation or face change or disappointment, they may feel so upset and bereft that they resort to their old
patterns of emotionally interchangeable addictive behaviors. Instead,
they need to learn to discuss feelings of loss and to find new ways to
repair relationships.

# Conclusion

The number of patients with both an eating disorder and an addictive
disorder is high. An appropriate integrated treatment approach will address the psychological issues behind both problems. The fact that most
individuals with both disorders do not get well easily demonstrates that
a merely symptom-oriented approach is inadequate.

When the eating disorder and drug dependence coexist, *both*
problems are priorities. Because the disorders are primary and
interdependent, they must be studied and treated simultaneously. An

understanding of psychodynamic principles helps us see these struggles as real, human ones, which enlarges the patient's worldview considerably. Patients must learn that there are good reasons why they have formed an identity around their addictive behaviors—even as they learn to recognize the physical and emotional costs of those reasons. Therapists can help these patients seek out the underlying causes of their problems, while providing them with anchors and supports in lives that often have been derailed by abandonment, abuse, family discord, and a dearth of inadequate parenting or parental role models.

Clinical experience shows that patients benefit enormously from the presence of a clear and sufficient amount of environmental stabilization. This provides them with an opportunity for gradual resocialization and emotional disclosure. However, the early emphasis on containment to prevent direct and indirect self-harm is gradually replaced by increasing the patient's self-responsibility for abstinence through participation in various therapies, including NA and AA, and finding ways of control and mastery through cognitive strategies and relapse prevention. Learning about the problem in educational classes is also helpful.

A sense of humor about self and others is a positive sign of flexibility that can moderate the harsh conscience that demands high achievement and sabotages success. Likewise, a person can move forward by developing the ability to tolerate painful and intense emotions while understanding that all relationships, though ambivalently perceived and ultimately imperfect, give support and stability. The treatment goal is for the patient to replace substances with people as the main source of soothing gratification and meaning in life. Enhanced caring for the self may then eventually translate into greater empathic attunement to others, leading the individual to develop the capacity to form and tolerate mutual, life-enhancing relationships.

# 11

# The Body at Risk: Medical Complications of Eating Disorders

When there's no getting over that rainbow
When my smallest of dreams won't come true
I can take all the madness the world has to give
But I won't last a day without you.

"I Won't Last a Day Without You"
Sung by Karen Carpenter
(Lyrics by Paul Williams)

When Karen Carpenter sang these lyrics of one of her most popular songs, no one expected that her life would be so brief. As
listeners of love songs, we all take for granted their hyperbole. We all
know that we can and will outlast the scars of Cupid's arrow, even as we
protest to our beloved that we cannot survive one moment alone. While
we rhapsodize that such a loss would kill us, we also deny the real perils
of existence that can bring about our demise any day.

Most of us function quite adequately in our world by denying death
(Becker 1973). Yet we quickly become aware of our own mortality when
we, or someone close to us, is struck down by a life-threatening illness or

accident. When someone as famous as Karen Carpenter dies young because of a potentially treatable illness, it pulls us back into stark awareness of the fragility of life and the mortality sometimes associated with an eating disorder. Sadly, she sang that she could not last a day without her "love." Instead, her relentless love of a distortedly thin body led to our loss of her and her beautiful voice.

Karen Carpenter's untimely death, though tragic, increased public awareness of the potentially fatal consequences of eating disorders. Anorexia nervosa and bulimia nervosa are two of the most life-threatening of all psychiatric illnesses. At least 5%–20% of all anorexic people will eventually die from the disorder. Outcome studies in this country and abroad show an increase in deaths due to anorexia linked to the length of time an individual has the disorder. If a person has the illness for 5 years, there is only a 5% mortality rate. But the mortality rate gradually increases to 18% for individuals who have the illness for 30 years.

In contrast to anorexia nervosa, there have been few well-conducted outcome studies on bulimia nervosa. Because this eating disorder has been studied in depth only since the mid-1970s, not enough time has elapsed for full follow-up of treated patients. However, many clinicians believe that bulimic patients will actually be shown to have a higher mortality rate than anorexic patients. This hypothesis is largely based on data collected in European treatment centers throughout the 1960s and 1970s. These reports concluded that individuals who had what was then called "bulimarexia"—alternating periods of self-starvation with bingeing and purging—actually had a much higher incidence of death than those with the disorder's purebred cousin anorexia.

In the United States, a number of reports from university medical centers suggest that the prognosis for people with severe and refractory bulimia is less favorable than for those with uncomplicated anorexia. The medical consequences are themselves higher, and the risk for suicide is greater. Despite the stark importance of these findings about absolute mortality, the data do not take into account the other long-term effects of either illness. Over half of all anorexic patients remain below normal weight despite their ongoing treatment. Some of these patients do improve with respect to their psychological functioning: their interpersonal relationships strengthen, they work through their sexual conflicts, and their work roles evolve. However, a large number of anorexic people remain troubled in the interpersonal, social, and cultural spheres of their lives. Anorexic patients have a continuing preoccupation with thinness that robs them of full participation in life. They also struggle with the physical consequences of their difficulties, such as impaired menstrual function.

Patients with bulimia nervosa have similar long-term problems. With successful treatment, their bingeing and purging may decrease in frequency or disappear altogether, but they remain burdened by the earlier physical effects of the problem (depression, anxiety, and impaired functioning in their personal lives). Both anorexia nervosa and bulimia nervosa are probably long-term conditions for a large number of the people who have them. Cure itself may therefore not be as realistic a goal as is long-term maintenance of a chronic condition.

The medical complications of the disorders can be quite severe. Arnold Andersen of the University of Iowa (1992) has likened the bouts of anorexia and bulimia to the rings of a tree. Each episode leaves a permanent, indelible impression, with the individual never being "normal" or ever quite the same after each one. Once we account for the body systems that are jeopardized by an eating disorder and for its grisly toll (e.g., morbidity), the cascading ravages of the disorder are shown in their true light. We must become aware of the impact an eating disorder can have on each organ and on the body as a whole.

Thus far, our review of the psychological costs of eating disorders has focused little attention on the specific medical complications of the illnesses. Yet every body system can be affected by an eating disorder. We should review, on a system-by-system basis, the physiological problems that occur when an individual enters a state of self-starvation or becomes caught in the vicious binge-purge cycle.

# What Happens When We Starve: The Work of Ansel Keys

As World War II drew to a close, one researcher working in the United States was making notable inroads in understanding metabolism and the effects of starvation. By taking a group of conscientious objectors and systematically starving them, Ansel Keys demonstrated that individuals whose body mass and weight are decreased undergo significant physical, behavioral, and emotional changes (Keys et al. 1950). Keys's work has recently been rediscovered, because many of the changes seen in his volunteer subjects are the same ones found among anorexic patients. His work offers much insight into what actually occurs when individuals starve themselves.

The healthy subjects Keys studied were asked to restrict their food intake until they lost 25% of their original body weight. Keys then focused on the effects of that weight loss on these men. He found that their bodies slowed down remarkably. Their heart rate, respiration, and body temperature all declined. Like anorexic people, these subjects experienced an increased obsession with food. They became so preoccupied with mealtime that it interfered with their other daily activities. Whenever the volunteers did eat, they tended to use an inordinate amount of salt and spices and mixed their food together idiosyncratically. Some of them were able to tolerate periods of hunger better than others. Those who could not adhere to the diet would episodically binge and then feel terribly guilty about what they had done.

Like the eating disorder patient seen in clinical practice, some of the subjects in the Keys study were able to tolerate long periods of food restriction, perhaps to avoid the fear of guilty self-recrimination. But like those volunteers who gave way to their impulse to eat, most people are unable to endure the pain of a fast or hunger for long. After a period of restriction, we all tend to overindulge with a large meal or some binge eating. In fact, on diets that are too low in calories (500–1,000 calories), we simply become so hungry that we often cannot maintain such a diet. We overeat, just as the subjects in the Keys study did, and we end up consuming more calories than if we had eaten sensibly in the first place.

From a psychological perspective, the Keys volunteers were considered to be even-tempered and emotionally stable human beings. Yet as they entered the starving state, they became irritable and angry. Many of them experienced depression, anxiety, and general physical malaise. During the period of normalization of nourishment, their emotional difficulties did not wane for quite some time. Likewise, their interest in sex declined dramatically, and their ability to concentrate and make good judgments was impaired.

One of the most compelling observations Keys made centered on his subjects' intrusive obsession with food. Like anorexic patients, the volunteers found themselves focusing all their attention on the timing, quantity, and quality of their next meal—even to the point of avoiding other life-sustaining activities. Although these men did not develop full-blown eating disorders after the experiment, their 3-month period of starvation led them to be preoccupied with body shape and fat for months after resuming a normal eating pattern. Like anorexic people, the men did not gain weight until they ate a significant number of calories. Some needed to eat as many as 10,000 calories a day to feel satiated. At follow-up a year later, however, most of these men had recovered from both their emotional struggles and their bizarre eating habits.

This experiment demonstrated a number of important clinical features helpful to those who observe and treat people with eating disorders. First, the starvation state alone clearly affects mood and behavior. Any treatment must therefore begin with nutritional care. This focus is the only way to sort out the effects of starvation on mood and thinking from any more deeply rooted psychological problems. Even under the best of circumstances, individuals who have starved themselves will need a long period—up to a year—to readjust their body image and reestablish normal eating patterns.

During the active phase of resuming a normal eating pattern, the anorexic patient will need many more calories to regain and maintain her lost weight than if she were already at her normal weight. Thus, a young woman who can maintain normal weight on a diet of 1,600–1,800 calories may need 3,200–4,000 calories per day if she is recovering from self-starvation.

Finally, many people who set out to lose weight and attempt to restrain their eating on a diet will periodically give in to impulse—that is, go on a binge. This tendency has led the noted investigator and clinician Craig Johnson to quip to his patients that "the best defense against bingeing is to eat regular meals" (Johnson and Connors 1987, p. 231). People ruin their diets by getting too hungry. Paradoxically, eating small meals and staying relatively full helps people avoid overeating by quelling hunger pangs and filling the void without too much food.

# Medical Complications of Anorexia Nervosa

Most deaths attributable to anorexia nervosa are thought to be caused by starvation and instability in the cardiovascular system. Although these individuals are all predisposed to many types of cardiac arrhythmia (irregular heartbeat), it is impossible to predict which ones will eventually have life-threatening symptoms. Common abnormalities can be spotted with an electrocardiogram, but this tool cannot help predict with certainty which patients will have the most dangerous complications. However, these individuals will commonly experience bradycardia (very slow heartbeat) and low blood pressure, which can cause lightheadedness, dizziness, and syncope (fainting).

When a starving person begins eating again, great care must be taken to ensure that the process occurs slowly. If treatment proceeds too quickly, the individual may experience congestive heart failure, which is potentially life threatening. For people considered at medical risk, the nutritional care procedure should be done within a hospital setting where signs of heart failure such as edema and shortness of breath can be monitored and treated quickly. A patient will often need to eat substantially more calories (i.e., 3,500 daily) before she begins to gain weight.

A well-known consequence of eating disorders concerns the problem of electrolyte imbalance, which can produce life-threatening complications. Lowered potassium and chloride (i.e., hypokalemia and hypochloremia, respectively) are among the most studied, although hypomagnesemia, hyponatremia, and hypophosphatemia (i.e., low magnesium, sodium, and phosphorus, respectively) also occur. Yet even regularly monitoring a patient's electrolyte status with routine laboratory tests may not protect against sudden and unsuspected crises. Many patients have normal levels for weeks, only to develop a sudden deficiency that requires immediate medical intervention.

❧ A patient, Margaretta H., was under the care of a competent and concerned family physician. Margaretta had refused all psychotherapeutic help until one day when her starving state led her to be hospitalized on an emergency basis. Because her serum phosphorus levels were low and unstable, her doctor valiantly tried to give her adequate supplements intravenously while providing her with intravenous feedings. Margaretta's physical condition had so deteriorated, however, that her body could not tolerate the challenge. Her 10-year illness had left her so exhausted and wasted that the medical intervention itself overly taxed her. When she died from congestive heart failure and electrolyte imbalance, she weighed only 52 pounds. Her plight led both her family and her doctor to wonder if Margaretta herself had wanted to die.

## Hematological System

Like cardiac irregularities, anemias also result from starvation. They can contribute to the individual's feelings of fatigue, malaise, inertia, and lack of concern and interest in usual activities. Establishing and maintaining good nutrition is the treatment of choice, although vitamin supplementation can also be used. Even in patients who attain their recovery weights, anemia secondary to the eating disorder may persist for many months.

## Musculoskeletal System

Women with anorexia nervosa have reduced bone mass that makes them vulnerable to developing fractures. Osteoporosis, which is not uncommon among elderly women, frequently occurs in adolescents and young women with anorexia nervosa. This condition not only predisposes them to an increased risk for fracture in everyday activities such as walking or stooping, but it may also lead to their assuming a posture usually seen among much older people. Long-term studies now suggest that even when anorexic individuals return to their normal body weight, their bone density remains low and may not normalize for a long time. Youngsters and adolescents who restrict their food intake may impede their growth, and adolescents and adult women will be prone to fractures of their vertebrae, sternums, and long bones *years after* their recovery.

## Endocrine System

Amenorrhea (cessation of menstrual period) is a core feature of anorexia nervosa. It can be expected to develop in 80% of women who have lost 12% of their ideal weight; even modest weight loss may thus be associated with menstrual irregularity. Interestingly, 30% of anorexic women report some history of amenorrhea prior to their significant weight loss. Those who recover tend to have regular menses, in contrast to the irregular menstrual cycles of chronically ill people with anorexia. Still, the return of menstrual periods usually lags behind weight restoration.

Although the cause of amenorrhea continues to be debated, it may occur in response to emotional stress, malnutrition, and weight loss. Many college-age women report losing their periods when they begin their freshman year or must cope with some other stressor. Thus it remains unclear whether the menstrual irregularities that accompany anorexia nervosa are due to dietary restriction, low hormonal levels, loss of fat tissue, or emotional stress. A great deal of evidence gathered over the past 20 years has also shown that women must have a certain minimum amount of body fat to begin and maintain normal menstruation and, consequently, have the ability to reproduce (Frisch 1988). Body composition affects fertility. Underweight women have an abnormal secretory pattern of gonadotropin-releasing hormone in the hypothalamus. The decline in this hormone affects the release of follicle-stimulating hormone, estrogen, and progesterone, all of which are essential in the development of eggs and ovulation. When fat is lost by diet or exercise, the hypothalamus (by a mechanism that is still unknown) sends signals that influence the ability to menstruate. Reproduction is curtailed by hypothalamic changes affecting circulating estrogen, temperature regulation, and the capacity to maintain normal metabolic rate.

Malnutrition has long been known to affect the number of offspring in a society (or species). Even Darwin observed that domestic animals who had a regular and plentiful food supply were more fertile than those relatives who lived in the wild and had less nourishment available to them. Likewise, poorly nourished women in the 1800s grew slowly, achieved menarche later in life, and had fewer births and more unsuccessful pregnancies. In contrast, the research of Rose Frisch has shown that well-nourished women have a higher rate of fertility, including the number of live, successful births and the rate of birth of fraternal twins. Fat stores probably provide energy needed to sustain pregnancy and lactation for 3 months following birth.

Undernutrition also affects the male's ability to procreate. Keys demonstrated that weight loss precipitated male subjects' loss of sexual interest and, over time, resulted in a decrease in sperm motility and longevity (Keys et al. 1950). Elite male athletes have hypothalamic dysfunction that lowers testosterone levels and may decrease fertility. Athletic women also increase their muscle mass and decrease body fat. Many of these athletes stop menstruating because their fat content drops, and their sex hormones (estrogen, follicle-stimulating hormone, and luteinizing hormone) also decline.

Anorexic people also find it very difficult to tolerate cold. This vulnerability may be linked to the loss of insulating adipose tissue peripherally and changes in the thyroid gland and hypothalamus. The starving body attempts to minimize heat and energy loss in all systems by cutting back on "nonessential services." By bundling themselves up in layers of clothing, anorexic women not only hide their emaciation but also attempt to compensate for their unpleasant shivering.

### Gastrointestinal Complications and Laxative Misuse

Persons who have insufficient dietary bulk will inevitably suffer from constipation. Any food intake may then create a sensation of abdominal pressure that perpetuates the feeling of being bloated. Thus anorexic persons who begin to eat can feel quite uncomfortable. However, the best treatment for constipation and abdominal bloating is a therapeutic, balanced diet that helps the individual achieve a metabolic balance.

Laxatives should be avoided whenever possible. If one must be used, a bulk agent such as Metamucil (psyllium hydrophilic mucilloid) or

Fiberall is best. Patients may find it easier to cope with the constipation and discomfort when they feel reassured that these problems will abate as they recover weight and establish good eating habits. Both anorexic and bulimic people can fool themselves and their loved ones when it comes to using laxatives.

🍎 Joy I., a 32-year-old singer, complained constantly to her physician and her mother that she was constipated. She refused to eat regular meals, and—even when her illness became so severe that she needed to be hospitalized—she demanded that her psychiatrist prescribe various laxatives for her.

Joy became very angry when these medications were denied. She even threatened to leave the hospital. She hid from both herself and her treaters the secret reason for taking more and more laxatives: she really wanted to avoid gaining weight. Little did Joy realize that laxatives are a most inefficient way to induce weight loss. Even taken in large quantities, they deplete the body of only a tiny amount of ingested calories.

Rapid eating of large quantities of food should also be avoided, because it can cause gastric dilatation and rupture, possibly leading to death. Fortunately, this is a rare complication. In most cases, stomach functioning returns to normal as weight is regained at a rate of 1–3 pounds a week. Medical supervision helps the woman proceed slowly but soundly toward healthy weight restoration.

## Cholesterol and Carotene

Despite the state of starvation, cholesterol levels increase in anorexic people. A disturbance in lipoprotein metabolism is the likely culprit. Carotene levels are also elevated, leading to a yellowish discoloration of the skin.

## Insomnia

Anorexic individuals frequently have difficulty falling asleep and staying asleep. Although insomnia may signal an underlying struggle with depression, it can also be caused by a sequence of malnourishment, anxiety, excessive exercise, and more self-imposed hunger. This combination of factors often leads an affected woman to seek prescribed and over-the-counter sedatives in an attempt to get satisfactory sleep. Yet this behavior itself is addictive and consequently self-defeating. Good sleep hygiene is an essential element of full recovery, because adequate rest is essential for anyone to be able to function at her best level.

## Dermatologic and Visual Findings

Patients with anorexia nervosa are commonly described by laypeople and clinicians alike as appearing to be "walking skeletons" or "looking like concentration camp prisoners." Indeed, their emaciated state truly makes them look as if they are just skin and bones. Meanwhile, they reinforce their body image disturbance by referring to themselves as "plump" and "fat" (see Chapter 7). The anorexic person's sunken and pallid face, deep eye sockets, and baby-fine hair convey a diminutive and sickly presentation. As a result, the anorexic patient may appear much older or much younger than she is in reality. Cataracts, atrophy of the optic nerve (which can cause blindness), and retinal degeneration may also accompany malnutrition.

## Neurological System

Brain abnormalities have been found to occur in patients with anorexia nervosa. Postmortem examinations, computed tomography (CT) scans, and magnetic resonance imaging (MRI) scans have all documented the occurrence of a variety of structural brain alterations. The therapeutic implications of these findings are not clear, and the tests are not routinely included in the workup for anorexia. Although some studies have shown that the brain returns to normal after a period of stable nutrition, other studies have documented that brain changes continue even after a normal body weight is maintained for a period of at least a year (Hall et al. 1989b; Ploog and Pirke 1987). While the precise meanings of these brain-based changes are still being investigated, patients and their families should seriously consider the studies that document that brain abnormalities occur in patients with anorexia nervosa.

# Medical Complications of Bulimia Nervosa

The medical complications of bulimia nervosa are just as numerous and serious as those of anorexia. Similarly, each system of the body can be ravaged by bingeing and purging. Common sense would dictate that the more frequent the episodes, the more pervasive the difficulties. Yet the physical complications of bulimia nervosa can also be highly individualized. Some people with severe bulimia may have only a few of the physical manifestations of the illness. Others may have a subclinical eating disorder by DSM-IV standards (American Psychiatric Association 1993; e.g., they do not meet all the full and specific criteria for bulimia) and yet manifest numerous physiological problems.

Bulimic people often seek medical treatment for a variety of physical symptoms, including swelling of the hands and feet, fatigue, abdominal fullness, swelling of the salivary glands, and dental problems. A wide range of physical symptoms is associated specifically with bulimia.

## Cardiovascular System

Patients with bulimia can easily become dehydrated. This tendency can cause a lowering of blood pressure secondary to a low intravascular volume. Electrolyte abnormalities, particularly hypokalemia and hypomagnesemia, can predispose the bulimic individual to cardiac conduction abnormalities.

The misuse of ipecac to induce purging is common among bulimic individuals. Abuse of ipecac or other purgatives irrevocably damages the heart and other muscular tissue. These over-the-counter preparations are therefore potentially quite dangerous for people with eating disorders. Chest pains, skipped heartbeats, and syncope can all indicate their overuse. Patients who take ipecac need to be honest with their treaters about using it, and therapists must question their clients about any potential misuse. (Some family members and clinicians are so concerned about the abuse of over-the-counter drugs like ipecac and diet pills that they have petitioned the U.S. Food and Drug Administration for more government controls. Congressional panels are currently considering this possibility.)

After purging, the bulimic individual will sometimes retain fluid in a rebound fashion, causing edema of the hands and legs. Still, the most frequent and serious problems leading to cardiac arrest and kidney failure are the low potassium, sodium, chloride, and magnesium levels caused by self-induced vomiting and laxative and diuretic abuse. Electrolyte disturbances cause a constellation of symptoms that patients must guard against, including generalized weakness, confusion, memory and thinking impairment, and emotional lability.

### Endocrine System

Although abnormalities in the menstrual cycle (dysmenorrhea) are common in bulimia nervosa, a full cessation of menses (amenorrhea) usually occurs only in those women who are also anorexic. About 30% of bulimic women will experience some abnormalities in their menstrual cycle and should be under the care of a family doctor or gynecologist. At The Menninger Clinic, we have observed a high frequency of premenstrual problems and other gynecological concerns among our bulimic patients over the years.

### Gastrointestinal System

Bulimic patients develop peptic ulcers and pancreatitis (inflammation of the pancreas) at a higher-than-expected frequency. Usually, the latter condition presents as severe abdominal pain, but on occasion it can be totally masked. Pancreatitis is a potentially life-threatening consequence of bulimia.

❦ A patient in the eating disorders clinic, Kali J., was diagnosed as having pancreatitis after having had several bouts of fever. Although pancreatitis is frequently a relapsing condition, Kali avoided telling anyone that she had had eight prior episodes of the disorder before entering the hospital. Treatment required putting Kali's gastrointestinal system to rest by using intravenous fluids. This treatment caused Kali to stop eating. In addition, she underwent a series of tests that necessitated the routine use of enemas and other cathartics. These procedures led her to want to return to abusing laxatives—self-destructive behavior she had put aside for several months.

Kali's case highlights the fact that routine medical procedures such as gastrointestinal cleansing and intravenous fluids can lead to a resurgence of bulimic symptoms. Kali's binge-purge cycle had been arrested for months before the return of her pancreatitis. Her case also demonstrates how a condition such as pancreatitis or peptic ulcer may recur in patients who have achieved good control over their eating disorder. Such interrelated problems provide an even stronger argument against developing an eating disorder or at least minimizing its effects by seeking early and definitive help (Zerbe 1992a, 1992c).

Gastric dilatation and rupture can occur in bulimic patients who consume massive quantities of food. Families of patients often ask what it means to binge. There is still no generally agreed-upon definition, but most people think of it as ingesting large quantities of food. Yet people who restrict their food intake will feel as though they have binged after eating only a small amount of food, such as two cookies or one candy bar.

In the television movie *Kate's Secret*, Meredith Baxter Birney plays a woman who goes on a big binge after she holds a party in her home. Numerous high-caloric foods are laid out before her in the kitchen, and she shoves handful after handful into her mouth. Such episodes are usually not so dramatic, although it is not uncommon to find individuals who can consume 10,000 to 15,000 calories of high-calorie carbohydrate foods such as chips, cookies, and doughnuts in a short time. No wonder stomachs are prone to rupture!

Gastric rupture has a mortality rate exceeding 80%. Some researchers believe that patients who alternate between anorexic and bulimic episodes are at an even greater risk for this problem. The phenomenon of "cruising"—roaming up and down the aisles of grocery stores and purchasing binge foods—can precipitate this dire consequence.

## Musculoskeletal and Dermatologic Systems

Electrolyte imbalance and the abuse of ipecac and laxatives often lead to weakened muscles among bulimic persons. Self-induced vomiting also causes abrasions on the back of the dominant hand or knuckles. Calluses form, creating what in medical parlance is called "Russell's sign." The bulimic person will also commonly have a pasty complexion, yellowish skin, and hair loss caused by chronic protein malnutrition.

## Neurological System

Secondary to the electrolyte imbalance and malnutrition brought on by bulimia nervosa are epileptic seizures. In addition, there can also be abnormalities in the bulimic person's electroencephalogram (EEG) pattern.

Bulimic patients have the same kind of brain-based changes found in anorexic patients. Atrophy (shrinkage) of the cortex that is not related to patients' having low body weights was observed in several studies. The mechanism causing the brain disturbance in bulimia nervosa remains unclear. Until this mechanism can be more thoroughly understood, patients must recognize that they might be irreversibly altering their brain structure and/or brain function because of their eating disorder.

## Dental Problems

People with bulimia have their share of dental problems. The acid content of regurgitated food causes erosion of the enamel of the teeth, creates gum abscesses, and obstructs the salivary glands. The resulting so-called "chipmunk face" is a telltale sign of bulimia. There have even been several case reports where young women were on the operating room table for what were thought to be tumors of the parotid gland. Before being administered anesthesia, the young women admitted to their surgeons that they were bulimic. Parotid swelling is more frequent in patients who binge and purge on a daily basis.

Additional dental problems that bulimic patients have include the development of cavities and the propensity to lose fillings more frequently than nonbulimic people. Ulcers on the lips, loss of taste papillae over the tongue, and halitosis are other complications. Dentists advise their patients to refrain from brushing their teeth after a purge because this leads to further erosion of the enamel. If a person must purge, it is better to rinse the mouth out with sodium bicarbonate or water.

## Hematologic System

Anemias, which are common among bulimic patients, tend to require a prolonged time to correct even after nutritional stabilization. This resistance may be linked to frequent use of over-the-counter laxatives such as Ex-Lax and Correctol, which contain large quantities of phenolphthalein. These compounds suppress the bone marrow, leading to a specific toxic effect and loss of early forms of blood cells.

Repeated bingeing and purging can also cause a variety of vitamin deficiencies. The loss of vitamins results in a cracking around the edges of the mouth, mucosal ulcers, and loss of hair. Vitamin supplementation is highly recommended for people with bulimia. A good over-the-counter therapeutic vitamin with iron is relatively inexpensive and can correct most minor vitamin deficiencies. Of course, the best way to correct for a vitamin problem is to eat normally.

## Caffeine Intoxication

An excessive intake of coffee, cola, and tea is common among patients who struggle with eating disorders. These drinks can create an artificial feeling of fullness while giving a bit of an uplift to someone beleaguered by a state of poor nutrition. Tremulousness, jitteriness, anxiety, and irritability are all symptoms that may point to a person's overuse of caffeine.

❦ One patient, Eden K., would come to her therapy sessions in midafternoon, always on the edge of her seat and flooded with anxiety. Her therapist, a savvy social worker practicing in a medical setting, believed that Eden's tenseness and furtiveness were precipitated by the difficult material the two were discussing in the sessions.

One day Eden developed a pounding in her chest that resulted in a spontaneous panic attack. Further evaluation showed caffeine to be the culprit. Eden was drinking two pots of coffee a day. Although the subjects she was bringing up in therapy were difficult to bear and may have added to her already compromised physical threshold for containing anxiety, her unwitting abuse of caffeinated beverages was the greatest precipitant of her difficulty.

## Substance Abuse

As I described in Chapter 10, polysubstance abuse plays a role in the lives of at least 30% of all bulimic patients. Educators, family members, therapists, and general physicians should always consider the possibility of a hidden drug or alcohol problem in these patients. Impulsivity, emotional lability, general anxiety, and difficulty with interpersonal relations may all herald a problem with substance abuse.

Substance abuse often is not restricted to street drugs. Benzodiazepines such as Valium, Librium, Dalmane, Xanax, and Halcion can also be abused by these patients, because their propensity toward insomnia may lead medical practitioners to prescribe such compounds for sleep. Both physical and psychological dependence can result if a sleeping aid is used for more than a brief time or for more than a circumscribed problem.

## Other Major Medical Problems

Patients with eating disorders often have additional physical problems unrelated to the eating disorder or its medical complications. For example, two of our patients also had the severe, hereditary, involuntary spasmodic movement disorder called Tourette's syndrome. Plagued with uncontrolled contractions of their arms, legs, and facial musculature, these patients needed a larger quantity of additional calories each day to attain normal body weight. Their extra body movements used up many additional calories.

Another patient struggled with both a severe seizure disorder and anorexia nervosa. Her insistence on maintaining thinness required the consulting neurologist to be even more careful in determining the optimal dose of medication for her. Eventually, surgical methods were needed to control her seizures. One factor that complicated the difficulty in getting the seizures under control was the patient's state of malnutrition.

It is also common to see diabetes mellitus and an eating disorder occur together. Diabetic individuals with bulimia sometimes misuse their insulin as a way of purging. Both illnesses involve lowered self-esteem, produce family dysfunction, and create conflicts about autonomy.

Unfortunately, diabetes brings with it a number of complications of its own that lead to lowered life expectancy overall and an impact on the individual's quality of life. When an eating disorder and diabetes occur together, medical complications increase. Most physicians believe that bulimic individuals who also have diabetes place themselves in even greater physical jeopardy. When a bulimic individual is struggling unsuccessfully to bring the diabetes under control, it may indicate the presence of a hidden eating disorder.

❦ Patrice L., a 32-year-old educator with special expertise in music theory, had a history of juvenile diabetes mellitus (since age 5) and major depression (since age 22). Although her psychiatric condition had improved with medication and supportive psychotherapy, her endocrinologist observed that her diabetes was more and more out of control. Her psychiatrist never considered that she had a hidden eating problem and worked instead in the traditional psychotherapeutic fashion with the issue of how diabetes affected her life. She confronted Patrice about her losses connected to the illness (the fact that Patrice could not have children), her decreased visual function, and her loss of self-esteem. (Patrice lost many days of work every year and was sensitive to the teasing of her friends and colleagues.) One day Patrice confided to her psychiatrist that she had been abusing her insulin in order to lose weight. For years she had also engaged in bingeing. She apparently was struggling with a diagnosable eating disorder in conjunction with her other medical and psychiatric problems, but neither of Patrice's physicians had been aware of it.

Investigation led to the insight that not only did Patrice wish to be thinner than her normal slightly plump appearance, but she also had been afraid to express anger at her therapist directly. Her misuse of insulin was a way to mistreat herself and unconsciously express anger to her therapist. One aspect of that anger was how it displaced onto the therapist the disappointment that Patrice felt toward her own parents. Neither her mother nor her father had been able to give Patrice the conflict-free life she had wanted. She had had many losses over the years, not the least of which was the loss of body integrity and self-esteem associated with her diabetes. She was furious that those people she saw as helpful and powerful could not miraculously cure her. Patrice also longed for a highly idealized maternal figure who would perfectly understand and take care of her. When neither support was forthcoming, she acted out by devouring large quantities of food, then purging by restricting her insulin.

Patrice's case underscores the interrelationship of a concurrent eating disorder and diabetes mellitus. Both the course of each illness and its treatment are complicated. Although some patients will improve with supportive treatment, education, and pharmacotherapy, others will need more extensive treatment. It is therefore critical for all physicians and therapists who are working on such cases to see themselves as a team and to convey their consistency and hope to the patient.

As in other medical conditions that occur alongside eating disorders, treatment should be tailored to the individual situation. For example, long-acting insulin (Ultralente) can be given if the individual believes she must or will binge. Patients and their treaters should be prepared to work together for a long time on both problems, always keeping in mind how the conditions may interact. Finally, any physical condition carries with it a sense of loss—the loss of an ideal body and an ideal future. Mourning must occur.

Likewise, the perceived loss of control over any part of the body may lead a person to turn to an eating disorder as an understandable but unconscious way of reestablishing control. To master both disorders, such individuals are helped to recognize that wish for bodily integrity and control. They are urged to express in words their feelings about the medical problems. Ultimately, the medical condition itself may not be susceptible to cure or change, but the way a person deals with it may be. Mastery requires a patient to have the courage to look at the conscious costs of the illness so that she can triumph in the best way over them.

## Somatization

As the eating disorder improves early in treatment, patients tend to somatize to other body systems. These patients are often referred to various medical subspecialists, because they complain of headaches, back pain, breathing difficulties, abdominal cramping and nausea, muscle and joint pain, and the like. It is tempting for both patient and treater to believe that a new and real physical problem has developed. No doubt the pain is real but misplaced. Raging internal emotions erupt in the body as the patient searches for a way to express feelings that were previously contained and enacted within the eating disorder.

This explanation is at best a partial understanding of a complicated phenomenon we know too little about. Yet treaters observe clinically how eating disorder patients somatize to multiple body systems and suffer greatly doing so. As patients find new ways to express their feelings in words, they develop the recognition that the aches and pains that accompanied the initial control of their eating symptomatology were indeed psychologically based. But this insight is hard won.

During times of painful somatic experience, the patient is convinced that she has a physical disorder that must be diagnosed and treated. She experiences her body as torturing her. She would much rather have a concrete and treatable physical condition than a diffuse, potentially untreatable and shameful psychological one. Ultimately, she wishes to avoid the abyss of dealing with her own inner pain and conflicts. These are terrifying and anguishing because she does not know or understand them. The interior of her body, even when at war with her, is more friend than foe.

## Conclusion

Anorexia nervosa and bulimia nervosa clearly cause serious and potentially life-threatening physical symptoms. Diagnosis is often hindered by the patient's reluctance to truthfully confide the actual symptoms and deal with the underlying eating disorder. Nonmedical therapists treating eating disorder patients need to be aware of the physical problems created by these disorders so that they can encourage their patients to seek medical evaluation and treatment. Pediatricians, internists, family practitioners, and psychiatrists who do not routinely deal with such patients should treat with suspicion anyone whose low or rapidly fluctuating weight or medical problems cannot be accounted for in other ways. Insurance companies also need to become more cognizant of the life-threatening nature of these disorders and should provide coverage for their treatment. But perhaps most crucial is the fact that patients and families must soberly regard the mortality statistics and the medical jeopardy of these disorders. This knowledge may then propel them to confront their difficulties directly, knowing that to do otherwise they risk their lives—if not a lifetime of impaired physiological functioning.

# 12

# Filling Up: The Biology of Nutrition and Eating Disorders

They now saw the French dinner coming upon them, a thing of incalculable nature and range . . . they gave themselves into their cook's hands. . . .

This woman is now turning a dinner at the Café Anglais into a kind of love affair—into a love affair of the noble and romantic category in which one no longer distinguishes between bodily and spiritual appetite or satiety.

Isak Dinesen
*Babette's Feast*

In Isak Dinesen's short story *Babette's Feast*, a group of self-denying followers of a Protestant sect partake of an elaborate and bountiful French meal prepared by Babette, a world-class Parisian chef. While sharing their feast, these ascetics are humanized. Their tongues wag eloquently as they drink champagne, what their innocent senses believe is a sparkling "lemonade" that "agreed with their exalted state of mind and seemed to lift them off the ground, into a higher and purer sphere" (p. 37).

As the group eats the sumptuous meal Babette has prepared, they

271

experience a spiritual grace they had not known by their religious pursuit of virtue, sacrifice, and self-denial. While the wine flows and the participants indulge themselves with friendship as much as with the hitherto untasted delicious morsels, hearts that "once slandered each other" are transformed "past the evil period in which they had been struck" (p. 41). Such fellowship is experienced as a blessing, which transports each supplicant into a "kind of celestial second childhood" where they sleep peacefully till late in the afternoon, "their hearts suddenly filled with gratitude" (p. 43) for their chef and the ecstatic experience her talent has wrought. Meanwhile, Babette is content to fulfill her destiny by demonstrating great culinary art. The friends had willingly "given themselves into her hands" (p. 25). Her only desire was to do her utmost to make them perfectly happy with her cuisine. Yet the camaraderie and fellowship that resulted from eating led to spiritual renewal, a seemingly unanticipated benefit!

The appeal of this story (which was made into a movie) rests on the magical but largely unconscious emotional sustenance most of us find when we eat a good meal. We identify ourselves with the frugal brothers and sisters of the village who find delight in the savoring of friendship and feast together. We also long to be magically transformed into happier, healthier human beings by what we eat. For centuries, humans have turned to special foods, meals, and diets to increase longevity, energy, potency, and spirituality. Our current fascination with diets is part of this ancient traditional desire to be restored and reformed by what we eat.

Cooking also becomes a valued act in the quest. Like Babette, many of us will attempt to turn into culinary purveyors, purchasing dozens of cookbooks and taking scads of cooking courses. Creating a luscious meal becomes the quintessential act of kindness that draws people to us like no other. We want others to sup at our table much as we, as infants, drank in physical and loving sustenance from our mother's breast. Indeed, this earliest feeding experience becomes equated in our mind with food, desire, and love itself. For humans, to feed is to humanize; to cook is to love. Babette's feast, like all feasts, is truly an act of love, full of human generosity and spirituality, and part of the popularity of the story lies in how deeply we resonate with this meaning.

But in this modern age, we also find ourselves asking whether or not food has more than symbolic meanings alone—whether a French dinner, for example, can have demonstrable physiological effects that promote physical as much as social well-being. Recent studies on the metabolism of food suggest that it does. Much of the psychological meaning we ascribe to food may have some biological basis as well. Investigations into the role of carbohydrate restriction and food craving, the important roles that certain neurotransmitters have in the development of eating disorders, and the neurosignals that tell us when to eat and when to stop are but a few of the biobehavioral mechanisms that play a role in everyday eating.

To be sure, the study of the psychobiology of human eating and eating disorders is still in its infancy. What has been learned over the past decade has nonetheless been extraordinary, making inroads into both our understanding of eating behaviors and eating disorders. In this chapter I discuss some of the most important research informing the treatment of eating disorders and provide practical tips for curtailing these disorders and improving nutrition. We also consider those mechanisms that are believed to play roles in the development of the eating disorders themselves. These notable ideas aid in development of treatment techniques and point the way for further research into complex neuroanatomical and neurotransmitter pathways that may be implicated in the development of anorexia and bulimia.

## Food Cravings

Let's begin with a bit of research that has practical implications for everyday life. In the 1980s, J. J. Wurtman and her colleagues found that meals low in carbohydrates alter neurotransmitters and affect mood (Wurtman 1988a, 1988b, 1990; Wurtman and Wurtman 1988). Looking specifically at the neurotransmitter serotonin, they found that a deficit in this chemical creates an appetite for carbohydrates. Additionally, the paucity of some large neutral amino acids that occurs when fasting actually furthers serotonin uptake into the brain. When one eats carbohydrate-rich meals, tryptophan levels are raised and one no longer hungers for the carbohydrate. Tryptophan is then converted to seroto-nin. Brain serotonin decreases alertness and increases drowsiness.

The investigators found that those people who tend to prefer carbo-hydrate snacks may do so because of the positive changes they produce on their moods. Noncarbohydrate snackers, on the other hand, want to avoid what they perceive as adverse moods such as drowsiness (caused by eating carbohydrates). Carbohydrate snacks may also be craved be-cause they create sensations of being soothed and lulled, desired internal experiences for many people at times of emotional stress.

Preferred binge foods tend to be rich in carbohydrates (as well as dietary fat). Bulimic individuals may tend to binge on carbohydrates to make up for a serotonin deficit in their brains. Interestingly, some anti-depressants (e.g., Prozac) that elevate brain serotonin have also been shown to be helpful in decreasing binge episodes. More and more evi-dence asserts that serotonin plays a role in modulating mood as well as, perhaps, bulimia nervosa. However, this research has implications for people who don't have an eating disorder and aren't depressed. A num-ber of popular weight reduction diets over the years have insisted upon reducing the quantity of daily carbohydrates because "they make you fat." Nothing could be more wrong. Carbohydrates are metabolized dif-ferently than proteins or fats. Because they meet our energy needs best, they are used to get us going and keep us going; they are not stored as fat unless eaten in very large quantities. Therefore, carbohydrates should comprise about 50%–60% of the food we eat. When deprived of them, we quickly become carbohydrate depleted and are prone to overeat them or binge. The body seems to be trying to restore itself by making more energy available and replenishing serotonin. When a person has enough intake of carbohydrates, and serotonin, carbohydrate craving stops.

A healthy diet will contain sufficient amounts of simple and com-plex carbohydrates such as vegetables, grains, fruits, legumes, pasta, rice, and cereals. Eating these may also help the bulimic avoid binges, be-cause they will not be serotonin depleted. Modern research thus tells us that one of the true "magic foods" for weight control, mood regulation, and possibly the control of eating disorders is the carbohydrate food group!

# More About Serotonin

A while back, the dietary supplement tryptophan was quickly taken off the market because of some impurities in its production. This was quite unfortunate, because tryptophan, in addition to being a precursor of serotonin, promotes sleep. The dietary supplement tryptophan helped some individuals fall asleep without the use of addictive medication. Tryptophan may also have helped selected patients get enough brain serotonin. To the extent that some individuals need to eat many carbohydrates to replenish brain serotonin, dietary tryptophan appeared to be one alternative to eating surplus calories in the form of starches, breads, sweets, and so on. However, when this dietary supplement of tryptophan was given in controlled trials to obese binge eaters, the individuals did not always reduced weight. How often logical scientific inferences fail to meet our expectations when tested in the laboratory; how often we must acknowledge the complexity and mystery of psyche and soma when our most treasured theories fall short.

Disturbances of serotoninergic systems of the brain have been postulated to occur in anorexia nervosa and bulimia nervosa patients. Walter Kaye and his team of researchers at the University of Pittsburgh believe that dietary abnormalities make a substantial contribution to both illnesses (Kaye and Weltzin 1991a, 1991b). Underweight anorexic patients have reduced serotonin activity, possibly based on a deficiency of dietary tryptophan. When weight is restored by normalized eating, serotonin in the cerebral spinal fluid (CSF) increases. Kaye believes that underweight anorexic patients have low CSF serotonin because of their malnutrition, but even among long-term weight-restored anorexic patients, there appear to be disturbances in serotoninergic activity.

Indeed, the persistence of low mood and obsessional symptoms described in anorexic patients and even some who have recovered may be due to impaired serotonin function. The elevated level of a serotonin metabolite, CSF 5-HIAA, in renourished anorexic patients may indicate increased serotonin activity predisposing the person to anxiety, obsessiveness, and inhibitions. These emotional problems are experienced every day among anorexic patients. Kaye's research suggests that anorexia may at least in part be biologically based.

It is still unclear that what is being measured in the CSF or the body's periphery reflects what is accurately going on in the structure of the brain. Current evidence points, however, to underweight anorexic patients having reduced brain serotonin activity. In contrast, long-term weight-restored anorexic patients have increased serotonin activity. Not only might an intrinsic disturbance in serotonin activity contribute to the rigid, ritualistic, and perfectionistic behaviors of anorexic patients, but it might be a cause for their inhibited feeding behaviors and weight loss. Although still speculative, anorexic patients may pursue weight loss to begin with to reduce the dysphoric feelings created by an innate hyperserotonergic (too much serotonin) state. As Kaye points out, anorexic patients report feeling better when they are restricting food, hypothetically lowering brain serotonin.

In regards to serotonin activity, Kaye further suggests that restricter and bulimic anorexic patients may occur along a continuum. The fact that antidepressants reduce bingeing behavior, independent of effects on mood, suggest that there may be abnormalities in one or more neurotransmitter pathways, such as serotonin. As reported, the serotonin system has a major role in modulating appetite. If this system is not functioning up to par (hyposerotonergic function), bulimia could result. Although evidence is conflicting, some interventions which diminish serotonin function or activation actually increase food consumption and promote weight gain. Theoretically, hyposerotonergic function in bulimia contributes to reduced satiety, increased meal size, longer meal duration, faster eating, and increased carbohydrate consumption.

Further evidence for the role of serotonin or other neurotransmitters in bulimia comes from the fact that antidepressants have been found useful in the treatment of bingeing and the mood problems associated with it. This does not necessarily mean that bulimic patients have a variant of depression (see Chapter 2). Sometimes antidepressants primarily decrease bingeing but do not affect eating normal-size meals; at other times they seem to have specific antibulimic properties. Additionally, it usually takes up to 4 weeks or longer for an antidepressant medication to have an effect on depression. Antibulimic effects often occur within one week of treatment. The antidepressants are no panacea for bulimia, however, because their effect often wears off quickly. Nevertheless, most authorities conclude that the response to antidepressants in reducing bingeing behaviors suggests a biological mechanism at work; the antidepressants are correcting a defect in the neurotransmitter systems, probably serotonin or another chemical regulator such as norepinephrine.

## The Role of the Hypothalamus—
## Brain Changes

Neuroanatomical and neurochemical changes in the hypothalamus have been implicated in anorexia nervosa and bulimia nervosa. Special nerve tracks in the nuclei of the ventral medial hypothalamus (VMH) and lateral hypothalamus (LH) have long been known to be associated with eating behavior. Lesions (e.g., injuries) in either of these two areas of the brain effect eating and other behaviors. To study particular brain areas and pathways, experiments have been conducted on animals. Lesions were made in animal brains in the laboratory and their effects verified. These investigations have yielded much information about the eating disorders.

If the VMH is lesioned, animals eat voraciously (hyperphagia) and hormonal and other metabolic functions are disrupted. If the LH of an animal is lesioned, the animal refuses food and water to the point of starving itself to death. Intricate research in the 1970s and 1980s has demonstrated how small and specific bundles of fibers in these areas are responsible for some of these behaviors. One important study by Keesey (1986) actually found that LH lesions might lower the set point for body weight. LH-lesioned animals maintain low body weight despite caloric increases and decreases. The greater the extent of the lesion, the lower the body weight tends to be.

Although a direct comparison cannot yet be drawn to anorexia, anorexic women fervently cling to a low body weight much as LH-lesioned animals do. Some have argued that these experiments show that the body set point can be modified neuroanatomically. An LH lesion results in the body weight being defended against despite forced feeding, food restriction, and diets. For example, if the LH-lesioned animals are force fed, their weight will eventually approach that of nonlesioned animals, but at the end of the forced feeding their weight will return to its postlesioned level. Likewise, if the LH-lesioned animals are restricted from food, they will lose weight. When refed they will gain, but only to their postlesioned level. The set point has been "readjusted" by these brain-based lesions in the LH.

The VMH may also play a part in anorexia nervosa. Leibowitz (1983) argued that in animals, a decrease in ventral medial hypothalamic epinephrine activation produces behaviors similar to that seen in human anorexia. That is, animals with VMH dysfunction lose body weight, decrease the rate of their eating, increase their activity, reduce carbohydrate intake, and have a tendency to rebound with overeating. Most authorities acknowledge that, because eating is a biological and psychological activity, drawing absolute parallels to a single hypothalamic change or lesion is probably unwarranted. Still, there may be important implications for future understanding and treatment of anorexia nervosa that may be culled from this brain-based research.

## The Hypothalamus—Chemical Changes

Amenorrhea (failure to menstruate) is such a well-known symptom of anorexia nervosa that it is part of the diagnostic criteria for the disease proposed for DSM-IV (American Psychiatric Press 1993). Interestingly, a significant percentage of anorexic patients, at least 10%–20% depending on the study cited, will develop amenorrhea before any significant weight loss occurs. Most of the time menstruation will normalize after a period of sufficient weight gain, but sometimes it does not do so despite appropriate treatment. This has led a number of investigators to suggest that chemical changes within the hypothalamus and the neuroendocrine system play a role in anorexia. For those patients whose periods do return and normalize, prognosis seems to bode better. Psychological and physical improvement may thus be judged, to some extent, on the return of menstruation, possibly reflecting a final common pathway of chemical change in the hypothalamic system. These brain-based changes signal not only menses but positive emotional shifts.

Already mentioned in an earlier chapter of this book was a case example where amenorrhea began when the patient went off to college. This is a very common occurrence. This stress-induced primary amenorrhea develops with many different types of emotional triggers such as peer or family problems. It may also be related to changes in the hypothalamus that occur as a result of stress or that have their basis in psychological conflicts and ineffective coping mechanisms. The biological and psychological aspects may also be related in a complex, but currently unknown, fashion.

In anorexia itself, the reproductive hormones, luteinizing hormone (LH), follicle stimulating hormone (FSH), and luteinizing hormone releasing hormone (LHRH) are all decreased or blunted but generally return with improved nutrition. Likewise, growth hormone (GH), and the thyroid hormones free triiodothyronine (T3) and thyroxine (T4) also drop. The reproductive, growth, and thyroid hormone levels improve with treatment and thus are felt to be caused by the poor nutritional state of the anorexic. They do not indicate a primary biochemical problem because refeeding reverses their imbalance.

## Other Neurochemical Changes

Anorexia and starvation can produce neurochemical changes that are quite similar. This has led some to suggest that starvation is a model for what transpires with anorexia. However, in some ways the two conditions are really very different.

Noted researcher Regina Casper (1992) has pointed out one major difference between starvation and anorexia that is quite provocative. When normal people are starved, they attempt to conserve energy. Their activity level decreases, they have less energy for life itself, and consequently they are not terribly productive. In contrast, anorexic patients tend to be hyperactive, despite their starvation state. This observation has been corroborated in a series of animal experiments. When animals are deprived of food, their activity level dramatically increases. They will pick whatever means of "exercise" is available to them such as racing on an activity wheel, and will continue unabated until fed or exhausted (Yates 1991). In clinical work, patients sometimes seem to have limitless energy that amazes the observer. Stress also appears to increase their activity level and is reflected in a competitive, driven demeanor.

For example, I can recall from my medical student days, a neighbor who was clearly anorexic and yet had the endurance to run around the apartment complex time after time as if she were training for a marathon. Even though I maintained a normal weight and good stamina, I was convinced that I would have collapsed from a fraction of her exertion. What allows the anorexic to "run the extra mile" even though her added exertion threatens demise? Casper suggests that the anorexic patient's caloric restriction, low body weight, and poor nutrition all induce central nervous system changes that cause her hyperactivity.

Besides serotonin, the neurotransmitters norepinephrine, dopamine, and the endogenous opioids may come into play. The latter have received particular attention in the past decade. It is now believed that beta endorphins serve to initiate eating behaviors; if a compound such as naloxone is used to block the endorphins, food intake decreases markedly. Studies of obligatory runners have suggested that beta endorphins increase with exercise, producing an "exercise high" that becomes difficult for the runner to give up. The endorphins probably also combat depression.

Although the specific roles the endogenous opiates play in eating behavior and activity levels of anorexic patients are unknown, it may be that they signal the urge to eat while driving activity up. The endorphins thereby potentiate anorexia by complex neurochemical responses still to be determined. In the coming decade, research will likely clarify these relationships more specifically.

One landmark study (Fichter et al. 1986) confirmed some of the neuroendocrine and psychological disturbances induced by fasting. They took five women between ages 21 and 25 who were of normal weight, psychologically healthy, and physically fit. Over four consecutive 3-week periods, the investigators alternated the subjects' feeding between normal caloric intake and fasting. They found that when the individuals were restricting their intake, disturbances in the hypothalamic-pituitary-adrenal axis did occur. The women's thyroid function, for example, varied; cortisone levels increased. When the women resumed eating normally, each of these parameters returned to normal.

This study confirmed what dieters and their loved ones have suspected for years: food restriction has an impact on mood. Although the particular effect of the endorphins were not determined, they likely cause some of the psychological deterioration that occurred with starvation. For the women in this sample, anxiety, depression, annoyance, and moodiness increased. The researchers concluded that the irritability that occurs when someone diets results in a neuroendocrine disturbance. This disturbance corrects itself when healthy eating patterns resume.

This study is important when one thinks about the etiology and impact of eating disorders: the emotional and physiological disturbances associated with them may be brought about by the actual dieting and purging maneuvers rather than being the cause of the mood swings. (See Chapter 11, Medical Complications, which describes the important work of Keys on male subjects who fasted.) As early as 1950, Keys noted similar behavioral, emotional, and cognitive changes that accompany starvation (Keys et al. 1950). Summarizing Keys' work from the perspective of contemporary eating disorders treatment, David Schlundt and William Johnson conclude:

> The changes in eating patterns and preoccupation with food during starvation were striking, as were the strong tendencies to break the diet with binge eating and the difficult adjustments encountered during the refeeding period. All in all, the study [Keys et al. 1950] points to the potential dangers of diets involving drastic and even moderate caloric reduction for prolonged periods. Many of the physical, behavioral, and psychological changes observed in these normal, healthy male volunteers are very similar to those occurring in people who set out to lose weight by dieting. (1990, p. 53)

In summary, to date the neuroendocrine disturbances that occur in people with anorexia can be compared to those of people who are starving but who do not have anorexia. Most of the hormonal changes seen appear to be a product of starvation. A specific neurochemical cause for the illness itself or one that links it to other psychiatric conditions such as depression has not yet been found. In contrast, the endocrine changes associated with bulimia nervosa have been much less studied. Nevertheless, it is becoming increasingly apparent that the hypothalamus, through a complicated set of neurochemical pathways, serves as a central hub for various signals that regulate feeding and satiety.

The reader is cautioned to take all of the above details about the role of neurotransmitters with a grain of salt. This is a rapidly evolving area of study where new findings are reported daily. They make what has been written out of date before the chapter is even published! The interested and concerned reader, nonetheless, desires to master the illness, in part by becoming familiar with the most compelling biological facts about the etiology of anorexia and bulimia. Just as I have stressed throughout the book the importance of psychodynamic, family, cultural, and dieting factors in the etiology of these disorders, so is it important to keep in mind that specific neurochemical factors, yet to be discovered, may also play a major role.

This particular summary is necessarily brief due to space limitations. Although important areas of interest have been reviewed, it has not included other potentially important biological mechanisms such as the gastrointestinal hormone cholecystokinin or the function of the vagus nerve. Abnormalities in these areas may interplay with other neurohormones to delay gastric emptying, potentiating anorexia or bulimia by creating sensations of abdominal fullness or distention. The interested reader is referred to the most up-to-date reviews on the biology of eating disorders by reading the *Journal of Clinical Nutrition*, the *International Journal of Eating Disorders*, or recently published textbooks and articles listed in the bibliography (Hsu 1990; Kaye and Weltzin 1991a, 1991b; Schlundt and Johnson 1990; Yates 1991).

## Genetic Factors

Family members always want to know if a hereditary factor—"something in the genes"—caused their loved one's illness. Likewise, concerned patients who either once had or currently have a disorder worry that they will pass it on to future generations. Besides the logical wishes to know about one's genetic endowment and predispositions so as to avoid future afflictions, patients and their families are likely feeling the pangs of guilt when they ask about the role of genetics in predisposing to certain difficulties. Given these psychological concerns and preoccupations, it is all the more important to know the limitations of our current knowledge regarding hereditary factors in anorexia and bulimia.

The recent history of psychiatry has been marked by many strides linking genetics to a range of behavioral problems, including depression and schizophrenia. Like these disorders, eating disorders have also been shown to have some heritable factors, although in these conditions the role of the environment appears to be more important. Still, a number of reports, when collated, show a greater concordance rate among monozygotic (identical) as compared to dizygotic (fraternal) twins. Identical twins share exactly the same genetic material, so when an inherited characteristic or attribute occurs in one, it is bound to occur in the other. Regardless of the specific research methodology used, among anorexic patients, 40%–56% of twins are concordant for the eating disorder. There are fewer published twin studies for bulimia nervosa, but those that are available demonstrate a marked difference in concordance for monozygotic and dizygotic twins. Evidence continues to mount showing bulimia nervosa to be a *heterogeneous disorder*, meaning to have a number of causes. Thus, in some eating disorder patients, heredity may play more of a role than in others (Fichter and Noegel 1990; Holland et al. 1988; Hsu et al. 1990; Strober 1991; Vandereycken and Van Vreckem 1992).

Although the methodology of the studies indicating the genetic link for anorexia has been greatly criticized, most authorities believe that the evidence indicating some heritability for anorexia nervosa is striking. However, because twins usually share the same environment, as well as genetic material, it is also quite conceivable that the high concordance rate among monozygotic twins is environmentally induced. Only future identification of genetic markers and adoption studies like those done for schizophrenia and obesity will discriminate between heritable and environmental factors. Still, one important case report by Crisp and Toms (1972) demonstrated how environmental factors may function. In this study, an anorexic male reared an adoptive son and permitted a girl to reside briefly with his family. Both children developed anorexia nervosa, indicating that the home in which one is reared may be influential if not insurmountable in the development of anorexia.

Hsu and colleagues (1990) also report preliminary information regarding the concordance rate among bulimic twins. They found that about one-third of monozygotic twins, as opposed to no dizygotic twins, developed bulimia. In each of the families, alcohol abuse and affective disorders were common. Hsu and colleagues believe that bulimic patients may be more environmentally predisposed to their disorder than anorexic patients. Still, the researchers suggests that a number of possibilities exist such as a real biological defect that predisposes to a lack of impulse control, neurotransmitter dysfunction, or poor affect tolerance.

Even establishing that a real genetic vulnerability exists tells us only part of the story about how one goes on to develop an eating disorder. Any genetic vulnerability does not necessarily condemn an individual to developing an eating disorder. Even inborn errors of metabolism, such as phenylketonuria, can be successfully treated with nutritional (i.e., environmental) manipulation. However, it would appear that an individual with a positive family history for an eating disorder is at greater risk for developing one herself if she embarks on a rigid diet (Hsu 1990, p. 91).

One must, therefore, take these genetic studies quite seriously while remembering that dieting, emotional stress, and family patterns supersede genetic vulnerability. For anorexia nervosa, a specific genetic loading for the disease may exist but is likely to be enhanced by the cultural preoccupation with thinness, the individual's personality strengths and weaknesses, other kinds of psychiatric difficulties, body image problems, and possibly neurochemical difficulties in the hypothalamus.

## Practical Implications of Research

These elegant areas of investigation are fascinating to read about, sometimes increase one's sense of mastery over the illness, and occasionally contribute to one's feeling powerless over what one can do about such a problem. After all, if you conclude as you read the reams of available biological research that your problem is largely physiologically based, you may be likely to give up on taking steps to help yourself overcome the difficulty. I would argue that this position would be unfortunate, unhelpful, and incorrect.

Looking at the role of biological factors that predispose to eating disorders underscores the often neglected role of nutrition in helping manage them. Developing sound eating habits not only is excellent practice for living fully and healthfully, but empowers the individual to take as much control of her life as she can. She may not be able to change a very early brain-based difficulty, but she can exercise wisely and eat those foods that correct neurochemical imbalance and help regulate body weight. Registered dietitians knowledgeable about eating disorders can be of great service, not only in providing good nutritional information to the client but helping to support her in emotionally stressful times. The dietitian's advice ensures nutritional adequacy of the diet while dispelling common myths and misconceptions about food.

Eating disorder patients are usually more familiar with nutritional guidelines and books about eating and diet than are their physicians, psychiatrists, and therapists. Eager for information about their illness and ways to cope with food, they have voraciously read from the popular literature—which is often, unfortunately, speckled with ideas that can be downright hurtful. Witness the high-protein diet craze popular in the last two decades. By suggesting that one eat large amounts of proteins and avoid carbohydrates, this proposed weight loss diet not only did little to aid weight regulation but potentiated bingeing in some vulnerable individuals by precluding carbohydrates from the diet. Apparently, the individuals who binged made up for a dietary lack of tryptophan, but got their energy source by metabolizing protein and fats. Glucose is essential in satisfying energy requirements, but this is an ineffective way to get the requirement met.

Using body protein up means all muscle mass, including heart mass, gets converted to glucose to meet the body's energy demands. Also recall from biology class how the body's protein is used up long before its fat stores are. These fad dieters compromised their health by burning their muscle mass because they needed energy but had restricted carbohydrates. They believed, from the diet propaganda, that they were really burning up excess fat. Additionally, this process resulted in a loss of fluid. Most of these dieters thought they were doing well on their high-protein regimen early on because they lost water weight. This temporary weight reduction was actually caused by obligatory fluid loss that occurs when any of us restrict carbohydrates. Soon our body stabilizes and the rate of loss decreases, causing frustration.

At The Menninger Clinic, we follow some very straightforward guidelines that aid patients to practice good nutrition and are relatively easy to implement. Recognizing that new diet plans are praised and published every day (e.g., pyramid system, juicing), we try to encourage interventions that make sense, are simple, and have stood the test of time. In this rapidly changing field, the best medical and research evidence still supports eating three balanced meals every 4 to 5 hours throughout the day and taking a nutritious snack for individual needs. A balanced meal consists of approximately one part protein and two or three parts carbohydrate foods. Vegetable protein, rather than animal, appears to be a healthier choice; hence the recent trend to eating more beans, legumes, and so on.

It is very difficult for the body to get the nutrients it needs when fewer than 1,000 calories are consumed. Our dietitian recommends a meal plan beginning with 1,200 calories that includes each of the basic food groups; because nutrient intake improves with a variety of foods, protein, vegetables, fruit, starches, and fat should be consumed every day. The greatest number of calories should be taken in breads, pastas, and rice (6 servings) followed by vegetables (3–4 servings) and fruit (2–3 servings).

For example, a typical 1,400-calorie diet would involve about 6 ounces of meat, but this could be substituted with certain meat alternatives such as cooked dry beans, nuts, eggs, or peanut butter. Two to three servings of milk per day would also be included. Again, one could substitute cheese, yogurt, tofu, or cottage cheese for milk in order to provide the necessary calcium intake for adults. (Teenagers and children need more servings of milk.) The same 1,400-calorie diet would include 4 servings of vegetables (1 cup of leafy greens or ½ cup of nonstarchy vegetables would be 1 serving), 4 fruits, 5 starches, and 3 fats. Serving sizes of individual nutrients are included in the appendix at the back of this book. Also included is a table describing the components of some popular combination foods like casseroles, breaded vegetables, tacos, and salads with dressing. This list shows the specific food groups constituting any one selection (i.e, pizza, potatoes au gratin, etc.).

The main point to emphasize is that all food groups can and should be part of the healthy daily diet. Red meat should be reduced but not avoided; most authorities recommend a maximum of 6 ounces of meat, poultry, or fish each day. (A way to approximate this is to say that a portion the width of a woman's palm is about 3 ounces.)

Because most patients with eating disorders fear carbohydrates, they will need to be supported by loved ones as they increase their intake of starches in the form of pasta, rice, bread, and legumes. It must be reinforced that the best source of energy for the body is the carbohydrates, and eating more fruits and vegetables will decrease the rate of stroke and heart attack in women by 40% and 22% respectively. This data, recently released from a Harvard University study, suggests that significant amounts of beta-carotene and carotenoids found in vegetables are protective to cells; they help modify so called "bad cholesterol" (LDL cholesterol) so that it does not stick to artery walls, decreasing the plaques that cause strokes and heart attacks.

If the desire is to lose weight, it is better to cut down on the portion size than to eliminate a food group altogether. Based on the earlier information about brain neurotransmitters synthesis and the still unknown subtle influences of diet in helping the body replenish its resources, one can easily see why. Each food group provides essential nutrients that are not available in the other groups.

We also recommend that the person with an eating disorder abstain from caffeinated beverages if possible and use alcohol only sparingly. Caffeinated beverages can make the individual feel full temporarily, but too many of them result in heightened anxiety (caffeinism). Several patients in our program appeared to be having full-blown anxiety attacks when, in reality, they had drunk over 10 cups of coffee and diet colas. There is also some evidence that caffeine actually interferes with normal eating patterns. Alcohol, on the other hand, loosens inhibitions, including the inhibition to eat. Bingeing, in some circumstances, may be precipitated by drinking too much alcohol at a social gathering.

Finally, all of us are much more prone to eat at times of stress. And we usually turn to snack foods that we know are not nutritious because they are so easy to find and require no preparation. Recall how carbohydrate intake increases tryptophan and then brain serotonin, causing sleepiness and soothing. We might tend to eat more carbohydrates at times of stress to create these calmer moods. For example, I remember the tension I experienced the first night of Desert Storm. As the news reported the bombing of Baghdad, my heart raced and I grabbed a bag of pretzels (fortunately a low-fat, high-carbohydrate snack). Before I knew it, I looked down and realized I had actually eaten half a bag of pretzels! Never a binger before, I now realize the fear that most of us experienced that evening had gotten to me as well!

In retrospect, a better strategy for coping would have been to take a long walk with my dog, invite friends over to talk about the issue or other day-to-day concerns, or involve myself in housework or a hobby. Eating to quench intense emotions is something we must all try to curb in a society where food is so readily available. Sometimes it appears temporarily easier to munch away one's problems rather than to problem-solve them adaptively.

## A Healthy Diet Versus Dieting

If your mother was at all like my own, you grew up in a household where the benefits of broccoli, green beans, salad, and all the rest of the vegetables were emphasized routinely. Much of what is discussed here will not be news for you because of what mother taught, although now there is more scientific evidence to back her up. Fortunately, as an adult I am somewhat more able to take advantage of my mother's advice than I was at 17, and therefore more able to follow these scientific guidelines!

The National Cancer Institute and the National Institutes of Health recently kicked off a 5-year, $33-million campaign to get people to eat 5 servings of fruit or vegetables daily because of the significant cut in risk of illness that will be made by this dietary readjustment. "An apple a day keeps the doctor away was good advice, but we're extending that," said Bernadine Healey, former director of the Nationals Institute of Health. "Five-a-day" is the new slogan to remind us to eat our vegetables.

Because most adults already eat an average of 3½ servings of vegetables per day, the new recommendation for five will not mean changing what one does very much. But there are many Americans who eat no vegetables, putting their health at risk in the process. If you begin the morning with a glass of tomato or orange juice, have a salad and fruit at noon, add an apple, pear, or carrot for a snack, and another vegetable or two with dinner, you have already hit the quota. You have also avoided some of the main food triggers of binges— snack foods.

Ice cream, potato chips, and candy bars are very high in fat and low in nutrient value. Their texture and taste make them easily consumed during a binge. By substituting low-fat foods such as raw vegetables, toast with jam or cinnamon sugar, fat-free yogurt, a pear, or plain popcorn, one has found not only a safe alternative to fatty snack foods but may have interrupted the beginning of a binge by thoughtful problem solving. The healthy foods also increase the sensation of fullness because of bulk, decreasing the tendency to eat more out of hunger and an "empty stomach."

Vegetables also provide the right amount of essential vitamins, minerals, and electrolytes needed to maintain the body's homeostatic regulation. Eating a variety of foods, but especially vegetables, provides sufficient quantities of most minerals and trace elements so that additional supplementation, which can be expensive, is avoided. Of course, if someone has restricted their food intake for a long period of time, a vitamin and mineral supplement may be necessary. But usually, with regular and nutritious eating, one will get what one needs from one's diet. This especially applies to the electrolytes such as sodium and potassium. Potassium plays a major role in muscle and heart function but cannot be stored by the body. With purging or nutritional deficiency, potassium levels are often dangerously low. Good nutrition prevents the irregular heart beats, muscle cramps, fatigue, and fainting associated with low potassium and magnesium levels.

Most women who have a deep hatred for their body fat must remember that certain fat-soluble vitamins are essential for health. The body stores them, but one must eat some fat to get them in the first place. If vitamins A, D, E, and K become too low due to starvation, many different types of physical problems result. Water-soluble vitamins, such as B complex and C, must be consumed daily. If they are not replenished quickly, other kinds of vitamin deficiencies develop. The reader is encouraged to learn about each of these essential vitamins, the recommended daily intake, and the food sources for them in Table 1 at the end of this book. By looking over this table, you will quickly agree with the need to have a variety of foods in your daily diet, because only then will you be able to be sure you have enough of all of the vitamins required to sustain good bodily functioning.

When preparing food it is a good idea to increase one's "fat awareness." By this I mean that many foods and ways of preparing food hide sources of fat. We end up eating more fat than we are aware of because we cook with it and use it to flavor our food. By substituting baking for frying, jelly for butter, and plain crackers for cakes and cookies, one begins to weed out the high fat foods from one's diet. The American Cancer Society and the American Heart Association have published low-fat meal plans and food lists that increase "fat consciousness" and facilitate more healthful eating. The benefits of a double portion of asparagus can be wrecked by two pats of butter.

Recently, I visited a friend I hadn't seen in several months. I was struck by her notable weight loss. For over 10 years she had fought a hard battle with her weight, especially after she had stopped smoking. She explained that the secret to her success was no expensive diet plan but rather the simple reduction of most of the fat from her diet. She did this by replacing a high-fat snack like buttered popcorn with plain popcorn, limiting her meat intake to 4–6 ounces per day, and avoiding "fatty add-ons." These are the usual hidden but high-fat sources found in salad dressing, butter, gravies, and sauces.

Her testimonial brought to life the recent scientific studies that have shown that people who reduce their dietary fat to 30% or less of the total calories eaten, lose weight even without restricting their overall caloric intake. In essence, they exchange the number of high-calorie fats with lower calorie carbohydrates. Schlundt and Johnson (1990) propose that a lifestyle change that limits fat intake and allows people to eat as many carbohydrates as they wish promotes long-term weight loss. Fat is reduced, but eating carbohydrates is permitted, so that feelings of food deprivation are minimized.

These very feelings of deprivation cause one to go off a good diet. It has long been known that reducing fat also reduces the incidence of cancer and heart disease, but this kind of diet is hard to maintain psychologically. If carbohydrates are substituted, a greater physiological feeling of satiety results along with the satisfying feeling of emotional fullness, helping the individual stay on a healthful, sensible diet. Less truly becomes more.

One must also consider the types of sugar products one eats and their impact on the body's physiology. Simple sugars like those used in baking or sprinkled over cereal increase the blood glucose level quickly, but then the effect falls off, leading to the desire to snack to restore energy. When other sugars like fructose (fruit sugar) are eaten, hunger does not come on as rapidly. One will be much less prone to binge eat if one takes in a balanced breakfast, because then one has a variety of nutrients being metabolized at different rates. Energy sources remain adequate so that one never becomes too ravenously hungry.

On the other hand, a doughnut or cinnamon roll couldn't be a worse way to start off the morning. Although delicious, they make the blood glucose level rise quickly, followed by an elevation in the insulin level, leading to a reactive hypoglycemia that will make the person who eats them want to eat larger amounts of food to compensate. Best to include juice, fresh fruit, and breads for breakfast to avoid a midmorning dash to the candy machine.

Finally, exercise must also be considered a part of good nutrition. According to the Tufts University *Diet and Nutrition Letter* ("Just what is a balanced diet, anyway?" 1992), exercise "enhances the benefits of healthful eating by helping to keep the body's cholesterol concentration at a desirable level, by keeping blood pressure down, and by improving bone density" (p. 5). Rigorous exercise may also reduce the risk of colon cancer by helping food move quickly through the intestines. This process reduces the amount of time "potentially harmful waste products come into contact with the colon," possibly decreasing the risk of cancer in the colon. Citing data from the Harvard University School of Public Health study that tracked 17,000 Harvard alumni over a period of more than 25 years, those alumni who burned 2,500 calories a week exercising developed colon cancer half as often as their sedentary counterparts. There is also some evidence that exercise also helps prevent adult-onset diabetes in both men and women.

# Conclusion

We are just beginning to understand some of the biological mechanisms that contribute to the eating disorders and weight regulation. Even though there is so much that we do not know, both experience with diets and contemporary scientific research tell us that eating from the basic food groups still makes sense. What we have learned about brain neurochemistry makes it all the more important to take more seriously what we put into our bodies. In this chapter we have reviewed some of the formal data, stressing the particular importance of eating carbohydrates and avoiding extra sources of fat. Knowing that bingeing can be brought on by a depletion in dietary carbohydrate to correct for depleted brain serotonin underscores the importance of eating from this food group. Mention was also made about the importance of limiting dietary fat by modifying lifestyle. Then one can eat most, if not all, of the carbohydrates one wants. When this is done, bingeing, obesity, and other eating disorders are much more likely to be curtailed.

Emphasis was also placed on the importance of regular exercise and the "five-a-day" vegetable regime to reduce disease and promote weight control. Cutting back on meat but not cutting it out altogether is a moderate step each of us can take to reduce the risk of cancer and promote health. Eating some meat ensures that one does not become deficient in vitamin $B_{12}$, zinc, calcium, and so on.

Most importantly, the individual who follows these scientifically based but simple suggestions also begins to practice healthful living and adaptive coping strategies that positively affect all of life. Only then can one justifiably say one has stopped betraying one's body and begun to wisely nurture it. Adequate care of our biology improves our psychology, and vice versa. Ultimately, this permits us to more fully experience life's non-food-related feasts, such as friendship, personal accomplishment, and the arts.

# 13

# When Calories Add Up to Pain: The Tolls of Obesity

More are slain by suppers than by the sword.

Ancient Proverb

Conventional wisdom places great emphasis on how obesity affects health. Without much reflection, we find ourselves concurring with the ancient maxim that food is a most dangerous weapon, at least in theory if not in fact. A recent article in the *Wall Street Journal* quoted Health Management Resources on some startling changes in American dietary practice. Twenty-five percent of Americans are more than 20% overweight.[1]

A high physiological and psychological price may be paid for being out of condition. All of us tend to gain weight with age but those among lower socioeconomic groups and in rural areas are especially vulnerable. In contrast, people in the higher socioeconomic brackets can afford to take part in the burgeoning diet industry. These programs—often ex-

---

[1] Thirty to forty percent of adult women in this country, particularly women of color, fall into the mildly to moderately obese category. Sixty percent of African American women over age 50 are obese (Stunkard 1977; Stunkard and Wadden 1992).

pensive because they provide their own food packages, group support, and medical supervision—tout high success rates through provocative testimonials by movie stars and sportscasters. Yet this desire to take off the weight and to improve appearance and increase longevity produces some ghastly statistics: a full 97% of the people who lose weight will regain it within a year.

Regardless of our weight-loss technique or diet plan, getting the pounds off and keeping them off can be frustrating. Individuals beset with the problem of being overweight or those who work to alleviate the suffering caused by it are perceptively asking a central question: what is causing the epidemic of obesity in our culture? In some ways, we are victimized by our own success. With the advent of highly processed foods and the availability of meats, rich pastries, and fast foods, our intake of dietary fat has increased 30% over the past 80 years. Conversely, Americans have reduced their physical activity by 75% during that same period. The results are less energy burned, more calories taken in, and more fat stored.

But diet is not the only culprit. Fascinating animal, family, twin, and adoption studies all point to a strong genetic factor. For example, a noted researcher on obesity reviewed the adoption records of 540 Danish men and women. Using the same population that had previously been studied for genetic influences on schizophrenia and alcoholism, Albert Stunkard (1959; Stunkard et al. 1986) found that body weights of adopted children were closely related to those of their biological parents, while totally unrelated to those of their adoptive parents. Obesity appeared to be strongly influenced by genetic factors yet was influenced little, if at all, by the adoptive family environment. We must therefore examine our heritage, and not just our willpower alone, in setting out to modify the contours of our bodies.

Studies of twins have also confirmed this viewpoint, while adding to our knowledge about how the environment may contribute to the development of obesity. Identical twins not only look the same but also have the same genetic programming for body size and weight. Interestingly, however, only twins of lean or medium build will tend to have the same body weight if they are reared apart. Overweight twins may have quite dissimilar body weights, depending on the environment in which they live. As Stunkard's work underscores, the genetic influence in human obesity is very real; but unlike hair color and eye color, it is not the only determining factor: "in the case of obesity, heredity is not destiny" (1990, p. 22).

Discussions with obese individuals often prove to be quite provocative to normal-weight listeners. Obese people believe they have a "metabolic imbalance" that propels them to gain more weight than the people around them. They persist in explaining that they can eat the same amount of food—or even less—than others they know of and still gain weight. They hate this aspect of their physical makeup and will go on at length about their metabolic problems.

Although such remarks often meet with derision, they may actually reflect an accurate perception about the predisposition to obesity. Studies of energy metabolism undertaken in the 1980s found a great difference between infants born to mothers who were lean versus those born to mothers who were obese. Energy expenditure is more than 26% less in infants who become obese by age one; in addition, half the infants of obese mothers became obese by age one. But lean mothers seldom produce obese children. Studies among widely varying cultural groups—such as Pima infants (and those of other Southwest American Indian tribes) and English infants—suggest that a low rate of energy expenditure contributes to obesity in families (Hsu 1990; Martin et al. 1991; Stunkard and Wadden 1992).

One interpretation of these data is that obese individuals use calories more efficiently, which may be an advantage in natural selection in preindustrial societies. At one time, food shortages commonly occurred every 2–3 years, so a woman with the biological capacity to store fat was at an advantage, as were her offspring. The art and customs of earlier societies implicitly recognized obesity as an asset. Because fat functions as a cushion against food shortages during pregnancy and lactation, fatness became a welcome sign of beauty, health, and prosperity. Some early societies even sequestered brides-to-be in fattening huts, to increase their physical desirability and perhaps even prepare them for the energy-draining reproductive years. Yet our own culture, where food is readily available, does not require a well-tempered, fuel-efficient energy machine; nor does the obese body pose the same survival advantage. In fact, it may actually put one at a disadvantage. By having greater metabolic efficiency, obese individuals are inclined to fatness, which may now predispose them to disease and rejection by their culture.

Other factors also lead to a body size larger than the cultural ideal. For example, the theory of body weight set points also helps explain why it is so difficult for many people to lose weight and keep it off. Although still incompletely understood, set point is currently defined as the tendency for each person, whether thin or heavy, to remain at the same weight for long periods. The concept is based on a person's body energy remaining level over time. Without being aware we do so, we control caloric intake and physical activity to maintain constant energy stores based on an internal body thermostat. No wonder the most ardent dieter might think that "the more things change, the more they stay the same." Despite exerting enormous effort, we may be unable to regulate our body size because the set point perpetuates physical equilibrium.

Set point theory fits well with the concept of "adaptive thermogenesis" (Martin et al. 1991). Nonobese subjects can consume foods high in calories, particularly those rich with carbohydrates or proteins, and not seem to gain much weight. This is because their resting metabolic rates increase to offset the period of overnutrition. As a result, many people may be surprised at not having gained more than a pound or two after a vacation during which they gorged on culinary delights. These lucky souls may be benefiting from their set point and their adaptive thermogenesis (perhaps in conjunction with an increased energy expenditure from exercising more than while working at a sedentary job). Those of us who diet from time to time and struggle to maintain even modest weight loss need to be aware of the set point theory (and adaptive thermogenesis), because it stresses a biological component to our habitual weight that may be impossible to override, much as we try.

To complicate matters, research has linked a variety of chemicals in the body to the genetic transmission of obesity. At excessive levels, the enzyme adipose tissue lipoprotein lipase (ATPLL), induces obesity by causing preferential deposits of fat in adipose tissue, which may exist in larger amounts in obese people. Adipsin, a newly discovered protein secreted by the fat cells themselves, may also help regulate the size of fat deposits. Lower levels of adipsin have been noted in obese rats. The hormone cholecystokinin, long known for emptying the gallbladder, may help mediate satiation when eating (Morley 1989).

A growing body of evidence suggests hunger is controlled by a hormone called neuropeptide Y (NPY). If NPY is not present or if its action is blocked, appetite wanes. It now seems likely that obesity may be caused by an overproduction of NPY, and anorexia may be caused by a defective response to it. If NPY causes obesity, a chemical clocking its action may aid weight control by reducing hunger. Research on NPY is currently under way, but we are still far from having an available drug to reduce eating by blocking NPY. Still, NPY is found in above-normal concentrations in obese animals. Eventually there may be some direct applications of NPY research in understanding and treating eating disorders in human beings.

These substances are only a few of a potential multitude of internal chemical regulators that play a role in developing and maintaining obesity. Indeed, the complex factors that lead to obesity may be responsible in part for the historic difficulty in treating the condition successfully. The Council on Scientific Affairs of the American Medical Association summarized the dilemma most succinctly but starkly: if a "cure" for obesity is defined as a reduction to a desired weight, with maintenance at that weight for 5 years, then one is more likely to be cured of most forms of cancer than of obesity (Council on Scientific Affairs 1988, pp. 2547–2551).

These discouraging findings are countered by one long-term study of the outcome of psychoanalytic treatment for obesity that was conducted under the auspices of the American Academy of Psychoanalysis (Glucksman 1989; Rand and Stunkard 1983). This landmark study is one of the few to include control and experimental populations to investigate the effectiveness of psychoanalytic treatment on weight reduction. The study examined 147 patients: 64 obese women and 20 obese men in the experimental group, and 46 normal-weight women and 17 normal-weight men in the control group.

Besides demonstrating specific psychodynamic issues associated with weight gain or weight loss and different deviant eating patterns among obese individuals, the AAP researchers found that weight loss could be maintained. After 4 years, a full 66% of the obese patients who lost more than 20 pounds had maintained their lower weights, and 25% had maintained a loss of more than 40 pounds. Perhaps most significant, though, was the finding that subjects in the experimental group improved their self-esteem and social adaptation by reducing their tendency to disparage their bodies. The positive effect of psychotherapy on weight loss is examined more fully later in this chapter. First, however, let us assess the physiological problems caused by obesity and the rationale behind losing weight.

## The Physical Costs of Obesity

For years, both the medical press and the media have stressed the health risks associated with obesity. A body weight that is 10% above average carries an increased risk of mortality (11% for men and 7% for women). When body weight rises to 20% above average, mortality increases dramatically— to 20% for men and 10% for women. However, these figures suggest a decreased risk of mortality when the body mass index (weight in kilograms over height in meters squared) ranges from only 25 to 30. That is to say, the effect on life expectancy of modest deviations in ideal weight is small, so that in all likelihood a woman can maintain a slightly plump figure without running any extraordinary health risk.

What may be more dangerous to health is the fluctuation of body weight brought on by repeated dieting. In 1991 the *New England Journal of Medicine* reported that the incidence of coronary heart disease and the risk of death increased in people whose weight varied frequently, presumably because they intermittently tried weight-reduction diets (Lissner et al. 1991). Although more research is needed on this link, scientific evidence argues for an avoidance of shifting weight patterns. Weight fluctuations may be more injurious to a person's health than a stable but higher-than-average weight.

The risks of death and disease undoubtedly increase dramatically with moderate to severe obesity. (Moderate obesity is defined as 41% to 100% above average weight or a body mass index [BMI] of 30–40; severe obesity is defined as 100% above-average body weight, or a BMI of more than 40). Yet individuals with moderate and severe obesity make up only 10% of the obese population. The rest are mildly obese (20%–40% above average body weight), with minor complications from their excess weight. Nonetheless, American women and men often live into their 70s or even longer despite our society's overall increase in body weight. (Women, for example, now weigh an average of 2–8 pounds more than they did in the 1950s). From a scientific perspective, those women who maintain a somewhat fuller figure but whose weight does not seesaw have no increased health risk. In all likelihood, then, many women and men can comfortably carry a few extra pounds over the upper limit of the normal weight range given in life insurance tables. These people can still be healthy, too, although being overweight may not be psychologically permissible.

Dieting patterns may have a greater impact on health than on weight per se. We now know that the high level of fat in the American diet contributes to an increased risk of cancer and coronary heart disease. Breast, colorectal, pancreatic, prostate, and uterine cancer are among the 35% of the cancers associated with dietary factors. Conversely, pollution, background radiation, and food additives—all of which have caused a great public outcry—cause only a small percentage of cancers—4% (Council on Scientific Affairs 1988). Dietary recommendations at the end of this chapter focus on minimal life-style changes that can be implemented by both lean and heavier individuals to reduce the incidence of cancer and the propensity for heart disease by decreasing cholesterol and triglyceride levels, which should ultimately lead to increased longevity.

Gross obesity is also associated with other serious medical disorders—hypertension, diabetes, and coronary disease. The physical and mechanical stress of maintaining a large body can also cause arthritis, sciatica, varicose veins, hiatal hernia, and embolism. Decreased ventilation capacity may result in sleep apnea syndrome, leading to chronic sleep deprivation and daytime sleepiness. As a result, job performance falters and the person's quality of life is diminished. A less well-known but potentially crucial complication for women is increased maternal mortality and toxemia during pregnancy. Moreover, obese mothers tend to produce obese infants. Obesity also predisposes a person to increased mortality before surgery and to greater complications during and after it.

Thus all of us would do well to try not to exceed the upper limits of normal weight and, in particular, to reduce body fat. This admonition is especially true for anyone in a medically high-risk group.

In the early 1960s, an undergarment manufacturer made a fortune through television commercials that adroitly sold girdles to hide "that midriff bulge." Now we know that fat in the upper body or midriff—so-called android obesity—carries a far greater health risk than does lower body fat localization (gynecoid obesity). Gym teachers and coaches of yesteryear who indoctrinated us with the wisdom of abdominal bends, sit-ups, and other exercises to firm up the tummy may have unknowingly helped us address this health factor. Upper body obesity in particular is associated with an increased risk of heart disease and cancer. More recent studies have examined how that fat is distributed (that is, whether inside or outside the abdominal wall) and have linked the fat inside to increased health risk. Unlike men, women tend to have more fat outside the abdominal wall and are therefore at lower risk for medical complications (Schapira 1991).

To determine our ideal weight, we must examine a number of factors, including body size, height, and location of fat deposits. For practical purposes, the most helpful determination of obesity involves measuring the body mass index and the ratio of waist-to-hips circumference. The "ideal weight" picture is complicated though, by research studies that indicate there may be some health benefits to being a bit plump. Underweight women carry double the risk of producing low-birth-weight babies, and underweight people in general are prone to a variety of physical illnesses, especially infections.

Sex is also affected by weight and by fat distribution. Researchers at Michael Reese Hospital in Chicago found that heavier women desired sexual intercourse more than did their thinner compatriots. Their quotient for erotic excitability and readiness was double that of thin women. This finding was supported by researchers at Loyola University's Sexual Dysfunction Clinic, who noted that heavier women desired romance and sex while anorexic women shunned them (Wolf 1990). Many factors, including hormonal ones, may be responsible for the increase in sexual response that accompanies some healthy fat stores. (Suffice it to say that these important data have influenced my own treatment and teaching efforts. I now encourage my women patients and students to indulge in an occasional chocolate mousse or apple strudel.) Apropos of that experience, evidence also suggests that sensation begets sensation; a good meal or good music may also lead to enhanced sexual pleasure and responsiveness.

## The Psychological Risks of Obesity

The diet industry is booming these days because of the psychological toll that obesity exacts on individuals. The societal contempt often directed at people who are obese causes them great emotional pain and can lead to interpersonal rejection and employment discrimination. Tragic stories of such complications abound. A 1991 story in the *Wall Street Journal* reported the saga of Ralph Falk and his daughter Carol. Falk was the founder of the multimillion-dollar Baxter International, Inc., company (Bailey 1991). When he died, he left $2 million to his son but only $100 to Carol. Why was Carol, who was the family pariah, cut out of her father's estate? She alleges that it was because she is fat, despite having spent most of her 66 years battling her weight and its attendant psychological problems. Carol's dramatic tale highlights the family disruption, poor self-esteem, and loss faced by obese patients every day.

Like anorexic and bulimic patients, those who are obese must also struggle with an alarming degree of bodily hatred and self-hatred that can lead to an ultimate betrayal of one's body and one's self. Depression and suicide are not uncommon. Indeed, the concomitant long-term, disastrous physical effects of obesity can be construed as a slow form of suicide that goes undetected, because the health problems are classified and tabulated under other medical rubrics such as those of heart disease or cancer.

Although overweight people show no increase in overt psychopathology on conventional psychological measurement scales, they nonetheless have many psychological problems. They may view their own bodies as loathsome and grotesque and may have been the target of hostility and contempt, even internalizing these critical peer and parental views of themselves. Some emotionally healthy obese people have no body image disturbance; but research has shown a strong prejudice against most obese people cuts across age, gender, race, and socioeconomic status. Although few studies have examined whether obese people are less likely to marry, one researcher found that only 12% of women who moved into a higher social class were obese, compared to 22% who moved into a lower class (Brownell and Wadden 1992; Stunkard and Wadden 1992; Vandereycken 1993; Wolf 1990). Appearance that is considered physically attractive may be an important predictor of marriage into a higher socioeconomic class. Adolescent girls who are obese are particularly vulnerable to narcissistic wounds caused by the teasing of their peers. Adult women are subject to a cultural double standard. Although the prevalence of obesity is equal between men and women, women participants in diet clinics outnumber men nine to one. As a result, women contribute a disproportionate amount of time and money to the $36 billion a year spent on the diet and exercise industry.

Severely obese people face the greatest discrimination and prejudice and pay a higher psychological price for their condition. Faced with constant humiliation for their size, they also have restricted physical mobility and may fail repeatedly at dieting. Their increased futility and depression leads to a pervasive sense of having failed to fit into a world of smaller people.

It is difficult to generalize psychological issues and trends among groups of individuals, regardless of the degree of obesity. Although sweeping generalizations should not be made, some notable trends add to a psychological understanding of the burdens of the condition for obese people and the professionals who treat them.

Conflict around dependency, such as whether to become independent or assume additional responsibility, is a major internal struggle. Many obese patients become frustrated in nondirective therapy, because they want the therapist to assume responsibility for them and to make decisions for them, much as they look to others outside of therapy. Control of their lives seems to lie outside themselves, and they do not view themselves as forceful and effective instruments in their own lives. Because of their repeated failures to control their weight, they tend to externalize control of their lives. For them, food has taken a major chunk—literally and metaphorically—out of their internal sense of agency by being something that is ungovernable by conscious means. Tragically, overweight people believe that their accomplishments or advances do not result from their own efforts but instead arise from luck or external influence. In this way, those who are obese are not unlike many highly successful and overtly independent career women of normal weight. Studies have also shown that these women are deferential and pathologically modest in staking claim to their own accomplishments (Brownell et al. 1986; Glucksman 1989; Wing 1992).

Obese individuals may be less sensitive to internal cues than are people of normal weight. Hilda Bruch (1973) theorized that eating disturbances are related to an inability to identify hunger, emotions, and other bodily states correctly. She suspected that a maternal gap in early learning behaviors resulted in the adult's development of a defective sense of effectiveness and an inability to modulate feeling. If such is the case, food may be used to quell disturbing feelings that remain unnamed. It may also compensate for an important relationship by providing self-soothing. For obese individuals, food may serve as a soothing object at times of emotional distance. It may help those who feel disconnected from their mothers to better withstand painful feelings. Food would thus fit Winnicott's (1957/1965) definition of the transitional object as a physical object, like a blanket or small toy, that soothes the toddler whose mother is absent. In times of anxiety, sadness, or angst, food helps quell a shaky spirit in all of us. But for obese people, food may be more than an occasional pacifier; it may be one of their few sources of emotional peace and calm. Eating thus functions as a form of self-medication against painful feelings, and in so doing it restores a sense of well-being by representing maternal ministrations, both unconsciously and symbolically. The following is a typical but unfortunate example of this state of affairs.

❧ Deborah M. was an appealing 46-year-old woman who was a homemaker and civil servant. Enveloped in a gloomy haze of depression, she described a paucity of maternal care during her childhood. Deborah longed for someone to step into the role of the idealized other, because she had experienced so many occasions of abandonment and feeling unloved and victimized at her mother's hand. On one level, Deborah defended against memories of early disappointments by becoming the champion of underprivileged people and taking up the cause of the indigent. Ambitious projects beyond her capabilities preserved her precarious sense of self-esteem. Yet her voracious hunger—she weighed more than 350 pounds at the beginning of therapy—spoke to her desire for love, nurturance, and adulation. Physical difficulties brought on by the complications of her obesity also helped Deborah to gain attention and caretaking from others: she could control them and demand the concern she felt was her due but that she had never been able to possess, even as a child.

For so many of those who are obese, periods of weight gain also exacerbate their feelings of unlovableness and disappointment in themselves and in others. In contrast, they associate periods of weight loss with greater self-satisfactions and more satisfying relationships. At lower weight, they can better tolerate their feelings of competition, particularly with other women. In fact, obese individuals are less competitive toward other women than one would expect. Discouraged from feeling as attractive to men as they would like, these women retreat from competing for the most attractive partners. At work, they shy away from professional competition with those of either sex. As a result, they may experience a pronounced feeling of aggression and frustration due to their thwarted competitive zeal.

Sexuality itself is avoided because it raises, among other things, thoughts of having more or doing better than other women. It may also put at risk a tenuous but sustaining unconscious source of maternal solace and support. Like the obese child who tries to elicit parental love or approval, an obese adult may adopt a posture of passive compliance in hopes that conformity will provide some reward and recognition. In reality, though, obese people continue to experience feelings of deprivation and gratification.

In summary, the symbolic meaning of food for obese individuals is that it helps fill emotional emptiness for people with eating disorders. Karl Menninger (1942/1970) wrote that we unconsciously equate food with love. Eating voraciously can thus be seen as a way to take in or incorporate the love a person wants—whether it is from a parental figure, a significant other, or a therapist. When love is thwarted, we tend to continue seeking it and may even be more inclined to use food as a substitute.

Overeating can also help us keep others at a distance. Fat serves a protective function. The anxiety and guilt we associate with our own sexuality or overt expression of hatred may seem less dangerous when surrounded by a protective layer of adipose tissue. When an individual is unable to resolve this struggle, any weight loss will probably be temporary, because the self-image and body image will not be fundamentally altered. It takes much time and effort for obese individuals to learn that they can safely expose hidden aspects of themselves and can directly express competence, tolerance, and affability toward themselves and others. Their tendency to view thin as good and fat as bad must give way to a more integrated and less rigid view of self and others.

❦ Obese individuals often have a personal history replete with losses. For example, Julie N. had been reared by a maternal aunt after losing her mother in a car accident when she was three and her father to a terminal illness when she was eight. Also separated from her sister because of her aunt's financial limitations, Julie had experienced both real and emotional abandonment and neglect. As an adult, she doubted that any other person would ever love her or even believe she was worthwhile.

In treatment, Julie recounted that one of the highlights of her childhood involved her memory of being sexually abused at the hands of a neighbor. Because Julie had so few memories of warmth in her life to hold on to, she searched endlessly for a "Prince Charming" who could provide her with love, fulfillment, and an idealized family life. Her inability to express her feelings in words led her to turn to food to modulate her feelings. Her compulsive eating behavior helped her cope with feelings of emptiness, loneliness, and angst.

Although Julie initially rejected therapy, she eventually forced herself to participate in both family and group modalities. As she began to risk losing the security of her own lonely isolation, she became more in touch with her feelings and could examine them within the confines of ambivalent human relationships. The supportive feedback of her group members and therapists helped Julie learn to value herself in a more loving manner. She learned to be more direct and assertive with her aunt, too, whereas previously she had "stuffed her anger" out of fear she would be abandoned. Family therapy gave Julie an opportunity to address old losses and grievances, particularly her aunt's failure in recognizing the neighbor's hurtful relationship with her.

## Binge-Eating Disorder

As early as 1959, Stunkard identified a group of people with eating disorders who have some special attributes. These are obese individuals who have disordered eating behaviors characterized by bingeing and psychosocial impairment. Binge eaters who do not purge have been categorized in the American Psychiatric Association's DSM-III-R as having an eating disorder not otherwise specified (eating disorder NOS). Binge-eating disorder will be included in the appendix of the DSM-IV (American Psychiatric Association 1993) as a subcategory of bulimia. This addition will help clinicians recognize those individuals who have episodic voracity. It has been hard for scientists and clinicians to verify enough facts to warrant a specific diagnosis, although this was considered for several years. Two of the difficulties are 1) defining a binge and 2) wanting to avoid stigmatizing obese individuals who binge. These individuals already feel so discouraged with their difficulties, tend to lack self-assurance, and blame themselves for failure.

For our purposes, a binge is defined as a lack of control over eating in a discrete period of time, such that the individual often feels she cannot stop eating or choose how much she eats. (Other criteria that describe behaviors of binges can be found in the appendix to this book.) The main difference from bulimia nervosa is that binge eaters do not purge. Some may be normal weight, but many are obese—hence the inclusion in this chapter. Subjectively, binge eaters find it difficult to fight their tendency to gobble their food or to keep eating in check, particularly during times of emotional distress (de Zwaan et al. 1992; Marcus et al. 1992; Patton 1992; Smith and Morgan 1990).

Although the exact prevalence of binge eating among obese individuals is not known, surveys over the past decade have reported this serious problem in 23% to 46% of obese individuals who seek treatment for weight loss (de Zwaan et al. 1992; Marcus et al. 1992). Binge eating seems more common in overweight women than in men, and it tends to be so discouraging to individuals that they are more likely to drop out of weight loss treatment than are obese patients who do not binge. Depression, guilt, embarrassment, and personal disgust are part of the descriptive criteria that reflect the psychological pain and poor self-esteem of the binge-eating population.

Marsha Marcus and her team of investigators at the University of Pittsburgh have studied obese binge eaters and have reported a number of other interesting findings (Marcus, in press; Marcus et al. 1990a, 1992). Marcus has shown that there are both obese and normal-weight individuals who have clinically significant problems with binge eating but do not purge. Normal-weight people who binge may differ from obese people who binge in ways that we do not yet understand. They may tend to stay at a normal weight because they use strict dieting or fasting between episodes to compensate for lapses when they binge. Among obese people who are binge eaters, symptoms of depression and sexual dysfunction, family histories of obesity, frequent but failed attempts to lose weight, and childhood obesity are common. Body image disturbance also tends to be high, leading some investigators to believe that this problem must be tackled by intensive treatment efforts that focus on changing the body image. We still have much to learn about binge-eating patterns, because there are still so few research studies in this area. In the next decade we can anticipate more studies that will show us how far-reaching binge-eating problems are among both obese and nonobese people in our society and how clinicians can help intervene effectively.

Because this group of patients struggles so much with what seems to be an affective disorder (e.g., depression), clinicians have turned to a host of medications to see what helps. The new selective serotoninergic reuptake inhibitors (SSRIs) like fluoxetine (Prozac) and fluvoxamine have not proved helpful to patients who binge. Interestingly, fluoxetine and behavior modification have been of considerable help in the treatment of obesity. According to the Marcus research, the effect of fluoxetine in the long-term treatment of obesity needs further evaluation but is nonetheless promising (Marcus et al. 1990b). Still, there is growing evidence that the weight loss that occurs with many patients who take fluoxetine for mood disturbance lessens over time. That is, initial weight loss drops off, and weight gain can occur.

Among obese people who binge and who have problems with depression, medication has not been found to be effective in helping their moods. Moreover, once the drug is discontinued, weight gain rapidly occurs. Clearly, more long-term treatment studies are needed to effectively help this group. In the meantime, a range of psychotherapeutic approaches may be tried, including psychodynamic psychotherapy, behavioral and cognitive therapy, and specific relapse prevention strategies, which are discussed at the end of the chapter.

Psychologically speaking, binge eaters have been found to have significant fears of abandonment. These patients also tend to eat when they are alone—often at home by themselves or in the evenings when not at work. These facts, derived from behavioral research, mesh well with the understanding of the disorder that psychodynamically oriented clinicians have expressed. This useful information helps patients develop their own coping strategies. For example, a person might try to increase her social supports at vulnerable times. Instead of relying on only one significant relationship, she might try to develop a host of support systems or a supportive network of people. Naturally, this is easier said than done.

Psychotherapy can be another avenue of support in addressing the underlying fear of abandonment. In psychotherapy, patients are encouraged to discuss anxieties they might have in developing a larger network of friends and thereby benefit from the therapist's skill and knowledge about community activities and support. Thus, people should first learn new cognitive skills related to the situations in which they are tempted to (and often do) binge. Then those high-risk times can be interrupted with productive activities and social support. Addressing the feelings and fantasies that have led to bingeing in the first place—particularly the loss of significant relationships, real or perceived abandonments, and the threat of total aloneness—also helps curtail bingeing.

Finally, it is important to differentiate a recently described "nighttime binge-eating disorder" from other kinds of binges. Mark Mahowald, a neurologist at the Minnesota Regional Sleep Disorders Center, has worked with a group of patients who each gained 13–67 pounds in what has seemed like a form of sleepwalking (Schenck et al. 1991). These patients binge without waking up, eating all kinds of "food"—from buttered cigarettes to salted cat food sandwiches. However, the next morning these nocturnal eaters don't remember what they have done and are aghast to find the remains of their unusual meals in the kitchen. Some patients have even scalded their mouths while drinking hot liquids or bruised themselves on furniture in their rush to the kitchen. One woman purportedly woke up as she was preparing to drink a bottle of ammonia.

Although Mahowald believes that this nocturnal eating disorder derives from a disturbance in the sleep-wake cycle, it could also be a hitherto unacknowledged dissociative disorder ("Nighttime eating disorder may be fairly widespread" 1993; see Chapter 9). For complex psychological reasons, nighttime eating may be totally split off or dissociated from awareness. This parallels what people who binge eat commonly describe in the waking state: a secret, unknown, misunderstood aspect of themselves overtakes them, leading to episodes of gorging followed by self-recrimination. Those who binge often speak of themselves as two distinct entities: one who can be in conscious control and function normally, and another who preferentially stays out of conscious awareness—"the binger." Binge eating in such an individual might be thought of as on the continuum of dissociative disorders, from mild to severe, sometimes to the point of having one "alter personality" who binges. In treatment, as she acknowledges her bingeing and lack of personal integration, she finds her temporary loss of self-control abhorrent and terrifying.

## Considerations for Treatment

As should be readily apparent from this discussion and the case examples, from a psychological perspective, obesity is a symptom. Because the emotional difficulties are often so long-standing, therapists must help these individuals consolidate and improve the picture of themselves, which often takes a long time. Along the way, there will often be many failed diets and outbursts of anger, because such far-reaching problems are not easily reversed. Besides real physiological and genetic limitations, obese individuals must resolve any developmental issues at the root of their problems. This fact is often difficult to tolerate, because of our all-too-human desire for a "quick fix" that will last forever. However, there is wisdom in approaching the situation realistically, knowing that its resolution will probably take much time and effort. This knowledge may be the greatest buffer for both the patient's and the therapist's frustration. Identifying one's feelings and finding oneself is not an easy quest, nor should it be entered into lightly.

Individual, family, or group therapy (or a combination of these) is usually helpful. A number of research studies have also demonstrated the effectiveness of support groups or leader-facilitated psychotherapy groups in treating obese people. One caveat appears to be that the individual must want to work in a group and not find it threatening. People who are reluctant to reveal their intimate thoughts and feelings to others may benefit more from an individual psychotherapeutic approach. Over time, however, even those who must struggle to face their own feelings will find that it becomes easier to talk, and therefore a group modality may eventually prove useful.

One deeply held fantasy that complicates the treatment of obesity centers on the idea that losing weight will make all of life's problems disappear and will magically transform the formerly obese individual. To arrive at a more mature appreciation of what is realistic and possible, this understandable wish must be confronted, discussed, and eventually worked through. Another benefit of ongoing therapy is that it provides opportunities for discussing the emotional crises that may arise during weight loss or if the weight reduction program fails. Being able to discuss the emotional impact that major reductions in weight bring about in self and body image can be facilitated by a professional therapist or support group.

Tolerating painful feelings from the past and dealing with day-to-day crises and triumphs are significant challenges for all of us. The dilemma faced by obese individuals is similar, inasmuch as they have used a behavior—eating—to increase their tolerance for painful feelings. Sometimes, it is necessary for them to learn a new repertoire of feelings by focusing on internal cues that have long gone unnoticed. This new ability will influence not only their behavior, but it will also help them to identify other emotions and bodily states. Moreover, by being encouraged to reveal their secret thoughts and fantasies, these individuals might be better able to retrieve those that are typically suppressed or forgotten.

One common fantasy among obese people is that weight control is possible without limiting caloric intake. People will sometimes acknowledge that they pay only lip service to the idea of eating less. Their tendency to deny what is actually eaten, while searching for easy solutions, is a primary resistance to treatment. But by understanding the emotional factors that provoke eating behavior, obese people can begin to master their problems with weight. Entering therapy is one way to confront these defensive styles and to get support during the times of greatest suffering over this refractory condition. Indeed, obese people must tackle any possible unconscious investment they have in maintaining an obese body image. This image prevents the self from expending much psychological energy on anything other than dieting. Yet a different view of one's self and the world is made possible by strengthening other parts of the self that are valued, such as competence at work, good parenting abilities, and a sense of humor. In the American Academy of Psychoanalysis study cited previously (Rand and Stunkard 1983), researchers found a correlation between weight loss and feelings of increased self-esteem and competence. During periods of weight loss, obese people also tend to report increased satisfaction in their relationships and in their ability to manage their own moods.

Of course, the dynamic issue of deprivation must be dealt with by finding ways other than through food to nurture oneself. Establishing and developing more intimate interpersonal relationships can help make this shift. Friendship and love not only help people deal with the feelings of separation and abandonment that often trigger episodes of overeating, but they also provide gratification in life that is different from food yet very substantial. The obese individual's conflicts with aggression, competition, and sexuality make change difficult, but treatment in a professional setting can provide the necessary shepherding.

Nothing is more crucial for individuals than to find a place where they feel valued for themselves as they are, regardless of what they weigh. At times, they may decry the therapist who takes a neutral stance about weight loss or weight gain. But this position rests on the understanding that individuals are of value regardless of their appearance. Because the desire for unconditional love is a universal quest, obese individuals must reckon with that desire and their own need to be cared for as they are. Likewise, any person must change because of a desire to do so—not in an effort to please a therapist, parent, spouse, or child. Such efforts will almost inevitably lead to failure, because they reenact previous experiences of feeling pushed or prodded to take some action to gain or ensure the love of another, usually a parent or parental substitute.

Ultimately, each person must develop self-acceptance without self-condemnation based on weight or any other perceived flaw. Looking inward, any of us might question our motivations, but the obese person might ask: Why am I doing what I do? Why do I think my weight is so bad? Who am I changing for? Am I following my own agenda for what I want, or am I trying to live out someone else's life plan? Am I following the internal commands of my parents or spouse? What is the internal price I will pay if I chart my own course? Are my goals about losing weight realistic and based on a quest for better health, or am I trying to change for appearance's sake alone?

Throughout this process of self-examination, the emphasis should be on *self-acceptance*, as well as on developing a realistic sense of what may be a biological limitation impeding thinness. Because genetic, familial, and set point factors all influence weight, obese individuals must recognize that change may be extremely difficult despite their best efforts. To paraphrase Nietzsche, obesity is not a problem to be overcome, it is one to transcend. Struggling to accept the fact that the ideal body image may never be attained can form a significant part of the psychological work. The loss of the ideal figure should be grieved, along with working through past losses not fully mourned. In psychiatric circles, it is often said that treatment is complete only after tracing one's losses and working on each of them to facilitate growth. Focusing on past losses as well as on the loss of the ideal body is particularly helpful for those who are obese. They lose the ideal but find the real; and in so doing, they may gain much more than they ever thought possible.

All of us can and should engage in positive health practices, such as maintaining a healthy diet and exercising regularly. Research data suggest that maintaining optimal weight is best achieved by increasing energy expenditure while voluntarily decreasing caloric intake. Walking a little farther and faster and cutting back on fat avoids costly diet programs and goes a long way toward losing weight permanently. In addition, one must plan meals wisely, because daily structure helps stop overeating and can also help in other areas of life. Skipping meals should be avoided, and one should eat at the same time every day. Cognitive-behavioral therapists recommend a daily regime of three meals and two snacks, because this lessens the tendency to binge after a period of food deprivation.

One must also strive for balance in choosing food, avoiding the tendency to defeat oneself by precluding certain favorite high-calorie foods. Usually it is impossible for any of us to give up all of life's delectable choices. If your expectation is that you can do so, any misstep will lower your self-esteem and your resolve to eat wisely. How many times we all begin to lose weight by thinking, "I just will never touch another piece of cheesecake." When we later give in, we are demoralized and think, "What's the use? I'll never lose weight. I'm a failure." We then find it much more difficult to pick up and start a structured, healthy meal plan again. Moderation in eating and exercise are keys to success, albeit not as glamorous as the latest diet rage promising fast results.

A 1,200-calorie diet, rich in texture, flavor, and aroma, is ideal. This level of intake avoids the deprivation (that is, on a diet of 500–800 calories) that leads to bingeing, yet also considers the research data that support a dependence on the sensory characteristics of food. Foods high in fat, for example, are particularly desirable because of their high sensory quality. A greater variety of low-calorie foods with full flavor, appearance, and taste helps those who are obese by providing sensory appeal. Future advances in this area of treatment might involve new psychotropic medications or the manipulation of neuronutrients such as chromium, carnitine, lipoic acid, or glycerol.

In the meantime, reducing the fat content in one's diet to less than 30% may drastically reduce the likelihood of heart disease and cancer. Although the American Heart Association suggests that this goal may be unrealistic for most Americans, because we relish processed food and meals high in fat, it would no doubt be beneficial for all of us to trim as much fat as possible from our diets. Psychologically, to do less might be regarded as not simply a careless act but a dangerous one as well, tantamount to driving without fastening the seat belt. Evidence is now accumulating that high levels of Vitamin A and beta-carotene also reduce the risk of cancer. Vitamin A does the job best when absorbed through eating fresh fruit rather than by taking dietary supplements. Thus eating more fresh fruit and cutting down on fats by avoiding fast-food restaurants and the like promotes weight loss and diminishes susceptibility to disease.

A high-fiber diet also reduces the incidence of colon cancer. In India, there is virtually no colon cancer among Hindus, who eat foods rich in cellulose, fiber, and roughage. In contrast, the Parsi community in Bombay has a more Western diet and has a rate of colon and breast cancer almost equal to our own. In addition, cruciferous vegetables (Brussels sprouts, broccoli, cauliflower, and cabbage) have been found to inhibit the development of colon, lung, and breast cancer. The exact mechanism of their protective effect is unknown. More research will most likely reveal other dietary manipulations that can help reduce health risk as well as weight.

Noted obesity researcher Kelly Brownell, in addition to advocating some of the life-style changes emphasized above, underscores the importance of individualized treatment in another way: There is really no "standard treatment" for obesity for everybody (Brownell 1988; Brownell and Wadden 1992). So little is known about this disorder that investigators cannot say for certain which diets or behavioral strategies will work for a particular person or group. Some individuals appear to be greatly helped by behavioral techniques and cognitive therapy. For example, changing one's eating pattern by keeping a diary of the types and amounts of food eaten, the circumstances under which one eats (and eats too much), and any other factors that might contribute to maladaptive eating behaviors are a few of the suggestions offered in these treatment protocols. The patient gains new insights and devises strategies for dealing with her weight problems. Some individuals have been successful at combining behavioral treatments with prescription weight-loss diets. Finally, some researchers believe that in the next 10 years, we will have a variety of medications to help.

Brownell maintains that some patients will benefit by individual treatments, whereas others can make good use of group therapy, all with a goal toward maintaining modest weight losses (Brownell 1988; Brownell et al. 1986). To lose as little as 10% of one's body weight helps normalize blood pressure, reduces cardiovascular risk factors, and promotes health. The goal is to help individual patients increase their awareness of the need to maintain an adequate exercise level *over time* and use their social supports to exert more conscious control of their eating. These principles, stressed by behavior and cognitive therapists, mesh well with long-held psychodynamic therapy, which emphasizes impediments to self-care and failed coping strategies.

To avoid the ill effects of "yo-yo dieting" that were described earlier, some experts have emphasized that a realistic goal for many patients is taking weight off in steps, only 10% at a time. George Blackburn, professor of surgery at Harvard Medical School and Director of the Center for the Study of Nutrition in Medicine at Deaconess Hospital, writes that no matter how overweight an individual is,

> He or she should first try to lose 10% [of body weight]. For example, a patient who weighs 200 pounds should try to lose 19–20 pounds over a 3-month period. This moderate amount of weight loss will allow the patient to look and feel better and more confident. (Blackburn et al. 1993, p. 3)

Blackburn and his colleagues underscore how maintaining weight loss is much more difficult than initial reduction. Easy answers must be avoided with this complicated problem. But an encouraging fact is that this stepwise program has been shown to be effective. As the dietary, exercise, and psychological changes I have emphasized in the chapter are incorporated into a person's life, the probability that that person can maintain weight loss is much higher. Thus, after you lose the first 10%

of your current body weight and maintain it for 6 months to a year, you might attempt to lose another 10%. By doing this, you maximize health benefits to yourself, because 90% of them can be achieved with only a 10% reduction in present body weight. This realistic approach also avoids the frustration and anger that occur with repeated failures at dieting.

As I have noted, drug treatments designed to help curtail obesity are again receiving medical attention. In the 1960s, men and women who grew weary of failed diets sought out medical practitioners who prescribed amphetamines for weight reduction. Often the results were disastrous. The patients lost weight, but amphetamines had their own range of serious side effects, including addiction, agitation, even psychoses.

Recently, a team of investigators at the University of Rochester led by Michael Weintraub (1992) have had good success in treating obesity using a combination of medications. Phentermine (Fastin, Ionamine) and fenfluramine (Pondimin) are two anorexiants (appetite suppressants) with very different pharmacological properties that have been shown to help long-term weight control when used in combination with behavior modification, exercise, and nutrition education. Although not all patients benefit from these medications, some people were able to use the drugs for more than 3½ years without serious side effects. The Weintraub team concluded that for some people, these medications may enhance weight loss more than behavior modification, exercise, and calorie restriction alone.

Investigators are working to see if other drugs might be useful. Caution in this area cannot be overemphasized. Quests to find miracle drugs to treat obesity have been going on for years. The research of Brownell (1988) and Weintraub (1992) underscores how no single drug will be helpful for everyone and that changes in life-style will inevitably need to be made. In addition to regular exercise and dietary adjustments, increased activity in daily life helps a lot. Walking to the mailbox, using stairs instead of the elevator, and standing while talking on the phone are just some of the ways we can counter our sedentary life-style. Making these changes does not alter our need for regular exercise, but it does burn calories and enhance fitness.

Recognizing the complexity of the problem physiologically as well as the shame that obese patients feel, Brownell summarizes, "It may be desirable to shift the focus of weight loss from aesthetic health issues to the concept of 'reasonable weight'" (Brownell and Wadden 1992, p. 509). We have noted clinically that many clients lose weight and experience important benefits (e.g., lowered blood pressure and improved self-esteem) but are discouraged because their goal weight still appears far off. As the weeks pass and weight loss becomes more difficult, these individuals may be at increased risk of relapse. Establishing an attainable, realistic goal may help prevent this (Brownell and Wadden 1992).

A simultaneous focus on physical and psychological health goes a long way toward remedying the mind-body duality inherent in Western thinking. Nowhere has the mind-body split been more pronounced than in the treatment of obesity, because thoughts and feelings seem to be detached from the self. To develop a true self, obese people must take into account both their physical and psychological needs and then integrate the two areas, putting formerly unspeakable feelings into words. The goal is not only bodily longevity but also the enhancement of a psychic vitality, anchored in self-worth.

## 14

# Life's Hurdles: Ways Eating Disorders Help Us to Cope

If one scheme of happiness fails, human nature turns to another; if the first calculation is wrong, we make a second better; we find comfort somewhere.

Jane Austen
*Mansfield Park*

When the French Impressionist Berthe Morisot became despondent over war and political injustices, the social constraints placed on women of her time, and the problem of finding a suitable mate, she turned her energies toward painting. The results of her endeavors are some of the most intriguing (albeit little known or appreciated) works of 19th-century Paris.

Like many other cultivated people of either gender, Morisot transformed personal suffering and struggles into productive work. Today, her prints and etchings are admired for their charm and style. We should doubly respect them as representative of her capacity to cope with severe depression and a social environment that redoubtably emphasized women's achievements as resting solely and squarely in the home. Any personal quest for a different kind of life—such as one filled with enriching friendships, affairs of the heart, and love of one's professional

319

work—was not socially acceptable in her time. Despite these restrictions, Morisot developed her innate artistic talent and led a life filled with good friends and a rich supportive network.

Morisot also used art to deal with the political and personal challenges that perplexed her and her long-standing tendency to feel depressed. This capacity, commonly known as the defense mechanism of sublimation, is but one aspect of the psychologically healthy person who is able to productively turn loving and aggressive strivings into a creative outlet and successful work. Life requires this adaptive capacity from each of us, and the more we are able to make use of it, the more we can succeed in a variety of ways.

No person can engage in every desirable love relationship or vent all the anger or rage that surfaces. To do either would lead to social chaos and great personal cost; friends would be lost, and we would be unable to take advantage of real possibilities in other relationships. We might feel continually fragmented by a rush of intense feelings that could not be channeled productively. We therefore need to develop our capacity to explore new outlets for our energies and interests. To function in life without resorting to harmful coping skills, such as eating disorders, we must first acquire a variety of healthy coping skills.

Most people use a host of defense mechanisms every day. For example, we may not be particularly enthralled with our mother's new boyfriend or a present from a relative. But to avoid causing pain to those we love, we try to stave off negative impressions and feelings and to exchange our loathing for acceptance. This process, which is called reaction formation, protects the self from the full experience of life's unpleasantness and promotes civility in human interactions. Simply put, we turn an attitude or interest into its opposite, which is more personally and socially acceptable. This indispensable skill enables us to maintain friendships without having to be absolutely—and brutally—honest about everything that comes to mind. Haven't you tried to act happy sometimes when someone phones, although you really wished you'd missed the call? Or you may tell a co-worker that her outfit is attractive, then wonder later why you said so because it was really hideous.

Reaction formation manifests itself in many different ways. The more we know about ourselves, the more we recognize we may not be, for instance, as unbigoted or as freethinking as we might believe we are. Only under the greatest self-scrutiny, such as in therapy or psychoanalysis, do we uncover what lies behind our reaction formations.

For example, a good friend of mine who is a law professor and mother of a child has become a champion of social causes and a mover in civil rights at a major Southeastern university. While undergoing psychoanalytic treatment because of work inhibitions, she discovered that her impassioned feelings about racial bigotry stemmed from unconscious racial prejudice. Her mother had been a zealous racist. Much as my friend had tried to disavow her similarity to her mother, she had actually incorporated many of her mother's views and values. As her self-insight grew in therapy, she realized, to her great chagrin, that her legal career had actually been predicated on an attempt to differentiate—or disidentify—from her mother. Much as she consciously wanted to be fair and to act as the antithesis of her mother, she found herself instead with very similar viewpoints. She struggled to promote an African American clerk in her office or to hire an Asian American housekeeper. She was appalled to learn through therapy that she harbored real hatred against other racial groups, much as her mother did.

One might suspect that after identifying this defense, my friend's interest in civil rights might take a major turn. She might decide to honestly acknowledge her bigotry or to stop defending her baser qualities by putting less time and energy into fighting causes. Such was not the case. Instead, as she learned more about herself and her underlying motivation, she felt freer to define her beliefs consciously and forthrightly. Her earlier work inhibitions lessened as she addressed her own disappointment and anger, which she had formerly hidden as a way to be pleasing and avoid making waves. She pursued her career as a social activist less anxiously but more effectively. She sublimated her energy by becoming a better litigator and orator, because she no longer had to stave off feelings of bigotry and hatred that she consciously despised.

Although sublimation and reaction formation are well-known and relatively healthy ways that we redirect our energies and ward off danger and adjust to life's challenges, eating disorder patients are prone to use some additional defense strategies. In fact, an eating disorder can itself be considered a coping strategy par excellence. Viewing it this way helps us see how the symptoms have been used to adapt to internal and external difficulties. At first blush, eating disorders may appear destructive and hurtful (as indeed they are), but they also serve less apparent functions. Patients who have revealed their struggles with these disorders often talk about how they used the eating disorder to cope with personal burdens. These patients are quite aware that they have not yet found a more adaptive way to confront life's challenges.

Elsewhere in this book, I have cited the high number of patients (at least 30%) who do not recover easily despite active treatment for their eating disorder. Studies show that another 30% improve without attaining the highest level of functioning either they or their treaters would like to see. Meanwhile, they are painfully aware that their eating disorder is hurting them, sapping their energy, and contributing to their sense of personal failure. Why is it, then, that these individuals cannot easily give up the eating disorder when other choices seem so apparent?

For most people, the symptom persists because it provides at least one (and probably more) ways of coping. As Boris (1984a) wrote about treating patients with eating disorders, "What we [therapists and family members] call their symptoms, they call their salvation" (p. 315). This "salvation" provided by bulimia or anorexia implies a nearly religious devotion these patients have to holding on to their symptoms. Little wonder that they usually keep the disorder secret from loved ones, who might even suggest they give it up. These individuals experience that suggestion as a form of damnation that forces them to live with inexpressible anxiety and guilt.

Eating disorders are ultimately self-defeating and dangerous, but their beguiling feature is that they appear essential to survival, even as they threaten it. Ultimately, the individual clings to the eating disorder to avoid something worse. It is only as the person recognizes what that "something worse" is and finds new and more adaptive ways of coping that she can be free to make the choice to give up the symptoms. In essence, she must find some other salvation—that is, she must develop new coping skills, such as creativity, assertiveness, and enjoyment of hobbies and interpersonal relationships. Treaters and loved ones can open a new door of understanding by helping the patient look at how the eating disorder actually helps her manage her life. This process also helps others to fully appreciate that the patient has done the best she can with the tools available, just as we all might do.

From the outset, I must stress that I am suggesting only a partial understanding of and purpose underlying the meaning of eating disorders. I have learned from my patients and their families that each woman has a unique story to tell; the many reasons for their eating disorders are complex and always quite different. They have relied on their eating disorders for novel reasons that have sometimes shifted over the course of their own lives. Thus, my patients have taught me more than any textbook about how efficiently and effectively an eating disorder can help someone deal with loss, sadness, abuse, poor self-esteem, abandonment, and sexual conflict.

So instead of presenting every possible meaning for an eating disorder, which would also be impossible, I suggest an approach based on fostering a relationship that explores the possible meanings of the eating disorder. Unraveling some of the ways it has been useful empowers individuals. People learn about their lives and the reasons for their struggles in the context of an open and trusting relationship. Both patient and therapist must be willing to delve into the patient's inner life, which will enhance her capacity to form intimate relationships later on. It will also help the patient learn about herself and how to speak with her own voice. In this context, psychotherapy often seems mysterious (if not dangerous) to nontherapists, but it shouldn't be.

Most therapists want to see their patients grow in their ability to take command of their lives by developing trust and being able to talk with friends and loved ones about their illness. As they grow in their appreciation of the psychological meanings of the eating disorder, it has much less power over them. They no longer rely on it as a salvation, because they understand it and have new tools to negotiate life's challenges. They also become more capable of using the insight derived from other people, movies, books, and the like and so enlarge their world.

Like an Impressionist painting, for these patients, the world is suddenly filled with color and vividness. They derive an appreciation for understanding and purpose they had not been aware of previously. Not surprisingly, friends and loved ones also become more psychologically sensitive. Both the eating disorder patient and her significant others thereby grow from the experience. The result is a deepening appreciation of the richness and complexity of life.

Let us look at the life stories of some of these patients themselves, which reveal how their symptoms helped them function and how they were eventually able to give them up and move on.

# The Terror of Needs

Most of us have experienced certain distressing and discomforting feelings. Whether we feel demoralized, angry, depressed, or anxious, we need to safely discharge these emotions somehow. But handling them constructively is a challenging task, especially when we are not aware of what is bothering us.

Although such dilemmas plague everybody, it is always easier to recognize the problem of misdirected emotions in somebody else rather than ourselves. From earliest infancy, we tend to rid ourselves of bad, painful feelings by projecting them out into the world or onto another person, usually our mother or primary caretaker, who can effectively and compassionately contain them.

Because young children do not yet have the internal reservoir to handle their feelings alone, the expectation is that our mothers will be able to reflect these feelings back to us in more manageable doses. Meanwhile, just as children need to get rid of what is bad, they also try to take in, or introject, what is good. Under the best of circumstances, loving and empathic parents or parental substitutes help children learn that their needs are acceptable and can be gratified by the environment.

Naturally, not all our needs can be met, perhaps because our constitutional or hereditary endowment places undue stress on the mother. Sometimes she cannot handle her child's needs—either because she is going through a stressful period herself or is just unable to intuitively match the child's urgent demands. As a consequence, the child begins to experience the world as unable to meet its basic requirements. Instead, the world seems abandoning, attacking, persecutory, and cruel. Whenever legitimate imperatives for nurturance are not met, such children develop the view that those very necessities are inordinately wrong. They may blame themselves for having needs; or they may feel damned and relegated to a world that persecutes them for their demands, which can cause self-hatred to develop.

One outcome of this dilemma is a defensive strategy in which the individual gives up on having her needs met. In effect, she says to everyone in her life, "I don't need anyone. I don't even need food." In this scenario, food becomes a symbol of persecution. At other times food may be used temporarily, like a drug, to dull the sensation of persecution through bingeing, only to be gotten rid of when the individual feels satiated or bloated. Purging becomes an ingenious way of getting rid of the internal persecutor, just as starving is a way to control the persecutor by not taking anything in.

In one scenario, the child senses that her parents have difficulty understanding and attuning themselves to her. Because their original message may have been that her needs were inordinate and unmanageable, the eating disorder patient now strives to control those needs. If no one can meet them, the patient will try to control them herself. As a result, a false sense of self-sufficiency causes the patient to do all she can to keep her distance both from food and from other people. To risk acknowledging one's needs for another person means handing over an inordinate amount of control and power. It implies dependence by indicating that the other person is important to the self, a possibility that can be frightening to anyone who has not found others to be soothing or kind. The perceived dependence invites attack or persecution, as the following case vignette illustrates.

❧ Samantha O. was a 40-year-old mother of three who was making considerable headway in the treatment of her 12-year struggle with anorexia nervosa. Subjected to severe parental neglect as a girl, Samantha longed for intense interpersonal relationships that would give her some of the parental care and concern she had not received as a small child.

Her expectations in relationships were always dashed, however, because no one could meet her demands. Samantha ended up hating herself for resenting other people's successes and their capacity to make commitments. By refusing to eat, Samantha tried to show people that she could get along without whatever they had to offer. Much as she wanted to be nurtured, she fought it in the form of refusing sustenance, because eating made her feel all the more deficient and aware of what she really coveted.

Samantha began psychotherapy out of desperation. Her husband could not meet all her needs, nor could her friends. Samantha felt lonely all the time and longed for care and understanding. As her psychotherapy process grew more intense and Samantha began to trust her therapist, her eating deteriorated. Her husband became understandably worried, yet he was furious because the treatment seemed to make her worse! After an additional 15-pound weight loss, Samantha finally had to be admitted to the hospital because her life was in jeopardy.

At this point her therapist was scheduled to take a brief vacation. But when she told Samantha about her plans, Samantha threatened suicide. She refused to eat and found no solace in the care of the eating disorder program staff members, her husband, or her peers. An experience of total aloneness over one weekend stirred intense feelings of neediness in Samantha that she tried to disavow. Without the immediate support of her therapist, she felt tortured by her own inner demands but was also envious of her therapist, whom she believed withheld healing. She also deeply resented this therapist for having so much more in life than she did. For example, even though Samantha was an excellent and devoted mother, she was convinced that her therapist was a better (if not a perfect) parent.

Although surrounded by other supportive people, Samantha seemed lost in a lonely crowd where the person who mattered most, her therapist, had abandoned her. Yet she would not make use of the help her therapist offered. Instead, Samantha foiled all attempts to reach her.

What led Samantha to become worse as her therapy actually became more important to her? This common reaction is based on (among other things) envy of the therapist's qualities and disavowal of the good inherent in one's own life. The patient reacts as if all that is good rests within the therapist or other people and none within herself. Even as she begins to understand herself better, she tries to defeat the therapist, because any insight or progress makes her aware that she is not totally self-sufficient. The knowledge that she must rely on other people creates an unsettling anxiety that must be disavowed. The therapist must be made to feel flawed and deficient and therefore unenviable. Better to defeat treatment than to acknowledge one's dependence on or admiration of another person! Consequently, Samantha stopped eating to teach her therapist an important lesson: She didn't need food—or treatment. In reality, her attempt to control the situation indicated that she really wanted to be (ful)filled, but instead had chosen to develop the inner power and backbone to triumph over human needs.

When Samantha's envy was pointed out by her astute therapist, she naturally denied it. With time, however, she came to see that all that was strong did not rest only within her therapist—it also was within her. This understanding decreased her envy and her need to spoil whatever love, support, and nurturance others gave her. As the eating disorder patient begins to recognize that not all riches, goodness, or abilities lie within the worlds of others, then she will naturally be less envious. She can then open up more to accept the genuine gifts and healing qualities of other people and to form sustaining attachments and ordinary dependencies. Yet to get to that point, the individual must be willing to recognize that one can sabotage a relationship because of envy and fear of attachment. Although all of us feel envious sometimes, most of us are aware that total self-sufficiency is impossible and not a good idea. We must risk ultimate rejection, too, if we allow ourselves to need and get involved in a relationship.

It is also important for family members, therapists, and friends to be aware that generosity may be particularly aversive to the individual with an eating disorder. It incites even more envy, because she feels so unable to give anything herself. She must then attempt to show others up, to deflate the value of those who seem to have more than she has. The anorexic patient, in particular, wants people to see her as self-sufficient. Her refusal to eat signals to others that they should want what she has and what she can do by refusing food, so that she becomes the object of envy herself. Her symptoms also vividly indicate that others have nothing she wants or needs, and thus they are not to be envied.

The eating disorder patient must relinquish her primary mode of self-defense to enable her to partake of the human sustenance of give-and-take relationships. Only after she understands and accepts that all of us thrive within the context of interpersonal bonds will she begin to deal with how much she loses by her position. The terror of neediness evokes memories and fantasies that can never be satisfied. She must confront the belief of the unhappy child within her that she can never be sustained by another person. Doing so permits her to accept the succor of human relationships without fearing that dependence will utterly overwhelm or destroy her.

## Fleeing Reality

From time to time, most people refuse to admit or acknowledge an unpleasant reality. This psychological process of denial makes life look rosier than it is by temporarily pushing away painful feelings or unwanted events. For example, when a dreaded disease such as cancer is diagnosed, most of us might react by shoving this knowledge aside—"forgetting" what is really going on so that we can cope with the situation. We also tuck away painful feelings of anxiety, sadness, loss, and even guilt. As a defense, denial allows us to go about our business acting fairly contented, as if nothing bothers or troubles us beneath the surface. A certain amount of denial is adaptive, even healthy. The problem arises when it is relied on to squelch experience. Too much of denial stifles growth. To temporarily protect the self, it can siphon off the full range of our emotions and reactions.

Eating disorders are significant ways of disavowing psychological pain. Just as people may flee from experiencing physical pain by using sedative drugs or anesthetics, those who misuse food may do so to hold certain feelings and experiences at bay. This distancing maneuver allows the patient to steadfastly forswear certain aspects of her past and present.

❦ Kelly P. was a lively anorexic woman. At age 22, she had already had her diagnosis for 6 years. In addition to self-starvation, Kelly compulsively exercised to the point of exhaustion. She had several stress fractures of her ankles because of her moderate osteoporosis and intense activity level. She never seemed to stop exercising, although the prescribed treatment for her fractures and her eating disorder was to rest her legs and gain weight.

Kelly denied her physical pain, her weight loss—even the state of her psychological health. She insisted that she was healthy and plump. Even after her podiatrist placed her ankles in casts, she managed to keep exercising her upper body. To burn up calories, she squeezed her fingers, clenched her hands, waved her arms, and turned her torso from side to side. Yet she already weighed 30% below her designated recovery weight.

What personal saga lay behind a compulsion so severe that it drove Kelly to exhaustion, if not physical compromise and injury, even as she insisted she was fit and energetic? Kelly had read many self-help books and was a veteran of several hospital programs that used pharmacotherapy, the 12-step approach, and cognitive and behavioral methods. As a result, she was understandably discouraged when her parents insisted she leave home for yet another treatment center. The treatment team at the new program began by letting Kelly and her family know that her treatment would be arduous. Nothing had worked so far, and Kelly did not seem motivated to change. The treaters told Kelly that they would first need to find out why any change seemed so difficult for her, and then they would help her discover the reasons underlying her anorexia.

Mr. and Mrs. P. seemed quite supportive of Kelly's investigation into her illness. But in some ways they also colluded with her denial by providing a meager history about the family's early life together. Over months of intensive treatment that incorporated nutritional care, individual and family therapy, group therapy, biofeedback, and severe restriction of exercise (which required 24-hour vigilance on the part of nursing staff), Kelly was forced to delve more deeply into her past. The treatment goal was to provide her with the emotional support she needed to refrain from life-threatening behavior. Only when her symptoms were under control could she begin to make use of what others might offer in terms of understanding and exploring her past.

On the surface, Kelly expressed anger at her mother for being alcoholic. She acknowledged that she had felt abandoned and betrayed whenever her mother left her with her father or a babysitter, only to go off and drink with her friends for what seemed like an eternity. When Kelly's mother returned to their chaotic household, she would emotionally abandon her daughter yet again as she turned her own reserves of emotional energy into screaming barrages at her husband.

In treatment, Kelly gradually began to experience the full force of feelings she had denied for years. Her use of exercise in particular had staved off the rage she felt toward both her parents for what she considered their emotional neglect and abandonment. Exercise also allowed her to avoid the depression and loss associated with this parental deprivation.

Only with difficulty could Kelly begin to see the deep ambivalence she harbored toward both her parents. True, they had been responsible for some realistic disappointments and deprivations in her life. But they had also tried their best to see that she was well-educated and cared for; they had sacrificed so that she could receive psychiatric treatment. She attempted to disavow her ambivalence as she did her need for food, but neither could be suppressed forever. Her emotional struggle surfaced instead in her life-threatening symptoms.

Kelly's actions also indicated that she could endure without her mother's succor; indeed, to have even one "sip" of nurturance might stimulate a desire for more, something her mother might be unable to give even now. By running, bending, shaking, and fasting, Kelly could take care of her own needs and wants that she was convinced no other person could ever satisfy.

Another way to illuminate Kelly's plight is to look at the extent of her helplessness when she was young. Despite her pleas and longings, she could not force her parents to clean up their acts. Her ineffectual position with them led her to feel chronically small, defeated, and impotent to change the course of her own life.

By becoming the "thinnest" or "the greatest sufferer," the anorexic patient creates within herself an illusion of power. Her target weight becomes a measurable, achievable goal. She then has the right to feel special, because she has finally "achieved something" grand—but she cannot accept this accomplishment for long.

Because people with eating disorders believe they have sacrificed their own lives for others, they also believe that they deserve to be treated better. They seem to feel entitled to special treatment and understanding. Finally, their illness permits them to turn the tables on those who symbolically or realistically deprived them of their childhood. For once, they hold the power to cause concern and worry; for once, they can demand the care they wish they had received and decide whether to take it or reject it. But these motivations cannot come into consciousness without hard work and a desire on the part of the patient to know herself.

It surprises many people that eating disorder patients, despite even high intelligence, often lack insight into their less apparent motivations for the longest time. Clearly, their poor nutritional state hinders their capacity to think. But even after they are well nourished, they must be helped to see that taking in food or taking in a relationship by talking does not equate with total dependency. Integrating this insight into the self takes time. It involves relying on the expertise of another and depending on that person, which can be scary for someone who has resolved to care totally for herself. To do so requires her to lose control and give up her own "competence." But as she understands more about the meaning of her symptoms, she empowers herself by these very discoveries and the knowledge that she can manage new interpersonal ties without feeling enveloped. She moves toward health when she can reckon with all her feelings and impulses, no longer taxing herself by the abject denial of her emotions.

## Is There a Monster Inside Me?

The philosopher George Santayana wrote this poignant aphorism about the passage of time: "We must welcome the future, remembering that soon it will be past; and we must respect the past, remembering that once it was all that was humanly possible."

This saying captures much of the basis of modern psychodynamic psychiatry. To be successful, treatment must help us welcome our future. But first we must be able to put our past into perspective and reckon with whatever positive challenges and pitfalls we have traversed to get to where we are. The future is bound to be unwelcome if what is remembered from the past is painful. Learning about ourselves helps us to change the present and the future by giving us insight into our own strengths and limitations.

Psychodynamic treatment helps us to examine the important memories and events of the past. Through it, we come to realize how all of us, regardless of our self-understanding, will inadvertently play out the past. We also come to see how our present realities are shaped by the significant qualities of our parents and other loved ones. Yet before treatment, we are rarely consciously aware of this process. In therapy we become more attuned to what those in psychiatric practice call our "identifications and incorporations."

Consider, for example, how often you hear a remark like this: "Little Susie's walk is really just like her father's." These common, everyday comments speak to the degree to which we incorporate aspects of our most intimate relationships, particularly those that are important in our childhood. As we are growing up, we also introject entire situational schemes, repeating them over and over to gain mastery.

A simple illustration of this phenomenon occurs frequently in clinical practice. A mother, never satisfied with the accomplishments of her children, reprimands them repeatedly. She wants them to do exactly what she tells them to do; when they disobey, she withdraws from them even for the slightest infraction. This parent probably learned this disruptive pattern of interaction from her own mother who, inadvertently but somewhat mean-spiritedly, forced her children to submit to her own whims rather than fostering their unique achievements. In any case, the rigid mother experiences herself as being a loving and good mother by enforcing such standards. In actuality, she may be behaving quite aggressively toward her child, unwittingly enacting a pattern that conveys more hate than love.

Children raised in such households often view their parents as cruel, but nonetheless long for their love. They cannot avoid taking in the baneful, erratic qualities they experienced but tend to keep them buried. On a conscious level, they love their parents and want to emulate and please them more than anything. So the child who has identified with the parental drive to control and punish may end up relentlessly punishing herself for any small infraction. Without knowing it, and to avoid being helplessly subjected to her parents' anger, she may also take on some of their haughty, exploitive qualities. Her unconscious intent is to achieve mastery over her environment by doing to others what had been done to her. In psychological terms, this process is called "identification with the aggressor." Individuals who identify with the aggressor are angry and often enrage other people.

❦ One individual, Whitney R., spewed forth recriminations that put even her closest friends on guard. She lashed out at so many different therapists that no one in her college town wanted to work with her, either in individual or group therapy. Among her peers, Whitney's hostility had earned her the nickname Junkyard Dog, a sobriquet that she wore with her irascibility like a badge of merit.

Whitney's bulimia was further evidence of her malevolence; with every purge, she became more convinced that she was bad. She called herself a monster. It confirmed to her that her father's early opinions had been right—that is, she was born deviant, ugly, unproductive, and hurtful. His angry tirades resulted in punishments that kept her from forming age-appropriate, positive relationships. When he became angry with her imperfections, he would punish her by grounding her for weeks on end. His tirades led to (among other things) Whitney's deep insecurity, which hindered her from forming good social relationships. For Whitney, the eating disorder and rampant hostility combined to confirm an early object tie with a punishing father. Unconsciously, she was treating herself just as she had experienced her father treating her. She also berated others, as she had experienced her father verbally abusing her, for not living up to an impossible ideal. With her patterns of restricting, bingeing, and purging, Whitney took revenge on herself for not attaining her own very high standards, hoping all the while to gain some control over her body.

Not until this repetitive pattern was identified for Whitney could she begin to change it. Naturally enough, she vehemently resisted any efforts on the part of her new therapist to explain her actions firmly yet forcefully. Whitney's therapist had to help her see how her actions were like those of her father, including her aggression against herself and others. This correlation could be made only within the context of a relationship where Whitney also felt accepted for who she was. The therapist realized that beneath Whitney's veneer of anger was really a scared child who had never known acceptance or love for herself. She had been expected to fulfill her father's wishes rather than her own. If this dynamic could not be addressed, Whitney would probably continue to punish herself and then pass on this maladaptive heritage to her own children. In all likelihood, she would not have found a way to overcome her eating disorder either, because behavioral control would have been purely symptomatic rather than addressing her underlying preoccupations.

Thus we see how self-punishing an eating disorder can be. Through self-punishment the individual manages to feel quite self-righteous and egotistical, at least temporarily. Her emphasis on perfection holds her to a higher standard than others around her. Yet her hope is to please the object whose love she craves—usually a parent. With the self-sacrifice and aggression she directs toward the self, perhaps she will finally win the love of the sought-after other.

The individual who has internalized a parent who finds her unlovable or despicable will be unable to nurture her own good qualities, such as intelligence and affability. Instead, she will behave like a monster and will deny her talents. She cannot take advantage of opportunities because she is filled with aggression that manifests itself in relentless self-punishment and "terror of the good." She will also purge to get rid of the monster within her.

What can be done when so much aggression is bottled up inside and cannot be discharged into effective work or positive accomplishments? It can be directed against the external world. Just as the original beloved objects treated her poorly, so she will be compelled to treat her friends and others poorly. Healthy relationships will be spoiled because only another masochist can tolerate the overt chidings and implied criticisms of one with so much inner self-hatred. The individual thus attempts to mask this aggression by projecting it outward or by making herself just like the caretaker who was perceived as hurtful and aggressive.

Change begins when the individual learns to speak of the anger that is wrecking her life. She is then freer to give voice to her feelings in a treatment process where her anger and desire for change can be acknowledged. Yet this therapeutic relationship must focus on how the individual is repeating her past and undermining her future by spoiling her relationships.

However, it is also essential for the eating disorder patient to develop friendships and love relationships that show her that healthy interdependence does not destroy independence. These relationships survive despite the individual's positive moves ahead. By "identifying with the aggressor," eating disorder patients cope with life, wreaking havoc on others as it was done to them. But in the end, they destroy anything that might be good for themselves, including the taking in of nutritious food. They are compelled to repeat their "bad past" over and over again, because it is the only past they have or know. But if they begin to permit themselves to have good things, including relationships and better control of their eating disorder, they will improve. Nothing succeeds for them like surviving success. Their relationships, including therapeutic ones, provide opportunities to practice dealing effectively with previous destructive feelings such as envy, jealousy, and competition. As they find new objects of identification to take delight in their success, they move forward to new styles of interaction and coping by having more avenues for self-expression and intimate interaction.

## Punishment Means Love

Sometimes a woman acts submissively to win over a person who has been harsh, abusing, or simply critical. Her past leads her to believe that suffering is the only way to connect with others and preserve relationships. She is compliant to win love; otherwise, she feels lonely and abandoned. To stop this pattern requires her to give up an all-important relationship. She is thus caught in a relentless struggle to find love but believes that she can get it only if she submits to control or pain. She might lose the other person if she puts her foot down, becomes assertive, or refuses to obey orders.

To win the person's love, this woman throws all she has into "seducing" the all-important original object, usually her mother. She is terrified of losing this vital tie. She equates eating, nurturing, and being criticized because of their temporal connection so early in life, and so develops an eating disorder as a particularly entrenched and devastating mode of self-punishment. If the eating disorder becomes severe, other people also begin to "punish" the patient by imposing restrictions on her such as structured eating, confronting her about her health, and insisting she enter treatment. Indeed, eating disorder patients unwittingly try to provoke their treaters into establishing a dramatic stance of control, because control is what they are used to. In an equally extreme attempt to get their needs met, they may also try to charm their treaters into a disavowal of the symptoms.

In any case, for some individuals, one hidden meaning behind the eating disorder is that it masks an attempt to bring another person psychologically close by being submissive. Although terrified of doing so, the person with an eating disorder may believe that submission is the only way to obtain love. The eating disorder then becomes a way to render punishment on the self while terrorizing the other person. Naturally, most people will rarely consciously accept this equation early in their treatment. Until a woman becomes conscious of how her self-punishment is a way to acquire love, she will continue to enact it. As Berliner (1947) observed, this "need for punishment or self-punishment is thus a bid for affection; it is the need for the love of a person who punishes" (p. 464).

Sometimes the individual has experienced so much pain and abuse at the hands of other people that she now has an additional wish for retaliation. In this case, she may need to destroy her treatment, her therapist, or her own important relationships out of a desire to punish her earliest objects whom she perceived as sadistic and hurtful but with whom she now identifies. In a sense, this self-destructive tendency also allows her to feel superior to others and devoid of any need for them.

When a parent is explosive, abusive, prone to addictions, or simply unable to communicate effectively with the child, it can result in a lack of holding and soothing. The child also fails to develop a language that allows her to speak her mind and to participate in mutual exchanges of meaningful verbal connections. She is left to struggle with herself, often without words and caught up in a myriad of feeling states that reinforce her badness and the fact that she deserves pain. If she knows only pain, it will naturally become the only way she can relate to others. And she will continue to perpetuate this cycle until she learns a different way of interacting.

🐾 Melissa S. was a severely anorexic young woman who had defeated many treatments. She allegedly had experienced numerous physical attacks at the hands of her mother. At age four, she was adopted by another family who brutalized her. She saw herself as the victim of others' multiple aggressions against her and bitterly complained that she had been mistreated throughout her life. Indeed, it was difficult to listen to Melissa, because it seemed as though she had never experienced even one positive, nonabusive relationship.

Melissa had a strong need to destroy her treatment because of her identification with the maternal figures who had abused her. She taxed the patience of even the most experienced therapists by making them feel that they had nothing worthwhile to offer her. Their slightest error or imperfection led Melissa to decry that evil had once again been done to her. She tried to corrupt her treatments by cashing insurance checks that should have been turned over to her treaters.

At one point, one of Melissa's group therapists was worried that Melissa might falsely accuse at least one of her treaters of a sexual boundary violation. This possibility seemed plausible, because Melissa had never described any good experiences with another human being. Although Melissa had presented factual evidence of her prior abuse, the therapist wondered if she had not used some hyperbole in doing so and noted that Melissa seemed to want to experience only the worst in life.

In actuality, Melissa's group therapist had uncovered a powerful dynamic that had slowed Melissa's treatment all along. Melissa was attempting to turn all those who could do her some good into destructive perpetrators. This reversal helped Melissa hold onto a relationship paradigm she had experienced since her youth—submission, suffering, and destroying the good as a condition for maintaining an important (albeit destructive) relationship. Love came only from punishment! Only after a prolonged experience in treatment was Melissa able to internalize others as basically beneficial. As she began to experience her treaters as caring and as keepers of good professional boundaries, she began to see that all people were not wrongdoers.

## "It's All in My Mind"

Clinical work with eating disorder patients confirms that as a group they are among the most extraordinarily bright and talented of people. Sometimes they have been able to accomplish impressively and dramatically in their chosen careers despite struggling with starving, bingeing, or purging. Some may not have been able to achieve to their fullest potential but are still shown to be quite intelligent and capable according to their psychological tests.

Both groups of the achieving and underachieving eating disorder population have this facet in common: given the opportunity, they can use their intellect either constructively or destructively. One potentially harmful way is to use intellectualization to avoid facing one's feelings or life circumstances. This defensive strategy temporarily helps the individual cope by providing emotional distance from pain, trauma, or loss while preserving self-esteem by asserting cognitive capacity. Life is lived only "in the mind." The person denies her physical body to focus instead on developing brilliant verbalization skills. Often the words are without much meaning. When taken to extremes, intellectualization blocks the expression of affect, or emotional catharsis. This process thus prevents the individual from experiencing important aspects of her personality. She can achieve intellectually but cannot win a final victory over her symptoms. She does not have a genuine knowledge of herself.

❦ Kristen T., age 20, was forced to leave college in her junior year despite her superior academic performance because of her bulimia and very low weight. On the surface, Kristen was committed to her treatment to control her symptoms and explain why she had turned to eating to express her feelings.

One afternoon in group therapy, Kristen poignantly related how her mother had fed her only tiny sandwiches while other members in the family received full-course meals. Her mother's own eating disorder and obsession with appearance had made Kristen feel "like a pig" from an early age. As treatment proceeded and Kristen began to eat differently but normally, she even gained a bit of weight and began struggling with how to integrate what she experienced as a shift in her body image.

During another group therapy session, Kristen became quite tearful as she talked about these changes. Then she began sobbing as she detailed her mother's militaristic control of her childhood diet. In the midst of this incident, Kristen suddenly shut off her tears, looked up and smiled at the group, and bluntly reported that she now understood the reasons for her long-standing anger at her family and the causes of her eating disorder. She then gave a detailed but highly intellectualized formulation of the cause of her difficulties. Beginning by reciting a litany of complaints against her mother who had made her care for an aging grandparent, Kristen concluded by focusing on her father's construction business as an activity that kept him away from home for weeks at a time. She relayed all this information without much feeling at all.

One of the group therapists pointed out that Kristen was avoiding her feelings by becoming so focused on a rational view of her experience. Then a peer encouraged Kristen to take risks by openly expressing her emotions rather than blocking her sad feelings, because the more she did so, the more she would be able to truly learn about herself. Those in the group sensed that Kristen felt devastated at not having had the kind of unconditional love from her parents she longed for; she was recognized only for her rigorous control of her body through diet, exercise, gymnastics, and academic accomplishments. Small wonder Kristen reverted to intellectualization as a defense: not only was it the only way she knew to cope with highly disturbing feelings, but it also had won her parents' favor and recognition from the time she was small. Human sympathy in Kristen's family was considered a supreme indulgence, so to express sorrow, joy, irritation, or any other feeling was the ultimate "pig out."

## The Search for the Golden Fleece

As young children, we all look for heroes and heroines, usually in the form of our parents. Later on we transfer our loyalty to other adults with charisma, star quality, or simply the ability to stir deeper admiration within us. Kohut (1971, 1977) understood this phenomenon as the developmental need to draw strength from another human being who is more powerful and perfect, recognizing it as age-appropriate idealization. But as development proceeds, children gradually become aware of their parents' flaws. Parents can facilitate this growth by not demanding perfection of themselves or their children, which enables them to learn to appreciate both strengths and weaknesses.

In a sense, idealization gives way to the child's realistic appraisal of the personal fallibility as well as the fallibility of others. John Steinbeck's story "The Red Pony" depicts this process. The story opens by focusing on the main character, a young boy who is enthralled with both his horse and the family's hired hand, who he believes can do no wrong. However, the boy's belief in the hired hand's omnipotence falters when the man is unable to keep his pony from dying. As the main character realizes that his hero is not as godlike as he had hoped, his idealization gives way to a more realistic and adult appraisal of talent leavened with human frailty.

Some eating disorder patients maintain tenacious idealizations in their relationships. These idealizations are best understood as a holdover from earlier development. Thus, along with the eating disorder itself, the person hopes to find perfection in the other, which may signal a failure to negotiate an essential developmental level.

The cost, of course, is that one can never find the kind of adulation in adult relationships that was longed for in youth. Inevitable disappointment accompanies each failure in empathy and understanding that occurs with human interactions. The life history of many people with eating disorders will include a series of failed relationships, even ones with treaters and treatment teams. Their tendency to feel disappointed in others occurs because they continue to search for the proverbial Golden Fleece—the mythical perfect human relationship.

🍂 Carol U., a 45-year-old stockbroker with severe bulimia, went to pieces in every relationship she established with a man. She usually began a relationship with an older but nonetheless stable suitor, then inevitably found him lacking after a few months. Likewise, she began treatment relationships but became disappointed when her bulimic symptoms did not remit quickly.

Carol was, in many ways, a remarkable woman. She could look ravishing in outfits that she had put together from secondhand stores, and she had accumulated impressive wealth during her career. She also had a surprising capacity to attract both men and treaters, all of whom fantasized that they could provide her with the compassion, caring, and cure she needed. This rescuer role played to the conceit and competitive zeal of the treaters, each of whom wanted to "be the best and brightest therapist" to help Carol.

The basis of Carol's search for the perfect other was her own defective sense of self. She needed to idealize others so that her connection with them would make her feel (temporarily) better and more perfect. Yet another side of her refused to get well. She defeated her treatment, as she defeated her lovers, by complaining that no one was ever good enough to help her. Carol first needed to recognize that a key part of her did not want to change her illness. Then she needed to mourn her wish for an idealized other, because no one that perfect or wonderful ever really exists for us.

Mourning was a keynote of her therapy. By letting go of her search for perfection in another person, Carol was able to negotiate the developmental roadblock of wanting perfection in herself. Ultimately, her striving for perfection was traced back to her childhood wish for perfect parents and her early belief that her parents wanted her to be flawless. In this process, Carol was supported by a therapist who herself was quite comfortable with her own imperfections. The therapist helped Carol deal with the errors in empathy and understanding inherent in any treatment process. On this most thrilling of journeys, there are always expectable fluctuations and missteps along the way.

Carol gradually realized that even her bulimia was related to her search for the Golden Fleece. She had used bingeing like a drug to make her feel whole and soothed, much like an infant in a blissful state of oneness with its mother. This fantasy kept alive the hope that a powerful therapist would fill the parental role and purge Carol of her defects. Meanwhile, she had attempted to rid herself of them by vomiting profusely. Although her eating symptoms were at center stage, they reflected Carol's deep desire to be taken care of by an omnipotent other. Only when she was able to accept the fact that perfection is neither desirable nor obtainable could she begin to heal herself.

## Paying as You Go

In "The Tyranny of the Should," Karen Horney (1950/1970) addressed the terrible toll exacted by feelings of guilt. The critical agency in the mind—the superego—helps rein in forbidden impulses and desires with an ongoing critical commentary (usually unconscious) about what should or should not be done. At other times, the superego may be more "beloved" or benevolent (Schafer 1960, p. 186). In healthy functioning, it guides us to carry through with legitimate ideals such as social activism, loving parenting, and career accomplishments.

Sometimes, however, it is impossible to take advantage of this loving aspect of the superego to move ahead in life because of the guilt feelings that accompany doing better than others. The resulting conflict can be undermining, despite a person's obvious potential in a given endeavor or field. This phenomenon is illustrated by those students who never manage to complete their degree or to have a healthy relationship—much as they themselves protest that they want to do so. The conflict frustrates those who want to achieve but feel blocked; it also perplexes their loved ones and friends. Those individuals who must bear witness to this emotional struggle can only wonder what happened to keep their friend stuck in an entrenched pattern where success seems impossible.

Unconscious guilt feelings lead many career and relationship pathways to a dead end. One might understandably ask what causes these feelings in the first place and why individuals, despite the knowledge that they are not achieving up to their potential, persist in failure. It is the task of good psychotherapy to solve the mystery behind such inhibitions.

Although each story is unique, there are some common pathways that lead to the pattern of "paying as you go" for the transgression of doing better. Many individuals unconsciously believe that success will damage their parents; if they outperform their parents, they may in turn be abandoned by them. Of course, as we reach adulthood we might expect to not continue carrying these childhood fears of loss and abandonment, but sometimes the fears linger anyway.

Furthermore, each individual possesses an internal "parent" who gives permission or forbids certain behaviors based on their accompanying punishment or prize. As a result, we may embark on our life journey with certain internal admonitions or scripts that preclude us from having anything good in our lives. A central belief then surfaces that more is not deserved and, if it is acquired, then it comes at the cost of being abandoned or punished. In wresting defeat from the jaws of victory, such individuals deal with life's hurdles by repeatedly refusing to jump over them. This self-defeating behavior often occurs in the face of significant talent and natural endowments—as Katarina's case will demonstrate.

❦ At the time she began psychotherapy, Katarina V. was 38, single, and had been anorexic for 15 years. Despite her professed desire to marry, she had only been able to engage a series of married men in adulterous affairs. Despite her beauty, charm, and wit that would seem attractive to a wealth of available men, Katarina continued to make destructive choices—although she felt quite ashamed of her past. When one of her lovers decided to divorce his wife and marry her, she became terrified at his proposal.

At this point, Katarina recognized the severity of her eating disorder and her conflict about men. She decided to enter treatment. She expressed a superficial desire to marry and have a family, but when presented with the opportunity, she fled from it. Katarina was in the dark as to what had led her to this self-defeating pattern. Her eating disorder also fueled her relationship difficulties by helping her maintain an aloof stance with men. Whenever she was ill, she could not maintain a romantic involvement, which was one way to protect herself.

Katarina was also worried about the fate of her elderly mother. As she spoke of her concern that her mother might die at home without her being there, a clue to the cause of Katarina's romantic failures surfaced. To have a man of her own would mean successfully competing with and doing better than her mother. This possibility seemed threatening to Katarina, who loved her mother deeply and did not want to hurt her.

Not surprisingly, Katarina was always deferential toward her female therapist and would not challenge her in any way. She maintained a childlike demeanor that did not place her in the more dangerous and adult role of competitor. In a similar way, her involvement with married men was a compromise. Katarina never attained the status of wife and thus never challenged her mother—in reality or in her own mind. Likewise, her anorexia helped her maintain a less womanly body that precluded more age-appropriate challenges.

Through it all, Katarina failed to achieve what she consciously wanted because of her unconscious feelings of guilt about doing as well as or better than her mother. Indeed, Katarina's sense of guilt was so severe that she needed to defeat both herself and her treaters. Her refusal to accept the understanding they offered and her attempts to derail the treatment by continual self-recrimination and lackluster involvement with others was based on the damage she believed she would cause if she aspired to more for herself.

# Conclusion

One way to understand eating disorders rests on viewing them as highly innovative psychological patterns for coping with life. Sometimes they are found alongside other symptoms that also alleviate diffuse anxiety, pain, and sadness. All the coping strategies explored in this chapter help to shore up the individual's flagging sense of self. They are heroic attempts to deal with life, albeit less successfully than would be ideal.

Yet psychotherapy can be used to unravel these defense mechanisms and help the individual find new and more adaptive behaviors. Along the way, the patient benefits by seeing how her therapist deals with life—and his or her own imperfections. It is crucial for patients to remember that their therapists cannot provide either perfect understanding or an immediate cure—nor would doing so be advisable. Instead, life is viewed as a process where growth and change are desirable. It takes time for the self to grow, but only personal growth will ultimately attenuate the eating disorder. Real healing in the therapy relationship comes not only from a striving for personal integration and integrity but also from the internalization of a new role model. As the role model is incorporated, the patient should gain the capacity to behave somewhat more reflectively, less rigidly, and much more kindly toward herself than at the beginning of treatment. Over time, the patient's own capacities grow. She becomes empowered by recognizing that she is not the passive recipient of the therapist's goodness but rather an active participant in her own treatment.

A skilled and caring therapist willingly shows the eating disorder patient that growth enhances and does not detract from their relationship. To develop the correct fit with a therapist, patients must be willing to work slowly and listen carefully. It is crucial for them to be good health care consumers, because it is their own interests that are paramount. They will recognize the right therapist as they learn to rely on their level of comfort and the ease with which the therapist can explore issues and meaning without becoming dogmatic.

The individual with an eating disorder must feel that her own point of view and strengths are appreciated. A good relationship with her therapist will help her recognize that neither party is the sole harbinger of wisdom in the patient-therapist dyad. A good measure of humility is therefore an important quality in a therapist, because both participants must be open to the discovery of fresh ideas and new potentialities. The healing process is an evolving one that welcomes life's hurdles as opportunities for growth and the exercise of newfound confidence.

# 15

# Treatment:
# The Body Reclaimed

Hard work keeps the wrinkles out of the mind and spirit.

Helena Rubinstein

When a woman undertakes psychiatric treatment, she may not be aware initially that it will be the hardest work she will ever face in her life. As she musters courage to begin her journey, she may feel a sudden burst of energy and well-being—what mental health professionals call a "flight into health." Yet her probing into the recesses of her soul will necessarily take her many new places. More often than not, she will find the reassurances of sensitive friends, family members, and her therapist that she is "doing hard work" as a veritable euphemism for the internal pain and unpredictability inherent in the treatment process. She will also find that a part of her resists giving up her illness and moving forward even as she consciously tells herself and others how much she wants to.

As a woman gets to know herself better along the way, she will begin to feel a renewal of spirit and a lifting of gnawing vexations and torments. She will also discover in herself potentially new capacities as she begins to exercise her freedom to reveal her unique gifts to the world. Thus hard work will produce its own reward: she will find herself more able than ever before to enjoy and to use her mind and spirit. Her life may not be worry- or wrinkle-free, but she will, in the words of the late Karl Menninger, become "weller than well."

Dr. Karl, as he was affectionately known, used this phrase to convey the idea that psychiatric treatment does not cure all of life's ills. Instead, it helps the individual deal with them so adaptively and constructively that the improved functioning is even better than what is considered normal. As the work of treatment gets under way, a patient soon realizes that it can never be fully complete, because life itself will always introduce fresh challenges and new choices throughout the life cycle.

The first step is by far the most difficult: how do you begin to ask for help? For any of us, this process is heartwrenching, because we must squarely examine ourselves, our flaws, and our difficulties. We must admit that we cannot take care of everything on our own any longer (nor should we try to); but admit it we must. My experience as a psychiatrist leads me to concur with advice columnist Ann Landers, who consistently points out that acknowledging the need to seek help solves 50% of the problem.

In this chapter, we will examine the lives of some of the most courageous women I have ever known. Their struggles with eating disorders, although challenging to the professionals who were trying to help them, have also been a source of unremitting inspiration to their treaters and a stimulus for growth to themselves.

The treatment relationship is really a journey taken by both the patient and the therapist—a rich enterprise that reveals many mysteries for both participants along the way. Each life history presented in this book could merit a book in itself. Like all life stories, they illustrate so much about the human condition—how people overcome difficult realities, physical illnesses, the limits of an unsupportive culture, and discrimination. Having an eating disorder is an additional challenge, perplexing to the individual, her family, and even her therapist.

As I have already demonstrated, there are a variety of possible therapeutic strategies for patients, depending on their needs. In other chapters of this book, we have sampled the various options and interventions offered by modern psychiatry. I will now explain how specific modalities can be used, depending on the unique needs and struggles of the patient.

My purpose is not only to emphasize the variety of options but also to acknowledge that some problems are difficult to solve quickly. Eating disorders are so interwoven with developmental struggles and challenges that the woman may be terrified of participating in treatment and moving forward. As one individual with anorexia repeatedly exclaimed, "I'd rather die than grow up!"

The subspecialty of eating disorders treatment has recently been enriched by the development of specific practice guidelines and treatment strategies. Under the auspices of the American Psychiatric Association (APA), Joel Yager, an eating disorders specialist at UCLA Medical Center, has chaired the APA Work Group on Eating Disorders, which is putting together a workbook that helps clinicians conduct state-of-the-art therapy (APA Work Group on Eating Disorders 1993). These guidelines address the range of useful treatments yet acknowledge that patients differ and may require one or more modalities (e.g., medication, group therapy, individual therapy).

To compile the specific treatment approaches, the task force worked with hundreds of experienced clinicians, who extensively reviewed each suggested strategy. Then the task force members studied each strategy's indications, efficacy, and safety through clinical and literature reviews to arrive at the most thorough yet cost-effective treatment recommendations. The DSM-IV guidelines (American Psychiatric Association 1993) ensure that consumers will receive the most up-to-date treatment, because the treatment strategies will be reviewed and updated regularly by the task force. Doctors are also urged to treat each patient individually, respecting differences and not necessarily using a cookbook approach.

As important as these guidelines are to both patient and practitioner, there is nothing like a real-life example to drive home the reality that treatment is multifaceted and challenging. In the following sections, treatment principles and alternatives will be brought to life to illustrate not only what can be useful, depending on individual needs, but also to show how individuals with long-standing complex problems can work with treaters to ameliorate their eating disorders and, ultimately, to change their lives.

The stories of these patients will show us that treatment can indeed be the most arduous work, taking a great deal of time and a large investment of energy and financial resources, all without the kind of guarantee or warranty we have come to expect of material acquisitions. Yet what these individuals have been able to achieve is much more valuable and substantive than anything money can buy. These women committed themselves over the long haul to overcoming their eating disorders. Like most patients, they realized that there were no simple or easy answers to their difficulties, though they (quite naturally) wanted them. Despite inevitable snags, disappointments, and relapses, they persisted in staying the course so that they could ultimately live their lives more effectively.

### ❦ Who Am I?

Penelope W., age 24, was by anybody's standards a "poor little rich girl." Raised in a household where every conceivable material advantage was her birthright, her chief complaint was having absolutely no idea who she was as a young woman. Her mother, with whom she had a highly enmeshed but all-too-gratifying relationship, could well have afforded to buy Penelope anything she wanted.

When Penelope came for an outpatient evaluation, her bulimia was so severe that it had eroded her teeth and caused her cheeks to swell up like those of a chipmunk. At the time, this otherwise attractive and personable young woman remarked, "If I could only buy an identity at a drug store, I know I would be all right. But money can't buy an identity when none exists. I have no idea who I am or where I'm going."

Penelope was terrified at the thought of being "turned into" a woman in her own right. Her intense relationship with her mother, which had been appropriate when she was very young, was now precluding her from pursuing other relationships and career gratifications. Outside her mother's orbit, Penelope had little idea of who she was or how she wanted to act. Her eating disorder helped her define herself. When she binged, she temporarily believed she had the power to "fill" herself up emotionally, but her anxiety about being her own person and doing anything secret from mother made her feel very guilty. After bingeing, Penelope vomited not only to purge herself of the large amount of food she had eaten but also to void her feelings of guilt and to return to a feeling of oneness with her mother. In the postpurge state, she felt totally soothed and comforted.

After a brief admission to the hospital to help control the eating disorder and stabilize her medical condition, Penelope began intensive individual psychotherapy and group therapy. Her psychiatrist was particularly skilled in psychopharmacology and wisely offered Penelope a choice of antidepressants. Like 30%–50% of other bulimic patients, Penelope received no benefit from adequate dosages and blood levels of several different antidepressant trials. Because medication did not prove helpful, it was fortunate that she was highly motivated to learn about herself in therapy. Her insight and intelligence made her an excellent candidate for both individual and group psychotherapy, and so she began to learn about herself and form her own identity.

As a way to help Penelope develop her imagination and begin to explore her own ideas, her therapist engaged her in a fanciful discussion one session when Penelope had little to say. The therapist wondered what Penelope would choose to be if she were an object that could be purchased. The patient reported, "An angora sweater—soft, pastel, and cuddly—a beautiful light blue, strokeable and warm."

The therapist commended Penelope for permitting herself to have such an evocative visual image. Yet the therapist also sensed that a hidden meaning of the image was its more highly tactile quality, which reflected Penelope's wish to be both comforting and comforted, to see herself as someone who could be pleasing to and pleased by others. Then the therapist told Penelope that she sensed that her "real self" intensely needed the structure provided by another person through emotional contact with and closeness to that person. After all, a sweater alone is a shapeless heap—until it is filled with the defining form of the individual who wears it. For the first time in her life, Penelope believed she was being understood as who she was.

Although Penelope's struggle to find an identity persisted, she used psychotherapy alone to achieve control over her eating disorder and to move toward developing a fuller life. Her therapist, sensitive to the warning signs of relapse in eating disorders, reminded Penelope of the signals of a return to bingeing. For her, these included obsessively thinking about food, feelings of hopelessness about her future and her life, and continually looking to others instead of herself to confirm her existence. The therapist's sensitivity to a tailored relapse prevention plan and acknowledgement of Penelope's real assets and struggles combined with the insights that occurred spontaneously in therapy to help Penelope establish autonomous control over her symptoms and her life. Most importantly, she began to discover an identity independent of her wealth or her mother that filled her with ideas of substance, of which she had hitherto been unaware.

## ❧ A Fire Within

Nell Y., a 42-year-old homemaker, mother of 3, and entrepreneur, came in for evaluation. At 5 feet 9 inches, she weighed only 105 pounds. Nell acknowledged that she had a host of psychological problems for which she had sought outpatient psychotherapy over the years; now the severity of her eating disorder had become life-threatening.

Although Nell had planned to kill herself with an overdose of medication the day after Christmas, she instead made an internal pact to starve herself to death. Her anorexic tendencies, which had begun 6 years earlier, were now in full force. Nell's outpatient psychotherapist, a nurse practitioner with expertise in nutrition, insisted that she be admitted to an inpatient unit to reverse her physical decline and seek out the roots of her self-destructiveness.

From the first, Nell reported a family history that had been brutal and sadistic. From Nell's perspective, her early years had been filled with relentless torture at the hands of her parents, both of whom had died when Nell was in her early 20s. Although she could recall almost no loving family memories from her elementary school years,

Nell remembered one teacher fondly. This supportive relationship had helped her through some of the most difficult times in her youth. Even after meeting her husband, who was a devoted and caring man, Nell found that her difficulties did not abate. In what she finally understood as an unconscious attempt to sabotage the only happiness she had known, she engaged in several extramarital affairs. Her husband displayed enormous understanding and patience, only to find his hopes for a better life with Nell dashed when she developed anorexia. As Nell herself said, "I am my own worst enemy. I can give to my kids but never to me. Sometimes I'd just rather give up. I'm not sure who will win the struggle." She felt utterly hopeless to move toward recovery.

In the hospital, Nell, like most anorexic people, complained about the large number of calories she was given in her meals (1,200 calories to begin with) and the required daily routine of three meals and a snack. But as her alliance with her treaters grew, she confided that she was "always hungry" and was able to risk asking for a calorie increase. Five weeks into treatment, Nell was eating close to 3,000 calories a day but was still unable to gain weight. We explained to Nell and her husband the scientific rationale for increasing her calories: these data explain that starving individuals sometimes need a very large number of calories to begin to gain weight.

Like many other eating disorder patients, Nell had a unique, insightful explanation for this physical reaction. She understood herself as "burning up all the food you can give me because of my internal war inside myself." As we explored what Nell meant, we discovered that some aspects of herself seemed determined to defy any of her attempts to get better by gaining weight. She was plagued by intrusive thoughts about her past. She was unable to gain weight not only because the raging fire within burned up all the calories she could eat, but also because it represented one crucially powerful way she could experience anger.

Once Nell's treaters knew what her inner experience was, they could help her express her anger more concretely in constructive outlets. In activity therapy, Nell began to work in clay to vent her rage in some tangible form. She carried this practice over into psychotherapy interviews and group therapy sessions, verbalizing her anxiety and discomfort as she told about her early life experiences and found new meanings for them. Without conscious awareness, she formed the clay into various shapes, all with symbolic meaning, that treaters could then question her about. The tubular structures she crafted looked like penises, while the urn-sharped containers resembled vaginas. It became apparent that Nell was preoccupied with sexual concerns too difficult to confide to anyone. Through her anxiety-releasing activity of molding clay, Nell conveyed to her treaters and her therapy group the alarming amount of dysphoria and discontentment she felt, particularly in relation to early sexual abuse and its residual effects.

When patients like Nell begin treatment, they often cannot put into words what has happened to them. This stalemate occurs in part because their bodies have experienced enormous physical pain during abuse or because words have so little meaning for them that they benefit more from "experiential therapies" instead. Pioneers in this aspect of the field, such as Ann Kearney-Cooke (1989, 1991), work to alleviate a patient's poor body image and vulnerable body boundaries by using guided imagery techniques in group and individual therapy sessions. Patients might be asked, for example, to imagine what it would be like to wake up in the morning, look in the mirror, and find themselves with completely different bodies. They are encouraged to fantasize what the day would be like. How would people treat them with their new bodies? Would the world be friendly and inviting or rejecting? As these patients imagine their new selves going through the day interacting with their parents and friends, they begin to reconsider the power inherent in their particular body types and to reexamine how their bodies feel.

These types of exercises are quite helpful for some patients. Psychologists Lynne Hornyak and Ellen Baker (1989) recommend a host of experiential therapies for people with bulimia and anorexia, including hypnosis, psychodrama, dance and movement therapy, art therapy, and music therapy. Because eating disorder patients have highly individualized histories—and treatment needs—each technique may play a special role in treatment. The psychodynamically informed Menninger program includes biofeedback training, movement therapy that combines dance and exercise, music therapy, and art therapy. These techniques can be integrated to help certain individuals allow their bodies to "speak." But just as medication carries with it side effects and risks, so too do verbal and experiential therapies.

For example, when Nell began biofeedback training, she was instructed to gain awareness and control over autonomic processes—one of the main goals of this modality—by listening to soothing music and thinking pleasant thoughts while receiving feedback from a machine that would indicate when her hands became warmer. This warming response indicates increased relaxation—a favorable response of the sympathetic nervous system, especially true for those who have eating disorders. These individuals, who have exerted control by eating or not eating, otherwise feel little control over their bodies and bodily responses. Because of this, they are often unable to relax. Instead, they are caught up in the experiences of being constantly aroused, tense, anxious, and hypervigilant.

During the biofeedback exercises, Nell began to recall horrific memories of abuse—a common experience of those who have been abused sexually and physically. As her sympathetic nervous system (fight-flight response) kicked in, her blood pressure skyrocketed. Because the thoughts that came to mind were so terrifying, Nell wanted to quit biofeedback. But we urged her to continue, because biofeedback training could eventually help her feel much more in control of her body so that she could experience it differently and increase her ability to be more at ease in anxiety-provoking situations. We believed that she could learn to deal more constructively with her destructive memories by learning to guide herself toward more fulfilling and comforting images.

In fact, the biofeedback training did enhance Nell's coping capacities. Over several months, Nell learned to increase her ability to warm her hands by calling to mind more pleasant visualizations. The therapist encouraged Nell to master the relaxation response by thinking of refreshing images of rolling hills and birds in flight. One startling observation the therapist made was the very narrow range of blood pressures and temperatures that Nell could maintain in her hands. The blood pressure and hand temperature of most people will vary a number of points over an hour, depending on the degree of stress or relaxation a person experiences. Nell's blood pressure shot up only in states of deep relaxation, where the unconscious memories of abuse were more available. Otherwise, Nell's readings showed almost no variability, as if she maintained the tightest involuntary control even over her physiological processes.

The results of Nell's biofeedback therapy led her treaters to suggest other modalities to increase her repertoire of relaxation exercises for self-soothing and self-relaxation. The goal was to enable Nell to feel the power within herself to deal with a range of feelings without having to maintain rigid physiological or psychological control. In this experiential therapy, the biofeedback therapist showed Nell how to keep her psychophysiologic arousal patterns (such as blood pressure or hand temperature) within a normal range while feeling more at ease in a number of real and imagined situations. This initial self-control permitted Nell to feel more at ease in a number of life situations, and her comfort in her own body grew tremendously.

It really wasn't surprising that Nell felt such a great need to be in control. As a child, she had been conditioned to conform to her parents' rigid expectations. Every time she opened her mouth, she seemed to elicit only blows. She remembered her parents' beatings both as physical assaults and as psychological attacks on her capabilities. She grew tall quickly and loved to sing, but, as she shot up in height, she was referred to as "a weed who should be seen rather than heard."

As might be expected, music therapy held some promise of helping Nell find her own voice. But although she was clearly drawn to music, singing was too terrifying for her to permit herself to engage in it. The music therapist had to repeatedly push Nell to participate in group events. Despite her lovely soprano, she had never felt relaxed enough to use it because of the threat that it would lead to a violent rebuke.

Music therapy helped Nell overcome her fears of retaliation in still another way. It became a legitimate outlet for a talent that she had hidden for years. Having long expected punishment whenever she sang, she now resisted opening her mouth and giving voice to inner sensations. As Nell began to use music therapeutically as a way to express a range of emotions, it increased her self-esteem and provided her with new avenues for social involvement. She could also listen to a range of musical selections that spoke directly to her emotions. Her participation in this expressive media formed a bridge to her other therapies where she verbalized and clarified her past.

Nell's ongoing depression and her intense, intrusive memories of abuse led her treating psychiatrist to suggest that she avail herself of the most up-to-date medication. After her nutritional status had improved, she could begin sequential trials of antidepressant medications if her despondency did not reverse itself. But Nell refused medication, wanting instead to "do it on my own." Because mind-altering drugs had been forced on Nell in the past, her psychiatrist decided not to push the point, although she continued to remind Nell of the benefits of medications such as the tricyclic antidepressants (TCAs), monoamine oxidase inhibitors (MAOIs), and Prozac.

The therapist especially emphasized how Prozac has been shown to alleviate intrusive memories of abuse, a potentially promising effect for Nell. Despite these suggestions, Nell categorically and repeatedly refused any medication. Fortunately, she improved significantly without it.[1] Nell's refusal was based to some extent on her wish to work out her problems psychologically and avoid external controls over her body, but it also spoke to her less conscious need to keep on suffering and avoid medication—as she had avoided food. While Nell engaged in an internal war that burned up all her food sources out of anger, she also used her internal war to avoid finding greater tranquility through medication therapy. The most tenacious battle she fought was within herself, where her masochistic tendencies derived from her past led to spoiling and self-defeat. As she said, "I'm proud that now I can say what will and will *not* go into me! You can't make me. I'd rather die than be forced to do what you want me to do, even if it means I feel more pain!"

---

[1] The use of medication is a major part of the APA guidelines, but not all patients will respond to or even accept a recommendation to begin psychopharmacological treatment.

Nell's case highlights one further characteristic typical of individuals with eating disorders. Their illnesses appear to intensify at times of developmental change and stress, when more is required of the individual than can be legitimately handled. In Nell's case, childhood trauma did not allow her to fully capitalize on her own genuine strengths. Therapy was designed to help her do so, but having to function as a wife and mother taxed her beyond her reserves. As a result, her inpatient stay allowed her to have an extended "time-out" where she could build a self and establish an identity. This phase of Nell's treatment, although expensive in terms of time and money, was priceless in the long run. It allowed her to mature and to achieve goals she might not have otherwise—particularly while she was needed to mother her own children. In essence, treatment gave her a portion of the nurturance she had missed as a little girl herself.

The nature of Nell's illness revealed, among other things, that she had not experienced the early parenting and nurturance that allow most people to give easily to others. Consequently, she had been unable to work or to function smoothly. Instead, her supreme quest was to fill the gaps of her early impoverished upbringing, so that she would finally obtain the caretaking she had always needed and that every child deserves. Understanding that her assumption of the roles of wife and mother had heralded her illness enabled Nell to seek out and benefit from supportive people and experiences, in addition to psychotherapy, when she left the hospital. This support increased her chances for healthy functioning.

Whenever new responsibilities or greater expectations in life up the ante, all of us need a modicum of additional support. Traditionally found in our extended family, support must be established in adulthood through friendships, support groups, church, and even therapy. In Nell's case, she had to learn to ask for help lest her identity fragment from inner despair and pain. She gradually found a host of resources on which to rely, and more important, she developed the courage to do so. As she garnered less rigid self-control and a broader self-knowledge through treatment, Nell participated in a greater range of interpersonal and reflective experiences, which helped her quell the inner terror of her own body and the fear she felt on becoming close to other people.

### ❦ Leather and Lace

Mora Z., a 28-year-old insurance sales representative for a successful Midwestern firm, looked more like a streetwise gamine when she appeared for an outpatient evaluation. Wearing a black leather jacket, sunglasses, and a Harley-Davidson T-shirt, Mora also sported an air of superficial bravado that hid her fears of closeness with other people. Like many bulimic patients, she had kept her symptom secret from her family and friends for years. She hated being overweight so much that she frequently abused laxatives, diuretics, and syrup of ipecac, and overexercised in an attempt to regulate her weight.

After laboratory studies indicated that Mora was in severe electrolyte imbalance, she was hospitalized. Only then did she reveal to the nursing staff that her mother had taken her to physicians for weight control since she was seven. Various doctors had prescribed diet pills, but to no avail. Mora's weight continued to be in the upper range of normal until she began self-starvation. By high school, she had developed a full case of anorexia, only to move into bulimic symptomatology when she could no longer continue self-imposed periods of starvation.

All Mora's prior attempts at treatment had fallen short, largely because of her poor motivation. Mora could see no way out from a lifetime of emphasis on her body. She allowed herself only one friendship, because she believed that other people would not want to get to know her. Indeed, her sunglasses and unconventional garb were a way to say "Back off!" to the outside world. Around other people, Mora felt vulnerable and naked, yet her social isolation fueled her bulimic rituals. These time- and energy-consuming symptoms gave her something to do rather than risk the terror she faced when in a new situation with people.

From the beginning, Mora's treaters openly discussed with her the seriousness of her situation. The treatment team had strong doubts about being able to help her. Her motivation for getting better was highly questionable, because she had been obsessed with her weight since she was a young child. Numerous medical problems had not frightened Mora into making use of available help earlier, and she seemed convinced of her own need to fail and make others angry with her before she even started.

One glimmer of hope centered on Mora's love of music. She would sit quietly in her room, strumming her guitar, sometimes chiming in on the wistful lyrics of well-known songs. One of her favorites was a hit by Stevie Nicks, "Leather and Lace," a song whose lyrics convey a woman's desire to be seen as strong and competent, yet also soft and gentle. The staff members appreciated Mora's musical gifts even while they heard her reach out in this song for a more full integration of self. Mora's difficulties seemed particularly tragic because psychological testing revealed that she was highly intelligent. Her academic interests had not been cultivated, however, because of her parents' early focus on her weight. Instead, Mora's identity had consolidated around a wish to be thinner, and at the time of her hospitalization, she talked about herself as if her only identify was that conveyed by the eating disorder. Mora especially feared any sexual interactions with men. She refused to undergo a physical examination by a male internist and avoided participating in group therapy sessions with a male cotherapist.

Because Mora was so afraid of getting close to anyone despite her desire to do so, one of the early treatment goals was to help her establish a range of comfortable relationships with the program staff. To arrive at this end, Mora's treaters focused on becoming allied with the healthy parts of her. Meanwhile, they also encouraged her to take part in psychoeducational activities about her illness, to establish a solid nutritional plan that would improve her eating behavior, and to leave behind—at least temporarily—the mayhem of her job, where she had to erect a "false self" to earn a living. This process first entailed acknowledging Mora's wish to control and understand her manifest symptoms. We began by encouraging her to write about her eating and how she experienced it in a daily journal.

The use of journal writing, which I alluded to earlier in this book, has been discussed extensively in the professional literature (Geist 1989; M. L. Miller 1991; Rabinor 1991). This process permitted Mora to begin to share not only what she was eating, but also—as she developed trust—how she felt about food, eating, and the urge to evacuate it from her body. As psychologist Judith Rabinor (a specialist in eating disorders who practices on Long Island) writes, journaling initially helps the patient realize that treaters take her eating seriously while simultaneously permitting "consolidation and growth of the self, which eventually culminates in the elimination of the eating disorder" (1991, p. 93).

As expected, journaling marked only the beginning of Mora's search for personal insight. Hospitalization finally broke her cycle of social isolation, because she was encouraged to talk with peers about her struggles and to interact with them instead of going off on her own to binge and purge. Her chaotic and unstructured life outside her job was replaced by a daily structure of healthy activities and group therapy sessions that she grew to enjoy. At first, like many patients, Mora adamantly hated group sessions and complained about the daily regimen of treatment. Her peers found her irritating and disagreeable and began to scapegoat her. But as her therapist gently confronted her about her attitude, Mora began to change. She offered more of her own insights to others and eventually became a revered group member and a leader in her hospital unit's patient government structure.

Mora's intelligence also proved to be an asset in her treatment. She began to thrive on the insights offered by her peers and treaters about the underlying conflicts contributing to her eating disorder. Not surprisingly, she was able to acknowledge a long-standing tendency toward depression. She expressed understandable anger toward both her parents for their undue emphasis on her weight when she was so young, and she began to understand how her assumption of the role of family arbiter had been detrimental to her. Only then did Mora realize that her social isolation and eating disorder also served to protect her. Her identity as the "sick member" of the family enabled her to escape from difficult family problems while also permitting her parents to focus on her problems rather than their own.

Like most of us, Mora wanted to live in the "perfect" family. Of course, there is no such thing. In structured family therapy sessions, the social worker addressed Mora's wishes for her parents to be perfect while helping her learn to tolerate a certain amount of family distress and discord. Soon Mora began to develop healthy personal ambitions. She decided to pursue advanced training as an exercise physiologist or plant ecologist. When her father actively discouraged her pursuits, she acknowledged her disappointment but was not deterred from following her own dreams. In individual and group therapy meetings, she worked to acknowledge and accept her father's limitations while also recognizing that her parents were truly trying to modify old, hurtful patterns of family interaction for the better.

As Norre and Vandereycken (1991) have pointed out, inpatient treatment sometimes gives an individual a "new chance" and can be a "turning point, breaking through an inescapable vicious cycle" (p. 62) of social isolation, physical deterioration caused by the eating disorder, impaired family and parental relationships, and poor motivation. One could reasonably argue that Mora might not have died even if her eating disorder had persisted, but breaking the cycle by addressing underlying deficits clearly improved her quality of life and may have helped save it. In fact, after discharge, Mora found that her life was far from perfect, because she still had to struggle with entrenched dysfunctional behavior. Yet she was in a much better position to pursue her goals. While working part-time, she finished a college degree and managed to avoid being rehospitalized despite some brief relapses into bulimia.

Mora's treatment program now consists of outpatient individual and group psychotherapy and monthly follow-up sessions at the eating disorders clinic. Ongoing family therapy sessions would also be useful, but distance precludes them. Mora reports that she is pleased with her progress. She has learned much about herself in the more than 3 years she has been in treatment, only 6 months of which were spent as an inpatient.

In an era of quick fixes, the duration of Mora's treatment can seem like a long time to those eating disorder patients and their families who expect instant miracles. As Mora's case demonstrates, the ability to change comes from an integration of personality structure that occurs only over time by learning to rely on oneself and others. When questioned about what she found most helpful in her treatment, Mora cited the trusting relationships she had formed in individual and group therapy. But she also highlighted the importance of the unit's relapse prevention groups that meet in the evening. These meetings, which are conducted by members of the unit's nursing staff, help participants recognize the warning signs that point to a relapse into eating disorder behavior. Patients are encouraged to aim for abstinence from bingeing and purging as much as possible. However, if they do relapse, they are also encouraged not to judge themselves too harshly—a tendency common among people with eating disorders, who usually set impossibly rigid and absolute standards.

A more realistic, nonabstinent approach is that advocated by Bemis (1985), which is followed by treaters at The Menninger Clinic. Because most patients can learn only over time to live without their bulimic behavior, which they use as a coping mechanism (see Chapter 14), they must be encouraged to tolerate occasional relapses. Under certain stressful circumstances, bulimic behavior will return. Meanwhile, a person can learn certain strategies to reduce the tendency to relapse. Patients should be encouraged to assume as much self-responsibility as possible and to avoid bingeing, and yet realize that this level of self-control may not always be possible. There may even be times when the bulimic behavior will increase, but this discouraging fact should not propel an individual to drop out of treatment.

Even severe relapses are reversible. Mora's individual relapse plan emphasized how isolating herself from others led her to binge and purge. She was cautioned about spending too much time by herself alone in her apartment. Because her natural physique tended to be a bit on the plump side, she was particularly cautioned against fantasies of having a slender figure. Her relapse prevention plan encouraged her to engage in forthright discussions with her treaters about secretiveness and to confront her self-destructive eating habits by planning her meals with the help of a registered dietitian. (A list of general relapse warning signs developed by the nursing staff of the Menninger Eating Disorders Program is included at the end of this chapter.)

Most important, Mora began to accept the fact that she could make slow but steady headway with her problems. A quick, total cure was as unrealistic for her as it is for most patients with eating disorders. This sober approach was at first disheartening; Mora had understandably hoped for a miraculous and definitive solution to her difficulties. Gradually, though, she accepted that a quick victory was not only unlikely but also undesirable. Growth always takes time, and worthwhile goals are seldom achieved overnight. A slower pace was ultimately more successful for Mora because it allowed her more time to consolidate gains and establish her ability to be true to herself. As Norre and Vandereycken (1991) state,

> The apparent willingness for a quick and drastic change is a trap. . . . A lot of patients expect direct and almost magic therapeutic interventions. This clearly reflects the unrealistic expectations and achievement orientation so typical for these patients. We try to convince them that the bulimic episode is not an enemy, but an ally; it is a signal that something is going "wrong" in their lives. Unfortunately, most patients do not realize the severity and complexity of their problems. (p. 56)

Mora's case clearly demonstrates a complexity of difficulties that she was able to come to grips with only over an extended period. A multidimensional treatment based on a continuum of care—beginning with an intensive inpatient phase but continuing into outpatient follow-up—addressed the complexity of her eating disorder and its impact on many other areas of her life. Her struggle with bingeing and purging was the manifest reason Mora entered treatment; but to gain mastery over her eating behavior, she ultimately had to examine long-standing individual and family dynamics. Her growing understanding of how personal and family conflicts influenced her eating led her to gradually give up bingeing. In its place, she put healthier ways of coping, such as socializing, going to school, and singing in public.

In our treatment setting, patients like Mora are encouraged to write down their individual warning signs and the plan of action they will take when the urge to binge and purge escalates. To help prevent future relapse, they should then discuss this information with their primary treaters. Keeping a log or journal can be especially helpful, because progress can be charted by referring back to realistic points of difficulty and how they were confronted. This process helps the patient avoid denying the symptom—to others or even to herself. Most important, a written record helps show how growth has truly come about over time. Growth thus becomes less frightening than was originally thought.

## The Use of Medication

Throughout this book, I have indicated that medication is useful in some cases of anorexia nervosa and bulimia nervosa. However, there is still no "magic bullet" for either disorder. In fact, various categories of drugs have been tested for both disorders with unclear and sometimes disappointing results. It is more than likely that treatment will continue to be tailored to each individual by focusing on an integration of cognitive, nutritional, behavioral, psychological, and pharmacological modalities. Emphasis must be placed on the individual's psychological struggles as well, because so much of what underlies these disorders seems to center on conflicts in growth and development. Yet despite the lack of a pharmacological panacea, which should be apparent from the case examples and courses of treatment outlined in this chapter, people need to be informed about the role of medication in treatment so that they can make good personal choices and can ask their treaters relevant questions.

Before reviewing the specific drugs themselves, let us reexamine one caveat about drug treatment. As I explained in Chapter 2, comorbidity complicates the treatment of those with eating disorders. When other psychiatric problems are also present, a particular medication may be chosen for a specific intervention. For example, if a person struggles with generalized anxiety and a panic disorder with agoraphobia, the psychiatrist might begin treatment with a trial of a TCA. This type of medication is reasonably safe and fairly cheap, and it has proven highly effective for panic disorder. If the patient also struggles with bulimia nervosa, the antidepressant may ameliorate that problem as well.

Recent studies comparing psychopharmacologic treatment with cognitive and interpersonal psychotherapy for eating disorders have shown that medication is not as likely to be helpful as either of the other two treatment modalities. One study from the University of Minnesota (Mitchell et al. 1990) showed that psychosocial therapy produced 51% abstinence from bulimic symptoms, in contrast to only 16% abstinence with placebo or antidepressant treatment. Combining medication with psychosocial therapy was no more effective than therapy alone, although the combination did reduce depression. These results were replicated in a Stanford University study reported in the *American Journal of Psychiatry* (Agras et al. 1992). The Stanford researchers, led by W. Stewart Agras, found that cognitive-behavioral therapy produced a 48% reduction in binge eating and purging. In comparison, the antidepressant desipramine (Norpramin or Pertofrane) produced a 33% reduction in symptoms. The combination of treatments led to no greater success with respect to abstinence, except that the antidepressant seemed to lessen the patients' preoccupation with eating. Agras and colleagues concluded that antidepressant medication, when used alone, is the least preferred treatment for bulimia nervosa.

> Over the short term, cognitive-behavioral therapy and combined treatment regimens seem equally effective. In addition, there may be some advantage of the combined treatment over the longer term. . . . One problem with the combined therapy was that patients who ceased to binge-eat and purge early in treatment were poorly motivated to pursue the important dietary and cognitive changes that are part of cognitive-behavioral therapy. . . . Further research is needed before the final place of the antidepressants in the treatment of bulimia nervosa can be established. . . . Even with the most effective treatment, between 30% and 50% of [bulimic patients] still do not respond optimally. (Agras 1992, p. 3)

More recently, the serotonin reuptake inhibitor fluoxetine (Prozac) has proven helpful with chronic, refractory anorexia nervosa and bulimia nervosa. In patients with anorexia, fluoxetine alleviates depressive symptoms and leads to weight gain. Despite the medical complications of anorexia, fluoxetine seems to be well tolerated and does not cause the weight loss that sometimes affects healthy volunteer subjects or depressed people of normal weight. Furthermore, fluoxetine benefited subjects who had had multiple failures with other medication treatment, and it decreased their obsessive thoughts and compulsive rituals about food. Fluoxetine has also reduced the frequency of bingeing and purging in both depressed and nondepressed bulimic patients.

Although additional research is necessary to define optimum treatment for both groups of patients, fluoxetine shows promise as an agent of change. It has relatively few side effects, it tends to elevate mood while decreasing obsessions and compulsions, and it has a favorable effect on both types of eating disorders. Because there is still no proven difference between available antidepressants, the selection of one will often be made based on potential side effects and costs. In some studies, episodes of bingeing and purging are reduced by antidepressants. Some people's eating disorder symptoms are not eased, but the depression associated with bulimia nervosa is clearly alleviated. Some physicians will also choose the TCAs because of their familiarity and lower cost. As a third option, they might prescribe MAOIs, but these carry the risk of more serious side effects because of the necessary dietary restrictions. Some individuals who have not responded either to fluoxetine or the TCAs will respond to the MAOIs. Thus, even in the 1990s, individuals should be aware that the choice of medication is still made on a trial-and-error basis. If one drug does not work out, another should be tried.

Patients with eating disorders can still take standard doses of medication. If a TCA is chosen, the standard dosage of 200–300 mg of desipramine may be prescribed. Therapeutic levels are now measured to make sure the drug is not reaching toxic levels in the blood. The standard dosage of fluoxetine is 20 mg per day, although patients with eating disorders sometimes need higher dosages (e.g., 60 mg per day). The length of time needed on the drug is still unknown, although the best data suggest at least a 6-month trial.

As we can see, antidepressants are the most widely used and researched medication for eating disorders. Other groups of drugs have been tried, including antipsychotics (neuroleptics), lithium carbonate, appetite stimulants (for anorexia nervosa), anticonvulsants, and miscellaneous drugs such as zinc and naloxone (Narcan). In treating anorexia nervosa, neuroleptics have been tried extensively and with good rationale. After all, the body image problems of patients with anorexia nervosa sometimes reach near-delusional proportions, leading some authorities to call this illness a monosymptomatic hypochondriacal delusional disorder. The anorexic patient's bizarre eating patterns also have a delusional quality. Controlled studies of these agents have shown only limited success, although some patients have been able to gain weight and alter their anorexic attitudes somewhat. Antipsychotics are not routinely added to treatment protocols, however, because of their severe side effects, including tardive dyskinesia. Nevertheless, these agents can be useful in selected cases of anorexia nervosa when anxiety levels reach psychotic proportions. To determine the best medication protocol, the physician should discuss the benefits and risks of each drug with the eating disorder patient, explaining that if there is no perceived benefit in the first few weeks of treatment, the drug can be discontinued.

The appetite stimulants tetrahydrocannabinol (THC) and cyproheptadine (CYP) have also been somewhat successful in helping the anorexic patient increase weight. Although not an adequate treatment by itself, a trial of CYP may be useful for some anorexic patients who restrict their intake of food but do not binge and purge. Some investigators have conceptualized bulimia nervosa as an illness similar to epilepsy, which might be treated in trials with anticonvulsant drugs like carbamazepine (Tegretol), diphenylhydantoin (Dilantin), and sodium valproate (Depakene). Although there have been some anecdotal reports of good responses to these compounds, their use is largely disappointing unless the eating disorder patient has epilepsy as well.

Lithium carbonate has also been used to treat patients with bulimia nervosa. Despite some initially impressive results, lithium has not proven particularly effective in reducing binge-purge episodes. In addition, there is a real potential for serious toxicity, given the deleterious effect of lithium on electrolytes and the serious problems faced by bulimic patients with electrolyte disturbance who purge or use laxatives and diuretics. The watchword is caution; lithium may be used, but greater care must be taken in monitoring electrolytes.

When a bulimic patient also has a manic-depressive disorder (bipolar disorder) or other instability of mood, the use of lithium may be warranted clinically. In such cases, the patient needs to work closely with her physician to minimize vomiting and abuse of laxatives and diuretics. If she is unable to refrain from these activities, she will require more frequent checks of the blood levels of lithium and electrolytes to avoid toxicity. Although lithium carbonate can be quite effective in alleviating certain mood disorders, it must be stopped when there are complications brought on by a serious eating disorder.

## Conclusion: Outcome and Future Research

Although the growth in the number of treatment modalities for eating disorders is encouraging, many unanswered questions remain. Future studies will help us identify the best treatments for specific patients who have unique constellations of problems. Until that time, a woman with an eating disorder will have to begin a trial of treatment with a treater or group of treaters she can grow to trust in an environment that will be safe and growth promoting.

In all likelihood, she will benefit from a combination of treatment modalities like those highlighted by the cases in this chapter. Although a single treatment may not be effective, a combination of treatments will address the multiple aspects of the self affected by the eating disorder. Recent research comparing antidepressants and psychotherapy has demonstrated the importance of combining treatments such as group therapy, nutritional counseling, a cognitive-behavioral approach, and psychodynamic techniques. Each has been shown to be more effective than just antidepressant treatment alone. For some fortunate individuals, medication may be all that is necessary, but these patients are probably in the minority.

Finally, the treatment of those with eating disorders will undoubtedly continue to pose a challenge in the coming decade, because follow-up studies tend to be quite sobering with respect to cure. Despite the currently available treatment tools discussed throughout this book, at least one-third of eating disorder patients remain severely ill at follow-up (Bemporad and Herzog 1989; Dennis and Sansone 1991; Herzog et al. 1991; Johnson 1991a; Johnson et al. 1990; Pyle et al. 1990). According to a pilot study at Massachusetts General Hospital, in which 30 bulimic subjects were followed up at 34 to 42 months, the cumulative probability of relapse was 63% (Herzog 1991). This finding speaks only to the control of the eating disorder symptomatology. Patients may also continue to struggle with unsatisfactory personal and sexual lives, family problems, severe depression, obsessive-compulsive disorder, and so on.

In a 10-year follow-up study of 76 anorexia nervosa patients, Katherine Halmi, Director of the Eating Disorders Unit at New York Hospital—Cornell Medical Center, found that a significant number of women had resumed their menses and were within 15% of their target weight (Halmi et al. 1991). Yet only 24% of the sample could be described as free of an eating disorder diagnosis. Thirty-five percent had problems with binge eating or a body image disturbance or preoccupation with food, while 20% met formal criteria for bulimia nervosa. Over the course of a lifetime, 68% had major depressive disorder, 32% had dysthymia (neurotic depression), 34% had a social phobia, and 26% had obsessive-compulsive disorder. During the 10-year follow-up period, 56% had multiple relapses. Clearly, the illness is costly. Fortunately, the study also found that aggressive treatment during the first year after hospitalization strongly indicated a favorable outcome.

Bulimia nervosa has been studied less extensively than anorexia nervosa because it has been prevalent only since the 1970s. Like anorexic patients, recovering bulimic patients may experience a short-term remission of symptoms that should not be confused with long-term cure. Even if there are fewer episodes of the eating disorder, the individual may still struggle daily with many other problems. Although the short-term effectiveness of cognitive-behavioral therapy and medication is encouraging, only long-term outcome studies can assess the substantial medical morbidity, psychological toll, and societal costs of this serious and complex illness.

In the next two decades, eating disorders researchers will most likely give us a greater understanding of the causes and the interactions that produce eating disorders. As we become better able to distinguish between high-risk and low-risk groups, treatment will become more specialized. We will also become better at assessing the heterogeneous nature of both anorexia nervosa and bulimia nervosa, which should maximize treatment effectiveness. As treatment options expand, based on sound clinical research, patients can be even more optimistic about their prognosis. In the words of Tamara Pryor, Director of the Eating Disorders Clinic at the University of Kansas School of Medicine in Wichita,

> All eating disorders patients probably will not have a similar response to the same treatment. Therefore, experimental groups should be more carefully selected in the future. Factors involved should not only include additional diagnoses but also personality structure, patient age, chronicity of the illness, patient weight, family history, and family structure. (Pryor et al. 1990, p. 721)

As greater refinement in our knowledge base aids patient care, treaters should nonetheless remain forbearing and humble in their efforts, because no patient can—or should—fit a standard treatment protocol to a T. Individuals demand individualized treatment plans. Both patients and therapists should be hopeful as they deal with this most personal of illnesses, which encompasses how we view ourselves, what we eat, and how we intimately relate to others. No study will ever be able to predict exactly which patients will recover or to tell us exactly why. In the long run, many patients do show promise in controlling their symptoms, if not in getting over their disorder. And no matter what the best research studies eventually indicate, patients will need to continue mustering the courage to confront the thorny problems that affect so many areas of their lives and sap their energy. A belief that one can master life's problems and develop attainable goals will always be essential to reclaiming one's own body.

A follow-up interview with Mora 3 years after her inpatient treatment illustrates this. Although she was still struggling with an occasional urge to binge, Mora had become involved in a satisfying romantic relationship and was pursuing her career. She worked part-time, played in two softball leagues, and often went bowling. As we reviewed her family's early highly stressful interaction pattern, we noted how her parents had changed through family therapy. Mora had also garnered strength from her individual psychotherapy process and the two different group therapy sessions she attended. But the biggest change was in her attitude about herself and her approach to life. When I asked her what advice she would give to other eating disorder patients, she said, "The more I was able to do what I really wanted—pursue my ultimate goals—the better I did. You find strength and it builds." The empowerment derived from making decisions and attaining mastery is the final common pathway of all successful treatment interventions. It may also be the entry point to successful and fulfilling living.

# Signs of Eating Disorders Relapse*

1. Experiencing an increase in obsessive thinking about food or weight.
2. Realizing a resurgence of ingrained self-defeating ways of thinking—despite increased self-knowledge and understanding of eating disorder symptoms.
3. Feeling a need to be in control all the time.
4. Feeling competitive with peers about who is thinnest.
5. Feeling hopeless about relationships, work, the eating disorder, or one's personal life.
6. Denying the relationship between stress, anxiety, and the eating disorder symptoms.
7. Feeling a need to escape, such as from a place, situation, person, or group.
8. Feeling guilty for having engaged in eating disorder symptoms that are difficult to put aside and resolve.
9. Engaging in fantasies of perfection: imagining that being the perfect weight, making the perfect grade, or finding the ideal living situation will provide total happiness.
10. Believing that success is based on the number of pounds shown on a bathroom scale or on the number of calories consumed.
11. Believing that one can purge "just once."
12. Believing that one's body is fat even though others say one is thin.
13. Being unable to rely on a support system.
14. Becoming isolated or showing little sociability.
15. Providing treaters with inaccurate reports about the symptoms being experienced.
16. Drinking an excessive amount of water to increase weight.
17. Looking at oneself continually in mirrors.

---

*Based on guidelines developed by members of the nursing staff of the Eating Disorders Unit of the C. F. Menninger Memorial Hospital, under the supervision of Regina Sebree, R.N., M.S., A.R.N.P.

18. Feeling comfortable only in loose-fitting clothes.
19. Refusing to look at one's naked body because of obesity.
20. Wanting to lose weight to alter a body part (e.g., thighs seem too big, or stomach protrudes).
21. Skipping meals.
22. Choosing only "safe" foods.
23. Engaging in ritualistic eating patterns.
24. Eating meals extremely fast.
25. Exercising excessively to compensate for food intake.
26. Ignoring pain or discomfort when exercising.
27. Failing to follow one's structured meal plan and exercise plan.
28. Having problems with meal planning: repeating the same foods several times a week, choosing foods that appear to have lower calories, omitting foods, becoming unable to complete a menu in the time allotted, or planning meals haphazardly.
29. Thinking about suicide, but not mentioning it in therapy.
30. Changing clothes several times a day.
31. Becoming hyperactive (restless, unable to sit still).
32. Being unable to tolerate the feeling of food in the stomach; feeling huge instead of satisfied.
33. Thinking "When I get out of treatment, I can eat, exercise, etc."
34. Being secretive; not telling the therapist when having a relapse or struggling to avoid having one.

# Epilogue

You gain strength, courage, and confidence by every experience in which you really stop to look fear in the face. . . . You must do the thing you cannot do.

Eleanor Roosevelt

One radiant June afternoon, Greer appeared for her therapy hour. Arriving after a tough day during her final year in college, she shared how much better she was feeling. Her eating disorder, now under much better control, was no longer the principal focus of her life. She still worried about relapses from time to time. But she was more concerned about her deepening intimacy with her boyfriend, her maturing relationship with her parents, and the decisions she faced as she sorted out her own career path.

As Greer spoke with pride about her real accomplishments in treatment and in life, she suddenly looked a bit dejected. She then confessed that, although she was changing and growing in many new ways, her life was not idyllic. She certainly had no wish to return to more entrenched eating disorder symptoms, but she also wished that life was not so hard. Exemplifying her more mature, adaptive coping skills, Greer had shared her hopes and fears with her best friend, Genevieve. It was Genevieve who encouraged Greer with the quotation from Eleanor Roosevelt, which Greer had then brought to her session. The two friends appar-

375

ently discussed the quotation when turning to each other for mutual support and sorting out what was meaningful and important in their lives. Greer now spoke the aphorism in therapy because she was moved by Eleanor Roosevelt's comment and wished to be like her, to develop her own capacity to move ahead with life. Greer wanted her therapist to know how much she was trying to confront her fears and what was helpful in her doing so.

Like all people, Greer was now facing some of the very real pitfalls that surface when one begins to grow. She was leaving her eating disorder behind but finding out that living was not carefree or effortless. Although she enjoyed her new accomplishments, she often felt twinges of pain about her relationship with her parents, which was still strained. Insecurities flared concerning her attractiveness and womanliness as she took risks with men. Even her friendships with women were not always easy. Genevieve had sometimes shared her own struggles with Greer; she also wasn't always available when Greer wanted her to be around. Like all relationships, theirs was not perfect. Despite all the limitations and injustices that Greer experienced in her life and in her relationships with others, she acknowledged that she now felt as though she knew herself better than ever before. Some days she even liked herself. She contrasted her new self-perceptions with the old ones, when her misery had been hidden behind a facade of contentment.

To many readers this description of Greer's progress might, at best, sound like the fanciful, overly optimistic musings of a clinician who wants to put a positive stamp on the treatment of eating disorders at the end of her book! This conclusion would be quite understandable. Likewise, one could argue that any case study is necessarily unscientific and selective, and thus too narrowly focused. These criticisms are also reasonable, although they do not take into account the perspective one derives by looking at individual treatment gains. Greer had good reason to refute them as she explained her perspective on how her life had changed for the better.

Somewhat of a researcher in her own right, on a recent trip home Greer had discovered some videotapes of earlier years with her family. She asked me if we might someday watch them together, because she wanted to point out some things she saw on the tapes. When I agreed to watch those tapes with Greer, I had no idea what they might reveal nor what Greer had perceptively ascertained when viewing the tapes by herself.

As we watched the videotapes together, Greer's family life came alive like never before. She showed a tape of an almost idyllic portrait of her family as they ate a pleasant holiday luncheon together. Then Greer moved to a segment taped at college, where she had practiced some student teaching: she presented an excellent (and very funny) lecture to her classmates on introductory physics. In the tapes, Greer seemed to move confidently and gracefully through both her family outing and her college presentation. Dumbfounded, I sat back and quizzically asked myself: what is wrong with this picture? How is it that Greer looked so cheerful and confident when, in retrospect, she was struggling mightily with a severe eating disorder and so much inner pain? Greer began to explain.

❧ Dr. Z., when you see me, doesn't it look like I'm perfectly normal, contented, and happy? Can you believe that only weeks after these tapes were taken I was rushed to the hospital because my eating disorder was out of control? No one would ever sense, by looking at my family, how much turmoil we were in and how much despair I felt. I know I seemed connected to everyone on the outside, but I felt far away and walled off from other people on the inside. Just look closely and you can even see how my hair was dull and my skin was pale. But what is worse is that even as I spoke to my class and seemed so "put together," I was outright lying to my teachers, counselors, and friends. They had no idea about the trouble I was in; I had successfully hidden my depression and my eating disorder from all of them. Every night I wanted to die, because I felt so alone and yet so unable to know where to turn. I did not want to grow up.

I was awestruck by Greer's admission of her inner life and desperation. I knew that life was not easy for her now, although I also believed that most of the time it was quite a bit better. I asked Greer what had made the difference and what continued to help her get through the tough times. I wondered what advice she would give others who wanted to seek help, but were fearful and desperate, just as she had once been. She replied,

❦ It's people, really. I found out that I could get close to others without being overwhelmed or exploited. I have learned that people really can care. But even that doesn't seem to help much sometimes. It certainly isn't "perfect caring." Like last week, for example. You weren't around to talk to. I went home and realized that things are really changing with my mother. Sometimes it seems like she's sad because I'm getting more separate, becoming my own person. That frightens me. And I'm not always sure about how my father feels about me growing up and having a boyfriend. Being thin, I must say, is a way that I still feel good about myself and something they still praise me for. Getting close to any guy raises my insecurity. But much of the time I know I am different. And, more than that, I want to keep trying. I would really like to be able to give something back to life. I want to help other people. I've accepted that I'm not always going to be happy—not every minute—but the lows are not nearly as long or as bad as they used to be.

Greer went on to summarize how she kept Eleanor Roosevelt's aphorism close to her as a way of reminding herself to push ahead in times of adversity, to stay on track and pursue her dreams even when she did not feel particularly up to it. She had no illusions about life's possibilities, but neither was she disillusioned by her present or her past. She told me how her friendships (especially with Genevieve) and her treatment had helped her confront her inner despair. Meanwhile, as I silently reflected on Greer's words, I recalled that she had achieved an admirable capacity first described by the late Paul Pruyser, psychologist and theologian at The Menninger Clinic. Greer was able to "maintain hope in adversity" (Pruyser 1986, p. 120).

This patient's perceptions highlight so much of what we have tried to examine in this book. She vividly describes the cost of covering up an eating disorder and other difficulties. By refusing to allow others to know her or her dilemmas, she maintained a false self. She was terrified of growing. Greer tells us how parts of her still resist change, a fact that all of us must face when we are honest. If change were easy, it would come to us after reading a self-help book, seeing an inspiring television show or movie, or hearing a charismatic speaker or performer. But as Greer explains, even positive moves ahead bring forth challenges and potential failure. The latter, in particular, pose the risk of losing one's hard-won yet fragile self-esteem.

For Greer, as for all of us, having a better life is not as simple as it sounds. Moving ahead means we all walk a potential tightrope that may culminate in triumph or tumult. If we progress too far, we leave others (especially beloved parents or friends) behind to some extent. To commit ourselves to a path means we must make hard choices. We are called on to delineate our goals and values over and over again. In the case of a long-held eating disorder, we must replace the inordinate value that thinness has held in our self-evaluation with something more substantial. We must face our deepest fears, especially about what it means to change and move forward.

So, all of us can empathize with Greer's plight. As she seeks to reach out into the world and touch other people's lives, she faces inner doubts of whether she is up to the task and the hard work it entails. Will she be able to turn her back on previous inhibitions and insecurities to confront life anew? Will she be able to do what she now believes she cannot do but desperately wants to find the courage and confidence to confront? I firmly expect that the next few years will pose many struggles for Greer. Her life will not be easy, and not simply because she has had a life-threatening eating disorder. The challenges of adulthood for all of us are never easy. Sometimes it seems that adversity is all we face. Living life means taking risks, particularly risks with oneself. And, although throughout this book I imply that positive shifts occur when one is called to question oneself, to learn, and consequently to change, the reality is that in life change is almost always arduous.

Yet the potential rewards are great. For the person with an eating disorder, some of the benefits are improved physical health, repair of family relationships, enhanced self-esteem, and greater investment in and appreciation of important interpersonal ties. But to attempt to rectify these eating disorders, one must begin by opening the Pandora's box of one's past, with all its attendant disappointments, disillusions, and aspirations. Just as in the myth, one can embark on the journey if one believes that hope remains and will help sustain the self through the often perplexing and soul-searching times ahead. It is this hope that Karl Menninger believed allowed the individual to "see himself not as a mere spectator of cosmic events but as a prime mover in them" (1959, p. 490). It also allows the person to begin to positively affect the lives of others, just as one has been able to change oneself. Courage is needed on both fronts—to believe one has something genuinely good to offer others even as one recognizes one's own limitations and ongoing personal struggles.

All of us can do much more than we think we can, including arresting the ravages of a severe eating disorder. Although many difficulties must be faced along the way, the potential for positive change and growth must never be underestimated. Greer said it best:

❧ I guess that there will be parts of me I will always be getting to know. But at least I know I've made a beginning. I like what I see at least some of the time. Now I also let people count instead of just the eating or how I look. And if I can let people count, I can make a difference too.

Like other patients in this book, Greer has begun the process of recovery—of walking the path that will really be a lifelong journey. In so doing, she is reuniting psyche and soma, body and soul. Her earnest search for knowledge and herself was launched in an effort to rescue her body and her self without betraying it so severely. Her legacy is one of hope. She tells us that positive change does occur over time and with much effort. In the process, the value of building relationships, facing fears, speaking openly, and maintaining hope in adversity can never be underestimated.

# Tables

**Table 1.** Functions and primary food sources of vitamins

| Vitamin | Fat-soluble vitamins | | |
| --- | --- | --- | --- |
| | Functions | U.S. RDA | Primary food sources |
| Vitamin A | Aids vision<br>Helps keep skin healthy<br>Helps keep lining of mouth, nose, throat, and digestive tract resistant to infection | 800 μg | Liver, butter, cheese, whole process, milk, egg yolks, sweet potatoes, carrots, dark green vegetables, pumpkin, squash, lettuce, tomatoes, apricots, nectarines |
| Vitamin D (calciferol) | Helps body use calcium and phosphorus | 5 μg | Fish-liver oils, fortified milk, exposure to sunlight |
| Vitamin E | Helps keep red blood cells intact | 30 IU | Soybeans, nuts, seeds, vegetable oils, whole grain products, spinach |
| Vitamin K | Necessary for clotting of blood | 60–65 μg | Broccoli; liver, asparagus, spinach, cabbage, turnip greens |

## Water-soluble vitamins

| Vitamin | Functions | U.S. RDA | Primary food sources |
|---|---|---|---|
| Vitamin C | Helps hold body cells together and strengthens walls of blood vessels<br>Helps heal wounds | 60 mg | Oranges, lemons, limes, green pepper, tomatoes, strawberries, cantaloupe, cabbage, broccoli, potatoes |
| Thiamine (B$_1$) | Helps the body get energy from food<br>Helps keep nerves in healthy condition | 1.1 mg | Pork, liver, Brazil nuts, pecans, barley, oatmeal, legumes, whole grain and enriched products |
| Riboflavin (B$_2$) | Helps the body get energy from food<br>Helps keep nerves in healthy condition | 1.3 mg | Milk, liver, meat, eggs, barley, cheese, greens, broccoli, asparagus, brewer's yeast, enriched breads and cereals |
| Niacin (nicotinamide, nicotinic acid) | Helps the body produce energy<br>Helps maintain health of skin, tongue, digestive tract, and nervous system<br>Aids digestion and good appetite | 15 mg | Lean meats, fish, poultry, liver, nuts, peanuts, peanut butter, peas, lima beans, whole wheat and enriched bread, cereals, corn, cottage cheese, steak, chicken |
| Folic acid | Necessary for building blood cells | 180 µg | Liver, asparagus, greens, broccoli, okra, Brussels sprouts, peanuts, almonds, orange juice, legumes |

**Table 1.**   Functions and primary food sources of vitamins (continued)

| Vitamin | Water-soluble vitamins | | |
| | Functions | U.S. RDA | Primary food sources |
| --- | --- | --- | --- |
| Pyridoxine (B12) | Helps the body use protein Promotes healthy skin, eyes, and clear vision | 1.6 mg | Liver, pork, chicken, fish, legumes, bananas, potatoes, greens, tomatoes, rice, whole wheat bread, milk, cottage cheese, avocados, walnuts |
| Cobalamin (B12) | Helps build blood cells Promotes a healthy nervous system | 2.0 µg | Liver, beef, ham, fish, eggs, milk, cheese |
| Biotin | Assists in energy metabolism | 0.3 mg | Beef liver, egg yolk, oatmeal, soybeans, milk |
| Pantothenic acid | Assists in energy metabolism | 4–7 mg | Liver, egg yolks, mushrooms, chicken, milk, grains, legumes |

RDA = Recommended Daily Allowance; IU = international unit.
*Source.*   National Academy of Sciences 1989.

**Table 2.** Recommended daily servings from each food group for graduated calorie levels

| Daily calorie intake | Estimated calorie values and number of servings Food group | | | | |
|---|---|---|---|---|---|
| | Protein | Vegetable | Fruit | Starch | Fat |
| Calories per serving | 75 | 25 | 50 | 100 | 50 |
| 1,200 | 6 | 4 | 4 | 4 | 2 |
| 1,400 | 6 | 4 | 5 | 5 | 3 |
| 1,600 | 6 | 4 | 5 | 7 | 3 |
| 1,800 | 7 | 4 | 5 | 8 | 3 |
| 2,000 | 8 | 4 | 5 | 8 | 6 |
| 2,200 | 8 | 4 | 6 | 9 | 7 |
| 2,400 | 8 | 4 | 7 | 10 | 8 |
| 2,600 | 9 | 4 | 7 | 11 | 9 |
| 2,800 | 11 | 4 | 7 | 11 | 10 |
| 3,000 | 11 | 4 | 7 | 12 | 12 |

**Table 3.**    Food groups and serving sizes

| | |
|---|---|
| **Protein:** | **P** |
| Meat (1 oz):  beef, pork, chicken, turkey, fish | |
| Meat | **R** |
| alternatives:  1 T peanut butter or nuts, 1 egg, | |
| 3 T cooked dry beans | **O** |
| | **T** |
| Milk (2–3 servings a day equals calcium needs): | **E** |
| | |
| 1 cup skim milk, 1 cup buttermilk, 1 oz cheese, | **I** |
| 2 T shredded cheese, ½ cup plain yogurt, | |
| ¼ cup cottage cheese, 4 oz tofu | **N** |
| **Vegetables:** | |
| 1 cup leafy greens, ½ cup nonstarchy (cooked) | |
| spinach, broccoli, green beans, wax beans, | |
| brussel sprouts, onions, peppers, squash, cabbage, | **C** |
| asparagus, carrots, cauliflower, mushrooms, | |
| tomatoes | **A** |
| **Fruit:** | **R** |
| 1 small piece, fresh 3-in. | **B** |
| apple, orange, ½ banana, peach, pear, nectarine, | |
| 2 plums, ¼ cantaloupe, 1 cup watermelon, | **O** |
| ½ cup grapes, ½ cup strawberries, | |
| ½ cup canned fruit in juice, | **H** |
| ½ cup juice (no added sugar) | **Y** |
| **Starch:** | **D** |
| Grains      ¾ cup unsweetened cold cereal | **R** |
| (1 box), 1 slice regular bread, | |
| 2 slices light bread, 1 muffin, 1 biscuit, | **A** |
| ½ English muffin, 4 regular crackers, | |
| 2 squares graham crackers, ½ cup rice, | **T** |
| 1 small pancake (4–5 in.), ½ cup pasta, | |
| 1 corn tortilla, 1 flour tortilla, 1 dinner roll, | **E** |
| ½ bun, ½ bagel, 3 cups popcorn, | |
| ½ cup hot cereal, ½ waffle, | |
| ½ cup starchy vegetables (corn, beans, peas, potato) | |
| **Fat:** | **F** |
| 1 tsp margarine, butter, oil, shortening, | |
| mayonnaise (½ pkg), 1 T regular salad dressing, | **A** |
| olives, cream cheese (½ pkg), imitation bacon bits, | |
| 2 T sour cream, gravy or sauce, 1 slice bacon | **T** |

## **Table 4.** Food group serving equivalents in combination foods

**Casseroles**

2 protein, 1 starch, 1 fat (¾ cup)

    beanie wienies, beef stew, Brunswick stew, chili with beans, chicken and noodles, chili roni, goulash, ham and noodles, hash, Italian casserole, macaroni and cheese, ravioli, tuna and noodles

2 protein, 1 starch, 1 fat (¾ cup)

    chicken chop suey, chicken chow mein, pork chop suey, shrimp creole, meat stir-fry

**Mixed entrees**

2 protein, 1 starch, 1 fat

| | |
|---|---|
| pizza (1 slice = ⅙ medium) | quiche (1 slice = ⅙ medium) |
| tamale (1) | lasagne (1 2½-in. piece) |
| stuffed pepper (½ large) | eggplant parmigiana (1 serving, and 1 vegetable) |

**Meat with sauce**

2 protein, 1 fat (½ cup)

    spaghetti sauce, creamed beef, almond chicken, chicken à la king, curried beef, sloppy joes

**Breaded and fried meat**

2 protein, 1 fat, 1 starch (½ cup or 3 oz)

    chicken fried steak, fried chicken, fried scallops, fried fish, fried shrimp

**Special meats**

    1 frankfurter (1 protein, 1 fat)

    1 oz sausage (1 protein, 1 fat)

    ½ cup spaghetti sauce with only vegetables (1 vegetable)

**Breaded and fried vegetables**

1 vegetable, 1 starch, 1 fat (½ cup)

    fried onion rings, fried mushrooms, fried okra, fried zucchini, fried eggplant

**Salad with dressing**

1 vegetable or fruit, 1 fat (½ cup)

    Waldorf salad, carrot raisin salad, coleslaw, banana nut salad, avocado grapefruit section salad, cucumbers in dressing

1 starch, 1 fat (½ cup)

    potato salad, french fries, potatoes au gratin, creamed potatoes, hash browns, stuffing

**Table 4.**    Food group serving equivalents in combination foods
*(continued)*

**Cream soups**
2 protein, 1 vegetable, 1 fat (1 cup)
   lentil soup, potato soup, cheese soup, pea soup, cream of broccoli soup,
   New England clam chowder, navy bean soup, cream of tomato soup

**Broth soups**
1 protein, 1 starch (1 cup)
   chicken noodle soup, beef noodle soup, chicken rice soup, beef rice
   soup, chicken vegetable soup, beef vegetable soup, minestrone

**Concentrated sweets    Below 1,600 calories, use only**
       **twice a week or less**

| | |
|---|---|
| pie (⅛) | 2 starch, 2 fruit, 2 fat |
| cake, frosted (1/16) | 1 starch, 2 fruit, 1 fat |
| cake, unfrosted (1/16) | 1 starch, 1 fruit, 1 fat |
| sweet roll, frosted (orange roll, pecan roll, caramel roll) (2½ in) | 1 starch, 2 fruit, 1 fat |
| cookie (1) | 1 starch |
| brownie (1) | 1 bread, 1 fruit, 1 fat |
| ice cream (1 dip) | 1 starch, 2 fat |
| sherbet (1 dip) | 2 starch |
| syrup, honey, jelly, jam, molasses, sugar (1 tsp) | 1 fruit |
| fruit yogurt (regular sweetened,1 cup) | 2 protein, 2 fruit |
| pudding (½ cup) | 1 starch, 1 fat |
| doughnut, frosted (1) | 1 starch, 1 fat, 1 fruit |
| cake doughnut, plain (1) | 1 starch, 1 fat |
| lite fruit yogurt (1 cup) | 1 protein, 1 fruit |
| frozen flavored yogurt (6 oz or ¾ cup round dip) | 1 protein, 1 fruit |

**Other foods**

| | |
|---|---|
| taco (1) | 1 starch, 1 protein, 1 vegetable |
| burrito (1 bean or meat mix) | 1 starch, 2 protein, 1 fat |
| hamburger, small | 2 starch, 2 protein |
| baked potato with ½ cup topping | 2 starch, 2 protein, 1 fat |
| pita pocket (1) | 1 starch, 2 protein |
| tostada (1) | 1 starch, 1 protein, 1 vegetable |

*Source.* Based on the nutritional guidelines developed by Shirley Allen, R.D.,
The Menninger Clinic.

# Appendix

**DSM-III Criteria**

### Anorexia Nervosa

A. Intense fear of becoming obese, which does not diminish as weight loss progresses.
B. Disturbance of body image, e.g., claiming to "feel fat" even when emaciated.
C. Weight loss of at least 25% of original body weight.
D. Refusal to maintain body weight over a minimal normal weight for age and height.
E. No known physical illness that would account for the weight loss.

### Bulimia

A. Recurrent episodes of binge eating (rapid consumption of a large amount of food in a discrete period of time, usually less than two hours).
B. At least three of the following:
   (1) consumption of high-caloric, easily ingested food during a binge
   (2) inconspicuous eating during a binge
   (3) termination of such eating episodes by abdominal pain, sleep, social interruption, or self-induced vomiting

    (4)  repeated attempts to lose weight by severely restrictive diets, self-induced vomiting, or use of cathartics or diuretics

    (5)  frequent weight fluctuations greater than ten pounds due to alternating binges and fasts

C.  Awareness that the eating pattern is abnormal and fear of not being able to stop eating voluntarily.

D.  Depressed mood and self-deprecating thoughts following eating binges.

E.  The bulimic episodes are not due to Anorexia Nervosa or any known physical disorder.

### Atypical Eating Disorder

This category is a residual category for eating disorders that cannot be adequately classified in any of the previous categories.

## DSM-III-R Criteria

### Anorexia Nervosa

A.  Refusal to maintain body weight over a minimal normal weight for age and height, e.g., weight loss leading to maintenance of body weight 15% below that expected; or failure to make expected weight gain during period of growth, leading to body weight 15% below that expected.

B.  Intense fear of gaining weight or becoming fat, even though underweight.

C.  Disturbance in the way in which one's body weight, size, or shape is experienced, e.g., the person claims to "feel fat" even when emaciated, believes that one area of the body is "too fat" even when obviously underweight.

D.  In females, absence of at least three consecutive menstrual cycles when otherwise expected to occur (primary or secondary amenorrhea).

### Bulimia Nervosa

A.  Recurrent episodes of binge eating (rapid consumption of a large amount of food in a discrete period of time).

B. A feeling of lack of control over eating behavior during the eating binges.

C. The person regularly engages in either self-induced vomiting, use of laxatives or diuretics, strict dieting or fasting, or vigorous exercise in order to prevent weight gain.

D. A minimum average of two binge eating episodes a week for at least three months.

E. Persistent overconcern with body shape and weight.

### Eating Disorders Not Otherwise Specified

Disorders of eating that do not meet the criteria for specific Eating Disorder.

### Examples:

(1) a person of average weight who does not have binge eating episodes, but frequently engages in self-induced vomiting for fear of gaining weight

(2) all of the features of Anorexia Nervosa in a female except absence of menstrual period

(3) all the features of Bulimia Nervosa except the frequency of binge eating episodes

### Proposed DSM-IV Criteria

### Anorexia Nervosa

A. Refusal to maintain body weight over a minimally normal weight for age and height (e.g., weight loss leading to maintenance of body weight 15% below that expected); or failure to make expected weight gain during period of growth, leading to body weight 15% below that expected.

B. Intense fear of gaining weight or becoming fat, even though underweight.

C. Disturbance in the way in which one's body weight, size, or shape is experienced. Undue influence of body weight or shape on self-evaluation, or denial of the seriousness of the current low body weight.

D.  In females, absence of at least three consecutive menstrual cycles when otherwise expected to occur (primary or secondary amenorrhea).

Specify type:

*Bulimic type:* During the episode of Anorexia Nervosa, the person engages in recurrent episodes of binge eating

*Nonbulimic type:* During the episode of Anorexia Nervosa, the person does not reengage in recurrent episodes of binge eating.

### Bulimia Nervosa

A.  Recurrent episodes of binge eating. An episode of binge eating is characterized by both of the following:
    
    (1)  eating, in a discrete period of time (e.g., within any two hour period), an amount of food that is definitely larger than most people would eat in a similar period of time
    
    (2)  a sense of lack of control over eating during the episode (e.g., a feeling that one cannot stop eating or control what or how much one is eating)

Criterion B: Options for compensatory behavior

Option B1: Restrict to vomiting or use of laxatives

B.  The person regularly engages in either self-induced vomiting, or the use of laxatives in order to prevent weight gain

Option B2: No change from DSM-III-R criterion but with the addition of purging and nonpurging subtypes

C.  A minimum average of two binge-eating episodes a week for at least three months

D.  Self-evaluation is unduly influenced by body shape and weight.

E.  The disturbance does not occur exclusively during episodes of Anorexia Nervosa.

Specify type:

*Purging type:* If the person regularly engages in self-induced vomiting or the use of laxatives or diuretics.

*Nonpurging type:* Use of strict dieting, fasting, or vigorous exercise, but does not regularly engage in purging.

### Binge Eating Disorder

A. Recurrent episodes of binge eating. An episode of binge eating is characterized by both of the following:
   (1) eating, in a discrete period of time (e.g., within any two hour period), an amount of food that is definitely larger than most people would eat in a similar period of time
   (2) a sense of lack of control over eating during the episode (e.g., a feeling that one cannot stop eating or control what or how much one is eating)
B. During most binge episodes, at least three of the following behavioral indicators of loss of control are present:
   (1) eating much more rapidly than usual
   (2) eating until feeling uncomfortably full
   (3) eating large amounts of food when not feeling physically hungry
   (4) eating large amounts of food throughout the day with no planned mealtimes
   (5) eating alone because of being embarrassed by how much one is eating
   (6) feeling disgusted with oneself, depressed, or feeling very guilty after overeating
C. The binge eating occurs, on average, at least twice a week for a six-month period
D. The binge eating causes marked distress.
E. Does not occur exclusively during the course of Bulimia Nervosa and the individual does not abuse medication (e.g., diet pills, thyroid medication) in an attempt to avoid weight gain

### Eating Disorder Not Otherwise Specified

1) Subthreshold Anorexia Nervosa:
   a)   all of the criteria for Anorexia Nervosa are met except the individual continues to have regular menstrual periods
   b)   all of the criteria for Anorexia Nervosa are met except the abnormally low weight requirement (e.g., an individual who, despite substantial weight loss, still has a weight in the normal range)
2) Subthreshold Bulimia Nervosa:
   a)   Binge Eating Disorder: eating binges accompanied by significant distress, but without any regular compensatory behavior (e.g., vomiting, laxative abuse)
   b)   eating binges with atypical compensatory mechanisms (e.g., abuse of thyroid medication or diet pills, an individual with diabetes mellitus who intentionally reduces insulin dose)
   c)   eating binges at a frequency of less than twice a week for three months
   d)   compensatory behavior in the absence of the consumption of sufficiently large amount of food to meet the criterion for a binge (e.g., self-induced vomiting after eating two cookies)
   e)   an individual who repeatedly chews, but does not swallow, large amounts of food (and instead spits it out)

# Bibliography

Abelin EL: The role of the father in the separation-individuation process, in Separation-Individuation: Essays in Honor of Margaret S. Mahler. Edited by McDevitt JB, Settlage CF. New York, International Universities Press, 1971, pp 229–252

Abelin EL: Some further observations and comments on the earliest role of the father. Int J Psychoanal 56:293–302, 1975

Abelin EL: Triangulation, the role of the father and the origins of core gender identity during the rapprochement subphase, in Rapprochement: The Critical Subphase of Separation-Individuation. Edited by Lax RF, Bach S, Burland JA. New York, Jason Aronson, 1980, pp 151–169

Adler A: The Neurotic Constitution: Outlines of a Comparative Individualistic Psychology and Psychotherapy. Translated by Glueck B, Lind J. New York, Moffat, Yard, & Co., 1917

Adler A: Individual Psychology. New York, Humanities Press, 1929

Agras WS: Nonpharmacologic treatments of bulimia nervosa. J Clin Psychiatry 52 (suppl 10):29–33, 1991

Agras WS: Bulimia nervosa: combining medication and psychological treatment. Eating Disorders Review 3:1–3, 1992

Agras WS, Rossiter EM, Arnow B, et al: Pharmacologic and cognitive-behavioral treatment for bulimia nervosa: a controlled comparison. Am J Psychiatry 149:82–87, 1992

Akiskal H: Chronic depression. Bull Menninger Clin 55:156–171, 1991

American Psychiatric Association: Diagnostic and Statistical Manual of Mental Disorders, 3rd Edition. Washington, DC, American Psychiatric Association, 1980

American Psychiatric Association: Diagnostic and Statistical Manual of Mental Disorders, 3rd Edition, Revised. Washington, DC, American Psychiatric Association, 1987

American Psychiatric Association, Task Force on DSM-IV: DSM-IV Draft Criteria. Washington, DC, American Psychiatric Association, 1993

American Psychiatric Association Work Group on Eating Disorders: Practice guideline for eating disorders. Am J Psychiatry 150:207–228, 1993

Ames-Frankel J, Devlin MJ, Walsh BT, et al: Personality disorder diagnosis in patients with bulimia nervosa: clinical correlates and changes with treatment. J Clin Psychiatry 53:90–96, 1992

Andersen AE: Males With Eating Disorders. New York, Brunner/Mazel, 1990

Andersen AE: Medical complications of eating disorders, in Special Problems in Managing Eating Disorders. Edited by Yager J, Gwirtsman HE, Edelstein CK. Washington, DC, American Psychiatric Press, 1992, pp 119–144

Anderson SC, Back CM, et al: Psychosocial sequelae in intrafamilial victims of sexual assault and abuse. Paper presented at the Third International Conference on Child Abuse and Neglect, Amsterdam, The Netherlands, April 1981

ANRED (Anorexia Nervosa and Related Eating Disorders) Alert: What are we doing to our children? ANRED Alert 14:3, 1993, p 2

Averbuch G: The Woman Runner: Free to Be the Complete Athlete. New York, Cornerstone, 1984

Bailey J: She might have inherited millions, but for her mother. Wall Street Journal, November 25, 1991, pp A1, A10

Bakan R, Birmingham CL, Goldner EM: Chronicity in anorexia nervosa: pregnancy and birth complications as risk factors. International Journal of Eating Disorders 10:631–645, 1991

Balch P, Ross AW: A behaviorally oriented didactic-group treatment of obesity: an exploratory study. J Behav Ther Exp Psychiatry 5:239–243, 1974

Balint M: On love and hate (1951), in Primary Love and Psychoanalytic Technique. New York, Liveright, 1965, pp 121–135

Balint M: The Basic Fault: Therapeutic Aspects of Regression. London, Tavistock, 1968

Barbach LG: For Yourself: The Fulfillment of Female Sexuality. New York, Doubleday, 1975

Basow SA: The hairless ideal: women and their body hair. Psychology of Women Quarterly 15:83–96, 1991

Bass E, Davis L: The Courage to Heal: A Guide for Women Survivors of Child Sexual Abuse. New York, Harper & Row, 1988

Battle with bulimia prevents Garrison from reaching no. 1. Kansas City Star, August 18, 1992, p C3

Becker E: The Denial of Death. New York, Free Press, 1973

Bell RM: Holy Anorexia. Chicago, IL, University of Chicago Press, 1985

Bemis KM: "Abstinence" and "nonabstinence" models for the treatment of bulimia. International Journal of Eating Disorders 4:407–437, 1985

Bemporad JR, Herzog DB: Introduction, in Psychoanalysis and Eating Disorders. Edited by Bemporad JR, Herzog DB. New York, Guilford, 1989, pp 1–3

Bemporad JR, Beresin E, Ratey JJ, et al: A psychoanalytic study of eating disorders, I: a developmental profile of 67 index cases. J Am Acad Psychoanal 20:509–532, 1992a

Bemporad JR, O'Driscoll G, Beresin E, et al: A psychoanalytic study of eating disorders, II: intergroup and intragroup comparisons. J Am Acad Psychoanal 20:533–542, 1992b

Benedek T: Parenthood during the life cycle, in Parenthood: Its Psychology and Psychopathology. By Anthony EJ, Benedek T. Boston, MA, Little, Brown, 1970, pp 185–206

Benjamin J: The Bonds of Love. New York, Pantheon, 1988

Bennett WI: Obesity is not an eating disorder. Harvard Mental Health Letter 8(4):4–6, 1991

Ben-Tovin DI, Walker MK: A quantitative study of body-related attitudes in patients with anorexia and bulimia nervosa. Psychol Med 22:961–969, 1992

Beresin EV, Gordon C, Herzog DB: The process of recovering from anorexia nervosa, in Psychoanalysis and Eating Disorders. Edited by Bemporad JR, Herzog DB. New York, Guilford, 1989, pp 103–130

Berliner B: On some psychodynamics of masochism. Psychoanal Q 16:459–471, 1947

Bion WR: Notes on memory and desire (1967), in Classics in Psychoanalytic Technique. Edited by Langs R. New York, Jason Aronson, 1981, pp 259–260

Birtchnell SA: Dysmorphophobia: a centenary discussion. Br J Psychiatry 153 (suppl 2):41–43, 1988

Black C: Double Duty: Sexually Abused. New York, Ballantine Books, 1990

Blackburn GL, Brotman AW, Rosofsky WG: Why and how to stop weight cycling in overweight adults. Eating Disorders Review 4:1–3, 1993

Blinder BJ, Goodman SL, Goldstein R: Rumination: a critical review of diagnosis and treatment, in The Eating Disorders: Medical and Psychological Bases of Diagnosis and Treatment. Edited by Blinder BJ, Chaitin BF, Goldstein RS. New York, PMA Publishing, 1988a, pp 315–329

Blinder BJ, Goodman SL, Henderson P: Pica: a critical review of diagnosis and treatment: in The Eating Disorders: Medical and Psychological Bases of Diagnosis and Treatment. Edited by Blinder BJ, Chaitin BF, Goldstein RS. New York, PMA Publishing, 1988b, pp 331–344

Boris HN: The problem of anorexia nervosa. Int J Psychoanal 65:315–322, 1984a

Boris HN: On the treatment of anorexia nervosa. Int J Psychoanal 65:435–442, 1984b

Bowlby J: Grief and mourning in infancy and early childhood. Psychoanal Study Child 15:9–52, 1960a

Bowlby J: Separation anxiety. Int J Psychoanal 41:89–113, 1960b

Bowlby J: Separation anxiety: a critical review of the literature. J Child Psychol Psychiatry 1:251–269, 1961

Bowlby J: Pathological mourning and childhood mourning. J Am Psychoanal Assoc 11:500–541, 1963

Bowlby J: Attachment and Loss, Vol I. Attachment, New York, Basic Books, 1969

Bowlby J: Anxiety and anger, in Attachment and Loss, Vol II: Separation. New York, Basic Books, 1973

Bray GA, York B, DeLany J: A survey of the opinions of obesity experts on the causes and treatment of obesity. Am J Clin Nutr 55:151S–154S, 1992

Brems C: Self-psychology and feminism: an integration and expansion. Am J Psychoanal 51:145–160, 1991

Brown LS: Women, weight and power: feminist theoretical and therapeutic issues. Women and Therapy 4:61–71, 1985

Brown S: Treating the Alcoholic: A Developmental Model of Recovery. New York, Wiley, 1985

Browne A, Finkelhor D: Impact of child sexual abuse: a review of the research. Psychol Bull 99:66–77, 1986. Reprinted as Chapter 8 in Annual Progress in Child Psychiatry and Child Development. New York, Brunner/Mazel, 1988, pp 555–584

Brownell KD: Lifestyle, Exercise, Attitudes, Relationships: The LEARN Program for Weight Control. Philadelphia, PA, University of Pennsylvania Press, 1988

Brownell KD, Wadden TA: Etiology and treatment of obesity: understanding a serious, prevalent, and refractory disorder. J Consult Clin Psychol 60:505–517, 1992

Brownell KD, Marlatt GA, Lichtenstein E, et al: Understanding and preventing relapse. Am Psychol 41:765–782, 1986

Brownmiller S: Femininity. New York, Linden Press, 1984

Bruch H: Eating Disorders: Obesity, Anorexia Nervosa, and the Person Within. New York, Basic Books, 1973

Bruch H: Eating Disorders. London, Routledge & Kegan Paul, 1974

Bruch H: The Golden Cage: The Enigma of Anorexia Nervosa. Cambridge, MA, Harvard University Press, 1978

Bruch H: Anorexia nervosa: therapy and theory. Am J Psychiatry 139:1531–1538, 1982

Bruch H: Conversations With Anorexics. Edited by Czyzewski D, Suhr M. New York, Basic Books, 1988

Brumberg JJ: Fasting Girls: The Emergence of Anorexia Nervosa as a Modern Disease. Cambridge, MA, Harvard University Press, 1988

Buchele B: Group psychotherapy for persons with multiple personality and dissociative disorders. Bull Menninger Clin 57(3):362–370, 1993

Bulik CM: Drug and alcohol abuse by bulimic women and their families. Am J Psychiatry 144:1604–1606, 1987a

Bulik CM: Eating disorders in immigrants: two case reports. International Journal of Eating Disorders 6:133–141, 1987b

Bulik CM, Sullivan PF, Rorty M: Childhood sexual abuse in women with bulimia. J Clin Psychiatry 50:460–464, 1989

Bynum CW: Holy Feast and Holy Fast: The Religious Significance of Food to Medieval Women. Berkeley, CA, University of California Press, 1987

Cash TF, Pruzinsky T (eds): Body Images: Development, Deviance, and Change. London, Guilford, 1990

Casper RC: Risk factors for the development of eating disorders, in Adolescent Psychiatry, Vol 18. Chicago, IL, University of Chicago Press, 1992, pp 91–103

Chandarana PC, Malla A: Bulimia and dissociative states: a case report. Can J Psychiatry 34:137–139, 1989

Charlier M: Fasting plans are fast becoming a popular way to combat obesity. Wall Street Journal, February 24, 1988

Chatham PM: Treatment of the Borderline Personality. New York, Jason Aronson, 1985

Chatoor I: Infantile anorexia nervosa: a developmental disorder of separation and individuation, in Psychoanalysis and Eating Disorders. Edited by Bemporad JR, Herzog DB. New York, Guilford, 1989, pp 43–64

Chernin K: The Hungry Self: Women, Eating, and Identity. New York, Random House, 1985

Chodorow NJ: The Reproduction of Mothering: Psychoanalysis and the Sociology of Gender. Berkeley, CA, University of California Press, 1978

Chodorow NJ: Feminism and Psychoanalytic Theory. New Haven, CT, Yale University Press, 1989

Clinton DN, Glant R: The eating disorders spectrum of DSM-III-R: clinical features and psychosocial concomitants of 86 consecutive cases from a Swedish urban catchment area. J Nerv Ment Dis 180:244–250, 1992

Comerci GD: Medical complications of anorexia nervosa and bulimia nervosa. Med Clin North Am 74:1293–1310, 1990

Conroy W: The many facets of adolescent drinking. Bull Menninger Clin 52:229–245, 1988

Cooper PJ, Coker SE: Psychological treatments for the eating disorders. Current Opinion in Psychiatry 3:337–341, 1990

Cooper PJ, Taylor MJ: Body image disturbance in bulimia nervosa. Br J Psychiatry 153 (suppl 2):32–36, 1988

Council on Scientific Affairs: Treatment of obesity in adults. JAMA 260:2547–2551, 1988

Crisp AH: Diagnosis and outcome of anorexia nervosa: the St. George's view. Proceedings of the Royal Society of Medicine 70:464–470, 1977

Crisp AH: Anorexia Nervosa: Let Me Be. London, Academic Press, 1980

Crisp AH, Harding B, McGuinness B: Anorexia nervosa: psychoneurotic characteristics of parents—relationship to prognosis: a quantitative study. J Psychosom Res 18:167–173, 1974

Crisp AH, Palmer RL, Kalucy RS: How common is anorexia nervosa? a prevalence study. Br J Psychiatry 128:549–554, 1976

Crisp AH, Toms DA: Primary anorexia nervosa, a weight phobia in the male: report on 13 cases. BMJ 1:334–338, 1972

Dally PJ: Anorexia Nervosa. New York, Grune & Stratton, 1969

Dally P, Gomez J: Anorexia Nervosa. London, Heinemann Medical Books, 1979

Davies E, Furnham A: The dieting and body shape concerns of adolescent females. J Child Psychol Psychiatry 27:417–428, 1986

Davis C, Yager J: Transcultural aspects of eating disorders: a critical literature review. Cult Med Psychiatry 16:377–394, 1992

Davis WN: Epilogue, in Holy Anorexia. By Bell RM. Chicago, IL, University of Chicago Press, 1985, pp 180–190

Dee S: Learning to live again. People, March 18, 1991, pp 86–94

Demitrack MA, Putnam FW, Brewerton TD, et al: Relation of clinical variables to dissociative phenomena in eating disorders. Am J Psychiatry 147(9):1184–1188, 1990

Dennis AB, Sansone RA: The clinical stages of treatment for the eating disorder patient with borderline personality disorder, in Psychodynamic Treatment of Anorexia Nervosa and Bulimia. Edited by Johnson CL. New York, Guilford, 1991, pp 128–164

Densmore-John J: Nutritional characteristics and consequences of anorexia nervosa and bulimia, in The Eating Disorders: Medical and Psychological Bases of Diagnosis and Treatment. Edited by Blinder BJ, Chaitin BF, Goldstein RS. New York, PMA Publishing, 1988, pp 305–313

de Zwaan M, Nutzinger DO, Schoenbeck G: Binge eating in overweight women. Compr Psychiatry 33:256–261, 1992

Dinesen I: Babette's Feast and Other Anecdotes of Destiny (1958). New York, Vintage Books, 1984

Dodes M: The psychology of combining dynamic psychotherapy and alcoholics anonymous. Bull Menninger Clin 52:283–293, 1988

Dolan B: Cross-cultural aspects of anorexia nervosa and bulimia: a review. International Journal of Eating Disorders 10(1):67–79, 1991

Dostoyevski F: The grand inquisitor on the nature of man (1880), in The Brothers Karamazov. Translated by Garnett C. Indianapolis, IN, Bobbs-Merrill, 1945, pp 292–314

Eckert ED, Mitchell JE: An overview of the treatment of anorexia nervosa. Psychiatr Med 7:293–315, 1989

Edelstein CK, King BH: Pregnancy and eating disorders, in Special Problems in Managing Eating Disorders. Edited by Yager J, Gwirtsman HE, Edelstein CK. Washington, DC, American Psychiatric Press, 1992, pp 163–184

Edelstein CK, Yager J: Eating disorders and affective disorders, in Special Problems in Managing Eating Disorders. Edited by Yager J, Gwirtsman HE, Edelstein CK. Washington, DC, American Psychiatric Press, 1992, pp 15–50

Erikson H: Childhood and Society, Revised Edition. New York, WW Norton, 1963

Fabian LJ, Thompson JK: Body image and eating disturbance in young females. International Journal of Eating Disorders 8:63–74, 1989

Fairbairn RWD: The repression and the return of bad objects (with special reference to the "war neuroses") (1943), in Psychoanalytic Studies of the Personality. London, Routledge & Kegan Paul, 1952, pp 59–81

Fairburn CG: A cognitive behavioral approach to the treatment of bulimia. Psychol Med 11:707–711, 1981

Fairburn CG: Cognitive-behavioral treatment for bulimia, in Handbook of Psychotherapy for Anorexia Nervosa and Bulimia. Edited by Garner DM, Garfinkel PE. New York, Guilford, 1985, pp 160–192

Fallon AE, Rozin P: Sex differences in perceptions of desirable body shape. J Abnorm Psychol 94:102–105, 1985

Federn P: Some variations in ego-feeling. Int J Psychoanal 7:434–444, 1926

Federn P: Ego Psychology and the Psychoses. New York, Basic Books, 1952

Feeling fat in a thin society (results of a Glamour survey). Glamour 82:198–201, 1984

Fenley J, Powers PS, Miller J, Rowland M: Untreated anorexia nervosa: a case study of the medical consequences. Gen Hosp Psychiatry 12:264–270, 1990

Fichter MM, Noegel R: Concordance for bulimia nervosa in twins. International Journal of Eating Disorders 9:255–263, 1990

Fichter MM, Pirke KM, Holsboer F: Weight loss causes neuroendocrine disturbances: experimental study in healthy starving subjects. J Psychiatr Res 17:61–72, 1986

Fields PJ: Parent-child relationships, childhood sexual abuse, and adult interpersonal behavior in female prostitutes. Dissertation Abstracts International 42:2053B, 1981

Finkelhor D: Child Sexual Abuse: New Theory and Research. New York, Free Press, 1984

Fisher S, Cleveland SE: Body Image and Personality, Revised Edition. New York, Dover, 1968

Fliegel ZO: Women's development in analytic theory: six decades of controversy, in Psychoanalysis and Women: Contemporary Reappraisals. Edited by Alpert JL. Hillsdale, NJ, Analytic Press, 1986, pp 3–32

Ford M, Dolan BM: Bulimia associated with repeated spontaneous abortion. International Journal of Eating Disorders 8:243–245, 1989

Fosson A, Knibbs J, Bryant WR, et al: Early onset anorexia nervosa. Arch Dis Child 62:114–118, 1987

Fraiberg S, Adelson E, Shapiro V: Ghosts in the nursery: a psychoanalytic approach to the problems of impaired infant-mother relationships. Journal of the American Academy of Child Psychiatry 14(3):387–421, 1975

Franzini LR, Grimes WB: Contracting and Stuart's three-dimensional program in behavior modification of the obese. Psychotherapy: Theory, Research, and Practice 17:44–51, 1980

Freud A: The Ego and the Mechanisms of Defence (1936). Translated by Baines C. London, Hogarth Press, 1937

Freud S: Letter 79 (1897), in Extracts From the Fliess Papers: The Standard Edition of the Complete Psychological Works of Sigmund Freud, Vol 1. Translated and edited by Strachey J. London, Hogarth Press, 1966, pp 272–273

Freud S: Fragment of an analysis of a case of hysteria (1905), in The Standard Edition of the Complete Psychological Works of Sigmund Freud, Vol 7. Translated and edited by Strachey J. London, Hogarth Press, 1953, pp 1–122

Freud S: Analysis of a phobia in a five-year-old boy (1909), in The Standard Edition of the Complete Psychological Works of Sigmund Freud, Vol 10. Translated and edited by Strachey J. London, Hogarth Press, 1955, pp 1–149

Freud S: Psycho-analytic notes on an autobiographical account of a case of paranoia (dementia paranoides) (1911), in The Standard Edition of the Complete Psychological Works of Sigmund Freud, Vol 12. Translated and edited by Strachey J. London, Hogarth Press, 1958, pp 1–82

Freud S: Some character-types met with in psycho-analytic work (1916), in The Standard Edition of the Complete Psychological Works of Sigmund Freud, Vol 14. Translated and edited by Strachey J. London, Hogarth Press, 1963, pp 309–333

Freud S: Beyond the pleasure principle (1920), in the Standard Edition of the Complete Psychological Works of Sigmund Freud, Vol 18. Translated and edited by Strachey J. London, Hogarth Press, 1955, pp 1–64

Freud S: Group psychology and the analysis of the ego (1921), in The Standard Edition of the Complete Psychological Works of Sigmund Freud, Vol 18. Translated and edited by Strachey J. London, Hogarth Press, 1955, pp 65–143

Freud S: The ego and the id (1923), in The Standard Edition of the Complete Psychological Works of Sigmund Freud, Vol 19. Translated and edited by Strachey J. London, Hogarth Press, 1961, pp 1–66

Freud S: Some psychical consequences on the anatomical distinction between the sexes (1925), in The Standard Edition of the Complete Psychological Works of Sigmund Freud, Vol 19. Translated and edited by Strachey J. London, Hogarth Press, 1961, pp 241–258

Freud S: The question of lay analysis: conversations with an impartial person (1926), in The Standard Edition of the Complete Psychological Works of Sigmund Freud, Vol 20. Translated and edited by Strachey J. London, Hogarth Press, 1966, pp 183–258

Freud S: New introductory lectures on psycho-analysis (1933), in The Standard Edition of the Complete Psychological Works of Sigmund Freud, Vol 22. Translated and edited by Strachey J. London, Hogarth Press, 1964, pp 1–182

Friday N: My Secret Garden: Women's Sexual Fantasies. New York, Trident, 1973

Friday N: Forbidden Flowers: More Women's Sexual Fantasies. New York, Pocket Books, 1975

Frisch RE: Fatness and fertility. Sci Am 258(3):88–95, 1988

Fromm-Reichman F: Principles of Intensive Psychotherapy. Chicago, IL, University of Chicago Press, 1950

Furnham A, Alibhai N: Cross-cultural differences in the perception of female body shapes. Psychol Med 13:829–837, 1983

Gabbard GO: Psychodynamic Psychiatry in Clinical Practice. Washington, DC, American Psychiatric Press, 1990

Gadpaille WJ, Sanborn CF, Wagner WW: Athletic amenorrhea, major affective disorders, and eating disorders. Am J Psychiatry 144:939–942, 1987

Gandhi DH, Prakash Appaya M, Machado T: Anorexia nervosa in Asian children [letter]. Br J Psychiatry 159:591–592, 1991

Ganzarain RC, Buchele BJ: Fugitives of Incest: A Perspective from Psychoanalysis and Groups. Madison, CT, International Universities Press, 1988

Garfinkel PE, Garner DM: Anorexia Nervosa: A Multidimensional Perspective. New York, Brunner/Mazel, 1982

Garfinkel PE, Garner DM (eds): The Role of Drug Treatments for Eating Disorders. New York, Brunner/Mazel, 1987

Garner D: It is time to abandon traditional treatment for obesity. National Anorexic Aid Society Newsletter 15:1–5, 1992

Garner DM, Bemies KM: Cognitive therapy for anorexia nervosa, in Handbook of Psychotherapy for Anorexia Nervosa and Bulimia. Edited by Garner DM, Garfinkel PE. New York, Guilford, 1985, pp 107–146

Garner DM, Fairburn CG: Relationship between anorexia nervosa and bulimia nervosa: diagnostic implications, in Diagnostic Issues in Anorexia Nervosa and Bulimia Nervosa. Edited by Garner DM, Garfinkel PE. New York, Brunner/Mazel, 1988, pp 56–79

Garner DM, Garfinkel PE, Bemis KM: A multidimensional psychotherapy for anorexia nervosa. International Journal of Eating Disorders 1(2):3–46, 1982

Garner DM, Garfinkel PE, Schwartz D, et al: Cultural expectations of thinness in women. Psychol Rep 47:483–491, 1980

Gartner AF, Marcus RN, Halmi K, et al: DSM-III-R personality disorders in patients with eating disorders. Am J Psychiatry 146:1585–1591, 1989

Gaskell E: Motherhood: A Gift of Love (1860). Philadelphia, PA, Running Press, 1991

Geist RA: Self psychological reflections on the origins of eating disorders, in Psychoanalysis and Eating Disorders. Edited by Bemporad JR, Herzog DB. New York, Guilford, 1989, pp 5–27

Gelinas DJ: The persisting negative effects of incest. Psychiatry 46:312–332, 1983

Giannini AJ, Newman M, Gold M: Anorexia and bulimia. Am Fam Physician 41:1169–1176, 1990

Gilbert S: The Pathology of Eating: Psychology and Treatment. London, Routledge & Kegan Paul, 1986

Gilligan C: In a Different Voice: Psychological Theory and Women's Development. Cambridge, MA, Harvard University Press, 1982

Giovacchini PL: The psychoanalytic treatment of the alienated patient, in New Perspectives on Psychotherapy of the Borderline Adult. Edited by Masterson JF. New York, Brunner/Mazel, 1978, pp 1–19

Glucksman ML: Obesity: a psychoanalytic challenge, in Psychoanalysis and Eating Disorders. Edited by Bemporad JR, Herzog DB. New York, Guilford, 1989, pp 151–171

Goldbloom DS, Garfinkel PE, Shaw BF: Biochemical aspects of bulimia nervosa. J Psychosom Res 34 (suppl 1):11–22, 1991

Gordon C, Beresin E, Herzog DB: The parents' relationship and the child's illness in anorexia nervosa, in Psychoanalysis and Eating Disorders. Edited by Bemporad JR, Herzog DB. New York, Guilford, 1989, pp 29–43

Gordon RA: A sociocultural interpretation of the current epidemic of eating disorders, in The Eating Disorders: Medical and Psychological Bases of Diagnosis and Treatment. Edited by Blinder BJ, Chaitin BF, Goldstein RS. New York, PMA Publishing, 1988, pp 151–163

Gwirtsman HE: Laxative and emetic abuse in bulimia nervosa, in Special Problems in Managing Eating Disorders. Edited by Yager J, Gwirtsman HE, Edelstein CK. Washington, DC, American Psychiatric Press, 1992, pp 145–162

Gwirtsman HE, Guze BH, Yager J, et al: Fluoxetine treatment of anorexia nervosa: an open clinical trial. J Clin Psychiatry 51:378–382, 1990

Hall RCW, Beresford TP: Medical complications of anorexia and bulimia. Psychiatr Med 7:165–192, 1989

Hall RCW, Beresford TP, Hall AKN: Hypomagnesemia in eating disorder patients: clinical signs and symptoms. Psychiatr Med 71:193–203, 1989a

Hall RCW, Hoffman RS, Beresford TP, et al: Physical illness encountered in patients with eating disorders. Psychosomatics 30:174–191, 1989b

Halmi KA: Pragmatic information on the eating disorders. Psychiatr Clin North Am 5:371–377, 1982

Halmi KA, Falk JR, Schwartz E: Binge-eating and vomiting: a survey of a college population. Psychol Med 11:697–706, 1981

Halmi KA, Eckert E, Falk JR: Cyproheptadine: an antidepressant and weight-inducing drug for anorexia nervosa. Psychopharmacol Bull 19:103–105, 1983

Halmi KA, Eckert ED, La Du TJ, et al: Anorexia nervosa: treatment efficacy of cyproheptadine and amitriptyline. Arch Gen Psychiatry 43:177–181, 1986

Halmi KA, Eckert E, Marchi P, et al: Comorbidity of psychiatric diagnoses in anorexia nervosa. Arch Gen Psychiatry 48:712–718, 1991

Hamburg P: Bulimia: the construction of a symptom, in Psychoanalysis and Eating Disorders. Edited by Bemporad JR, Herzog DB. New York, Guilford, 1989, pp 131–140

Hamilton NG: Self and Others: Object Relations Theory in Practice. Northvale, NJ, Jason Aronson, 1988

Hardesty S, Jacobs N: Success and Betrayal: The Crisis of Women in Corporate America. New York, Random House, 1986

Harris L: Inside America. New York, Vintage, 1987

Hart KJ, Ollendick TH: Prevalence of bulimia in working and university women. Am J Psychiatry 142:851–854, 1985

Hays K: Journal writing with clients: an introduction and case history, in Innovations in Clinical Practice: A Source Book, Vol 7. Edited by Keller PA, Heyman SR. Sarasota, FL, Professional Resource Exchange, 1988, pp 127–135

Herman JL: Father-Daughter Incest. Cambridge, MA, Harvard University Press, 1981

Herman JL: Trauma and Recovery: The Aftermath of Violence. New York, Basic Books, 1992

Herzog DB: Antidepressant use in eating disorders. Psychosomatics 27 (suppl 11):17–23, 1986

Herzog DB: Recent advances in bulimia nervosa: cause and outcome. Paper presented at the annual meeting of the American Psychiatric Association, New Orleans, LA, May 1991

Herzog DB: Eating disorders: new threats to health. Psychosomatics 33:10–15, 1992

Herzog DB, Copeland PM: Eating disorders. N Engl J Med 313:295–303, 1985

Herzog DB, Keller, MB, Lavori, PW, et al: The course and outcome of bulimia nervosa. J Clin Psychiatry 52 (suppl 10):4–8, 1991

Herzog DB, Keller MB, Lavori PW, et al: The prevalence of personality disorders in 210 women with eating disorders. J Clin Psychiatry 53:147–152, 1992

Hesse-Biber S: Report on a panel longitudinal study of college women's eating patterns and eating disorders: non-continuum versus continuum measures. Health Care for Women International 13:375–391, 1992

Holland AJ, Sicotte N, Treasure JL: Anorexia nervosa: evidence for a genetic basis. J Psychosom Res 32:561–571, 1988

Horney K: Neurosis and Human Growth: The Struggle Toward Self-realization. New York, WW Norton, 1950

Horney K: The tyranny of the should (1950), in Neurosis and Human Growth: The Struggle Toward Self-Realization. New York, WW Norton, 1970, pp 64–85

Hornyak LM, Baker EK (eds): Experiential Therapies for Eating Disorders. New York, Guilford, 1989

Hsu LK: Outcome of anorexia nervosa: a review of the literature (1954–1978). Arch Gen Psychiatry 37:1041–1046, 1980

Hsu LKG: Lithium in the treatment of eating disorders, in The Role of Drug Treatments for Eating Disorders. Edited by Garfinkel PE, Garner DM. New York, Brunner/Mazel, 1987, pp 90–95

Hsu LG: The etiology of anorexia nervosa, in The Eating Disorders: Medical and Psychological Bases of Diagnosis and Treatment. Edited by Blinder BJ, Chaitin BF, Goldstein RS. New York, PMA Publishing, 1988, pp 239–246

Hsu LKG: Eating Disorders. New York, Guilford, 1990

Hsu LKG: Outcome studies in patients with eating disorders, in Psychiatric Treatment: Advances in Outcome Research. Edited by Mirin SM, Gossett JT, Grob MC. Washington, DC, American Psychiatric Press, 1991, pp 159–180

Hsu LKG, Chesler BE, Santhouse R: Bulimia nervosa in eleven sets of twins: a clinical report. International Journal of Eating Disorders 9:275–282, 1990

Hsu LKG, Crisp AH, Callender JS: Psychiatric diagnoses in recovered and unrecovered anorectics 22 years after onset of illness: a pilot study. Compr Psychiatry 33:123–127, 1992

Humphrey LL: Family relationships, in Psychobiology and Treatment of Anorexia Nervosa and Bulimia Nervosa. Edited by Halmi KA. Washington, DC, American Psychiatric Press, 1992, pp 263–287

Jacobson A, Herald C: The relevance of childhood sexual abuse to adult psychiatric inpatient care. Hosp Community Psychiatry 41:154–158, 1990

Janet P: Les Medications Psychologiques (3 vols). Paris, Felix Alcan, 1919. Reprint: Paris, Societé Pierre Janet, 1984. English Edition: Principles of Psychotherapy (2 vols). New York, Macmillan, 1976

Jimerson DC, Lesem MD, Kaye W, et al: Low serotonin and dopamine metabolite concentrations in cerebrospinal fluid from bulimic patients with frequent binge episodes. Arch Gen Psychiatry 49:132–138, 1992

Johnson C (ed): Psychodynamic Treatment of Anorexia Nervosa and Bulimia. New York, Guilford, 1991a

Johnson C: Treatment of eating-disordered patients with borderline and false-self/narcissistic disorders, in Psychodynamic Treatment of Anorexia Nervosa and Bulimia. Edited by Johnson CL. New York, Guilford, 1991b, pp 165–193

Johnson C, Connors ME: The Etiology and Treatment of Bulimia Nervosa: A Biopsychosocial Perspective. New York, Basic Books, 1987

Johnson C, Stuckey MK, Lewis LD, et al: Bulimia: a descriptive survey of 316 cases. International Journal of Eating Disorders 2(1):3–16, 1982

Johnson C, Connors ME, Tobin DL: Symptom management of bulimia. J Consult Clin Psychol 55:668–676, 1987

Johnson C, Tobin D, Enright A: Prevalence and clinical characteristics of borderline patients in an eating-disordered population. J Clin Psychiatry 50:9–15, 1989

Johnson C, Tobin D, Dennis AB: Differences in treatment outcome between borderline and nonborderline bulimics at one-year follow-up. International Journal of Eating Disorders 9:617–627, 1990

Johnson WG, Schlundt D: Sports that require lean build may cause increase in eating disorders. Obesity '91 Update, January 1991, p 7

Jones A, Cheshire N, Moorhouse H: Anorexia nervosa, bulimia and alcoholism: association of eating disorder and alcohol. J Psychiatr Res 19:377–380, 1985

Jong E: Fear of Flying. New York, NAL Dutton, 1973

Jordan JV, Kaplan AG, Miller JB, et al: Women's Growth in Connection: Writings From the Stone Center. New York, Guilford, 1991

Joseph A, Wood IK, Goldberg SC: Determining populations at risk for developing anorexia nervosa based on selection of college major. Psychiatry Res 7:53–58, 1982

Just what is a balanced diet, anyway? Tufts University Diet and Nutrition Letter 9(11):3–5, 1992

Katz JL: Eating disorders: a primer for the substance abuse specialist, I: clinical features. Journal of Substance Abuse 7:143–149, 1990

Katz JL: Substance abuse and eating disorders, part 1: an important area of co-morbidity. Eating Disorders Review 2(3):1–3, 1991

Kaye WH, Weltzin TE: Neurochemistry of bulimia nervosa. J Clin Psychiatry 52 (suppl 10):21–28, 1991a

Kaye WH, Weltzin TE: Serotonin activity in anorexia and bulimia nervosa: relationship to the modulation of feeding and mood. J Clin Psychiatry 52 (suppl 12):41–48, 1991b

Kearney-Cooke A: Reclaiming the body: using guided imagery in the treatment of body image disturbances among bulimic women, in Experiential Therapies for Eating Disorders. Edited by Hornyak LM, Baker EK. New York, Guilford, 1989, pp 11–33

Kearney-Cooke A: The role of the therapist in the treatment of eating disorders: a feminist psychodynamic approach, in Psychodynamic Treatment of Anorexia Nervosa and Bulimia. Edited by Johnson CL. New York, Guilford, 1991, pp 295–318

Kearney-Cooke A, Steicher-Asch P: Men, body image, and eating disorders, in Males With Eating Disorders. Edited by Andersen AE. New York, Brunner/Mazel, 1990, pp 54–74

Keesey RE: A set-point theory of obesity, in Handbook of Eating Disorders: Physiology, Psychology, and Treatment of Obesity, Anorexia, and Bulimia. Edited by Brownell KD, Foreyt JP. New York, Basic Books, 1986, pp 63–87

Kendler KS, MacLean C, Neale M, et al: The genetic epidemiology of bulimia nervosa. Am J Psychiatry 148:1627–1637, 1991

Kent A, Lacey JH, McCluskey SE: Pre-menarchal bulimia nervosa. J Psychosom Res 36:205–210, 1992

Keys A, Brozek J, Henschel A, et al: The Biology of Human Starvation. Minneapolis, MN, University of Minnesota Press, 1950

Khantzian EJ: Psychotherapeutic interventions with substance abusers: the clinical context. J Subst Abuse Treat 2:83–88, 1985a

Khantzian EJ: The self-medication hypothesis of addictive disorders: focus on heroin and cocaine dependence. Am J Psychiatry 142:1259–1264, 1985b

Khantzian EJ: Self-regulation and self-medication factors in alcoholism and the addictions: similarities and differences, in Recent Developments in Alcoholism, Vol 8: Combined Alcohol and Other Drug Dependence. Edited by Galanter M. New York, Plenum, 1990, pp 225–271

Khantzian EJ: Self-regulation vulnerabilities in substance abusers: treatment implications, in The Psychology of Addictive Behavior. Edited by Dowling S. Madison, CT, International Universities Press (in press)

Kierkegaard S: Either/Or (1844). Translated by Swenson DF, Swenson LM. Princeton, NJ, Princeton University Press, 1971

Kluft RP: Incest-Related Syndromes of Adult Psychopathology. Washington, DC, American Psychiatric Press, 1990

Kohut H: The Analysis of the Self: A Systematic Approach to the Psychoanalytic Treatment of Narcissistic Personality Disorders. New York, International Universities Press, 1971

Kohut H: The Restoration of the Self. New York, International Universities Press, 1977

Kohut H: How Does Analysis Cure? Chicago, IL, University of Chicago Press, 1984

Kramer S: Object-coercive doubting: a pathological defensive response to maternal incest. J Am Psychoanal Assoc 31 (suppl):325–351, 1983

Krejci RC, Sargent R, Forand KJ, et al: Psychological and behavioral differences among females classified as bulimic, obligatory exerciser and normal control. Psychiatry 55:185–193, 1992

Kuechler J, Hampton R: Learning and behavioral approaches to the treatment of anorexia nervosa and bulimia, in The Eating Disorders: Medical and Psychological Bases of Diagnosis and Treatment. Edited by Blinder BJ, Chaitin BF, Goldstein RS. New York, PMA Publishing, 1988, 423–431

Lacey JH, Smith, G: Bulimia nervosa: the impact of pregnancy on mother and baby. Br J Psychiatry 150:777–781, 1987

Laessle RG, Wittchen HU, Fichter MM, et al: The significance of subgroups of bulimia and anorexia nervosa: lifetime frequency of psychiatric disorders. International Journal of Eating Disorders 8:569–574, 1989

Lasch C: The Culture of Narcissism: American Life in an Age of Diminishing Expectations. New York, WW Norton, 1979

Lask B, Bryant-Waugh R: Early onset anorexia nervosa and related eating disorders. J Child Psychol Psychiatry 33:281–300, 1992

Lee S: Anorexia nervosa in Hong Kong: a Chinese perspective. Psychol Med 21:703–711, 1991

Leibowitz SF: Hypothalamic catecholamine systems controlling eating behavior: a potential model for anorexia nervosa, in Anorexia Nervosa: Recent Developments in Research. Edited by Darby PL, Garfinkel PE, Garner DM, et al. New York, Alan R Liss, 1983, pp 221–229

Leichner P, Gertler A: Prevalence and incidence studies of anorexia nervosa, in The Eating Disorders: Medical and Psychological Bases of Diagnosis and Treatment. Edited by Blinder BJ, Chaitin, BF, Goldstein RS. New York, PMA Publishing, 1988, pp 131–149

Leichtman M: The occupational hazards of having a physician father, in Medical Marriages. Edited by Gabbard GO, Menninger RW. Washington, DC, American Psychiatric Press, 1988, pp 103–119

Lerner HG: The Dance of Anger: A Woman's Guide to Changing the Patterns of Intimate Relationships. New York, Harper & Row, 1985

Lerner HG: The Dance of Intimacy: A Woman's Guide to Courageous Acts of Change in Key Relationships. New York, Harper & Row, 1989

Lerner HG: Masochism in subclinical eating disorders, in Psychodynamic Treatment of Anorexia Nervosa and Bulimia. Edited by Johnson CL. New York, Guilford, 1991, pp 109–127

Lerner HG: The Dance of Deception: Pretending and Truth-Telling in Women's Lives. New York, Harper & Row, 1993

Levin AP, Hyler SE: DSM-III personality diagnosis in bulimia. Compr Psychiatry 27:47–53, 1986

Levin RW: Somatic symptoms, psychoanalytic treatment, and emotional growth, in Psychoanalytic Perspectives on Women. Edited by Siegel EV. New York, Brunner/Mazel, 1992, pp 44–62

Levy AB, Dixon KN, Stern SL: How are depression and bulimia related? Am J Psychiatry 146:162–169, 1989

Liebert RS: The concept of character: a historical review, in Masochism: Current Psychoanalytic Perspectives. Edited by Glick RA, Meyers DI. Hillsdale, NJ, Analytic Press, 1988, pp 27–42

Lissner L, Odell PM, D'Agostino RB, et al: Variability of body weight and health outcomes in the Framingham population. New Engl J Med 324:1839–1844, 1991

Lissner L, Steen SN, Brownell KD: Weight reduction diets and health promotion. Am J Prev Med 8:154–158, 1992

Luhrmann G: Treating addictions and eating disorders. Eating Disorders News 2:1–3, 1991

Maloney MJ , McGuire JB, Daniels SR: Reliability testing of a children's version of the Eating Attitude Test. J Am Acad Child Adolesc Psychiatry 27:541–543, 1988

Maloney MJ, McGuire J, Daniels SR: Dieting behavior and eating attitudes in children. Pediatrics 84:482–489, 1989

Marcus MD: Binge eating in obesity, in Binge Eating. Edited by Fairburn CG, Wilson GT. New York, Guilford (in press)

Marcus MD, Wing RR, Ewing L, et al: Psychiatric disorders among obese binge eaters. International Journal of Eating Disorders 9:69–77, 1990a

Marcus MD, Wing RR, Ewing L, et al: A double-blind, placebo-controlled trial of fluoxetine plus behavior modification in the treatment of obese binge-eaters and non-binge-eaters. Am J Psychiatry 147:876–881, 1990b

Marcus MD, Smith D, Santelli R, et al: Characterization of eating disordered behavior in obese binge eaters. International Journal of Eating Disorders 12:249–255, 1992

Marcus RN, Katz JL: Inpatient care of the substance-abusing patient with a concomitant eating disorder. Hosp Community Psychiatry 41:59–63, 1991

Martin RJ, White BD, Hulsey MG: The regulation of body weight. American Scientist 79:528–541, 1991

Maser JD, Cloninger CR: Comorbidity of Mood and Anxiety Disorders. Washington, DC, American Psychiatric Press, 1990

Masterson JF: Primary anorexia nervosa in the borderline adolescent: an object-relations view, in Borderline Personality Disorders: The Concept, the Syndrome, the Patient. Edited by Hartocollis P. New York, International Universities Press, 1977, pp 475–494

McDougall J: Plea for a Measure of Abnormality. New York, International Universities Press, 1978

McDougall J: Theaters of the Body: A Psychoanalytic Approach to Psychosomatic Illness. New York, WW Norton, 1989

Menninger KA: The Human Mind (1930). New York, Knopf, 1965

Menninger KA: Man Against Himself. New York, Harcourt, Brace, 1938

Menninger KA: Love Against Hate. New York, Harcourt, Brace, 1942

Menninger KA: Hope. Am J Psychiatry 116(6):481–491, 1959

Menninger KA: Sparks. Edited by Freeman L. New York, Thomas Crowell, 1973

Menninger KA, Mayman M, Pruyser P: The Vital Balance: The Life Process in Mental Health and Illness. New York, Viking, 1963

Miller J: The Body in Question. New York, Random House, 1978

Miller JB: The development of women's sense of self, in Women's Growth in Connection: Writings From the Stone Center. Edited by Jordan JV, Kaplan AE, Miller JB, et al. New York, Guilford, 1991, pp 11–26

Miller ML: Understanding the eating-disordered patient: engaging the concrete. Bull Menninger Clin 55:85–95, 1991

Minuchin S, Fishman HC: Family Therapy Techniques. Cambridge, MA, Harvard University Press, 1981

Minuchin S, Rosman BL, Baker L: Psychosomatic Families: Anorexia Nervosa in Context. Cambridge, MA, Harvard University Press, 1978

Mitchell JE: The treatment of eating disorders [editorial]. Psychosomatics 31:1–3, 1990

Mitchell JE: Recent advances in bulimia nervosa: comorbidity and medical complications of bulimia nervosa. Paper presented at the annual meeting of the American Psychiatric Association, New Orleans, LA, May 1991

Mitchell JE, Hatsukami D, Eckert ED, et al: Characteristics of 275 patients with bulimia. Am J Psychiatry 142:482–485, 1985

Mitchell JE, Sein HC, Colon E, et al: Medical complications and medical management of bulimia. Ann Intern Med 107:71–77, 1987

Mitchell JE, Hoberman H, Pyle RL: An overview of the treatment of bulimia nervosa. Psychiatr Med 7:317–332, 1989a

Mitchell JE, Pyle RL, Hatsukami DK, et al: A 2–5 year follow-up study of patients treated for bulimia. International Journal of Eating Disorders 8:157–165, 1989b

Mitchell JE, Soll E, Eckert ED, et al: The changing population of bulimia nervosa patients in an eating disorders program. Hosp Community Psychiatry 401:1188–1189, 1989c

Mitchell JE, Pyle RL, Eckert ED, et al: A comparison study of antidepressants and structured intensive group psychotherapy in the treatment of bulimia nervosa. Arch Gen Psychiatry 47:149–159, 1990

Mitchell JE, Specker SM, de Zwaan M: Comorbidity and medical complications of bulimia nervosa. J Clin Psychiatry 52 (suppl 10):13–20, 1991

Mitchell JE, Pyle RL, Specker S, et al: Eating disorders and chemical dependency, in Special Problems in Managing Eating Disorders. Edited by Yager J, Gwirtsman H, Edelstein CK. Washington, DC, American Psychiatric Press, 1992, pp 1–14

Morgan HG, Russell GFM: Value of family background and clinical features as predictors of long-term outcome in anorexia nervosa: four-year follow-up study of 41 patients. Psychol Med 5:355–371, 1975

Moriarty D, Moriarty M: Sports/fitness programs and sociocultural influences on eating disorders. CAPHER Journal 52:4–9, 1986

Moriarty D, Moriarty M: The incidence, detection, and treatment of eating disorders among athletes and fitness participants. Paper presented at the 10th annual meeting of the Anorexia Aid Society, Columbus, OH, October 1991

Morley JE: Appetite regulation: the role of peptides and hormones. J Endocrinol Invest 12:135–147, 1989

Morley JE, Silver AJ, Miller DK: The anorexia of the elderly, in The Psychobiology of Human Eating Disorders: Preclinical and Clinical Perspectives. Edited by Schneider LH, Cooper SJ, Halmi KA. New York, New York Academy of Sciences, 1989, pp 50–59

Mullahy P: The Beginnings of Modern American Psychiatry: The Ideas of Harry Stack Sullivan. Boston, MA, Houghton Mifflin, 1973. (Originally published under the title of Psychoanalysis and Interpersonal Psychiatry: The Contributions of Harry Stack Sullivan. New York, Science House, 1970)

Mumford DB, Whitehouse AM: Increased prevalence of bulimia nervosa among Asian schoolgirls. BMJ 297(6650):718, 1988

Nash JD: Eating behavior and body weight: psychosocial influences. American Journal of Health Promotion 2(a):5–13, 1987

Nasser M: Comparative study of the prevalence of abnormal eating attitudes among Arab female students of both London and Cairo Universities. Psychol Med 16:621–625, 1986

National Academy of Science: Recommended Dietary Allowances, 10th Edition. Washington, DC, National Academy of Science, 1989

Newman M, Berkowitz B, Owen J: How to Be Your Own Best Friend: A Conversation with Two Psychoanalysts. New York, Random House, 1971

Newman MM: The dual dilemma: substance abuse in patients with eating disorders. Psychiatry Letter 8:1–8, 1991

Newman MM, Gold MS: Preliminary findings of patterns of substance abuse in eating disorder patients. Am J Drug Alcohol Abuse 18:207–211, 1992

Nighttime eating disorder may be fairly widespread. Lawrence Journal World (AP Special Features), March 1993

Norre J, Vandereycken W: The limits of out-patient treatment for bulimia disorders. British Review of Bulimia and Anorexia Nervosa 5:55–63, 1991

Notman MT, Nadelson CC (eds): Women and Men: New Perspectives on Gender Differences. Washington, DC, American Psychiatric Press, 1991

Novick J, Novick KK: Some comments on masochism and the delusion of omnipotence from a developmental perspective. J Am Psychoanal Assoc 39:307–331, 1991

Nussbaum MC: Love's Knowledge: Essays on Philosophy and Literature. Oxford, England, Oxford University Press, 1990

Ogden TH: The Matrix of the Mind: Object Relations and the Psycho-analytic Dialogue. Northvale, NJ, Jason Aronson, 1986

Ogden TH: The Primitive Edge of Experience. Northvale, NJ, Jason Aronson, 1989

Orbach S: Fat is a Feminist Issue: The Anti-Diet Guide to Permanent Weight Loss. New York, Paddington Press, 1978

Palmer RL, Oppenheimer R, Dignon A, et al: Childhood sexual experiences with adults reported by women with eating disorders: an extended series. Br J Psychiatry 156:699–703, 1990

Patton CJ: Fear of abandonment and binge eating: a subliminal psychodynamic activation investigation. J Nerv Ment Dis 180:484–490, 1992

Phillips KA: Body dysmorphic disorder: the distress of imagined ugliness. Am J Psychiatry 148:1138–1149, 1991

Ploog DW, Pirke KM: Psychobiology of anorexia nervosa. Psychol Med 17:843–859, 1987

Pope HG, Hudson JI: Are eating disorders associated with borderline personality disorder? a critical review. International Journal of Eating Disorders 8:1–9, 1989

Potok C: The Book of Lights. New York, Knopf, 1981

Price WA, Babai MR, Torem MS: Anorexia nervosa in later life. Hillside J Clin Psychiatry 8:144–151, 1986

Pruyser P: Maintaining hope in adversity. Pastoral Psychology 35:120–131, 1986

Pryor T, McGilley B, Roach NE: Psychopharmacology and eating disorders: dawning of a new age. Psychiatric Annals 20:711–714, 717–722, 1990

Pumariega AJ: Acculturation and eating attitudes in adolescent girls: a comparative and correctional study. Journal of the American Academy of Child Psychiatry 25:276–279, 1986

Putnam FW: Diagnosis and Treatment of Multiple Personality Disorder. New York, Guilford, 1989

Pyle RL, Mitchell JE: The epidemiology of bulimia, in The Eating Disorders: Medical and Psychological Bases of Diagnosis and Treatment. Edited by Blinder BJ, Chaitin BF, Goldstein RS. New York, PMA Publishing, 1988, pp 259–266

Pyle RL, Mitchell JE, Eckert ED, et al: Maintenance treatment and 6-month outcome for bulimic patients who respond to initial treatment. Am J Psychiatry 147:871–875, 1990

Rabinor JR: The process of recovery from an eating disorder: the use of journal writing in the initial phase of treatment. Psychotherapy in Private Practice 9:93–106, 1991

Rand CS, Stunkard AJ: Obesity and psychoanalysis: treatment and four-year follow-up. Am J Psychiatry 140:1140–1144, 1983

Reich W: Character Analysis (1945). Translated by Carfagno VR. New York, Farrar, Straus, Giroux, 1972

Rigotti NA, Neer RM, Skates SJ, et al: The clinical course of osteoporosis in anorexia nervosa: a longitudinal study of cortical bone mass. JAMA 265:1133–1138, 1991

Rinsley DB: Treatment of the Severely Disturbed Adolescent. New York, Jason Aronson, 1980

Rinsley DB: Borderline and Other Self Disorders: A Developmental and Object-Relations Perspective. New York, Jason Aronson, 1982

Rinsley DB: Developmental Pathogenesis and Treatment of Borderline and Narcissistic Personalities. Northvale, NJ, Jason Aronson, 1989

Rizzuto AM: Transference, language, and affect in the treatment of bulimarexia. Int J Psychoanal 69:369–387, 1988

Rodin J, Silberstein LR, Striegel-Moore R: Women and weight: a normative discontent, in Psychology and Gender (Nebraska Symposium on Motivation, Vol 32). Edited by Sonderegger TB. Lincoln, NE, University of Nebraska Press, 1985, pp 267–307

Rogers F: Body image and its modification. Pa Med 93(12):42–43, 1990

Rothstein A: The Narcissistic Pursuit of Perfection. New York, International Universities Press, 1984

Russell GFM: General management of anorexia nervosa and difficulties in assessing the efficacy of treatment, in Anorexia Nervosa: A Monograph of the National Institute of Child Health and Human Development. Edited by Vigersky RA. New York, Raven, 1977, pp 277–289

Sacksteder JL: Psychosomatic dissociation and false self development in anorexia nervosa, in The Facilitating Environment: Clinical Applications of Winnicott's Theory. Edited by Fromm MG, Smith BL. Madison, CT, International Universities Press, 1988, pp 365–393

Salmons PH, Lewis VJ, Rogers P, et al: Body shape dissatisfaction in school children. Br J Psychiatry 153 (suppl 2):27–31, 1988

Sansone RA, Fine MA, Seuferer S, et al: The prevalence of borderline personality symptomatology among women with eating disorders. J Clin Psychology 45:603–610, 1989

Satter E: Childhood eating disorders. J Am Diet Assoc 86:357–361, 1986

Satter E: Childhood disordered eating: precursor to eating disorders? National Anorexic Aid Society Newsletter 14:1–5, 1991

Schafer R: The loving and beloved superego in Freud's structural theory. Psychoanal Study Child 15:163–188, 1960

Schafer R: Those wrecked by success, in Masochism: Current Psychoanalytic Perspectives. Edited by Glick RA, Meyers DI. Hillsdale, NJ, Analytic Press, 1988, pp 81–91

Schapira DV: Diet, obesity, fat distribution and cancer in women. J Am Med Wom Assoc 46:126–130, 1991

Schenck CH, Hurwitz TD, Bundlie SR, et al: Sleep-related eating disorders: polysomnographic correlates of a heterogeneous syndrome distinct from daytime eating disorders. Sleep 14:419–431, 1991

Schilder P: The Image and Appearance of the Human Body: Studies in the Constructive Energies of the Psyche (1950). New York, International Universities Press, 1970

Schlundt DG, Johnson WG: Eating Disorders: Assessment and Treatment. Boston, MA, Allyn & Bacon, 1990

Schneider JA: Gender identity issues in male bulimia nervosa, in Psychodynamic Treatment of Anorexia Nervosa and Bulimia. Edited by Johnson CL. New York, Guilford, 1991, pp 194–222

Schotte DE, Stunkard AJ: Bulimia vs. bulimic behaviors on a college campus. JAMA 258:1213–1215, 1987

Schwartz H: Never Satisfied: A Cultural History of Diets, Fantasies, and Fat. New York, Free Press, 1986

Schwartz HJ (ed): Bulimia: Psychoanalytic Treatment and Theory. Madison, CT, International Universities Press, 1988

Schwartz HJ: Psychoanalytic psychotherapy for a woman with diagnoses of kleptomania and bulimia. Hosp Community Psychiatry 43:109–110, 1992

Searles HF, Kernberg OF, Masterson JF, et al: Discussion (of The psychoanalytic treatment of the alienated patient, by Giovacchini PL), in New Perspectives on Psychotherapy of the Borderline Adult. Edited by Masterson JF. New York, Brunner/Mazel, 1978, pp 20–39

Selvini-Palazzoli M: Self-starvation: From Individual to Family Therapy in the Treatment of Anorexia Nervosa. New York, Jason Aronson, 1978

Shure J: Sexual abuse linked to eating disorders. Renfrew Perspective 3:1–6, 1989

Sibley DC, Blinder BJ: Anorexia nervosa, in The Eating Disorders: Medical and Psychological Bases of Diagnosis and Treatment. Edited by Blinder BJ, Chaitin BF, Goldstein RS. New York, PMA Publishing, 1988, pp 247–258

Simpson WS, Ramberg JA: Sexual dysfunction in married female patients with anorexia and bulimia nervosa. J Sex Marital Ther 18:44–54, 1992

Slade PD: Body image in anorexia nervosa. Br J Psychiatry 153 (suppl 2):20–22, 1988

Smith JE, Morgan CD: The neglected bulimic: the nonpurger. Journal of Psychopathology and Behavioral Assessment 12:103–118, 1990

Snow DL, Held ML: Group psychotherapy with obese adolescent females. Adolescence 8:407–414, 1973

Sontag S: The double standard of aging. Saturday Review 54:29–38, 1972

Sours JA: Starving to Death in a Sea of Objects: The Anorexia Nervosa Syndrome. New York, Jason Aronson, 1980

Spitz RA: A Genetic Field Theory of Ego Formation: Its Implications for Pathology. New York, International Universities Press, 1959

Steiger H, Goldstein C, Mongrain M, et al: Description of eating-disordered, psychiatric, and normal women along cognitive and psychodynamic dimensions. International Journal of Eating Disorders 9:129–140, 1990

Steiner-Adair C: New maps of development, new models of therapy: the psychology of women and the treatment of eating disorders, in Psychodynamic Treatment of Anorexia Nervosa and Bulimia. Edited by Johnson CL. New York, Guilford, 1991a, pp 225–244

Steiner-Adair C: When the body speaks: girls, eating disorders, and psychotherapy, in Women, Girls, and Psychotherapy: Reframing Resistance. Edited by Rogers AG. New York, Haworth, 1991b, pp 253–266

Steinhausen HC, Glanville K: Follow-up studies of anorexia nervosa: a review of research findings. Psychol Med 13:239–249, 1983

Stiver IP: The meaning of care: reframing treatment models, in Women's Growth in Connection: Writings from the Stone Center. Edited by Jordan JV, Kaplan AE, Miller JB, et al. New York, Guilford, 1991, pp 250–267

Stone MH: The Fate of Borderline Patients: Successful Outcome and Psychiatric Practice. New York, Guilford, 1990

Strauman TJ, Vookles J, Berenstein V, et al: Self-discrepancies and vulnerability to body dissatisfaction and disordered eating. J Pers Soc Psychol 61:946–956, 1991

Striegel-Moore RH, Silberstein LR, Rodin J: Toward an understanding of risk factors for bulimia. Am Psychol 41:246–263, 1986

Strober M: Family genetic studies of eating disorders. J Clin Psychiatry 52 (suppl 10):9–12, 1991

Strober M, Salkin B, Burroughs J, et al: Validity of the bulimia-restricter distinction in anorexia nervosa: parental personality characteristics and family psychiatric morbidity. J Nerv Ment Dis 170:345–351, 1982

Stunkard AJ: Eating patterns and obesity. Psychiatr Q 33:284–295, 1959

Stunkard AJ: Obesity and the social environment: current status, future prospects. Proceedings of the New York Academy of Sciences 300:298–320, 1977

Stunkard A: Research on a big problem: obesity. Psychiatric News, March 2, 1990, pp 22–23

Stunkard AJ, Wadden TA (eds): Obesity: Theory and Therapy, 2nd Edition. New York, Raven, 1992

Stunkard AJ, Sorensen TIA, Hanis C, et al: An adoption study of human obesity. N Engl J Med 314:193–198, 1986

Sugarman A, Kurash C: The body as a transitional object in bulimia. International Journal of Eating Disorders 1(4):57–67, 1982

Swift WJ: Bruch revisited: the role of interpretation of transference and resistance in the psychotherapy of the eating disorders, in Psychodynamic Treatment of Anorexia Nervosa and Bulimia. Edited by Johnson CL. New York, Guilford, 1991, pp 51–67

Swift WJ, Letven R: Bulimia and the basic fault: a psychoanalytic interpretation of the binging-vomiting syndrome. Journal of the American Academy of Child Psychiatry 23:489–497, 1984

Swift WJ, Stern S: The psychodynamic diversity of anorexia nervosa. International Journal of Eating Disorders 2(1):17–35, 1982

Taylor MJ, Cooperc PJ: Body image disturbance in bulimia nervosa. Br J Psychiatry 153 (suppl 2):32–36, 1988

Theander S: Anorexia nervosa: a psychiatric investigation of 94 female patients. Acta Psychiatr Scand Suppl 214, 1970

Thomas HK: Emily Dickinson's "renunciation" and anorexia nervosa. American Literature 60:203–225, 1988

Tice L, Hall RCW, Beresford TP, et al: Sexual abuse in patients with eating disorders. Psychiatr Med 7:257–267, 1989

Titus M: Eating and vomiting in the service of maintaining a differentiated self-experience. Paper presented at the annual meeting of the American Psychological Association, Los Angeles, CA, August 1981

Titus MA, Smith WH: Contemporary issues in the psychotherapy of women. Bull Menninger Clin 56:48–61, 1992

Tobin DL, Johnson CL: The integration of psychodynamic and behavior therapy in the treatment of eating disorders: clinical issues versus theoretical mystique, in Psychodynamic Treatment of Anorexia Nervosa and Bulimia. Edited by Johnson CL. New York, Guilford, 1991, pp 374–397

Toner BB, Garfinkel PE, Garner DM: Affective and anxiety disorders in the long-term follow-up of anorexia nervosa. Int J Psychiatry Med 18:357–364, 1988

Torem MS, Curdue K: Dissociative states presenting as an eating disorder. Am J Clin Hypn 29:137–142, 1986

Torem MS, Curdue K: PTSD presenting as an eating disorder. Stress Medicine 4:139–142, 1988

Treasure J: Anorexia nervosa and bulimia nervosa. Current Opinion in Psychiatry 5:228–233, 1992

Tufts New England Medical Center Division of Child Psychiatry: Sexually Exploited Children: Service and Research Project: final report for the Office of Juvenile Justice and Delinquency Prevention. Washington, DC, U.S. Department of Justice, 1984

Vaillant GE: The Natural History of Alcoholism. Cambridge, MA, Harvard University Press, 1983

Van der Kolk BA: Psychological Trauma. Washington, DC, American Psychiatric Press, 1987

Van der Kolk BA, Saporta J: The biological response to psychic trauma: mechanisms and treatment of intrusive numbing. Anxiety Research 4:199–212, 1991

Van der Kolk BA, Van der Hart O: Pierre Janet and the breakdown of adaptation in psychological trauma. Am J Psychiatry 146:1530–1540, 1989

Van der Kolk BA, Van der Hart O: The intrusive past: the flexibility of memory and the engraving of trauma. American Imago 48:425–454, 1991

Vandereycken W: The sociocultural roots of the fight against fatness: implications for eating disorders and obesity. Eating Disorders 1:7–16, 1993

Vandereycken W, Meermann R: Anorexia Nervosa: A Clinician's Guide to Treatment. Berlin, Germany, Walter de Gruyten, 1984

Vandereycken W, Van Vreckem E: Siblings of patients with an eating disorder. International Journal of Eating Disorders 12:273–280, 1992

Vanderlinden J, Norre J, Vandereycken W: A Practical Guide to the Treatment of Bulimia Nervosa. New York, Brunner/Mazel, 1992

Viorst J: Necessary Losses. New York, Simon & Schuster, 1986

Voltaire: Candide (1760). Translated by Bair L. New York, Bantam, 1959

Walsh BT: Pharmacotherapy of eating disorders, in The Eating Disorders: Medical and Psychological Bases of Diagnosis and Treatment. Edited by Blinder BJ, Chaitin BF, Goldstein RS. New York, PMA Publishing, 1988, pp 469–476

Walsh BT: Fluoxetine treatment of bulimia nervosa. J Psychosom Res 35 (suppl 1):33–40, 1991

Walsh BT: Psychopharmacologic treatment of bulimia nervosa. J Clin Psychiatry 52 (suppl 10):34–38, 1991b

Walton BE, Jimerson DC, Franko D, et al: Alexithymic symptoms in bulimia nervosa. Paper presented at the 4th International Conference on Eating Disorders, New York, April 1990

Wardle J, Foley E: Body image: stability and sensitivity of body satisfaction and body size estimation. International Journal of Eating Disorders 8:55–62, 1989

Weintraub M: Long-term weight control study: conclusions. Clin Pharmacol Ther (suppl May):642–646, 1992

Weltzin TE, Fernstrom MH, Hansen D, et al: Abnormal caloric requirements for weight maintenance in patients with anorexia and bulimia nervosa. Am J Psychiatry 148:1675–1682, 1991

Westheimer R: Dr. Ruth's Guide to Good Sex. New York, Crown, 1983

White JH: Women and eating disorders, part I: significance and sociocultural risk factors. Health Care for Women International 13:351–362, 1992a

White JH: Women and eating disorders, part II: developmental, familial, and biological risk factors. Health Care for Women International 13:363–373, 1992b

White TH: The Once and Future King (1939). New York, Putnam, 1958

White WC, Boskind-White M: An experiential-behavioral approach to the treatment of bulimarexia. Psychotherapy: Theory, Research, and Practice 18:501–507, 1984

Whitehouse AM, Freeman CP, Annandale A: Body size estimation in anorexia nervosa. Br J Psychiatry 153 (suppl 2):23–26, 1988

Willard SG, Anding RH, Winstead DK: Nutritional counseling as an adjunct to psychotherapy in bulimia treatment. Psychosomatics 24:545–551, 1983

Wilson CP: Dream interpretation (1983), in Fear of Being Fat: The Treatment of Anorexia Nervosa and Bulimia. Edited by Wilson CP, Hogan CC, Mintz IL. Northvale, NJ, Jason Aronson, 1985, pp 245–254

Wilson JD, Braunwald E, Isselbacher KI, et al: Harrison's Principles of Internal Medicine, 12th Edition. New York, McGraw-Hill, 1991

Wing RR: Behavioral treatment of severe obesity. Am J Clin Nutr 55:545S–551S, 1992

Winnicott DW: Primitive emotional development (1945), in Collected Papers: Through Pediatrics to Psycho-analysis. New York, Basic Books, 1958, pp 145–156

Winnicott DW: On the contribution of direct child observation to psycho-analysis (1957), in The Maturational Processes and the Facilitating Environment. Madison, CT, International Universities Press, 1965, pp 109–114

Winnicott DW: Ego distortion in terms of true and false self (1960), in The Maturational Processes and the Facilitating Environment: Studies in the Theory of Emotional Development. New York, International Universities Press, 1965, pp 140–152

Winnicott DW: The Maturational Processes and The Facilitating Environment: Studies in the Theory of Emotional Development. New York, International Universities Press, 1965

Wise TH, Cooper JN: Group therapy during a modified fasting diet: themes and process. Int J Psychiatry Med 13:233–238, 1983–1984

Wold PN: Eating disorders symptoms in affective disorder. Journal of Psychiatric Neurosis 16:204–208, 1991

Wolf N: The Beauty Myth: How Images of Beauty Are Used Against Women. London, Vintage, 1990

Wonderlich SA, Mitchell JE: Eating disorders and personality disorders, in Special Problems in Managing Eating Disorders. Edited by Yager J, Gwirtsman HE, Edelstein CK. Washington, DC, American Psychiatric Press, 1992, pp 51–86

Woodside DB, Garner DM, Rochert W, et al: Eating disorders in males: insights from a clinical and psychometric comparison with female patients, in Males With Eating Disorders. Edited by Andersen AE. New York, Brunner/Mazel, 1990, pp 100–115

Wooley SC: Uses of countertransference in the treatment of eating disorders: a gender perspective, in Psychodynamic Treatment of Anorexia Nervosa and Bulimia. Edited by Johnson CL. New York, Guilford, 1991, pp 245–294

Wooley SC, Kearney-Cooke A: Intensive treatment of bulimia and body-image disturbance, in Handbook of Eating Disorders: Physiology, Psychology and Treatment of Obesity, Anorexia, and Bulimia. Edited by Brownell KD, Foreyt JP. New York, Basic Books, 1986, pp 476–502

World Health Organization: International Statistical Classification of Diseases and Related Health Problems, 10th Revision. Geneva, Switzerland, World Health Organization, 1992

Wurtman JJ: Carbohydrate craving: a disorder of food intake and mood. Clinical Neuropharmacology 11 (suppl 1):S139–S145, 1988a

Wurtman JJ: Carbohydrate craving, mood changes, and obesity. J Clin Psychiatry 49 (suppl 8):37–39, 1988b

Wurtman JJ: Carbohydrate craving: relationship between carbohydrate intake and disorders of mood. Drugs 39 (suppl 3):49–52, 1990

Wurtman JJ, Wurtman RJ: Do carbohydrates affect food intake via neurotransmitter activity? Appetite 11 (suppl 1):42–47, 1988

Yager J: The treatment of eating disorders. J Clin Psychiatry 49 (suppl 9):18–25, 1988

Yager J, Landsverk J, Edelstein CK, et al: Screening for Axis II personality disorders in women with bulimic eating disorders. Psychosomatics 30:255–262, 1989

Yager J, Young RT: Eating disorders and diabetes mellitus, in Special Problems in Managing Eating Disorders. Edited by Yager J, Gwirtsman HE, Edelstein CK. Washington, DC, American Psychiatric Press, 1992, pp 185–203

Yager J, Gwirtsman HE, Edelstein C (eds): Special Problems in Managing Eating Disorders. Washington, DC, American Psychiatric Press, 1992

Yates A: Compulsive Exercise and the Eating Disorders: Toward an Integrated Theory of Activity. New York, Brunner/Mazel, 1991

Yates A, Leehey K, Shisslak CM: Running: an analogue of anorexia? N Engl J Med 308:251–255, 1983

Yeary JR, Heck CL: Dual diagnosis: eating disorders and psychoactive substance dependence. J Psychoactive Drugs 21:239–249, 1989

Zakin DF: Eating disturbance, emotional separation, and body image. International Journal of Eating Disorders 8:411–416, 1989

Zerbe KJ: Recognizing eating disorders. American Rowing 18(8):42–43, 1987

Zerbe KJ: Through the storm: psychoanalytic theory in the psychotherapy of the anxiety disorders. Bull Menninger Clin 54:171–183, 1990

Zerbe KJ: Management of countertransference with eating-disordered patients. Psychodynamic Letter 1(9):4–6, 1991

Zerbe KJ: Eating disorders in the 1990s: clinical challenges and treatment implications. Bull Menninger Clin 56:167–187, 1992a

Zerbe KJ: Why eating-disordered patients resist sex therapy: a response to Simpson and Ramberg. J Sex Marital Ther 18:55–64, 1992b

Zerbe KJ: Recurrent pancreatitis presenting as fever of unknown origin in a recovering bulimic. International Journal of Eating Disorders 12(3):337–340, 1992c

Zerbe KJ: Whose body is it anyway? understanding and treating psychosomatic aspects of eating disorders. Bull Menninger Clin 57:161–177, 1993a

Zerbe KJ: Selves that starve and suffocate: the continuum of eating disorders and dissociative phenomena. Bull Menninger Clin 57:319–327, 1993b

Zerbe KJ, Marsh SR, Coyne L: Comorbidity in an inpatient eating disordered population: clinical characteristics and treatment implications. Psychiatric Hospital 24(1/2):3–8, 1993

Zimmerman M, Coryell W: DSM-III personality disorder diagnoses in a nonpatient sample: demographic correlates and comorbidity. Arch Gen Psychiatry 46:682–689, 1989

Ziolko HV: Bulimia and kleptomania: psychodynamics of compulsive eating and stealing, in Bulimia: Psychoanalytic Treatment and Theory. Edited by Schwartz HJ. Madison, CT, International Universities Press, 1988, pp 523–534

# Index

Page numbers printed in **boldface** *type refer to tables or figures.*

431